Flatbreads
and Flavors

Flatbreads and Flavors

A Baker's Atlas

Jeffrey Alford and Naomi Duguid

WILLIAM MORROW AND
COMPANY, INC.

New York

The following recipes first appeared, slightly altered, in *Bon Appétit* and are reprinted with permission: Tibetan Buttermilk Barley Bread; Afghan Home-style Naan; Uighur Nan with Cumin and Onion. A number of other recipes first appeared, in slightly different form, in *Eating Well* and *Food & Wine*.

LIBRARY OF CONGRESS CATALOGING-IN-PUBLICATION DATA

Alford, Jeffrey.
Flatbreads and flavors / Jeffrey Alford and Naomi Duguid.
p. cm.
Includes index.
ISBN 0-688-11411-3
1. Bread. 2. Cookery, International. I. Duguid, Naomi.
II. Title.
TX769.A486 1995
641.8'15—dc 20 94-30892
CIP

Printed in the United States of America
First Edition

1 2 3 4 5 6 7 8 9 10

BOOK DESIGN BY BARBARA M. BACHMAN

MAP DESIGNS BY JACKIE AHER

We each grew up in a tolerant, loving household where curiosity

about the world was encouraged and travel was seen as a nor-

mal part of life. This book is dedicated to our parents: to Ann

and Jack Alford, with love and thanks; and to Robin and

Adrian Duguid, remembered with

gratitude and love.

Preface

This cookbook is in part a journal, a travel diary, a record of events and mem-
ories expressed in recipes. In the course of our travels we've filed away recipe after
recipe, but with almost every one, in our minds we've also filed away images of
places and people, and their lives. How a food tastes has much to do with the asso-
ciations we make with it. To pass on a recipe for Afghan snowshoe bread without
also telling about the Mujahideen in refugee camps in Pakistan feels like an incom-
plete recipe, like leaving out the oven temperature or the amount of salt in the
bread.

We're two people caught in the grip of wanderlust—have been for a long
time. We first met in the fall of 1985 in the dark on the roof of a small hotel in Lhasa,
Tibet. We talked for hours, each almost immediately recognizing in the other a fellow spirit. Naomi was at the time on a five-month leave of absence from a career as
a lawyer in Toronto, but had already decided not to return. I was a cook and a baker,
about to begin a bicycle trip from Lhasa to Kathmandu, through the Himalaya.

In a few weeks, we rendezvoused in Kathmandu, and we've been together
ever since: Six months later, we were bicycling together from China to Pakistan,
through the Pamir and Karakoram mountains. The following summer we bicycled
in Western Tibet, and down through the Kun Lun mountains into the Taklimakan

Desert. Each trip was a remarkable adventure, giving us a chance to live side by side with people whose lives were very different from our own: Tibetan nomads in the high-altitude Changtang region; Kirghiz and Tajik villagers and nomads; Hunzakot and Wakhi villagers in the Karakoram; and Uighurs—desert people—living in the oases of the Taklimakan. From all of them we had so much to learn: practical things, like how to make a fire out of goat dung, and how to keep it going at an elevation of sixteen thousand feet. And little things—in reality, the big things—lessons about sharing food with strangers, about patience, about how bread tastes when bread is the only food there is to eat.

The following year, we began to work seriously on this book. We began traveling specifically in search of flatbreads, to Europe, to Yemen and Egypt, to what were then the Soviet republics of Georgia, Turkmenistan, Tajikistan, and Uzbekistan.

With language in common or without, we keep trying to plop ourselves down next to people who make flatbreads as a way of life. We have gone to Morocco, Tunisia, and Israel, to Syria, Turkey, Armenia, and Azerbaijan, to Mexico, Vietnam, and India. On farms and in homes, in markets and in neighborhood restaurants, people are almost without exception open and patient with our inquiries. Whenever we travel with our children, people are particularly kind, and then share the language not only of food, but of family.

Our flatbread journeys will continue, but here, in this collection of recipes and stories, is at least a part of all that has been so generously shared with us.

Acknowledgments

Because the recipes and experiences chronicled in this book were accumulated over many years, we both owe a great deal to people whose names we have forgotten or never knew: the Wakhi family in Khaibar in northern Pakistan who taught us to make roti; the Tajik nomad families in the Pamir Mountains who gave us bread and yogurt; Tibetan nomads at various grazing grounds in the Changtang, who welcomed us and shared tea and meat with us; the Kurdish nomads living in eastern Turkey who brought Jeffrey in from the rain; many other strangers and chance-met acquaintances, nomads and market merchants who answered questions or helped with language difficulties, tolerated photographs, and simply made us feel welcome. To all of them, thank you.

In Tibet, thanks to Tenzing Namgyel, for welcoming us many times at the Snowland and helping with translation and information; to Nawang Losang, and to three anthropologists met in Lhasa: Mel Goldstein and Cynthia Beall of Case Western Reserve University, for insights into what is and is not understood about the high-altitude life of Tibetan nomads, and Corneille Jest of the CRNS in Paris. In Tajikistan, thanks to Luda, Rosa, and Tanya. In Turkmenistan, special thanks to Dr. Shokrat Kadirov, for generous explanations; to Olya from Baghir; and to Armik. Thanks too to Dr. Shirin Akiner of the London School of Soviet and East Asian Studies.

In Vietnam, thanks to Dang Anwei of Pheonix Travel. Thanks also to Lam and Lum in Saigon, and to Kiem Lien in Hanoi. In Penang, a big thank you to Varusai, for his openness as well as his chapattis.

In India, thanks to Professor Kunjusankam Pillai and family, and to Balu Pillai and family.

In Israel, we were taken care of, introduced around, and made to feel entirely at home by Alisa Poskanzer; thanks for generous and thoughtful hospitality during our stay in Jerusalem, and thank you to Rabbi Steinsaltz, and to Mellia and Naomi Hellner, for help with matzoh; to Ettie Cohen, for information about the Kurdish community; and to Flora Shelomof the Babylonian Jewery Center in Or Yehuda.

Thanks to Latifa; Ouza and family; Abdullah and family; and Fatiha in and around Taroudant, Morocco. Thanks to Mr. Beshir Bouneb in Djerba, and a special thanks to Mokhtar, for his help.

In Georgia, special thanks to Nino and Karol; thanks also to Evelina and Temur, to Lianna, and to Mkrtech, all in Tbilisi.

Thanks to the Zuber family, in Mulhouse and elsewhere, and to Jacques and Aline Lemordant, from the Grenoble area. Thanks too to Sabine Monnier and to Ella Maillart.

In Oaxaca, thanks to Claudia and Mercedes, and to Elizabeth and Julietta at the Miseo Frissell in Mitla. At Hopi Mesa, thanks to Isabel and family, and in Santa Fe to the Greens at Glenn Green Gallery and to Dale Doremus.

A big thank you to traveling companions Ella Maillart, Ted Kerasote, Lee Day, Pat and Baiba Morrow, Wendy Baylor and Jeremy Schmidt, Deb Olson, Antony Southam, Rajan Gill, and Jon Schuetz.

Home from travels, we have been helped by cultural and culinary advice and information from many patient people, including Kathy Wazana, Ma'an Lababneh, Ed Keall, Wahid Azizi and his mother, Jeremy Fox, He Jian Shan, Lou Bagby, Souad Sharabani and Juliette Hanna, Judy Amundson, Anna Buchnea, Luigi Orgiera, the staff of the Woodland reserch center at Six Nations, Grace Buie, Mary Moran, Laura Simich, Annie Hurwitz, Molly Tharyan, Scott Welch, Ann Buttrick, and Helen Wearne. Many thanks.

We are grateful for all the recipe testing provided by Cassandra Kobayashi, Don Stewart, and Melanie Robitaille, and for testing by Hilary Buttrick, Karen Krupa, and Judi Stevenson. thank you to Almaz Kaplan for making Quick Injera for the jacket photograph.

For help and encouragement too diverse and sustained to describe, we thank Lesley Wischmann and Larry Jansen, Judy Nisenholt and Ethan Poskanzer, Cassandra Kobayashi, Trisha Jackson and Ramsey Derry, Rick Smith, Deb Olson, and Dina Feyerman, cookbook collector extraordinaire.

To everyone at Oldways Preservation Trust in Boston, a big thank you for encouraging the appreciation of traditional foodways, and for giving us the opportunity to talk to many people about flatbreads and agricultural traditions. Thanks too to Nancy Jenkins, for encouragement and introductions.

To photographers Jim Alford and Lee Day, thank you for many years of help, inspiration, and positive criticism. To Tina Ujlaki of *Food & Wine* and to Barry Estabrook and Rux Martin, we are deeply grateful for all of your advice and support. Thank you to Barbara Fairchild of *Bon Appétit,* who published our first article on flatbreads, and to Patsy Jamieson and Susan Stuck of *Eating Well.* Jeffrey Steingarten gave us advice on baking stones; Paula Wolfert, follow-up information on Tunisian breads; and thanks to Joyce Goldstein and baker Dan Glazier at Square One.

To all the people without whom this book wouldn't be a book: book designer Barbara Bachman and jacket designer Don Morris; food photographers Andrea Gentl and Marty Hyers and food stylist Dee Walsh. It was fun working with such talented, imaginative, sweet-tempered people. Thanks to copy editor Judith Sutton, and to Deborah Weiss Geline and Amy Broderick of William Morrow for their patient attentiveness. Thank you to Maria Guarnaschelli for first believing in this book, and then setting it out on a good course.

We are very fortunate to be able to rely on the sound advice, fine judgment, and friendship of both our agent, Susan Lescher, and our editor, Ann Bramson. It is one thing to be able to rely upon the skill and insight of those you work most closely with; it is another, rarer pleasure to be able to enjoy the process so entirely.

And finally, thank you to Dominic and Tashi, for being who you are.

Contents

▲▲▲

India, Nepal, and Sri Lanka ... 121

Eastern Mediterranean ... 173

Morocco, Tunisia, and Ethiopia ... 239

Armenia, Georgia, and Azerbaijan
(the Caucasus) ... 281

Europe ... 321

North America ... 361

Flatbreads
and Flavors

Introduction

We began this book with a passion for flatbreads, in love with the taste of freshly ground grain baked as bread on a hot iron griddle or on the walls of a tandoor oven and intrigued by all the different shapes and textures of flatbreads, all the different ways in which they are cooked and eaten. We had little idea at the time of just how enormous the world of flatbreads really is, or of how essential and important they are to the people who eat them every day.

Flatbreads are the world's oldest breads. People have been making them for well more than six thousand years. And over that time, the tradition of making flatbreads has not been confined to one or two regions of the world, but has developed simultaneously almost everywhere there is a perennial supply of grain, from Mesopotamia and Persia to southern India and Armenia, from antique Rome and preconquest Mexico to modern-day China and Italy.

Flatbreads can be made from every grain imaginable: wheat, rye, corn, oats, millet, sorghum, teff, rice, buckwheat. They can also be made from tubers, such as potatoes, and from legumes, such as chickpeas and lentils. They can be unleavened or leavened. They can be made so thin that they become transparent, like a very thin crepe, or they can be two inches thick and sliceable. Flatbreads are oven-baked, grilled, fried, skillet-baked, steamed, or even, as in southern Algeria and Tunisia, baked beneath the hot desert sand.

Though it is almost impossible to trace the exact origins of different flatbreads, we know that certain ones, such as Armenian lavash, and Bedouin fatir, are made today in much the same way they have been for several thousand years; they have, as Samuel Johnson said of Shakespeare, "pleased many and pleased long." Flatbreads are simple and straightforward to prepare and to eat, they are nourishing, and they make efficient use of locally available food resources.

Armenian lavash is a good example. This bread, also known as *khubz mahk-ouk* in the mountains of Lebanon, as *nane silli* to the Kurds, and as *roomali roti* in India, is paperthin and dries out soon after it is made. Traditionally, a large amount is made at one time so that it can be stored in dried form. When fresh bread is needed, it is simply sprinkled with water and wrapped in a towel; this makes it moist and supple almost immediately. The practice of drying bread for later use is also found with bread rings in Central Anatolia and with Finnish rye rings, which hang from the rafters through the winter until needed. In places where winter is long and a supply of grain must last through the cold months, it is an ideal solution.

In many parts of the world, having sufficient fuel for cooking has been an ever-present problem. Flatbreads, unlike loaf breads, tend to cook very quickly, requiring only a limited amount of fuel to provide heat. Millions of people all across northern India make chapattis once or twice a day. Across North Africa, where fuel is also sometimes very scarce, ovens have been designed to maximize the heat of a small fire. Beehive-shaped ovens made from mud and straw allow the heat to transfer rapidly from the sides and the breads to cook quickly.

But more than any other one reason, most flatbread traditions have been kept alive because they represent a good-tasting and healthy way of turning hard grain into edible food. In Central Asia, a fresh hot whole wheat naan baked on the walls of a tandoor oven fueled by smoky juniper probably tasted and smelled just about as wonderful two thousand years ago as it does today. (We can't imagine how it could taste any better!)

After years of doughs and rolling pins and bags of flour, and after years of talking with people about their breads, we have come to feel, if anything, even more passionate about flatbreads than when we began our flatbread journey. As if individual breads were people grown into old friends, we've become immensely fond of them, of their individuality and of all that they represent. When we cook bannock in a skillet in our kitchen, or tear off a piece of soft warm Turcoman sourdough naan from a basket set out on the table, we feel somehow more connected with the world in which we live, past and present. We delight in one of life's great wonders, in the remarkable transformation that happens when flour and water become bread.

The main distinction between the different flatbreads in this book is between unleavened breads and leavened, whether they be yeasted, sourdough, or soda-risen breads. Unleavened breads are always fairly thin. Risen flatbreads are more difficult to categorize, as there are so many different kinds. A yeasted bread may be paperthin, as in the case of lavash, but some, like Ethiopian Spice Bread and Hunzakot Apricot and Almond Bread might even be considered loaf breads, as they rise almost two inches high. Naans, a broad category of flatbreads from Central Asia, are usually rounds or ovals about an inch thick, risen with a sourdough or with commercial yeast. A number of leavened flatbreads, such as pizza and the Georgian cheese breads, have toppings or are filled. Most yeasted flatbreads are traditionally eaten as an essential part of a meal, much the way we eat bread with soup or the way bread is served as part of a meal in France.

There are two things that commonly keep would-be bread makers from making bread: yeast and kneading. With yeast there is a fear that if it is not treated correctly, it will fail and die, while kneading seems to many people a mysterious and difficult process. In fact, yeast is very forgiving and easy to work with, and kneading is an uncomplicated and pleasurable activity. Almost half the flatbreads we've included here are risen with yeast and require kneading; they are in no way difficult to make.

If you are just starting out with bread making, read carefully through the chapter entitled Flatbread Basics, then launch into making pita (page 185), an easy bread that is a good introduction to yeasted flatbreads. Start with a new supply of flour and of dry active yeast. Simply follow the recipe, and your bread will turn out well.

Kneading is a simple process of folding the dough over on itself over and over again. The first time will probably feel a little awkward, like any new technique, but you'll soon become accustomed to the basic motion. To get a good feel for it, try baking three days in a row, or several times in one week—by the end of that time you'll be well on your way to being a confident baker.

As for that question of time: We like to think of flatbreads as one of the world's great fast foods. When you read through a recipe and it says "Allow the dough to rise two to three hours, or even overnight," this may seem anything but fast. But think about how little time you spend actually working to make the bread: a total of only thirty minutes to one hour mixing, kneading, cleaning up, rolling out, and baking, depending upon the type of flatbread you are making.

When you become comfortable making bread, working with a big dough is as easy as working with a small one, so for many home bakers the size of their average dough gradually gets larger and larger. Bread freezes and reheats extraordinarily well. If you are cooking for a family, or you don't have much time to be in the kitchen but still want homemade bread, think about working with large doughs and using your freezer effectively. If you have made a large dough and baked only part of it, as we often do, wrap the remainder in a large plastic bag and put it in the refrigerator. For breakfast the next morning, cut off only as much dough as you will need, then roll out a few flatbreads and bake them in a hot oven or on your stove top in a dry cast-iron skillet. Or, if you're going on a picnic, or over to a friend's house for an outdoor barbecue, take your skillet and dough along and bake fresh hot breads over an open fire (see the instructions on page 21 for making stove-top pita, for example).

If you are an experienced bread maker, making flatbreads will introduce you to interesting new techniques as well as new tastes and flours. Try your hand at Hunza Sprouted Wheat Breads or Kurdish Bulgur Bread made from bulgur and minced onions. If you want to learn unusual techniques, make the Malaysian Flung and Folded Griddle Bread, which is flung through the air to become paperthin, then folded and twisted before being cooked on an oiled griddle. Also try Rajasthani Salt and Spice Bread or Xichuan Pepper Bread; both are rolled out flat and sprinkled with flavorings, then coiled before being rolled out flat again.

Flour does not need gluten to work well in flatbreads so wheatless flatbreads abound. Many of the flours that play only a minor role in baking loaf breads are much more significant in the world of flatbreads—the subtle nutty taste of blue corn flour and the exotic purple-brown of Ethiopian teff flour are unusual and delicious examples. We are particularly fond of sorghum flour, which is used in making San'a Sorghum Bread. For people with wheat allergies or celiac disease, trying to find wheatless loaf breads can be discouraging, but wheatless flatbreads are a perfect solution (see Index).

If you are looking for new tastes, try sweet Armenian Aromatic Festive Bread flavored with mahleb, the kernel of an Eastern Mediterranean black cherry. Very common but little known outside Asia is another aromatic seed called nigella, which is sometimes referred to as black onion seed. When used sparingly on a Afghan Snowshoe Naan, it imparts a flavor that goes so well with the bread that the two seem inseparable.

Fresh warm flatbreads bring a special touch to almost any meal. If you want to dazzle your dinner guests, serve Sardinian Parchment Bread alongside an Italian meal, or set out homemade High-Tech Crackers with pâté as an hors d'oeuvre. Berry Bannock is so perfect with a Thanksgiving feast that it has become for us the most essential part of the meal.

If you have children looking for an afterschool snack, or if you are an inveterate snacker yourself, try flatbreads. Of all the different recipes presented here, there are very few that aren't ideal as a between-meal snack—High-Tech Crackers, Unyeasted Date Rounds, and Savory Sesame Bread Rings, to name just a few. They're as nutritious as can be, satisfying a craving without a lot of oil and salt. And with all the fun of rolling, shaping, and flavoring flatbreads, they're a great way of getting your children involved in bread making.

For every flatbread recipe included in this book, there are two or three additional ones for dishes to accompany the bread. With tortillas there is a black bean mole and an ancho chile salsa; with dosas there is coconut chutney and a spicy lentil curry; with naan there are grilled chunks of lamb marinated in onion juice and a yogurt dip with garlic and mint. We've tried to include as many of these traditional combinations as possible so that you can make not only the flatbreads but the meals they inspire.

In addition, in the serving suggestions that accompany every recipe, you'll find ideas for how various breads and foods can be brought together to create a delectable meal, whether traditional or a cross-cultural combination of foods that work well together.

Flatbreads and Flavors is divided into chapters based on geographical regions. Each chapter opens with a map—to help identify the part of the world being discussed—and a short introduction to the region to help define and explain the breads and cultures included. Within each chapter, the recipes are grouped by country or culture.

The book begins with a chapter on Flatbread Basics, which is an introduction to bread making and flatbread techniques, from buying flour to kneading to rolling and shaping. A section called Selecting a Flatbread to Make zeros in on the best breads to wow your guests with, the best breads to make on a regular basis, the best breads to make for a light evening meal—in short, the perfect bread for every occasion.

In the Glossary at the back of the book you will find a detailed description of less familiar ingredients and where they can be found. We were surprised at how few ingredients needed to be included in the glossary, given that the book contains recipes from places as diverse as Mexico, Ethiopia, and Vietnam. Many ingredients have several alternate names, so check the Index to find where the ingredient is listed and explained in the Glossary.

Flatbread Basics

The art of making bread involves elements of intuition, of skill and practice, of play and creativity. Having a bread turn out the way you want it to turn out has to do with chemistry, and then again with feel and touch. In asking people all around the world how they make the bread they make, we quickly realized that there is only so much we can learn through hearing a recipe or by being taken through a process. We might be able to make the bread—and have it turn out deliciously—but the art of making a perfect injera, or of turning out a paperthin lavash, is something different. The art of bread making has to do with those subtle things, the smells, touch, and sensibilities we acquire over time, especially if we grow up in a culture where a particular bread is the most important food in our life.

This chapter is anything but definitive; the world of breads, and of flatbreads in particular, is much too big for that. What we discuss here are tools, techniques, ingredients, ideas, and observations that have over time helped us in bread making. If you've never before baked bread, you will find everything here that you need to know to get happily started. And if you're already an experienced hand, then you will find a few new twists on old problems, or an answer or two to why something happens the way it happens.

Flatbreads are forgiving. A pita that doesn't balloon, a Uighur nan that balloons too much—in the end it's not a worry. A warm, welcoming smell of bread baking will be there in the kitchen, and fresh hot homemade breads will be around for, well, about as long as it takes to start a new batch.

Ingredients

FLOUR

Most of the flatbreads presented in this book are made from wheat flour, the flour that is most adaptable and easy to handle for bread making. We concentrate here on wheat flours, the different kinds and where to find them, with a brief note on where to buy less-common flours such as teff, sorghum, corn, rye, and barley. For more background on wheat varieties and the specific characteristics of different wheat flours, see More About Wheat, pages 401–407.

Wheat Flours for Bread: Many of our flatbread recipes call for hard flour, either unbleached white or whole wheat flour, also known as bread flour or as hard wheat flour. Hard flour is generally made from hard winter or hard spring wheat and has a high protein content, between 12 and 15 percent. (For a more complete discussion of hard versus soft wheat, please see More About Wheat.)

You can substitute all-purpose flour, with a protein content of 10 to 11 percent, in whole or in part, in recipes that call for unbleached hard white flour; all-purpose flour generally produces a slightly softer, weaker dough with a tender texture. We also find that it has a blander, less distinctive taste than hard unbleached or whole wheat flour.

Most wheat grown in England, France, and Italy is slightly "softer" than North American bread flour; it has a lower protein content than wheat grown in the hot dry plains of North America. Consequently, a lower-protein flour comes closer to reproducing the texture of most French and some Italian breads. To approximate European-style bread flour, we blend all-purpose and soft wheat flours in a proportion of roughly 2:1. (See the recipe for Olive Ladder Bread, page 323.)

Shopping for Flour: Finding a good reliable source for flour can be one of the most difficult aspects of baking bread. Whenever possible, we use organic flour, that is, flour that has been milled from organically grown wheat. We find it generally has a better flavor. Flour should be reasonably fresh: Very old flour has a soft feathery texture and will not make good bread. Try looking at flours sold in bulk to become familiar with the difference in look and feel of fresh and old flour.

Don't be surprised if, when you go into a store and ask for an organic, freshly ground hard winter wheat flour, say 12 to 14 percent protein, the salesperson rolls his or her eyes and sighs. We hope this won't happen, and that the person serving you will know exactly what you mean and be able to help you, but what if he or she can't? Then it's time to work with the best of what's available. We order twenty-kilogram bags of organic unbleached hard white flour and organic hard whole wheat flour from a local distributor. We keep the flour in a very cool dry place, and go through it quickly; for our small family of big bread eaters, this amount works out well. In the summer heat, though, we tend to buy whole wheat flour in smaller quantities and store it in the freezer, for the oils in the flour can quickly go rancid in warmer weather. We also keep on hand a fresh supply of atta flour, which we purchase in small quantities from an Indian grocery.

Other Flours: The less common flours, such as rye, barley, corn, and oat flour, can be found in health food stores; rye flour is also available in most supermarkets. Other flours, such as rice flour, spelt, kamut, and teff can be found in health food stores or in shops specializing in foods of a particular region: Southeast Asian groceries for rice flour, Mexican or Latin American groceries for masa and corn flour, Ethiopian groceries for teff. Sorghum flour is available from Indian grocery stores.

LEAVENING AND FERMENTATION

Why talk about leavening—yeast, sourdough starters, baking soda—in a book about flatbreads? Nearly half of the bread recipes included in this book call for some form of leavening, if only for texture and flavor. Pita, naan, and pizza are all leavened breads. So too are Tibetan Barley Skillet Bread, Moroccan Anise Bread, and Apricot and Almond Bread.

Yeast: Yeast is a wonderfully mysterious thing. The yeast we rely upon for baking leavens our bread and lends its appetizing smell and taste. As a single-celled fungus, yeast works in bread by feeding first upon the sugars in the dough, and later upon the maltose produced as starch granules are broken down by malt enzymes. As the yeast metabolizes the sugars, it produces carbon dioxide and alcohol, a process in bread making referred to as fermentation.

Fermentation: While the yeast continues to grow and reproduce, thus creating more and more alcohol and carbon dioxide, the carbon dioxide begins to enter and expand air pockets that have been trapped by the gluten during kneading. The alcohol, the other product of fermentation, eventually turns to water (which is why a leavened dough is moister after it has been left to rise). During fermentation, other lesser chemical processes are also taking place that ultimately affect the flavor the yeast will impart to the bread.

When the bread is put into the oven to bake, the carbon dioxide expands in the heat—and as it does, it enlarges all the little air pockets by stretching the gluten (this is the process called "oven spring"), eventually resulting in a higher, lighter-textured bread than an unleavened one. While this is obviously of importance to loaf breads, it is also important to many flatbreads. If you have ever had a doughy pizza, you know what we mean.

Though it's generally agreed that fermentation is one of the key factors in determining how a bread will taste, there are many different theories about how best to ferment a dough. One way of thinking about the activity of yeast in a bread—and about fermentation—is that certain ingredients and conditions (such as salt, oil, and cold temperatures) inhibit the growth of the yeast, while others (such as sugars and warm temperatures) encourage growth. It's the balance of these factors that is important for successful leavened bread. Different people, with different theories on fermention, go about trying to achieve this balance in different ways, but it's a proper balance that everyone is aiming for.

Slow-rise Doughs and Sourdoughs: We are advocates of a long, slow period of fermentation. For us, the best flavor comes when the entire process is slowed way down. We like to give the dough plenty of time to do its first rise, unhurried by excess yeast, sugar, or warmth. This means that many of our recipes use less yeast than standard recipes call for. We also set doughs to rise at room temperature, purposefully avoiding those places in our kitchen that are "extra warm."

Historically, many of the leavened breads described in this book would have been made with some kind of sourdough starter, not with dry yeast, and some of the breads are still to this day made with sourdoughs, though in many places sourdoughs are being replaced by yeast. We decided to convert a number of recipes from sourdough to dry yeast, for several different reasons. First, using dry yeast can be more convenient and practical. Second, the process is more predictable. And third, we have more success in producing a reliably good flavor when using dry yeast than we do with sourdough starters.

This is not to say that we are "anti-sourdough"—far from it. Several recipes using sourdoughs—recipes we've found to be particularly reliable—are included here: Turcoman Sourdough Bread, Rice and Black Lentil Crêpes, and Ethiopian Sponge Breads. If you have a sourdough starter that works well for you, don't hesitate to replace the yeast in a particular recipe with your starter, and to experiment.

Buying Yeast: If you are planning to bake with any frequency, you are probably better off going to a health food store and buying dry baking yeast (not brewer's or nutritional yeast, neither of which has any rising properties), which is sold in bulk. You can also buy packages of dry yeast at the supermarket. We keep ours well sealed in small plastic bags in the refrigerator. It keeps for about six months. If you think your yeast is old, discard it and buy some fresh; that way you won't have to worry about its strength. Fresh yeast (as opposed to dry yeast), can be bought in cakes from specialty stores and bakeries (and sometimes from supermarkets). It has different baking and keeping characteristics from dry yeast. We call for dry yeast rather than fresh yeast because it is generally more available.

Baking Soda: Baking soda produces bubbles of carbon dioxide when it is placed in a moist acid environment, such as buttermilk or soured milk, or when it is combined with an acid salt in baking powder and mixed into a liquid. The gas production is very rapid—much more rapid than that of yeast—and happens both as you mix the dough and as the bread bakes. Georgian Cheese-Filled Quick Bread and Berry Bannock are both soda breads, as are Finnish Barley Bread and Fry Bread, but so little soda goes into them that they lack the distinctive soda taste of, say, a loaf of Irish soda bread.

WATER

"The bread in Samarkand is much better than here," confided a Tajik friend, Luda, as we shared bread and a bowl of tea one evening in Dushanbe. "It's because of the water. The water in Samarkand is clear, clean, and sweet, not like here."

The quality of the water, we've been told over and over again, is as important as the quality of the flour—maybe even more important. Our basic rule for using water in bread is that if the water tastes good, then it will be good for the bread. Avoid distilled water, which is very soft, or water that is excessively hard. Water from the tap in some cities can have a strong taste of chlorine, so for bread—and for drinking—we prefer to use locally bottled spring water.

SALT AND SWEET

In the recipes, we generally call for "salt," without any more detail. We prefer to use sea salt when possible, because it has a fresher taste, without the added chemicals in iodized free-running salt. Use whatever you have available.

Many yeast-leavened recipes call for mixing a small amount of sweetening into the liquid before adding the yeast. The sugars feed the yeast and help it grow. Sometimes we call for honey, sometimes for sugar. You can choose to always use honey or to substitute an equal amount of sugar for honey if you prefer. Honey gives a slight extra depth of flavor to bread and we generally prefer it, or brown sugar, to white sugar. Be sure to use a mild-flavored honey such as clover; if you use strong-tasting honey such as buckwheat for a sweetener, its flavor may overpower the taste of the bread.

Equipment

BOWLS, BOARDS, SPOONS, AND SCRAPERS

We are creatures of habit when it comes to bread making. We tend to mix our bread in the same bowl every time, be it a large dough or a small dough. We use our same favorite wooden spoon for stirring, the same measuring cup for scooping flour.

What makes a good bread bowl? A good bread-making surface? A good mixing spoon? The most important factor is that they feel good to you. If they feel good, and they work, then you will use them over and over again and they will take on special status. Some people like to knead on a countertop, others like marble, still others prefer wood (our preference).

Bread Bowls: We use a large ceramic bread bowl that Jeffrey found at a garage sale, sold as a pot for an enormous impatiens plant. It is heavy and has a two-inch rim around the outside that can be easily grabbed. It is a classic old bread bowl, off-white and thick, large enough to mix a bread dough that will feed a family for a week. Size is important. If you make a large dough and you find that it is hard to contain all the flour as you are mixing, then find a larger bowl for the next time.

Spoons: The spoon we use is not really a spoon at all, but a wooden implement with a flat blade like an oversize wooden spatula. The advantage of this shape is that excess dough can be easily scraped off. The handle of the spoon is thick and strong, another important characteristic of a good bread-mixing tool.

Kneading Surfaces: For a bread board, that is, a surface on which to knead bread, we have always used a wooden board like those used in drawing and design courses: It is twenty by twenty-six inches and half an inch thick. Our board doubles as a cutting board; we use one side for cutting vegetables and the other for bread making. We clean and oil the vegetable side frequently, while we scrape but never oil the bread side. We like this board because it is portable and lightweight, yet heavy enough not to warp. It is large enough to accommodate rolling out large flatbreads, such as pizzas.

Dough Scrapers: Wherever you knead and whatever you knead on, it's important to keep the surface smooth while you work, which brings us to one other essential bread-making tool: a dough scraper. Dough scrapers come in different shapes and sizes, but what all have in common is a stiff flat surface that can be used to lift the dough from its underside. Dough scrapers are usually rectangular in shape with a handle running along one side. The scraping edge is a thin, flat, stiff piece of steel, blunt but strong, with squared edges. Dough scrapers are ideal for scraping bread boards, for cutting dough, for lifting particularly sticky masses of dough, and for unsticking parts of a flatbread dough as you roll it out.

Plastic Wrap: At several points in the recipe—while the dough rises, for example—bread recipes classically call for the dough to be covered with a damp cloth. The purpose of covering the dough while it is rising or resting is to prevent the top surface from drying out and forming a crust. We find a damp towel more trouble than it's worth: The dough may stick to it or the towel may dry out, especially if the dough is being left to rise slowly. Instead we call for plastic wrap. Actually, we use large plastic garbage bags, because they are strong, clean, and perfectly smooth and they fit easily over our large bread bowl or around a big dough. If we bake only part of a dough, the rest can be stored in the refrigerator, sealed in the garbage bag.

Techniques

MAKING A DOUGH

Now you have a bread bowl, a spoon for mixing, a surface for kneading, flour, water, salt, maybe yeast: You're ready to start mixing.

Starting with Liquids: Flour can be old and dry and absorb a great deal of water, or it can be just the opposite—so the amount necessary for each recipe will differ slightly from batch to batch. Partly for this reason, we tend to work from a measured amount of water, not flour. Most of the recipes in this book have been developed and tested in this manner.

You may have encountered bread recipes that work in the other order, starting with the flour, then stirring in the liquids. Starting with dry ingredients means there is less tendency to dry out the dough by adding too much flour (which we will talk more about in relation to kneading); even so, starting with liquids and then adding flour remains the best method in our view, because of the ability it gives you to develop the gluten well and to thoroughly moisten the flour so that it can properly absorb the liquid and knead easily.

When working with corn flour or chickpea flour, or other nonwheat flours, it is best to add flour to the water and let it sit ten to fifteen minutes. The flour will absorb a great deal of water in that time, and when you come back to it to continue the recipe, it will be easier to work.

When making soda-risen doughs or batters, first mix all the wet and dry ingredients separately, and then combine them. Recipes for soda-risen breads are frequently written with exact measurements for both flour and liquid, but the problem with the variable absorbency of the flour is just the same as with other breads—so add more liquid or flour as you think necessary.

The Sponge Method: Many of the recipes give instructions for the *sponge* method. We are great believers in first making a sponge whenever possible. A sponge is made by adding to the liquid and yeast only half of the flour the recipe calls for, and stirring the flour, yeast, and water together until a batter forms. If the recipe calls for sugar or honey, add it to the sponge, for it will help the yeast grow. But don't add salt or oil to the sponge, as they inhibit the growth of the yeast.

If you are mixing a yeasted dough, you will be mixing with gluten and the well-being of your yeast in mind. In many of our recipes, you will see the instruction "stir the batter one hundred times in the same direction." The stirring helps develop the gluten. By stirring in only one direction, you avoid cutting or tearing the new little strands of gluten. Then set the sponge aside at room temperature, covered, for anywhere from thirty minutes to eight hours; the longer resting time can only improve the quality of your bread—both its taste and its texture—not to mention making kneading that much easier.

A sponge is also a good way to get started baking on a day where you may be busy with other things. Make a sponge, which takes only a few minutes to stir together, and come back to it later. (Make sure your bowl is large enough for the sponge to expand.)

Mixing: When it comes time to add the salt, oil, remaining flour, and whatever else is going into the dough, add the ingredients little by little, by sprinkling them over the surface of the sponge. Begin with the salt, then the oil, and then add the flour. Don't stir the dough at this point, as stirring can cut the strands of gluten, but incorporate the new ingredients by folding them in with your spoon. Take your spoon to the bottom of the bowl, then bring the bottom of the dough up, folding in whatever is on top. Work in as much flour, little by little, as you can this way, while still keeping the dough in the bowl—and then work in a little more. If you're working with a large dough, this part of the process may feel messy and unwieldy, but the more flour you can work in at this stage, the less sticky your dough will be when you turn it out of the bowl. When you really can't work in any more flour, it is time to turn out the dough onto a floured surface and to begin to knead.

KNEADING

Kneading bread dough is a pleasure, to be taken on easily and at your own pace. The reason we knead dough is to further develop the gluten in the dough and to incorporate air into the dough, especially in the case of yeasted wheat doughs. As we knead a dough, air is taken into the dough and dispersed in smaller and smaller pockets throughout. The carbon dioxide produced by the yeast during fermentation fills all the little air pockets created during kneading. In a well-kneaded dough, these pockets will be many and small, and as a result the finished bread will have a fine, even texture.

This all may sound like something relevant to loaf breads, not to flatbreads. Most flatbread doughs, however, depend on kneading just as loaf breads do. Chapattis, tortillas, puris—to name a few unyeasted flatbreads—are at their best when they puff up, or "balloon," in their final stage of cooking, producing a lighter, finer bread. So are pitas, which are yeasted. Other flatbreads, especially thicker ones such as Olive Ladder Bread, Three-Color Focaccia, and Afghan Home-style Naan, depend on a well-kneaded dough to give them texture and to help them rise and cook evenly.

Some doughs, on the other hand, must not be kneaded. When we first tried carasau, Sardinian Parchment Bread, for example, we mistakenly kneaded it. The bread ballooned in the oven—just what we didn't want—rather than staying in the flat thin sheet required. Kneading had developed the gluten and produced a kind of oven-baked semolina chapatti. Instead of kneading, the idea is simply to wet the flour, then to roll the dough out directly and slip it into the oven. Similarly, with lefse, the potato-based Norwegian Wrapping Bread, kneading is to be avoided. The gluten developed by kneading makes the bread tough rather than tender and soft to the bite.

Kneading Technique: Kneading can be accomplished in many different ways, but the standard method of hand kneading is a process whereby the dough is folded over upon itself, compressed, folded over again and compressed, over and over again. Find a place that is comfortable and make sure that your kneading surface doesn't move when you do. Push the dough out and away from you, then grab the end that is farthest away and pull it toward you until it folds over the rest of the dough. Now compress the dough by pushing the top portion into the bottom portion and pushing it down and away from you, using your shoulders and whole body, not just your hands and arms (especially important when kneading large doughs). Turn the dough a quarter turn, again grab the end farthest away and pull it forward, and again compress and push away. It may take a little while to master the motions as you think your way through the process, but soon you will find a rhythm. Depending upon the size of your dough, kneading can be done with one hand, using the other hand for guidance, or with two hands.

Troubleshooting: If the recipe calls for ten minutes of kneading and after three or four minutes you are tired, then you are probably using only your arms and not the rest of your body. Think about gently swaying back and forth, moving into the dough with all of your body. If your kneading surface is too high, using your body will be difficult; if the surface is too low, you may find your back getting tired before your arms do.

Your kneading surface must be floured before you turn the dough out to begin kneading. Flouring helps prevent the dough from sticking to the surface. As you knead, flour from the surface will become incorporated into the dough; when the dough begins to stick, scrape the surface clean with your scraper and sprinkle on some more flour. Some doughs, such as those made with rye flour or made with potatoes, can be particularly sticky at first. For these doughs, our recipes call for a generously floured surface; here again, you will probably have to reflour the surface as you go along.

If your hands get coated with sticky dough, rub them together to scrape it off, then flour your hands lightly. With very wet doughs, begin by generously flouring your hands as well as the surface, but resist the temptation to sprinkle flour directly onto the dough. You want additional flour to be incorporated gradually, not to form lumps or pockets of flour in the dough. Similarly, try not to add any more flour to your kneading surface than absolutely necessary. You want your dough to stay moist and elastic.

If the dough begins to feel stiff, and you start to have great difficulty folding it over during kneading, pick the dough up by one end and slap it down hard on the counter once or twice. The banging loosens the gluten strands, which have been tightened by the folding and refolding during kneading. If your dough is large and therefore difficult to lift and thump down, try pressing it out flat on the kneading surface. This will help lengthen the gluten strands and give you a dough which is easier to fold over on itself. Then continue kneading.

Knowing When You're Finished: How to know when the dough has been sufficiently kneaded? The best way is to look at a clock when you begin and to not stop until you've kneaded for at least the amount of time called for in the recipe. Especially with whole-grain breads, which generally require more kneading, the tendency is to stop before the dough is sufficiently kneaded. A well-kneaded dough will start to soften slightly and to develop a smooth sheen and increased elasticity. Overkneading is only really possible when using a dough hook or a food processor; an overkneaded dough will begin to break down and get sticky.

PROCESSORS AND OTHER MECHANICAL AIDS TO BREAD MAKING

We have friends in Wyoming who bake lots of breads and rolls every day. They own two small, relaxed restaurants, and the breads they make are the best of the restaurants' many attractions. But they do all this bread making by hand; they won't use a dough hook to help with the kneading. We think they're crazy—wonderful in their persistence, but crazy nonetheless. A dough hook kneads large doughs very efficiently and easily. If the bread is then finished off with a little hand kneading, the heavy labor has been taken out of the process but the dough has still been well handled.

We tend not to love mechanical devices, but we have come to acknowledge their usefulness in some situations. Hence the mentions in many recipes of food processors and spice grinders, side by side with instructions for using a large mortar and pestle. We have enjoyed experimenting with kneading in our food processor, and it does work beautifully with many doughs, particularly unleavened ones.

We have given instructions for using a food processor with breads we think particularly appropriate to it. However, a processor can be more trouble than it's worth for a really large dough, because it means having to do small batch after small batch in the processor. If you are using a processor, the important thing to remember is that you must not knead the dough too long, or the gluten strands will become overextended and begin to break down.

The general approach to processor mixing and kneading is to combine the dry ingredients in the processor, then add the liquid (with the yeast dissolved in it if the bread is yeasted) in a steady stream while the blade is spinning. With a standard-sized food processor, we add no more than about three cups of dry ingredients at one time. If the dough requires, for example, six cups of flour, we process the dough in two separate batches, then combine the two doughs and knead by hand for a short time. Even if the dough is small, we still like to knead for a short time by hand to get a feel for the dough. (For a more detailed description of kneading in a food processor, see High-Tech Crackers, page 392.)

ROLLING

There are many reasons we are enthralled with flatbreads, not the least of which is that we love to use rolling pins. A large drawer just under the counter where we knead is full of rolling pins, rolling pins from all around the world. All the pins are made from wood, but that is the only thing they have in common.

We have a favorite rolling pin approximately eighteen inches in length and gently tapered at both ends. It is by far the best pin we have for rolling breads out very thin; the tapered ends allow us to roll from the center out, which is important when we want an even, thin bread.

Troubleshooting: Rolling out breads should be a pleasure; one of the very few obstacles which can make the experience not so pleasurable is dough that insists upon sticking to your board. To prevent this from happening, first make round flat discs of the pieces of dough you will be rolling. Shape the discs between your palms, and then press them onto a well-floured surface, flouring both sides of each disc. If you have a large batch of dough, divide the dough into pieces, shape all of the pieces into discs, and flour them well before starting to roll. Cover the remaining discs with plastic wrap while you roll out breads one at a time. Once you begin rolling out the breads, you want to use only as much flour as you need to keep the dough from sticking, so work as much flour as you can onto the discs when you first shape them, and then be as sparing as possible with extra flour when you roll out the bread. If the top of the dough sticks to your rolling pin, flour your rolling pin, not the bread. If it still sticks, turn the bread over onto a light dusting of flour and continue rolling.

Another way to keep dough from sticking to the board is to move the bread gently in quarter turns with the tips of your fingers as you roll it out. Roll the bread from the center outward, then turn the bread a quarter turn and roll again, and so on. With this method you can develop an easy rhythm. It also keeps the thickness of the bread fairly even and allows you to maintain the shape you want (circular or oblong). Turning the bread between strokes of the rolling pin may become impossible as your bread gets larger and larger, but with most skillet-sized breads it is easily done. Keep a little sprinkling of flour on your board so that you can move the bread gently from place to place around the board. If you are rolling out a very large thin flatbread, try rolling toward you, using one hand, while at the same time pushing the far side of the bread gently in the opposite direction, stretching it even more.

Most bread doughs containing gluten, and yeasted doughs in particular roll out more easily when the dough is given time to rest at different intervals. If you have ever rolled out a particularly "strong" pizza dough and had the dough shrink back upon itself every time you rolled it out, you know what we mean. Strands of gluten, like bands of elastic, have a tendency to pull back when stretched. Rather than struggle to get the dough rolled out, it's much better to roll it out only as far as it will go, and then switch to a second piece of dough, rolling it out only as far as it wants to go. Then return to the first dough, which has had a chance to rest, and you will find that the gluten has relaxed and stretched and the bread is much easier to roll out. When worked with patiently in this way, high-gluten doughs can be rolled out as thin as you like.

SHAPING AND STAMPING

What differentiates one flatbread from another in many parts of the world is how the breads are shaped. The dough may be exactly the same, but the breads have a different shape or pattern, and as a result, frequently a different taste and texture. A simple flatbread called naan is made all the way from northern India to the Middle East, but there are dozens of different naan, many distinguished simply by the way in which they are shaped and their top surfaces stamped or pricked or slashed with a design.

Stamping and Pricking: If a dough is pricked with a fork or stamped, and therefore not allowed to "balloon," it makes a stronger bread. In Central Asia, often the center of a flatbread will be stamped, while the outside edge is left like a pizza crust to rise unimpeded, giving the bread two textures in one bread. Stamping is a deliberate way of individualizing a bread. In our kitchen we have a small collection of stamps, most from Central and West Asia. They vary from the ornate and elaborate to the simple and crude. A common Central Asian stamp has a wooden handle and a circular bottom surface studded with sharp nails. The bread is stamped right through with the nails to make concentric circles of tiny holes. Stamping of this kind can easily be done with a fork. A fork is also used to prick and decorate Moroccan Anise Bread and Finnish Barley Bread.

Similarly, we know of several distinctive ways of shaping matzoh, using a comb or a nail to make decorative holes or lacy patterns in the bread. The edges of the pierced places have a crisper texture than the rest of the bread; the holes also help prevent the bread from puffing up during baking. Olive Ladder Bread and Afghan Home-style Naan are also cut through, to give more crust and a distinctive shape to the loaf.

Slashing: Slashing the top surface of a bread, a common practice in loaf baking, allows the bread to expand and to rise higher. Marking a loaf with a slash or with fingertips, as for Ethiopian Spice Bread, Tibetan Barley Skillet Bread, and Aromatic Festive Bread, among others, is also a way of making a bread distinctive.

BAKING

While many traditional methods of cooking flatbreads translate without any diffi- culty whatsoever into a North American kitchen, others must be adapted in one way or another. Using quarry tiles and an upside-down wok are two ways we have found to successfully approximate traditional methods of baking.

Oven Baking—Quarry Tiles and Baking Stones: In many recipes, we call for using unglazed quarry tiles placed on the bottom rack of the oven. The main reason for using quarry tiles is to produce breads with a firm, tasty bottom crust and a softer top surface, very like tandoor-baked breads (see Tandoor Ovens, page 35). The tiles, much the same as a clay tandoor surface, absorb moisture from the dough, creating a crusty bottom surface. They also help to distribute heat more evenly in the oven.

Inexpensive unglazed quarry tiles are available at most tile stores. Before heading off to the tile store, measure a rack in your oven. Buy tiles that will fit side by side to cover the rack, but leave a one-inch gap all around so that the heat can freely circulate around the oven. (We recommend buying two or three more tiles than you need, so you have extras.)

You can also use one of the baking stones designed to be placed on a rack in your oven. We have not used these stones, but they make a more than adequate substitute for unglazed quarry tiles. Baking stones are available from specialty cook- ware stores. Because some of the breads in this book are long, you need a stone that is almost as large as your oven, not just a round pizza stone. The thicker the stone, the more evenly it will distribute the heat and the less likely it is to break. Place it on an oven rack in the same way as the recipes direct for quarry tiles, leaving a one- inch gap between the edge of the stone and the oven walls. The advantage of bak- ing stones is that they will not shift around as quarry tiles sometimes do. However, they are substantially more expensive than quarry tiles.

When using quarry tiles or a baking stone for flatbreads, preheat your oven for fifteen minutes longer than it takes to bring your oven to the correct tempera- ture. The extra preheating will ensure that the tiles (or stone) are well heated and will help the breads to rise, and to balloon if they are intended to.

Transferring Breads In and Out of the Oven: Placing a large, soft, pliable flatbread onto hot quarry tiles in a very hot oven can sometimes be tricky. Professional bak- ers use a peel, a large flat wooden paddle with a long handle, which allows them to slip breads in and out of the oven while maintaining a safe distance from the heat. Peels are fun to use and work effectively when you have a large oven with a smooth baking surface. But when baking in a home oven, a peel can be more trouble than it is worth because a small kitchen and/or a small oven leave little room for maneuvering.

We prefer simply laying or tossing the breads onto the tiles. This might at first feel intimidating, but with a little practice, you'll soon have the hang of it. The first thing to do is to take out the other oven rack before you preheat the oven, which will give you more room to work in. (You can use the extra rack for cooling breads as they come out of the oven.)

When baking extra-large flatbreads like a pizza directly on quarry tiles, use the back side of a baking sheet, or a peel, to transfer the breads to the oven. Liberally dust the surface with flour or cornmeal before placing the bread on top. When placing the bread into the oven, gently slip the back edge of the dough onto the back edge of your hot tiles, and then let the rest of the dough slide down onto the tiles as you remove the baking sheet or peel. Some bakers do this with a masterful in-out motion of their wrist, almost jerking the bread off, but this doesn't always work well in a small space.

For taking flatbreads out of the hot oven, we use a large, long metal spatula, the kind used for outdoor grilling, to quickly flip breads out of the oven.

Stove-top Cooking—Griddle and Sajj: Baking breads on a griddle or in a cast-iron skillet is another one of those baking processes with its own little mysteries. Why does one skillet or griddle work so well and another so poorly?

One general rule with cast-iron griddles and skillets (which we generally prefer over non-stick surfaces) is that the heavier and thicker the skillet, the better it is. There is nothing better than a dependable griddle for turning out good stove-top breads, so it is worth experimenting until you find a good one.

Several flatbreads in this book, such as Bedouin Barley Bread and Paperthin Lavash, are traditionally cooked on a sajj, a convex dome-like pan that is placed over a fire or burner. We usually improvise for a sajj by using a wok turned upside down over our gas burner. As with griddles or skillets, a heavier weight wok (ours is of spun steel) works best to distribute the heat evenly and prevent hot spots.

When cooking stove-top breads, it is worth remembering to trust your feel and not necessarily the precise times or temperatures given in a recipe.

Baking Over an Open Fire: One of the most pleasing and flavorful ways of turning dough into bread is over an open fire, exactly the way many traditional breads are still made. If you are planning to have a campfire, do consider taking flour and making breads. The easiest campfire griddle bread we know is Soft Whole Wheat Skillet

Bread, though it is also quite easy to take a sajj or an inverted wok and make Bedouin Barley Bread. Bannock is another great campfire bread, quickly mixed and then cooked in a well-greased griddle. Most of these breads come from nomadic or hunting traditions, where portability and simplicity are vital. If you have a yeasted dough, you can cook it over an open fire in a skillet, or if it is rolled out thin, on an upside-down wok.

We have also tried making thin strips out of yeasted dough, coiling each in a spiral along and around the end of a long stick, and then baking them as we would roast marshmallows or hot dogs. The bread turns out well as long as it is baked over very moderate heat (you should be able to hold your hand at the same distance from the coals for thirty seconds—usually at least six inches from coals). If the bread is too close to high heat, it cooks too quickly on the outside while staying uncooked inside.

STORING THE DOUGH

In several of these recipes, we suggest that once the dough has had a first rise, you bake part of it and store the rest well sealed in a plastic bag in the refrigerator. Refrigerated dough gets weaker over time; consequently, refrigerating doughs is not a good idea for loaf breads. But for yeasted flatbreads, particularly those less than one inch thick, refrigerator storage is an ideal, flexible way of having fresh bread quickly available. We usually store doughs for no longer than a week in the refrigerator.

If you have a dough in the refrigerator and want to bake a few fresh breads for breakfast or for unexpected guests, cut off the amount of dough you want and leave the rest well sealed in the refrigerator. (You will notice after a day or two that the dough is wetter than when you put it into the refrigerator; if it is particularly moist, knead it briefly on a lightly floured surface.) On a lightly floured surface, divide into pieces the dough to be baked, and flatten each piece lightly. Cover with plastic wrap to rest and come to room temperature.

Dough must be at room temperature to bake successfully. If it is too cold, the outside will overcook before the inside is done, resulting in a doughy texture. Of course, the thinner your breads are rolled before baking, the more quickly they will lose their chill and the more evenly they will bake. If you are in a real hurry, make very thin breads and use the heat of your hands to help warm the dough, by flattening each piece with the palm of your hand, then picking it up and flattening it in the air between your palms.

CLEANING UP

Cleaning up after making bread is simple if you do it as soon as you finish; leaving bits of dough in the bowl, putting the bowl aside, and forgetting to clean it out for an hour or two, will make clean-up a chore. (The same goes for wooden spoons, dough scrapers, and more or less anything you used that came into contact with a sticky dough.)

We have a cooking-class habit of running a sinkful of hot, soapy water whenever we come into a kitchen to cook, and this applies when we make bread as well. Whenever we finish using a spoon or a bowl or a measuring cup, we throw it into the water. We don't need to wash it right that minute, but by the time we get around to washing, everything can be easily cleaned.

KEEPING BREAD: DRYING, FREEZING, AND REHEATING

When a bread or batch of flatbreads comes hot out of the oven, there are two choices about what to do next. If the breads are to be eaten within a short time, they should be stacked and wrapped in a cotton cloth or kitchen towel. If the breads are meant to last for several days or longer, they should be set out on a rack to cool thoroughly before being stored.

Wrapping breads traps both heat and moisture, keeping the breads soft, warm, and pliable—but the moisture also makes the breads more susceptible to spoilage. A rule of thumb is that all thicker flatbreads, as well as flatbreads made in large quantities to feed a household over a number of days, should be placed on racks to cool. Excess steam will be given off as the breads cool, and the crust will firm up. When they are completely cool, wrap the breads in a plastic bag and seal it securely; they will keep well at room temperature for several days. Do not store breads in the refrigerator; they will become stale more quickly than at room temperature.

Drying Breads: Many of the world's oldest flatbread traditions revolve around another option for baked breads, and that is drying. In the case of Paperthin Lavash, Norwegian Crispbread, Finnish Rye Hardtack Rings, and a host of other breads from Anatolia to Switzerland to Central Asia, drying bread has for hundreds of years been a successful method for preserving grains. After baking, the breads are left out to dry completely, and then can be stored for months. Dried breads are traditionally revived with a sprinkling of water, or crumbled into soup or tea and eaten like a bread soup or porridge. Dried bread is also light to carry—witness the Sardinian Parchment Bread, which is carried by shepherds as they follow their flocks through the hills.

Several of the flatbreads in this book can be preserved by drying. If you have extra pita, or any of the breads discussed previously, set a few out to dry. Make sure that they dry out completely; if need be, place them on an oven rack in a preheated 250 degree oven, and then check on them every ten minutes or so, until they are completely dry. Then let cool, and wrap in a plastic bag. (If you've made a hole through each one, they can be hung up with piece of string, like the Finnish Rye Hardtack Rings.)

You can use dried pita and similar breads to make Middle Eastern Toasted Pita, for soups (see Yemeni Yogurt Soup), salads (see Bread Salad), or main dishes (see Layered Chicken and Yogurt Casserole). Alternatively, break the breads into a hot soup to add body, texture, and flavor. Having an assortment of croutons is always more interesting than having just one kind.

Freezing: Our modern method for preserving food—freezing—works well for most flatbreads, so well in fact that it can sometimes be difficult to tell a warm, moist, reheated bread from a fresh bread. As a reheated bread cools, however, it becomes drier and tougher than freshly baked bread, particularly if it was reheated in a microwave. We freeze flatbreads in small batches, well sealed in plastic bags, so we can take only the breads we need out of the freezer.

Reheating: What is the best way of reheating bread? It depends upon the type of bread. Thin flatbreads, such as pita, wheat flour tortillas, and chapatti, can be quickly and easily reheated on a griddle over medium-high heat. If they are at room temperature, less than a minute on the first side and twenty seconds on the second should suffice. Thin flatbreads that are still frozen should be partially defrosted, then griddle-heated; they will take a little longer. Stack reheated breads and wrap them in a towel to keep in moisture and warmth. A very attractive way of reheating pieces of thin-crust pizza, or pita, naan, or other thin to medium-thick leavened breads, is to place them on a heated grill for a few moments. The grill will leave black grid lines on the breads and, if charcoal fired, will give the breads a pleasing, slightly smoky taste.

Thicker breads, such as Afghan Home-style Naan, Tibetan Barley Skillet Bread, and Three-Color Focaccia, are best reheated in a 350°F degree oven. Place the bread in a brown paper bag and fold it closed, then sprinkle the bag liberally with water and place it on the middle oven rack. The sprinkled water keeps the paper from burning in the heat of the oven and the paper keeps the bread's moisture (which turns to steam as it heats) from escaping. Depending on the size of the bread, it will take from ten to twenty minutes to reheat (be careful when opening the bag to avoid the hot steam which may have built up inside). Once the bread comes out of the bag, wrap it immediately in a cloth to keep it warm and moist until serving.

Reheating in a microwave causes bread to lose a great deal of moisture. You can retain some moisture by sealing the bread in a brown paper bag before placing it in the microwave oven, though using a paper bag can result in a slightly soggy crust. For these reasons, we avoid using the microwave for reheating.

A hot broiler is another good way of reheating many flatbreads, but, as is the case with reheating in a microwave, once a bread has been reheated under a broiler, it should be eaten immediately. Place the bread on a rack as close as possible to the broiler, then watch carefully as the bread reheats and toasts, letting your eyes and nose be the judge of when it is ready.

Selecting a Flatbread to Make

Use this list of breads by category to select an appropriate flatbread for a specific occasion. These breads are our favorites in each category.

BREAKFAST BREADS: Sri Lankan Coconut Breakfast Bread, Spelt Breakfast Bread, Berry Bannock, Scottish Oatcakes

FILLED BREADS: Georgian Cheese Boat Breads, Potato-and-Herb-Filled Bread

SWEET BREADS: Aromatic Festive Bread, Date-Bread Morsels, Apricot and Almond Bread, Norwegian Wrapping Bread, Sweet Bread Rings, Buckwheat Honey Country Bread

SAVORY BREADS: Bulgur Bread, Olive Ladder Bread, Uighur Nan with Cumin and Onion, Three-Color Focaccia, Pizza with Rosemary and Garlic, Lamb and Tomato Breads

MILDLY SPICED BREADS: Ethiopian Spice Bread, Moroccan Anise Bread, Aromatic Festive Bread, Thyme Bread, Afghan Snowshoe Naan, Fenugreek Corn Bread

STRONGLY SPICED BREADS: Chile Bread, Xichuan Pepper Bread, Rajasthani Salt and Spice Bread, Fresh Coriander, Ginger, and Chile Crêpes

GREAT BREADS FOR SNACKING: High-Tech Crackers, Sardinian Parchment Bread, Pueblo Sunflower Seed Breads

CRISP BREADS: Norwegian Crispbread, Sardinian Parchment Bread, High-Tech Crackers, Crisp Lentil Wafers

FLAT LOAVES FOR SLICING: Ethiopian Spice Bread, Tibetan Barley Skillet Bread, Apricot and Almond Bread

BREADS USED AS WRAPPERS: Beijing Pancakes, Wheat-Flour Tortillas, Fresh Rice Papers, Norwegian Wrapping Bread, Rice and Black Lentil Crêpes, Fresh Coriander, Ginger, and Chile Crêpes

BREADS USED FOR SCOOPING: Soft Whole Wheat Skillet Breads, Deep-Fried Whole Wheat Breads with Cumin, Blue Corn Tortillas, Corn Tortillas

BREADS USED AS A "SPONGE" FOR OTHER FLAVORS: Ethiopian Sponge Breads, Rice and Black Lentil Crêpes, Fresh Coriander, Ginger, and Chile Crêpes

BREADS FOR DUNKING IN SOUP: Afghan Home-style Naan, Moroccan Anise Bread, Ethiopian Spice Bread, Olive Ladder Bread, San'a Sorghum Breads, Apricot and Almond Bread

BREADS FOR APPETIZERS: Pizza with Rosemary and Garlic, Lamb and Tomato Breads, Three-Color Focaccia, Olive Ladder Bread, Georgian Cheese-Filled Quick Bread

BEST BREADS FOR BEGINNERS: Pita, Soft Whole Wheat Skillet Breads, High-Tech Crackers

BREADS MADE USING AN INTERESTING TECHNIQUE: Ethiopian Sponge Breads, Rice and Black Lentil Crêpes, Flung and Folded Griddle Breads, Hunza Sprouted Wheat Breads, Lacy Coconut Milk Pancakes, Pebbled Persian Bread

BREADS USING A SOURED DOUGH: Rice and Black Lentil Crêpes, Paperthin Lavash, Turcoman Sourdough Bread

BREADS TO MAKE WITH CHILDREN: High-Tech Crackers, Pizza with Rosemary and Garlic, Berry Bannock

FLATBREAD "CLASSICS": Pita, Corn Tortillas, Afghan Snowshoe Naan, Paperthin Lavash, Soft Whole Wheat Skillet Breads

YEAST-FREE FLATBREADS (A SMALL SELECTION): Soft Whole Wheat Skillet Breads, High-Tech Crackers, Sardinian Parchment Bread, Bulgur Bread, Hunza Sprouted Wheat Breads, Unyeasted Date Rounds

WHEAT-FREE FLATBREADS (A SMALL SELECTION): Ethiopian Sponge Bread, Rice and Black Lentil Crêpes, Fresh Rice Papers, Corn Tortillas, Rye Hardtack Rings, Scottish Oatcakes, Lacy Coconut Milk Pancakes, Finnish Barley Bread

1. Uighur Nan with Cumin and Onion
2. Afghan Home-style Naan
3. Afghan Snowshoe Naan
4. Apple Turnovers
5. Hunza Sprouted Wheat Breads
6. Apricot and Almond Bread
7. Pebbled Persian Bread
8. Sweet Persian Bread
9. Turcoman Sourdough Bread
10. Tibetan Barley Skillet Bread

Central Asia

Central Asia is a landlocked complex of high mountains, high-altitude grasslands, and vast deserts punctuated by fertile oases. It extends from the deserts and mountains of China's Xinjiang Province to Uzbekistan and Turkmenistan, from Hunza and Tibet to Afghanistan and Iran.

With little water and an extreme continental climate, much of Central Asia is suited to little but nomad or seminomad cultures: Herds of sheep and goats survive on meagre pastures in Turkmenistan's deserts and in much of Afghanistan, while in the high-altitude plateaus of Tibet and the high valleys of the Afghan, Tajik, and Chinese Pamirs, goats and yaks are the main animal resource. The herds provide milk and meat, as well as wool, which can be traded for grain. Seminomads live in villages and cultivate grain—wheat where the climate permits, barley in colder high-altitude areas—as well as maintain herds, which move from pasture to pasture in the mountains or grasslands.

Turkmenistan: Stamping bread before baking

In the desert oases, grain is grown, along with a great variety of fruits and vegetables, which thrive given ample water and protection from the harsh desert winds. Here too, on the margins of the oases, herds of sheep and goats are maintained to supply meat and milk, while chickens are kept in most households for both eggs and meat.

The breads baked by Central Asian nomads are elegant responses to the problem of scarce grain and fuel resources. Most often they are thin rounds quickly cooked over a fire in a skillet or sajj. Where there are permanent settlements, leavened breads are baked in household tandoor ovens or purchased from a local

baker. The tandoor breads are slightly thicker than nomad breads, with a crusty bottom surface and softer top. They are made to be dipped in tea or yogurt or torn and eaten wrapped around pieces of grilled lamb or chicken. The home-style breads may be made tender with the addition of a little yogurt or milk,

Xinjiang: Baker lifting naan from tandoor

while the bakery breads are straightforward combinations of wheat flour, leavening, salt, and water, shaped distinctively.

Where the climate is moderate and water is available, a greater variety of foods results in a more elaborate cuisine. In Central Asia, the most influential and highly developed cuisine is from ancient Persia, now Iran. Classic Persian savory dishes are sophisticated blends of tart and sweet; fruits are combined with meat, and fresh herbs are served with every meal. Persian cuisine influenced cultures in all the more fertile areas of Central Asia, such as the valleys of Hunza and Tajikistan and the desert oases of Uzbekistan.

Chinese Pamirs: Tajik girl by yurt

Uighur Nan with Cumin and Onion

Kashgar, Xinjiang, China

Kashgar, an oasis town on the edge of the Taklimakan Desert in the far west of China, has throughout its history been a crossroads between the worlds of the east and west. It is home to the Uighurs, a Turkic population who are the majority (far outnumbering the Han Chinese) in China's Xinjiang Province. Wheat is the staple food of the Uighurs, as it is for most other Central Asians, and the main crop of the oasis.

Kashgar is a flatbread paradise. There are flatbreads on every street corner and in every little eatery: breads with cumin seeds and onion, breads with garlic, breads with sesame seeds, bagel-like flatbreads—breads, breads, and more breads. There are also homemade noodles and shashlik, and more varieties of melons than you will see anywhere else in a lifetime. Tomatoes in Kashgar taste the way tomatoes should taste, and chiles are added to everything without restraint.

Uighur nan, like the flatbreads of much of Central Asia, are traditionally cooked in tandoor ovens (see page 35). (The tandoor technique can be very successfully and easily reproduced in a North American kitchen using unglazed quarry tiles or a baking stone.) This version of Uighur nan is round, with a flat center sprinkled with cumin, scallions, and salt. The rim has a thick crust, good for tearing off and dipping in tea.

2 teaspoons dry yeast

2½ cups lukewarm water

5 to 6 cups hard unbleached white flour

Approximately 1 tablespoon salt

Approximately 3 tablespoons finely chopped scallions (white and tender green parts)

Approximately 1 teaspoon cumin seed

You will need a large bread bowl, unglazed quarry tiles to fit on a rack in your oven (see page 20) or one or two baking sheets, a baker's peel or large baking sheet, a rolling pin, a bread stamp (see page 19) or a fork, and an optional spray bottle.

Sprinkle the yeast over the warm water in a large bowl. Stir to dissolve. Stir in 3 cups flour, a cup at a time. Then stir the dough 100 times in the same direction, about 1 minute, to develop the gluten. Add 2 teaspoons salt, then continue adding flour until the dough is too stiff to stir. Turn out onto a lightly floured bread board, and knead until smooth and elastic, about 8 minutes, adding more flour if necessary to prevent sticking.

continued

Rinse out, wipe, and lightly oil the bread bowl. Add the dough, cover with plastic wrap, and let rise until doubled in volume, about 1½ hours.

Position a rack in the lower third of your oven and arrange quarry tiles on the rack, leaving a 1-inch gap between the tiles and the oven walls. If you have no quarry tiles, instead place one large or two small baking sheets on the rack to preheat. Preheat the oven to 500°F.

Uighur nan for sale in Xinjiang

Punch the dough down and turn out onto a lightly floured surface. Divide into 6 pieces. Using lightly floured hands, flatten each piece into a 4- to 5-inch round. Cover the rounds with a dry cloth. Keeping the remaining pieces covered as you work, roll each dough round out on a lightly floured surface into a 10-inch round. The dough may spring back as you roll; it's best to work on 2 or 3 dough rounds at a time, alternating between them, to give the gluten time to stretch before you resume rolling. Then cover the large rounds with plastic wrap and let rise for 10 minutes.

Working with 2 breads at a time, using a bread stamp or a fork, stamp the center portion of each bread; work from the center out until the dough is thoroughly pricked and flattened, leaving 1½- to 2-inch rim all around. Sprinkle a scant teaspoon of scallions, a generous pinch of cumin seed, and a generous pinch of salt over the center of each bread, then dip your fingers in water and sprinkle the centers of the breads.

Slide each round onto a baker's peel or flour-dusted baking sheet, and slide off onto the quarry tiles or preheated baking sheet. Bake until the tops of the breads begin to brown, 8 to 10 minutes.

Transfer to a rack to cool for 5 minutes, then wrap in a cloth to keep soft and warm. Repeat with the remaining dough, scallions, cumin, and salt. Serve warm.

▲▲▲▲▲▲▲▲▲▲▲▲▲▲▲▲▲▲▲▲▲▲▲

Makes 6 large round flatbreads about 10 inches in diameter.

Serve with Spicy Cumin Kebabs (page 33), Sweet Onion Salad (page 65), and Oasis Peppers (page 34). These are also great on their own, dipped into Mint and Yogurt Sauce (page 43).

Spicy Cumin Kebabs

Xinjiang, China

This spicy grill is the classic street food in all the oasis towns that rim the Takliamakan Desert in western China. The small skewered pieces of lamb are first rubbed with dry spices, then quickly grilled with a sprinkling of salt. The spices bake onto the meat, giving the kebabs a tasty, aromatic surface to bite into.

2 pounds boneless leg of lamb	1 teaspoon black peppercorns
1 tablespoon cumin seed	1 teaspoon salt, or more to taste
1 teaspoon cayenne	

You will need 12 to 15 small wooden or metal skewers, a charcoal or gas grill, and a spice grinder or mortar and pestle.

If using wooden skewers, soak them in water for at least 1 hour.

Prepare the grill.

Remove excess fat from the meat, and cut the lamb into ½-inch chunks. Thread them onto the skewers.

Grind or pound together the cumin, cayenne, and black pepper to a powder. Rub the spice mixture over the skewered meat.

Grill the lamb for 5 to 8 minutes over hot coals, turning to cook on all sides. Halfway through the cooking, sprinkle the salt on the kebabs. Serve hot.

Alternatives: Using the same technique, rub the Georgian Spice Blend (page 304) over the lamb before grilling; serve with Sour Plum Sauce (page 309).

▲▲▲▲▲▲·▲▲▲▲▲▲▲▲▲··▲▲▲

Makes 12 to 15 skewers of grilled lamb chunks.
Serves 4 to 6 as part of a bread-based meal.

Serve hot with Mint and Yogurt Sauce (page 43), Sweet Onion Salad (page 65),
Oasis Peppers (page 34), and plenty of Uighur Nan (page 31).

Oasis Peppers

Xinjiang, China

Whenever we see beautiful bell peppers in an assortment of bright colors, we think of Oasis Peppers. This easy stir-fry has become one of our summertime favorites. With a touch of garlic, salt, and sugar, it keeps the freshness and the color of the peppers and at the same time transforms them into something new. A basket of fresh warm Uighur nan, a plate of stir-fried peppers, a cold glass of beer, and we are quite content.

Uighur man stretching noodles

> 1½ pounds bell peppers of assorted
>   colors (green, red, yellow, and orange)
> 1 to 2 tablespoons vegetable oil
> 1 tablespoon finely chopped garlic
> ½ teaspoon salt
> ½ teaspoon sugar

You will need a large wok or skillet.

Cut the peppers lengthwise in half and take out the veins and seeds. Slice crosswise into very thin slices.

Heat a large wok or skillet over high heat. When hot, add the oil. When the oil is hot, add the garlic and stir-fry until lightly golden. Toss in the peppers, and cook, stirring constantly, until tender, 1 to 2 minutes. Add the salt and sugar, toss and stir for another 30 seconds, and then turn out onto a plate. Serve hot with flatbreads.

▲▲▲▲▲▲▲▲▲▲▲▲▲▲▲▲▲▲▲▲▲

Serves 4 as a side dish.

This makes a great combination with Uighur Nan (page 31) and Spicy Cumin Kebabs (page 33).

TANDOOR OVENS

*For millions of people across Asia, and in small pockets of Africa as well, flat-*breads and tandoor ovens go together "like a horse and carriage." Many of these people rely upon tandoor breads for far more than half the calories they eat each day, giving the bread (and the oven) an importance the equivalent of which we really don't have in contemporary Western culinary traditions.

At their best, there is nothing we would rather eat than tandoor breads, and even at their worst, they are still good. Like food cooked over an outdoor grill, they always impart a trace of the tandoor, giving the breads a flavor of the fire and of roasted grain. The taste and smell of the breads arouse appetites—day after day, year after year—in a way that only simple, life-sustaining foods can do.

Tannur ovens for sale in Yemen

The word *tandoor* with its variants *tannur, tennur, tandir, tandore, tamdir, tandur, tanir, tanoor,* and even more, is the general word for oven in a multitude of languages, including Hebrew, Farsi, Kurdish, Arabic, Aramaic, Assyrian, Persian, and Tajik, as well as Turkish and the Turkic languages of Central Asia (Kazakh, Uzbek, Kirghiz, Uighur, Turkmen). The basic tandoor design seems to have originated in what is now Iran, or in areas nearby, and then to have traveled east to China and India; west to Yemen, Tunisia, Morocco, and Mali; and north to Turkey and Georgia. Perhaps the oven was originally developed for firing pottery and then someone realized that it could be used for baking. Or maybe the discovery went in the other direction.

Every tandoor, whether it is a large Afghan tandoor or a simple Yemeni household tannur set into a kitchen counter, works on the same principle. Lined with clay and shaped more or less like a barrel, tandoors stand vertically and are usually encased in mud, concrete, or some other type of support and insulation. The fire, made from wood, dung, coal, or gas, burns fiercely at the bottom of the oven, preheating the oven walls. When the tandoor is sufficiently hot, the fire is dampened to produce a bed of coals (or, in the case of gas, the flame is lowered), to maintain heat without singeing the breads. The flatbreads are usually moistened, then placed on a baker's pillow, a padded dome with a handle on the back. The baker picks up the pillow by the handle and uses it to slap the breads against the hot inside walls of the oven, where they bake in a very short time. Baking on the hot walls gives the breads a firm well-browned bottom crust, while the tops are cooked by the hot air traveling up from the coals below. Other foods cooked in the tandoor, such as tandoori chicken in North Indian Punjabi cooking, are pierced or threaded onto long metal skewers, which are placed into the hot tandoor.

Bicycling high in the Chinese Pamirs, we stopped several times one morning to look at groupings of three or four tandoor ovens set out like offerings in the beautiful wide-open landscape. Each oven was surrounded by a circle of rocks, used to hold down the perimeters of a tent. Later the same day, as we came over a small hill, we saw in the distance three dark felt yurts surrounded by small herds of sheep and goats. Children immediately came running across the landscape to see who we were, then waved us over to the campsite.

The families we found there were Tajik herders living a seminomadic existence, moving their herds from one meager pasture to another, depending on the

Turkmenistan: Slapping bread on a tandoor wall

season. When they return to certain pastures, their ovens are there, waiting for the shelter of the yurts. These ovens, circular columns built of mud and rock with a narrow slit at the front, are strong and easily brought back into working order. After we laid our bicycles down by one yurt and were escorted inside, we were thrilled to see the tandoor, set in the center of the yurt, already hot and in use. Handwoven carpets and blankets were folded and neatly stored around the walls of the yurt, along with twenty-kilo bags of wheat. A shaft of light coming down from an open flap of felt in the roof fell just to one side of the oven. The atmosphere inside the yurt was incredibly warm and welcoming with the smell of bread, fire, and earth. The ovens on the landscape and in this Tajik yurt gave us new meaning for the hearth—a movable hearth, a nomadic hearth.

In Yemen, tannurs are portable: You can purchase one at the market and walk home, carrying your oven on one shoulder. An arm's breadth in circumference and two and a half to three feet high, a Yemeni tannur is made from baked red clay. The oven is set down into a mud or concrete casing in the kitchen. It resembles the small portable clay kanoon oven of Morocco, which is also sometimes used for baking tandoor-style breads (see Portrait of Ouza, page 253). Of particular interest in Yemen, a country with an amazingly wide assortment of breads all baked in different ways, is the fact that tannur-baked breads are almost solely the domain of home bakers, seldom finding their way into the marketplace.

Traditional tandoor baking is an art learned over years of experience. On the edge of the Ashkabad oasis in Turkmenistan on a drizzly cold November day, I was reminded of just how tricky tandoor baking can be. As I came by on the road, a young woman was just starting to heat her oven, a dried mud-and-plaster beehive beside her house; I asked if I could watch. She gave me a distracted nod of assent and went back to the oven. She got a great blaze going—flames shooting out through the hole at the top of the oven—and then it died down into coals. Her mother-in-law appeared, carrying the breads out of the house on a tray. One by one, she pricked the large thick rolled-out breads with a stamp and placed them on the baker's pillow. Then the young woman picked up the pillow, leaned into the oven from above, and slapped the breads carefully against the heated inside walls of the oven. But—misery—the oven wasn't hot enough, and soon several of the breads began to sag. If the oven had been hotter, the top side of the breads would have dried and baked very quickly. As it was, the heavy uncooked dough started to detach itself from the bottom surface of the breads and to slide slowly down the oven wall. The mother-in-law pursed her lips, the daughter-in-law bowed her head, hiding tears.

Afghan Home-Style Naan

This Afghan home-style bread is a classic Central Asian naan, delicious on its own or as an accompaniment to almost any meal. Unlike Afghan Snowshoe Naan, which is much thinner, this bread is thick, soft, and almost rich in taste.

2 teaspoons dry yeast	Approximately 5½ cups hard whole wheat flour
½ cup warm water (105°F to 115°F)	2 tablespoons safflower or corn oil
1 cup well-chilled plain whole-milk yogurt	2 teaspoons salt
1 cup boiling water	6 tablespoons sesame seeds

You will need a large bread bowl, a medium-sized bowl, unglazed quarry tiles (see page 20) to fit on a rack in your oven or a baking sheet at least 10 by 14 inches, a baker's peel or another large baking sheet, a rolling pin, and a razor blade or sharp knife.

Sprinkle the yeast over the warm water in a large bowl. Stir to dissolve.

Place the yogurt in a medium bowl, and gradually stir in the boiling water. Let cool to tepid (105°F to 115°F).

Stir the yogurt mixture into the yeast mixture. Stir in 3 cups flour, ½ cup at a time. Then stir for 2 minutes in the same direction: You now have a sponge. Cover with plastic wrap and let stand for 30 minutes.

Sprinkle the oil and salt onto the sponge. Mix in enough of the remaining flour, ½ cup at a time, to form a dough. Turn out onto a lightly floured surface and knead until smooth and elastic, adding more flour if the dough is sticky, about 10 minutes.

Wash out and lightly oil the large bowl. Add the dough, turning to coat the entire surface. Cover with a damp kitchen towel or plastic wrap and let rise until doubled in volume, about 1 hour.

Position a rack in the lower third of the oven and arrange quarry tiles on the rack, leaving a 1-inch space between the tiles and the oven walls. Or place a 10- by 14-inch, or larger, baking sheet in the oven to preheat. Preheat the oven to 450°F.

Punch the dough down. Divide into 6 pieces. Using lightly floured hands, flatten each piece on a lightly floured work surface into a 4- to 5-inch round. Cover the rounds with a kitchen towel or plastic wrap and let rest for 10 minutes.

Lightly flour a baker's peel or the back side of a large baking sheet. Working with one dough round at a time, roll out on a lightly floured surface until the dough begins to stretch (keep the remaining dough covered). Brush the flour from the work surface, and sprinkle 1 tablespoon of the sesame seeds onto the work surface. Lay the dough on the seeds and roll out into a 6- by 10-inch rectangle. Turn the dough over. Using a razor blade or the tip of a sharp knife, cut five 1-inch-long slits evenly spaced around the dough, radiating out from the center like sun rays or flower petals. Slide the dough onto the baker's peel or prepared sheet. Then slide the dough onto the quarry tiles or preheated baking sheet and bake until the top begins to brown, about 5 minutes. Transfer the bread to a rack. Repeat with the remaining dough rounds and sesame seeds.

Serve warm or at room temperature.

▲▲▲▲▲▲▲▲▲▲▲▲▲▲▲▲▲▲▲▲▲

Makes 6 rectangular flatbreads, about 5 inches by 9 inches.

Serve with Chicken Street Kebabs (page 44) or Aziz's Apricot Noodle Soup (page 51).

Afghan Snowshoe Naan

Afghanistan, Iran, and Turkey

I never quite figured out the daily routine of the neighborhood bakery just around the corner from the small hotel in Kabul where I was staying. Early in the morning, late in the evening, midday—there was never a set schedule, yet no matter when they'd bake, there would immediately be a line of people waiting with out-stretched arms for breads. At least it was easy to know that they were baking, as the warm, welcoming smell of the tandoor—and of the juniper coals inside—would make its way quickly through the neighborhood. In Kabul the air is crisp and dry, and smells travel well—especially the smell of hot bread.

The bakery was unlike any other bakery I had ever seen. When baking wasn't actually in progress, there were no breads, no people, nothing. The bakery wasn't even a building. It looked something like a neglected piece of wooden scaf-folding, a project long ago started and abandoned. But once the baking got under-way, a group of seven or eight men and boys would climb up onto the scaffolding, and each would take his special place around the enormous burning hot tandoor—a little bit like a rock band coming on stage, the show about to start.

Oven hot, crew ready, out would come the breads—large, thin, whole wheat breads, stacks of them, hundreds of breads. People would line up and carry away ten breads, twenty breads. I could eat three—I did eat three—three times a day, leaving not much room for anything else. Which was quite all right; it was some of the best bread I have ever had.

Some years later we were in the town of Peshawar in northwestern Pakistan, which at the time was home to several hundred thousand Afghan refugees. It was midsummer and unbearably hot, well over 105°F. We'd come in search of an Afghan bakery, but we weren't allowed into the camps, so for days we'd searched with no luck.

One afternoon I hailed a rickshaw and asked my usual question: "Afghan naan?" The man immediately turned around: "Afghan naan?" I nodded. And away we went. About a mile down the road he stopped, turned around, and asked again, as if to make sure: "Afghan naan?" "Afghan naan," I nodded.

I'm not sure where we went, but it was far. We rode and we rode and we rode, at last pulling off the road at a small strip of five or six cinder-block buildings, a Pakistani version of a 1960s shopping mall. We rode up to the last building and there got out, at a cinder-block Afghan bakery.

In a back room a group of rough, tough, mean-looking men—and a few boys—sat watching television. The rickshaw driver introduced me as best he could:

"Afghan naan." A few men nodded and smiled. I sat down to watch TV. A bowl of spicy chickpeas arrived, and a plate of pureed spinach. Then an Afghan naan came, served on a plate, cut into small pieces, good but not hot. A man walked over and pointed at his watch: thirty minutes.

Half an hour later the television was turned off. Everyone got up and headed for the tandoor. The oven was hot, and people took their positions: The show was about to start. "Climb up here," the head baker, a thoughtful-looking, tall, long-limbed man, called out to me in English. By his side I looked into the tandoor. Four or five feet deep and two feet wide at its mouth, the oven was fired by natural gas and radiated intense heat.

The first bread baked was for me, a bread made double in size, a perfect snowshoe. As more breads were baked, we talked, about Afghanistan, about the war, about bread. All the men baking—and the boys—were Mujahideen. They seemed sad as a group, but serious and determined.

At one point the baker explained that in Peshawar natural gas is cheap, and wood scarce and expensive. "In Afghanistan we use wood, wood that smells of the country, of home," he said. "It makes the naan taste much better, like Afghan naan should taste."

▲▲▲▲▲▲▲▲·▲▲▲▲·▲▲▲··▲▲▲

In our house snowshoe naans are a favorite standby for parties, as well as a frequent everyday bread. They are easy to make and very beautiful: long and oval or snowshoe-shaped, less than half an inch thick, with lines of soft ripples on the surface. There is an attractive sprinkling of nigella, a small black seed sometimes called black onion seed, on each bread. Nigella has a pungent slightly oniony tang, hence its name. It is used commonly on breads all across Central Asia, as well as in the north of India, and is available in South Asian groceries. The taste of nigella is savory and appetizing, but a little goes a long way—in other words, don't overdo it.

2½ cups lukewarm water

1 teaspoon dry yeast

2 cups hard whole wheat flour

3 to 3½ cups hard unbleached white
   flour

1 tablespoon salt

Scant ½ teaspoon nigella
   (see page 417)

You will need a large bowl and unglazed quarry tiles (see page 20) to fit on a rack of your oven.

Place the water in a large bread bowl, add the yeast, and stir to blend. Add the whole wheat flour and stir well. Then stir 100 times, about 1 minute, in the same direction to develop the gluten. Cover this sponge with plastic wrap and let stand for 30 minutes to 3 hours.

Sprinkle salt over the sponge, then add 1 cup of the white flour and stir well. Continue adding white flour ½ cup at a time and stirring until the dough is too stiff to stir. Turn the dough out onto a lightly floured surface and knead thoroughly, until smooth and easy to handle, about 10 minutes.

Clean out the bowl, and oil lightly. Return the dough to the bowl, cover with plastic wrap, and let rise for 2 to 3 hours, until more than doubled in volume.

Gently push down the dough and turn out onto a lightly floured surface. Divide the dough into 4 equal pieces and shape each into a flat oval shape approximately 6 inches wide by 8 inches long. Cover with plastic wrap and let rise for approximately 20 minutes.

Place quarry tiles on the bottom rack of your oven, leaving a 1-inch space between the tiles and the oven walls to allow air to circulate. Preheat the oven to 450°F.

Five minutes after the oven has reached 450°F, begin shaping the first bread. Place a small bowl full of cold water at the edge of your work surface. Dip your fingertips in the water and then, beginning at one end of a disc of dough, make tightly spaced indentations all over the surface of the dough so that it is deeply and uniformly pitted. Now stretch the dough into a long oval strip by draping it over both hands and pulling them apart gently. The dough should gradually stretch and give, and after several tries will extend to make a long oval 16 to 18 inches long, with attractive stretch marks along it from the indentations (hence the name "snow-shoe bread"). There may also be a few small holes in the dough; don't worry about them—for many people, the slightly crisper areas around such holes and thin patches are the best part of the bread.

Place the bread back on the work surface, and sprinkle with a scant ⅛ teaspoon of nigella. Then, using both hands, place the bread on the heated quarry tiles, and bake for about 4 minutes, until the bread has golden patches on top and a crusty browned bottom surface. While the bread bakes, shape the next bread. You will soon develop a rhythm so that you can bake 2 breads side by side, one going in when the other is half-done.

To keep the breads warm and soft, let cool for 5 minutes, then wrap them in a cotton cloth. Serve warm or at room temperature.

▲▲▲▲▲▲▲▲▲▲▲▲▲▲▲▲▲▲▲▲▲

Makes 4 flatbreads approximately 5 inches wide and 16 to 18 inches long.

Serve with Mint and Yogurt Sauce (page 43) and Chicken Street Kebabs (page 44), with Pomegranate and Meatball Soup (page 60) or with Prune-Stuffed Kufta Soup (page 316).

Mint and Yogurt Sauce

Afghanistan

Similar versions of this garlic-yogurt dip can be found all the way from India to Egypt, for obvious reasons. It is simple and nutritious, and a delicious accompaniment to an enormously wide variety of different foods and tastes. Serve it with Spicy Cumin Kebabs or Aziz's Apricot Noodle Soup, or simply with warm naan. Yogurt, bread, and a little meat: the basic diet of the nomadic and seminomadic peoples of Central Asia.

1½ cups plain yogurt (see Note)

1 cup packed fresh mint leaves, finely chopped

1½ tablespoons minced garlic (3 to 4 cloves)

½ teaspoon salt

½ teaspoon black peppercorns, crushed or coarsely ground

You will need a medium-sized bowl.

Combine all the ingredients in a medium bowl and blend well. Refrigerate until chilled. (The sauce can be prepared up to 6 hours ahead and refrigerated, covered.)

Serve the sauce in individual bowls or in a larger serving bowl, with a spoon, so guests can spoon the sauce over grilled meats or scoop it up with flatbreads.

Note: If your yogurt is fairly liquid, or for a thicker sauce, drain yogurt in a cheesecloth–lined colander for 20 minutes before proceeding with the recipe.

▲▲▲▲▲▲▲▲▲▲▲▲▲▲▲▲▲▲▲

Makes about 2 cups sauce.

Serve with flatbreads, such as Afghan Home-style Naan (page 38) or any of the Central Asian breads, and drizzle over grilled meats such as Chicken Street Kebabs (page 44), Spicy Cumin Kebabs (page 33), or Marinated Lamb Kebabs (page 176).

Chicken Street Kebabs

Afghanistan

This is an approximation of a kebab I had almost fifteen years ago in a tiny little restaurant just off Chicken Street in Kabul. Our recipe may be somewhat off the mark, but the taste of the kebab still seems fresh in my mind. I went to the same restaurant every day, and ordered the same delicious little kebabs, wrapping them in pieces of naan torn off from a three-foot-long bread. For these savory kebabs, small pieces of boneless chicken are marinated in yogurt and spiced with turmeric and fresh mint before being grilled in the oven or on skewers over a charcoal grill. They are easy and delicious.

2 pounds boneless chicken legs, thighs, or breasts

m a r i n a d e

1 cup plain yogurt

⅛ teaspoon saffron threads, crushed and dissolved in 2 tablespoons water

¼ teaspoon turmeric

½ teaspoon freshly ground black pepper

½ teaspoon salt

1 cup fresh mint leaves, finely chopped

You will need 12 to 15 wooden or small metal skewers, a medium-sized bowl, a shallow nonreactive bowl, and a charcoal grill or a broiler.

If using wooden skewers, soak them in water for 30 minutes to 1 hour.

Cut the chicken into ½-inch pieces, discarding any skin, fat, and tough connective tissue.

Combine the yogurt with the spices and seasonings in a medium-sized bowl and mix well. Stir in the mint leaves.

Place the chicken in a shallow bowl, pour the marinade over, and stir to ensure that all of the chicken is well coated. Cover and let stand, refrigerated, for 3 to 4 hours.

Prepare a charcoal grill or preheat a broiler.

When the grill is almost ready, thread the chicken pieces on skewers. Place only a few pieces of chicken on each skewer and avoid crowding the pieces together. (If they are too tightly packed, they will not cook evenly.)

Grill over hot coals, on a rack 5 to 6 inches from the coals, turning the skewers to ensure even cooking, for 5 to 8 minutes. Alternatively, set the skewers over a baking pan and broil about 5 inches from the heat.

Serve with a fresh salad, a plate of fresh herbs, such as basil, tarragon, and flat-leafed parsley, and plenty of warm bread.

▲▲▲▲▲▲▲▲▲▲▲▲▲▲▲▲▲▲▲

Makes 12 to 15 skewers of grilled meat. Serves 4 to 6.

Serve with Mint and Yogurt Sauce (page 43), Sweet Onion Salad (page 65), an Herb Plate (page 291), and stacks of Afghan Home-style Naan (page 38) or Afghan Snowshoe Naan (page 40).

Apple Turnovers
Afghanistan

Among travelers making their way overland from Europe to India in the 1960s and 1970s, a small bakery in Kandahar, Afghanistan (I've never known its name), earned a huge reputation for fresh, warm, fabulous turnovers, simple, not too sweet, and packed with apple goodness.

Those turnovers have been for us an inspiration. Now we use the same dough for wrapping other fruits such as pears and plums, lightly dusted with sugar and spice. The dough is a simple flatbread dough—flour, salt, and water—no oil, no flaky pastry, just a straightforward, vital taste of wheat. There's no end to the yummy things that can be wrapped in flatbread doughs and baked.

These large half-moon–shaped breads are filled with apples, slightly sweetened with raisins and touched with cinnamon, which cook and soften as the turnovers bake—a wonderful midafternoon treat or satisfying dessert.

2 cups hard whole wheat flour

1 cup hard unbleached white flour

1 teaspoon salt

1½ cups water

2¼ pounds apples (preferably Pippin or Granny Smith)

½ cup brown sugar

1 cup raisins

1 tablespoon ground cinnamon

Juice of 1 lime

¼ cup apple juice or water

You will need two medium-sized mixing bowls, a rolling pin, and two small baking sheets that fit side by side in your oven.

continued

In a medium-sized bowl, mix together the flours and salt. Make a well in the center and pour in the water. Stir vigorously in one direction until all the flour is absorbed. When the dough becomes too stiff to stir, turn it onto a lightly floured bread board. Knead for 5 minutes, adding more flour if the dough is sticky. Cover with plastic wrap and let rest for 30 minutes.

Cut the apples into small chunks (peel or don't peel as you like). In a medium bowl, mix the apples with the brown sugar, raisins, cinnamon, lime juice, and apple juice or water. Mix well. Position a rack in the center of the oven, and preheat the oven to 350°F. Lightly grease two small baking sheets.

Divide the dough into 12 equal pieces. Between floured palms, pat each piece into a flat disc. With a rolling pin, roll out each disc until approximately 7 inches in diameter. If the dough is too soft and sticky, use flour to help in rolling. Put ½ cup of the apple mixture just slightly off-center on each round. Fold the dough in half to enclose the apple mixture, creating a turnover. Pinch together the edges and flute in a decorative way. (If the edges are not tightly sealed, some of the apple filling will ooze out during baking.)

Arrange the turnovers on the baking sheets, and bake for 20 to 25 minutes. Cool on a rack before serving.

▲▲▲▲▲▲▲▲▲▲▲▲▲▲▲▲▲▲▲▲▲▲▲

Makes 12 large half-moon–shaped turnovers.

Serve with tea or coffee as a snack. Alternatively, serve as a substantial dessert following a meal, perhaps of Chicken Street Kebabs (page 44), Mint and Yogurt Sauce (page 43), Lentil and Sultana Salad (page 57), and Afghan Home-style Naan (page 38).

Hunza Sprouted Wheat Breads

pitti • Hunza Valley, Pakistan

The people of the Hunza Valley in northern Pakistan, known as Hunzakots, are famous for their longevity. Much has been written about their traditional diet of apricots, yogurt, and wheat, on the assumption that their longevity is somehow diet-related. Another factor often given credit is their water, rushing down through this spectacular rugged valley from the glaciers of the Karakoram Mountains.

But there is now some skepticism about the famous longevity. "The number of very old people in Hunza has been exaggerated," we were told by an anthropologist who had worked in the valley, "and the age that people say they are is not always accurate." But many people do live long, healthy lives, as the environment is relatively pollutant-free and life here requires a high level of physical fitness.

The Hunzakot diet may not be a miracle secret to longevity, but apricots, yogurt, and wheat find their way into a great many delicious meals (see also Apricot and Almond Bread, page 49, and Aziz's Apricot Noodle Soup).

▲▲▲▲▲▲▲·▪▪▲▲▪▪▪▪▪▲▪▲▲▪

These sprouted wheat breads combine wheat berry sprouts and apricots, and come out tasting as wonderful as you might expect. Like other sprouted wheat breads, pitti have a wonderful natural sweetness and a chewy texture. If you have never worked with sprouted wheat doughs, definitely try these flatbreads. The entire process takes several days, but not that much work. The breads themselves are forgiving, and they smell more delicious as they bake than any other bread we know. Serve them, as they do in the Hunza Valley, with a young goat cheese and apricot preserves, and you have a delicious meal.

6 cups hard wheat berries	1½ cups unsulfured dried apricots
Spring water for soaking	1 tablespoon salt

You will need a large bread bowl, a tea towel, a lid or plate to cover the bowl, a large towel, a food processor, two small baking sheets (10 by 14 inches) that fit side by side in your oven, and a rolling pin.

In a large bread bowl, soak the wheat berries in room temperature spring water to cover for 18 hours, leaving plenty of room for the berries to expand.

Drain the wheat berries and rinse well under lukewarm water. Return the wheat berries to the bowl and cover with a damp tea towel and a lid or a large plate. Let stand for 12 hours, then rinse again.

continued

By now, the wheat berries should be starting to sprout, so from this point on, keep an eye on the length of the sprouts, and rinse the sprouts two or three times a day. When the sprouts are one third the length of the berries, rinse one last time. (The total time for soaking the wheat berries is approximately one and a half to two and a half days.)

Lay the sprouts out on a large towel and pat them relatively dry. Now you can begin to grind them. A food processor with the metal blade is by far the best tool for grinding the sprouts. Add 2 cups of sprouts to your processor along with the ¼ cup of apricots and ½ teaspoon of the salt. Process until the berries have broken down and a ball of dough is circulating around the processor; turn off immediately. Depending on your food processor, this will take approximately 1½ to 3 minutes; don't let the grinding continue, or the dough will be overkneaded and begin to break down. Take the dough out and put it into a bread bowl, and continue with the rest of the wheat berries, apricots, and salt.

When you have ground all the wheat berries, set the dough out on a lightly floured surface and knead for 2 to 3 minutes. Cover with plastic wrap and let rest for at least 1 hour. (This dough can also be put in a plastic bag and refrigerated for up to 48 hours. Bring back to room temperature before proceeding with the recipe.)

Preheat your oven to 325°F. Lightly oil two small (10- by 14-inch) baking sheets.

Divide the dough into 3 equal pieces, and set aside 2 of the pieces, keeping them covered. Divide the dough you are working with into 4 equal pieces. Pat each piece between floured palms into a disc about 4 inches in diameter. With a rolling pin, flatten each piece until it is ¼ inch thick and approximately 7 inches in diameter. Place on the prepared baking sheets, cover, and let sit for 20 minutes.

Place the breads in the middle of your oven and bake for 25 minutes. Remove and cool slightly before serving. Have the next batch of breads ready and resting while the first batch is baking, and similarly for the third batch. Serve warm or at room temperature.

▲▲▲▲▲▲▲▲▲▲▲▲▲▲▲▲▲▲▲▲▲▲

Makes 12 flatbreads, about 7 inches in diameter and just over ¼ inch thick.

Serve on their own, with tea or coffee, or with apricot preserves or a little fresh goat cheese, or to accompany Aziz's Apricot Noodle Soup (page 51).

Apricot and Almond Bread

kimochdun • Hunza Valley, Pakistan

In the summer, when tall green wheat blankets the intricately irrigated fields, and sage-green Russian olives cast their jasmine-like perfume out across the barren rocky landscape, the small villages of the Hunza Valley are alive with activity. Everywhere, you hear the familiar chunk-chunk-chunk of grain mills grinding and turning, powered by the rush of glacier-fed mountain streams. In the dry mountain air the smells of fires and breads baking drift by seductively. Gnarled trees are loaded with fresh apricots and plums, and steep snow-capped mountains stretch out in every direction.

During our bicycle trip down through the steep gorges and river valleys of Hunza, we learned three different methods of preparing kimochdun, a skillet bread often made for the celebration marking the end of Ramadan, Islam's month-long dawn-to-dusk fast. (With more time, we're sure we'd have been taught half a dozen more.) The only thing all three breads had in common was that they were baked in a heavy covered skillet, which was placed in and covered with hot coals.

·‥▲▲▲▲▲‥▲▲‥▲▲▲‥▲

This particular version of kimochdun is made with goat's milk, apricots, and almonds. It is a delicious, festive bread, suitable for celebrating the end of Ramadan, and tasting of the essential foods of the place from which it comes. The bread is traditionally cut into wedges and served warm.

2 cups goat's milk or whole milk

2 tablespoons honey

2 teaspoons dry yeast

½ cup lukewarm water

5 to 6 cups hard whole wheat flour

1 tablespoon safflower or other
   vegetable oil

1 tablespoon salt

⅔ cup unsulfured dried apricots,
   quartered

⅔ cup unblanched whole almonds
   (approximately 3 ounces)

You will need a heavy medium-sized saucepan, a large bread bowl, a cast-iron or other heavy 10-inch ovenproof skillet with 2- to 3-inch-high sides, and a sharp knife or razor blade.

Scald the milk in a heavy medium saucepan. Remove from the heat, and stir in the honey, and cool to lukewarm.

continued

Sprinkle the yeast over the warm water in a large bowl; stir to dissolve. Stir in the goat's milk, then stir in 3 cups flour, a cup at a time. Stir 100 times, about 1 minute, in the same direction to develop the gluten. Cover the bowl with plastic wrap and let this sponge stand at room temperature for 30 minutes.

Sprinkle the oil and salt onto the sponge. Stir in enough of the remaining flour, ½ cup at a time, to form a stiff dough. Turn the dough out onto a lightly floured surface and knead until smooth and elastic, adding more flour as necessary to prevent sticking, about 10 minutes.

Rinse out and dry the bread bowl, then oil lightly. Add the dough, cover the bowl with plastic wrap, and let stand until the dough has doubled in volume, 1 to 1½ hours.

Punch the dough down gently, and let it rest 5 minutes. Then turn out onto a lightly floured surface and roll out to a thickness of 1 inch. Sprinkle the apricots and almonds over the dough, and roll up into a cylinder like a jelly roll. Shape the dough into a ball and gently knead to distribute the fruit and nuts.

Lightly oil a heavy ovenproof 10-inch skillet with 2- to 3-inch-high sides. Gently roll the dough out on a lightly floured surface to a 10-inch round. Transfer to the prepared skillet. Cover with plastic wrap or a dry cloth and let rise until almost doubled, about 30 minutes.

Position a rack in the center of the oven, and preheat the oven to 350°F.

With a sharp knife or razor blade, cut a ½ inch deep X across the surface the dough. Bake until the top is light golden brown and the bread sounds hollow when tapped on the bottom, about 45 minutes. Place the bread on a rack to cool.

▲▲▲▲▲▲▲▲▲▲▲▲▲▲▲▲▲▲▲▲▲▲

Makes 1 flat loaf, about 10 inches across and 2 inches high.

Serve with Aziz's Apricot Noodle Soup (page 51) or eat plain, or with honey or fresh fruit jam, with tea or coffee for breakfast or a snack.

Aziz's Apricot Noodle Soup
mo'otch • Upper Hunza, Pakistan

Shisper Lodge sits all alone at the bottom of a long, beautiful, white glacier in the middle of the Karakoram Mountains in northern Pakistan. The lodge is run by a man named Aziz, a Wakhi who has lived his entire life in one of the world's most rugged mountain regions. His father carried mail for the British in the thirties and forties, crossing both the Karakoram and the Pamir mountains to deliver the post from Hunza to Kashgar. Aziz, no doubt like his father before him, has energy that knows no limit, especially so when it comes to preparing meals or telling a tale.

Shisper Lodge is a one-man show. Aziz not only looks after the guests, but he feeds the chickens, waters the apricot trees, and tends the garden. When we asked if we could learn to make his apricot noodle soup, he took us step-by-step through the recipe, all the while retelling mountain adventures.

Properly made, mo'otch should be cooked over a campfire with a glacier nearby, and a few eight-thousand-meter peaks in view. But it is also very good on a cold winter night in the middle of Toronto.

The soup's main ingredients are dried apricots and homemade noodles. A dollop of plain yogurt and a sprinkling of slivered almonds turns this simple mountain dish into elegant fare.

noodles

1 cup hard unbleached white flour or hard whole wheat flour

½ teaspoon salt

1 teaspoon vegetable oil (optional)

Approximately ⅔ cup water

soup

1 tablespoon vegetable oil

1 large onion, chopped

3 cloves garlic, finely chopped

1 cup unsulfured dried apricots, coarsely chopped

½ teaspoon dried chile pepper flakes

8 cups chicken broth, preferably low-salt

2 tablespoons fresh lemon juice

1 teaspoon salt

½ teaspoon freshly ground black pepper

garnish (optional)

2 cups plain yogurt

½ cup slivered toasted almonds

You will need a medium-sized mixing bowl, a large heavy pot, a rolling pin, and a knife.

continued

To make the noodles: Place the flour and salt in a medium bowl. Add the oil, then gradually stir in water until you have a stiff dough. Turn out onto a floured surface and knead for 5 minutes, until the dough is elastic and smooth. Let stand while you prepare the soup. (Or wrap in plastic wrap and refrigerate until you are ready to roll out the noodles.)

To make the soup: Heat the oil in a large pot. Add the onion and garlic, lower the heat to medium-low, and cook for 15 to 20 minutes, stirring frequently. Add the apricots, chile flakes, and chicken broth, increase the heat, and bring to a boil. Add the lemon juice. (The soup can be prepared to this point and then removed from the heat until about 20 minutes before serving, when the noodles should be rolled out and cut.) Let the soup simmer while you roll out and cut the noodles.

Roll out the noodle dough on a lightly floured surface. We prefer our handmade noodles to have a bit of bite, so we suggest that you concentrate on getting dough to an even thickness of about ⅛ inch, rather than trying for extreme thinness. It is much more important to have a uniform thickness, so the cooking time for all the noodles is the same, than to have them especially thin. Then use a knife to cut into strips about ¼ inch wide.

Bring the soup back to a rolling boil. Add the salt and black pepper, and then drop in the noodles. Boil until cooked through but still al dente; because they are fresh, they'll cook quickly even if they're thick, so keep a close eye on them.

Serve hot. Yogurt and slivered almonds make attractive accompaniments: Place a tablespoon of yogurt in each bowl of soup, then sprinkle it with some almonds. Then place a dish of each on the table so your guests can help themselves to more.

▲▲▲▲▲▲▲▲▲▲▲▲▲▲▲▲▲▲▲▲▲▲▲

Makes about 2 quarts soup. Serves 6.

Serve with plenty of fresh bread. Apricot and Almond Bread (page 49) and Hunza Sprouted Wheat Bread (page 47) both are especially good with mo'otch.

KIRGHIZ ENCOUNTER

She had beautiful bones and a long, ground-covering stride. She lived with her two sons in a flat-roofed stone house built into the hillside above a broad valley at the confluence of the Gez and Consiver rivers in the Chinese Pamirs—one of the most beautiful landscapes we had ever seen.

We had stopped to do minor bicycle repairs by the side of the rocky dirt-and-gravel track that was the Karakoram Highway. Above were the glacier-laden shoulders of Mount Kongur and across the valley were huge sand dunes, rising against more snow-covered mountains, which marked the border with Tajikistan. In all that vast sweep of country, there was little sign of human habitation. The only sounds were the soft swoosh of a breeze rustling the grasses by the side of the road and the clink of metal on metal as we struggled with a bottom bracket.

Suddenly a young boy appeared out of the landscape, then ran off. Moments later his mother came striding toward us and gestured for us to follow. The hillside looked empty of all but a few grazing goats. The family's house was far from the road, tucked behind a large boulder, its dry stone walls camouflaged by the rock and grasses in the landscape. Behind it was a small enclosure, also bulit of stacked gray rock.

We had no common language, but she invited us to stay in the house, a clean-swept single room, with folded rugs and blankets piled against one wall and a hole in the ceiling above the cook fire. We asked, again in gestures, if instead we could set up our tent just outside, to be out of her way. She smiled in understanding and agreement, and we realized how grave-faced she had been. Later, after her son Sok had helped us with the tent, she asked us in for tea. Pointing to herself, she proudly said, "Kirghiz," the name of her people.

It was Ramadan, the Muslim fasting month, so she wasn't eating or drinking until after sundown, but she insisted that we and Sok have some flatbread and tea. She showed us a man's photograph and we understood that it was her husband, who had died just a month earlier, from some problem in his chest. We tried to imagine life for her and her two sons in this isolated, beautiful place, the nearest village an hour's walk away.

In the middle of the afternoon, two horsemen rode up. They had come over from a village fifteen miles away. As the woman greeted them and ushered them into the house, she gestured to us to come in too. The men were there to help with ritual prayers for the dead, to grieve with her. She sat in the corner, head turned to the wall, and began to wail and keen, rocking back and forth. The visitors began saying things to her in response. We couldn't understand the words, but the feelings and meaning of the ritual were universal. "Oh, he's gone and gone from me forever," she would wail. "He was a very good man; he is in God's hands," the response would come. Time seemed to stop as emotions filled the room. Sok stood watching solemnly.

Then it was over. She composed herself, and showed her visitors out and off into the landscape. At sunset, Sok's older brother appeared with the five yaks and two camels he'd been shepherding all day. Goats were milked and all the animals were penned for the night. Then it was time to sit down and break the fast.

Next morning, while we packed up to go, she stood on the hillside, sweeping the landscape with our binoculars, scrutinizing the mountains and valleys that framed her world. As we headed to the road with our loaded bicycles, she handed us fresh flatbreads for the journey, then stood with Sok, watching.

Lhasa, Tibet: Nomad pilgrims at Potala

Pebbled Persian Bread
hushva nan • Iran

Hushva nan is tender and lightly yeasted, and made only of whole wheat. Like its close cousin, the ancient Persian bread *sanguake*, it has a very bumpy, irregular, pebbled surface and texture. The method we use for baking hushva nan is similar to that used in baking Hot Chile Bread (page 201) and Thyme Bread (page 207), and it is an interesting baking process to experiment with. The breads are first cooked on top of the stove in a skillet, then the skillet is transferred to the broiler. The result is a fairly thick and soft bread, with a glossy top surface and crusty bottom. Be sure to use lots of water in working with the dough, as it gives the bread its distinctive sheen.

1 tablespoon dry yeast	1 tablespoon salt
3½ cups warm water	1 tablespoon vegetable oil
7 cups hard whole wheat flour	

You will need a medium-sized bowl, a large bread bowl, and one or two cast-iron skillets or griddles at least 8 inches in diameter.

In a medium-sized bowl, sprinkle the yeast over 3 cups of the warm water. Stir and allow the yeast to dissolve.

In a large bread bowl, combine the flour and salt and mix well. Make a well in the center of the flour mixture, and pour in the yeast mixture and the oil. Stir in the same direction until all the flour has been absorbed, then turn out onto a lightly floured bread board and knead for 7 to 8 minutes. This dough should be on the moist side; if it isn't, add more water by wetting your hands as you knead.

Wash out and wipe the bread bowl and oil it lightly. Return the dough to the bread bowl, cover with plastic wrap, and let rise until doubled in volume, 1 to 1½ hours.

Gently punch down the dough. Add the remaining ½ cup warm water and knead into the dough (still in the bread bowl). This may seem a little messy and unorthodox, but the water will be absorbed after 2 to 3 minutes of kneading. Cover and let rise for another 30 to 60 minutes until almost doubled in volume.

Punch down the bread again. Divide into 8 equal parts and cover with plastic wrap or a kitchen towel.

Position an oven rack about 6 inches below the broiler element. Preheat your broiler. Have ready a bowl of water.

continued

Heat a lightly oiled 8-inch or larger skillet or griddle over high heat. Wet your hands and pick up one ball of dough. Start patting out the dough between your palms, moistening your palms as necessary to keep it from sticking. Then place the dough on a moistened work surface and push and flatten it with your fingers, to a 7- to 8-inch round. The surface of the dough will be irregular and bumpy with your fingermarks; that is one of the characteristics of the bread.

Flatbreads for sale

Place the dough in the very hot skillet or griddle, bumpy side up, and immediately reduce the heat to as low as possible. (If you are working with an electric stove, you may have to use two burners, keeping one very hot and the other very low, and move the skillet back and forth from one to the other.)

Cook for 3 minutes. Then transfer the skillet or griddle to the broiler, 4 to 6 inches from the heat source. Broil for 4 minutes, or until the top has begun to brown. Because of all the water, the surface should be somewhat shiny. Remove the bread to a rack. Allow to cool a few minutes before transferring to a warm towel if the bread is to be served soon; alternatively, let cool completely on the rack before wrapping in plastic.

If you feel comfortable with the process, heat two griddles, and proceed with two breads at once. Otherwise, keep going with one until all the breads have been baked. Serve warm or at room temperature.

▲▲▲▲▲▲▲▲▲▲▲▲▲▲▲▲▲▲▲▲

Makes 8 round breads, about ½ inch thick and approximately
8 inches in diameter.

Serve with any of the Central Asian dishes. These are particularly appropriate with
Persian dishes such as Pomegranate and Meatball Soup (page 60) or
Herbs and Greens Egg Pie (page 58).

Lentil and Sultana Salad

Persia

Lentil salads are such pleasing staff-of-life sort of food. Eaten on their own they are nutritious and satisfying, and when combined with Paperthin Lavash or Pebbled Persian Bread and a fresh salsa, like Cutting-Board Salsa, they make a delicious vegetarian meal.

This particular Persian salad combines lentils, rice, and sultanas with mild onion, parsley, and lemon juice. It tastes even better the second day, after the various flavors have had a chance to blend. Because the leftovers are so good, we like to make this salad in the large quantity suggested here. It is also an easy-to-eat, dependable snack for children.

2 cups brown lentils (approximately 12 ounces), washed and picked through

4 cups boiling water

1½ cups long-grain white rice or 3½ cups cooked rice

1 medium red onion, finely chopped

1 cup sultanas

3 tablespoons fresh lemon juice

3 tablespoons olive oil

½ cup finely chopped flat-leafed parsley

1 teaspoon salt

½ teaspoon freshly ground black pepper

You will need a large bowl, a large saucepan with a lid, and, if starting with uncooked rice, a medium-sized saucepan with a tight-fitting lid or a rice cooker.

Place the lentils in a bowl and cover with the boiling water. Let soak for 1 hour, then drain.

Transfer the lentils to a large saucepan, add 4 cups water, and bring to a boil. Lower the heat and simmer, covered, until tender but not mushy, about 40 minutes. Drain and set aside.

Meanwhile, if using raw rice, wash the rice under cold running water until the water runs clear. Place in a medium saucepan and add enough cold water to cover the rice by ¾ inch. Bring to a boil, cover with a tight-fitting lid, lower the heat, and simmer without removing the lid, for 20 minutes. Remove from the heat. Alternatively, cook the rice in a rice cooker, according to the manufacturer's instructions.

Whisk together the lemon juice and oil.

continued

In a large serving bowl, combine rice, lentils, onion, and sultanas, and mix well. Pour the dressing over and blend well. Let stand, covered, in the refrigerator for at least 1 hour (or even overnight). Just before serving, add the parsley, salt, and pepper and mix well.

▲▲▲▲▲▲▲▲▲▲▲▲▲▲▲▲▲▲▲▲▲▲

Makes 7 to 8 cups salad. Serves 4 as a main course or 8 to 10 as a side salad.

Serve with Pebbled Persian Bread (page 55) as a simple meal, accompanied by a plate of sliced tomatoes sprinkled with finely chopped mint and some Yogurt Cheese balls (see page 206).

Herbs and Greens Egg Pie
koukou·ye sabzi • Iran

Koukouye are Persian baked egg dishes, distant cousins of Italian frittatas. The eggs bind together a subtly spiced mixture of herbs and vegetables. This dish is traditionally served at the Persian New Year, in the month of April, as the color green symbolizes new life and growth. It is also an easy everyday dish. Koukouye makes a great hors d'oeuvre, cut into wedges and served with sliced ripe tomatoes, or an attractive light main course, accompanied by a salad and plenty of bread.

1 cup finely chopped well-washed leek
(1 medium leek, white and tender green part)

1 cup spinach leaves, washed, stemmed, and shredded

½ cup shredded leaf lettuce

½ cup finely chopped scallions

½ cup chopped flat-leafed parsley

½ cup chopped fresh coriander

2 tablespoons finely chopped fresh dill

8 large eggs

½ cup walnut pieces, finely chopped

2 teaspoons unbleached hard white flour or unbleached all-purpose flour

2 tablespoons water

¼ teaspoon baking soda (optional; see Note)

2 tablespoons plain yogurt (optional; see Note)

½ teaspoon salt

Coarsely ground black pepper

1 tablespoon olive or vegetable oil

You will need a large bowl, a medium-sized mixing bowl, a small bowl, and a 9- to 10-inch heavy ovenproof skillet or a flameproof 8-inch square baking pan.

Preheat the oven to 325°F.

In a large bowl, mix together all the chopped vegetables and herbs.

In a medium bowl, beat the eggs well. Stir in the walnuts. Place the flour in a small bowl, add the water, and blend to a paste. Stir the paste into the beaten eggs, then stir in the optional baking soda and yogurt. Add the salt and pepper to taste, and pour the egg mixture over the vegetables and herbs. Blend well.

Heat a 9- or 10-inch cast-iron or other heavy ovenproof skillet or an 8-inch square baking pan over medium-high heat. Add the oil and swirl to coat the pan with oil. Remove from the heat and immediately pour in the egg mixture.

Bake in the upper third of the oven until golden on top and the eggs are set, about 35 to 40 minutes. Serve warm or at room temperature with plenty of fresh bread.

Alternatives: If you prefer, sprinkle the walnuts on top of the egg mixture just before baking instead of mixing them in with the eggs.

Note: Baking soda and yogurt make the koukou a little lighter and moister, but they can be omitted.

▲▲▲▲▲▲▲▲▲▲▲▲▲▲▲▲▲▲▲▲▲

Serves 6 to 8 as an appetizer, 8 to 10 as part of a mezze table (see page 203), or 4 to 6 as part of a light lunch.

Serve with Pebbled Persian Bread (page 55). This makes a satisfying vegetarian lunch, served with a bowl of plain yogurt and Lentil and Sultana Salad (page 57), or a sophisticated appetizer, followed by Prune-Stuffed Kufta Soup (page 316).

Pomegranate and Meatball Soup
ash • Persia

The Iranian ash is a substantial soup, a close cousin of the meal-in-one soups and stews found throughout Central Asia. The variety of ingredients used in Persian cuisine is wider than in the less hospitable regions of Central Asia, and the spicing consequently more subtle. Persian cuisine is also known for its use of sweet and sour in savory dishes. Pomegranates are often used as a sour element, but since pomegranates and pomegranate juice available in North America are generally sweet, in converting recipes, lemon or lime juice must be added to give the necessary tartness.

This thick soup, with subtly spiced meatballs floating in a broth both sweet (from a pinch of sugar) and sour (from pomegranate juice and lemon juice), is a wonderful example of Persian flavorings. Despite the number of ingredients, it is very quick and uncomplicated to prepare. Rolling the meatballs takes about twenty minutes and can be done ahead. The soup takes another twenty to twenty-five minutes to cook. It is served with lime wedges so guests can add extra tartness, and with an aromatic blend of dried spearmint, salt, and pepper sprinkled on top.

meatballs

1 pound lean ground beef

½ pound (2 medium) onions, grated

Scant ¼ teaspoon ground cinnamon

½ teaspoon salt

½ teaspon freshly ground black pepper

soup

12 cups water

1½ teaspoons salt

1 cup long-grain rice, such as basmati or Thai jasmine

1 cup spinach or chard leaves, well washed and shredded

1½ cups flat-leafed parsley, coarsely chopped

1 cup finely chopped scallions

2 cups fresh pomegranate juice or unsweetened cranberry juice

1 tablespoon sugar

2 tablespoons fresh lemon juice or less, if using unsweetened cranberry juice (see Note)

garnish and accompaniments

3 tablespoons dried spearmint

1 teaspoon salt

1 teaspoon freshly ground black pepper

2 to 3 limes, cut into wedges

You will need a large mixing bowl, a large pot with a lid, and a small bowl.

To make the meatballs: In a large mixing bowl, combine the meat, onions, cinnamon, salt, and pepper. Mix well with a spoon, then knead with your hands to produce an elastic mass of even consistency.

To form the meatballs: Scoop out heaping teaspoons of the meat mixture and roll them between your palms into firm round balls. Place the balls on a plate as you work. You should have 45 to 55 meatballs. (The recipe can be prepared ahead to this point and the meatballs stored, well wrapped, in the refrigerator for 24 hours or in the freezer for 1 week.)

To make the soup: Put the water in a large pot. Add the salt and bring to a boil. Toss in the rice and boil over medium heat for 5 minutes. Add the remaining soup ingredients and the meatballs, and bring back to a boil. Reduce the heat and simmer gently, partially covered, for 15 minutes, or until the rice is tender but not mushy and the meatballs are cooked through. Remove from the heat.

Rub the mint to a powder between your palms, and combine with the salt and pepper in a small bowl.

Serve the soup in large bowls and sprinkle a generous teaspoon of the mint mixture over each bowlful. Place the remaining seasoning powder on the table if you wish. Serve with lime wedges, so that your guests can temper the soup's sweetness with tart lime juice, and have stacks of fresh breads on hand.

Note: Because pomegranate juice is sometimes difficult to find, we have also tried this recipe with unsweetened cranberry juice and find it an very acceptable substitute.

▲▲▲▲▲▲▪▪▪▲▲▪▪▪▪▲▲▲▪▪▲▲▲

Serves 4 to 6 as a meal-in-one, accompanied by flatbreads.

Serve with Afghan Home-style Naan (page 38), Pebbled Persian Bread (page 55), or Afghan Snowshoe Naan (page 40).

Sweet Persian Bread

nane sheer • Persia

These breads are more like cookies than flatbreads, but they are so simple and delicious we had to include them. They are made with milk and flavored with brown sugar and vanilla. We should warn you that they can be somewhat hard-to-the-bite once they've cooled, so enjoy them as they are customarily served, with a cup of hot tea or coffee, and dunk the breads to soften them. They are also delicious dunked in hot milk for a milk-and-cookies-style snack.

2 cups hard unbleached white flour, or more as necessary

¼ teaspoon salt

½ cup brown sugar

1 teaspoon baking powder

¾ cup milk, or more as necessary

1 teaspoon vanilla extract

You will need a medium-sized mixing bowl, two small (10- by 14-inch) baking sheets that can fit side by side in your oven, a rolling pin, and a sharp knife or pizza cutter.

Preheat the oven to 300°F.

In a medium-sized bowl, combine the flour, salt, sugar, and baking powder. Whisk or stir together. Make a well in the center and pour in the milk and vanilla extract. Stir the flour into the milk until a soft, kneadable dough begins to form. If the dough is too sticky, add a little more flour; if too dry, add a little more milk. Turn out onto a lightly floured bread board and knead for 2 to 3 minutes.

Dust two 10- by 14-inch baking sheets with flour. Divide the dough in half and roll out each piece to the size of the baking sheets (the dough should be less than ¼ inch thick).

Place in the center of your oven, and immediately turn the heat down to 250°F. Bake for 50 minutes. Remove from the oven. Working with one sheet at a time, turn out onto a large cutting board, and cut into 3- to 4-inch squares while the bread is still warm; it will harden quickly as it cools.

▲▲▲▲▲▲▲▲▲▲▲▲▲▲▲▲▲▲▲▲▲▲

Makes approximately 2 dozen 3- to 4-inch square thin flatbreads.

Serve with Mint Tea (page 268) or coffee or to accompany Fruit Compote with Scented Waters (page 237) or fresh fruit.

Turcoman Sourdough Bread

chorek • Turkmenistan

In Turkmenistan, breads are baked in tandoor ovens of various designs.
Tandoor baking gives breads a crisp, firm bottom crust and a tender, almost steam-cooked, upper surface (see Tandoor Ovens, page 35). The standard tandoor bread in Central Asia is called naan, but the Turcoman word for basic tandoor-cooked bread is *chorek*. Chorek is made with soured dough and usually contains milk and fried lamb fat. The fat is there to keep the bread moist and fresh-textured. Though we've skipped the mutton fat, we have included goat's milk in this bread. Goats are, along with sheep and camels, the main animal resource in the region. The desert climate is too hot and dry to support dairy cattle.

We wanted to translate traditional Turcoman bread to the North American kitchen but still produce a bread that tasted as local and "real" as possible. Leavened breads in Turcoman and other nomadic cultures are traditionally made with a soured dough. This usually involves keeping back a bit of dough from a batch of dough, mixing it with water and flour, and then letting the batter sit out for a day to sour and ferment. The process gives the bread flavor as well as leavening. A reliable way of reproducing the taste and textures of those traditional breads is to begin with a sponge made with only a smidgeon of yeast, then let it sit out for several days to pick up flavor and to ferment. Once the sponge has fermented, more flour is added to it to make a dough. Then the dough is kneaded and left to rise like any yeasted dough.

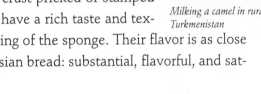

Milking a camel in rural Turkmenistan

These breads are large, with a soft crust pricked or stamped to stop the bread from "ballooning." They have a rich taste and texture from the goat's milk and the long souring of the sponge. Their flavor is as close as we can get to a home-cooked Central Asian bread: substantial, flavorful, and satisfying.

sponge

4 cups goat's milk (see page 415)

⅛ teaspoon dry yeast

2 cups hard unbleached white or unbleached all-purpose flour

1½ cups hard whole wheat flour

dough

1 tablespoon plus ½ teaspoon salt

1½ cups hard whole wheat flour (see Note)

1½ cups hard unbleached white or unbleached all-purpose flour, plus extra for kneading

continued

You will need a medium saucepan, a large bread bowl, unglazed quarry tiles (see page 20) to fit on a rack in your oven, a rolling pin, a bread stamp (see page 19) or a fork, and a baker's peel (optional).

Place the goat's milk in a medium saucepan and heat over medium-high heat until very hot but not boiling. Remove the scalded milk from the heat and pour into a large bread bowl. Let cool to lukewarm. (When testing the milk for temperature, stir first, because the milk in the center will be hotter than milk at the edges.)

When the milk feels just warm to the touch, stir in the yeast. Stir in the white flour, a cup at a time, then stir in the whole wheat flour. Then stir 100 times, about 1 minute, in the same direction to help develop the gluten. Set this sponge aside, covered with plastic wrap, for about 48 hours to sour.

Sprinkle the salt over the sponge, and stir in gently with a wooden spoon, again in the same direction. (Remember that the gluten has had time to develop and you want to treat it kindly.) Stir in the whole wheat flour, then the white. Then turn the dough out onto a lightly floured surface to knead it. Knead for 10 minutes, adding more flour as necessary. The dough will become smooth and somewhat elastic, though still soft.

Lightly dust your work surface again with flour, place the dough on it, and cover with plastic wrap. Let rise for 3 to 4 hours, or until doubled in volume. (If you have no convenient counter space, clean out your bread bowl, oil it lightly, and place the dough in it to rise, covered by plastic wrap.)

When ready to bake the breads, place quarry tiles on a rack just below the middle of the oven, leaving a 1-inch gap between the tiles and the oven walls. Preheat the oven to 450°F.

Transfer the dough to a work surface. With a sharp knife, cut the dough in quarters. (This will give you 4 pieces of dough, weighing about 1 pound each.) On a lightly floured surface, roll each piece of dough out into a round or oval about 10 inches across and ½ inch thick. Cover the breads with plastic wrap and let stand for 10 minutes.

Work with 2 breads at a time. With a bread stamp or a fork, stamp or stab the center area of the breads all over, leaving a 2-inch edge unstamped. The stamping or pricking will prevent the flattened area from ballooning during baking. Transfer to quarry tiles by hand or using a baker's peel, and bake for 10 minutes or until golden on top and firm and crusty on the bottom. Just before the first breads are ready to come out of the oven, stamp the remaining breads. Then bake once the oven is free. Place the baked breads on a rack to cool, or wrap in a cotton cloth if you wish to keep them soft and warm.

Note: To obtain a traditional Turcoman taste (although these days hard to find even in Turkmenistan because not much sorghum is being grown there now), substitute ½ cup sorghum flour (see page 418) for the same quantity of whole wheat flour when making the dough.

▲▲▲▲▲▲▲▲▲▲▲▲▲▲▲▲▲▲▲▲

Makes 4 large round or oval flatbreads, about 10 inches in diameter.

Serve with Chickpea and Onion Stew (page 67), or with Marinated Lamb Kebabs (page 176), or Chicken Street Kebabs (page 44) with Mint and Yogurt Sauce (page 43), and Sweet Onion Salad (page 65) on the side.

✻

Sweet Onion Salad

Uzbekistan

The late afternoon sunlight lengthened my shadow as I walked down a mud-walled lane in old Samarkand after a visit to the Gur Emir, tomb of Tamerlane. Off to the right I heard music, then I walked past an open doorway and caught sight of what I was hearing. There was an Uzbek wedding party in full swing in the court-yard, with lines of tables laden with food. A singer, backed by several musicians on traditional Uzbek instruments, was entertaining the wedding guests as they dined. I walked on, pleased with my glimpse of the festivities. Then came a calling out and a shouting. When I glanced back, there were several older men standing in the door-way and waving to me to come in.

Perhaps it would have been more polite to refuse, but the invitation was too tempting. I was seated on a bench at one of the tables, a place was quickly laid, and then plates of food appeared, passed down by my neighbors at the table: sweet onion salad sprinkled with cayenne and a handful of pomegranate seeds; lamb kebabs on flat metal skewers; piles of flatbreads; a plate of sliced radishes, dill, and parsley; a cucumber salad; bowls of yogurt; plates of fresh cheese; slices of fresh melon. . . . It seemed an endless array. The men were all drinking some kind of lethal homemade vodka, while the women drank fizzy fruit juices. Several of the older men came over to talk: Where was I from? Was I married? Did I have children? What did I think of Samarkand? Did I like the food? Seeing my enthusiasm, they pressed more food upon me. Meanwhile, the singer sang and swayed, the musicians behind her smiled and played. And I never saw the bride or the groom.

▲▲▲▲▲▲▲▲▲▲▲▲▲▲▲▲▲▲▲▲

continued

In this tasty salad, mild red onions are salted and allowed to drain for twenty minutes, then rinsed. This eliminates any strong onion flavor and leaves only a refreshing taste, which is well matched by the coriander tossed into the salad. If you can get fresh pomegranate, it's worth the trouble to decorate the salad with some pomegranate seeds. Sweet onion salad is delicious wrapped in bread and makes a great complement to grilled lamb.

2 medium red onions, thinly sliced (about 2 cups)	1 cup loosely packed coriander leaves, coarsely chopped
1 tablespoon coarse salt	½ teaspoon cayenne
3 tablespoons cider vinegar	Handful of pomegranate seeds (optional)
1 teaspoon sugar	

You will need a colander, a bowl, and a cotton towel or salad spinner.

Place the onions in a colander and place it over a bowl to catch the drips. Sprinkle the salt onto the onions and toss with your hands to ensure that the salt is well distributed. Let stand for 20 minutes, then rinse under cold water and pat dry with a towel, or dry in a salad spinner.

Transfer the onions to a shallow serving bowl. Mix together the vinegar and sugar and pour over the onions. Add the coriander and toss gently. Sprinkle the cayenne on top and, if available, a handful of pomegranate seeds. Serve at room temperature.

▲▲▲▲▲▲▲▲▲▲▲▲▲▲▲▲▲▲▲▲▲▲

Makes approximately 2 cups salad. Serves 4 to 6 as a side dish or 6 to 8 as part of a mezze table (see page 203).

Serve with Marinated Lamb Kebabs (page 176), Spicy Cumin Kebabs (page 33), or Chicken Street Kebabs (page 44), accompanied by Turcoman Sourdough Bread (page 63) or Afghan Home-style Naan (page 38).

Chickpea and Onion Stew

Tajikistan

Tajikistan, now an independent state, was a republic in the USSR, and before that was often controlled, at least in part, by the powerful emirs of Bokhara, now a city in present-day Uzbekistan.

The markets of Dushanbe, the mostly modern Soviet-style capital of Tajikistan, with a view of snow-covered peaks, are colorful with the bright prints and silks of Tajik and Uzbek women and, in the summer and fall, with mountains of fresh vegetables. Sweet onions and carrots are stacked beside heaps of fresh green herbs. Lentils, chickpeas, and other legumes are scooped out from huge sacks. A Tajik woman sells home-baked flatbreads from the back of a small cart: "Taste!" she commands. I do, and then buy a stack of six.

▲▲▲▲▲▲▲▲▲▲▲▲▲▲▲▲▲▲▲▲▲▲

Winters in Tajikistan are harsh, and there are few vegetables to be had. Root vegetables and legumes, like grains, can be stored and used when other vegetables are not available. The winter version of this dish would substitute onions and perhaps sliced carrots for the tomatoes.

With cooked or canned chickpeas on hand, this recipe takes about thirty minutes to prepare and cook. The chickpeas give body and flavor, the onions are sweet, the tomatoes colorful and a touch acidic. The spice blend—saffron, coriander seed, cumin, chile, and a hint of cinnamon—tints the dish a golden yellow and adds a complex and subtle flavor.

1 cup dried chickpeas (see page 409), soaked overnight in 3 cups water, or 2 cups canned chickpeas, rinsed and drained

Approximately 4 cups vegetable stock or water (less if using canned chickpeas)

1 tablespoon vegetable oil

1 pound (1 extra-large or 2 medium) Spanish onions, thinly sliced

1 pound (2 to 3 large) ripe tomatoes, coarsely chopped (drained canned tomatoes can also be used)

½ teaspoon saffron threads, crushed and dissolved in ¼ cup warm water

½ teaspoon dried chile pepper flakes, or more if you like chile heat

½ teaspoon coriander seed, crushed, or ¼ teaspoon ground coriander

½ teaspoon cumin seed, crushed, or ¼ teaspoon ground cumin

¼ teaspoon ground cinnamon

2 teaspoons salt

½ teaspoon sugar

accompaniments
1 to 2 cups plain yogurt
1 to 2 ripe tomatoes, finely chopped
1 sweet red bell pepper, julienned

continued

You will need a large deep pot with a lid and a cast-iron or other heavy skillet or large saucepan.

If using dried chickpeas, place in a large pot, add water to cover by at least 2 inches, and bring to a boil. Boil for 5 minutes, skim off any foam, and drain.

Return the chickpeas to the pot and add stock or water to cover. Bring to a boil, then reduce the heat, cover, and simmer until tender but not mushy, about 1 to 1½ hours, checking frequently to make sure there is enough liquid and that the chickpeas are not sticking; add more hot stock or water if necessary. If using canned chickpeas, place in a large pot with enough stock or water to cover, bring to a boil, and simmer, covered, until heated through, about 5 minutes.

Meanwhile, heat the oil in a cast-iron or other heavy skillet or large saucepan. Sauté the onion slices over medium heat, stirring constantly, until golden brown, about 10 minutes. Handle the onions gently, as part of the appeal of the dish is the intact rings of onions.

Add the sautéed onions to the chickpeas. Then add the saffron with its liquid, the spices, salt, and sugar and simmer over medium heat, covered, until the chickpeas are very tender, about 20 minutes. Serve hot with side dishes of yogurt, chopped fresh tomatoes, and julienned red pepper, as well as a stack of flatbreads.

▲▲▲▲▲∙∙▲▲∙∙∙∙▲▲∙∙▲▲▲

Makes 4 cups stew. Serves 3 to 4.

This stew goes well with any of the Central Asian flatbreads, such as Pebbled Persian Bread
(page 55), Turcoman Sourdough Bread (page 63), or Afghan Snowshoe Naan (page 40).

PILGRIMAGE

Autumn is pilgrim season in Tibet. The harvest over, people start traveling, heading for Lhasa. Pilgrims who have come from faraway villages and nomad encampments visit the temples and climb the long stairways that lead to the front door of the Potala, palace of the Dalai Lamas. They are strong-looking people, usually dressed in sheepskin *jubas* (long belted coats), the women with braided hair and a child or two to carry. They are devout, prostrating themselves full-length before the holiest of the temples in Lhasa, the Jokhang, or before revered Buddha images, lighting juniper branches, making traditional offerings of butter, fingering their well-worn prayer beads as they recite mantras and prayers. The scent of the juniper mingles with the smell of well-worn sheepskin and the rancid tang of aged butter. The air hums and resonates with prayer around the Barkhor, the wide flagstone pathway that circles the Jokhang Temple. For a Tibetan Buddhist, walking clockwise around the Jokhang is in itself a form of prayer, as is circumambulating any holy place or object.

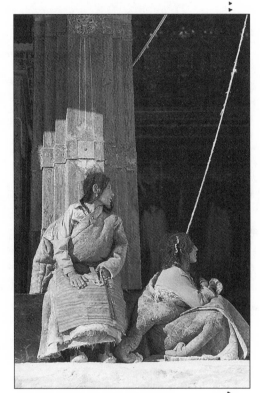

Changtang region, Tibet: Nomad family

The Barkhor is also a place of business: People set up small stalls and sell prayer flags, old jewelry, safety pins, almost anything, while others sit praying or begging as the crowd passes by. Pilgrims stop and stare, finger and barter, mingle and mix, always moving in the same clockwise direction around the Jokhang.

Tucked behind the Jokhang Temple, down a narrow lane leading off the Barkhor, is a small temple whose walls are covered with the remnants of wonderful frescoes. Children play in the courtyard and on the steps. One fall day in 1985, one of the children led me around a corner and up a narrow wooden staircase. There, in a small room, sat a very old monk, praying. I sat and watched and listened until well after dark, then bowed my way out. I don't think he noticed. The next evening I went back, and then each evening until I left Lhasa. On return trips to Lhasa I went back to find him, each time expecting him to be gone, each time finding him frail but very alive. So in hopes that he is still there, and because he is very much alive in memory, I write in the present tense.

Imprisoned for nineteen years by the Chinese government, and released in 1982, he prays for most of the day and well on into the evening, sometimes reading aloud from scriptures, often chanting from memory. One evening, through one of his novices who spoke some Chinese, the monk talked about prayer, and showed us where he slept, a small spare wooden room up another ladder. After prison and suffering, how did he feel? He laughed, waved his hand gently as if to brush the thought aside, picked up his beads, and began praying again.

Pilgrims stopping for tea on the way to Mt. Kailas in western Tibet

Tibetan Barley Skillet Bread
amdopali • Tibet

Barley is the staple food, and grain of preference, in all regions of Tibet.
Amdo, the large northeastern region of Tibet, gives its name to this Tibetan barley flatbread. The present Dalai Lama is from northern Amdo, a region known for its large monasteries, which functioned as important centers of learning until the Chinese takeover in the 1950s.

Oven-baked breads like this leavened barley and buttermilk loaf are generally found in settled valleys of Tibet. Tibetan nomads, who live in high-altitude grasslands, trade their wool and salt for barley from farmers living at lower altitudes or from traders; they eat the barley not in bread, but as *tsampa*.

Tsampa is barley that has been roasted or parched and then milled to the texture of flour. The roasting cooks the grain and makes it digestible without further cooking. Tsampa is a very portable food, ideal for long journeys where there is little fuel for cooking. It is eaten with Tibetan tea, which is flavored with salt or soda and aged butter. The tsampa is sprinkled into a bowl of tea to make a kind of dry porridge, which is then eaten in small lumps. For those not used to the combination, a little goes a long way, but it has been a lifesaver for nomads and travelers in Tibet for centuries.

When we traveled in western Tibet, tsampa was one of our staples. We experimented with it not just as a cereal to be mixed into hot tea, but also as an ingredient for flatbreads cooked over an open fire. When combined with a little atta flour purchased from Nepali traders near the border, the tsampa made particularly delicious bread.

▲▲▲▲▲▲▲▲▲▲▲▲▲▲▲▲▲▲▲▲▲▲▲

This Tibetan bread is more sophisticated than our rough-and-ready campfire breads: It is a yeasted oven-baked flat loaf, rich with buttermilk and full of the nutty aromatic taste of roasted barley. The key to using barley flour in flatbreads is to roast the flour before making the bread; roasting brings out the full flavor of the grain.

3 cups barley flour

Approximately 1¾ cups hard unbleached white flour

1 cup hard whole wheat flour

2 teaspoons salt

4 tablespoons unsalted butter, at room temperature

1 cup well-chilled buttermilk

1 cup boiling water

¼ cup firmly packed brown sugar

2 teaspoons dry yeast

½ cup lukewarm water

continued

You will need a large heavy skillet, a large mixing bowl, a medium bowl, a small bowl, a heavy 10-inch ovenproof skillet, and a razor blade or sharp knife.

Toast the barley flour in a heavy skillet over medium-low heat, stirring constantly, until slightly darker in color, about 10 minutes. Transfer to a large bowl. Cool.

Add 1 cup white flour, the whole wheat flour, and salt to the barley flour and mix well. Cut in the butter until the mixture resembles coarse meal. Set aside.

Combine the buttermilk, boiling water, and sugar in a medium bowl and mix well. Cool to lukewarm.

Sprinkle the yeast over the warm water in a small bowl; stir to dissolve, then stir into the buttermilk mixture. Make a well in the center of the dry ingredients. Pour the buttermilk mixture into the well and stir until a dough begins to form, about 5 minutes. Turn the dough out onto a lightly floured surface and knead until smooth and elastic, adding more white flour as necessary to prevent sticking, about 10 minutes.

Clean and wipe out the bread bowl, oil it lightly, and place dough in it to rise, covered with plastic wrap, until doubled in volume, about 1½ hours.

Butter a heavy 10-inch ovenproof skillet.

Punch down the dough. Knead briefly on a lightly floured surface until smooth. Shape into a 10-inch round. Transfer the dough to the prepared skillet. Cover with plastic wrap and let rise until almost doubled in volume, about 30 minutes.

Preheat the oven to 350°F.

Just before baking, cut three ¼-inch-deep parallel lines across the top of the dough, using a razor blade or the tip of a sharp knife. Bake in the center of the oven until the top is brown and the bread sounds hollow when tapped on the bottom, about 50 minutes. Invert the bread onto a rack, turn right side up, and cool completely.

▲▲▲▲▲▲▲▲▲▲▲▲▲▲▲▲▲▲▲▲▲▲▲

Makes 1 flat loaf, about 2 inches high and 10 inches across.

Serve in slices with a bowl of thick yogurt to dip the bread into as you eat. It is also a delicious accompaniment to soups and stews or eaten with honey as a snack with hot tea.

Tibetan Dried Meat

Tibet

The nomads of the Changtang region of Tibet live an extraordinary existence in a spare and beautiful high-altitude landscape. Winters are harsh and the air is thin at elevations ranging from 14,500 to 18,000 feet above sea level. The nomads, or Goloks, as they call themselves, move their herds of sheep, yaks, and goats from grazing ground to grazing ground throughout the year. In the winter the men usually travel to the salt pans near the northern edge of the Changtang to gather salt, which they trade for brick tea and grain, usually barley.

The other commodity the Goloks have to sell is wool. Every spring and summer, when the snow melts, Nepali traders make their way over the passes north through the Himalaya to the market villages on the Tibet-Nepal border. The nomads travel down on foot from higher elevations, with their herds of sheep and goats for shearing, and to trade with the Nepalis.

One of the major summer markets is in Burang, a village nestled into the mountains at a river junction near the point where Tibet, Nepal, and India all come together. Just outside the cluster of old stone buildings that make up the village, herds of sheep are moved into stone-walled enclosures and, one by one, they are sheared. The wool is roughly carded, twisted into huge ropes, and wound into balls six feet across. Porters hired by the buyers carry these giant skeins up over the Himalayan passes to Nepal. In Kathmandu, after a two-week trip—most of it on foot—the same wool will sell for almost ten times the price paid to the Golok sheepherders.

In our encounters with Goloks, we have been struck by both their tough resourcefulness and their generous hospitality. Invited into their tent by a Golok family in the Changtang, we were fed buttered tea, tsampa (ground roasted barley), and dried mutton, still on the haunch. As the leg was passed around with a large hunting knife, we each in turn hacked off a small piece of meat, then sat slowly chewing.

Sok and his mother in the Chinese Pamirs

On a later trip, we arrived in Lhasa determined to make our own dried meat for what would be a long trip westward. Vinegar and soy sauce are available in Lhasa, so we were able to add flavor by first marinating the meat. We used yak meat bought in the Barkhor market, and after marinating it, we laid the meat in the sun to dry, with one person appointed to whisk away stray flies and prowling dogs. The dried meat strips that resulted were lightweight and a great treat out on the road bicycling in western Tibet. We added them to stews and snacked on them for courage on particularly difficult days.

In this recipe we have substituted beef for yak meat. You could also use lamb, but removing all the fat would be more work. In the thin dry air of the Changtang, and even in Lhasa, meat dries quickly in the sun. If you live in a very dry area with lots of sun, try drying the strips in the sun. Otherwise, use the low-temperature oven suggested in the recipe. If you are sun-drying the meat, be sure to protect it from flies.

1 pound lean beef, all traces of fat removed and cut across the grain into thin strips

marinade

½ cup vinegar (wine, cider, or white)

¼ cup soy sauce

2 to 3 cloves garlic, crushed and coarsely chopped

½ teaspoon dried chile pepper flakes

½ teaspoon minced ginger

You will need a wooden mallet or a pestle, a large shallow bowl, and a large baking sheet.

With a wooden mallet or pestle, pound the meat strips to tenderize them.

Mix together all the marinade ingredients in a large shallow bowl. Place the meat in the marinade, turn to coat, and let stand, covered, in the refrigerator, for 6 to 12 hours.

Lay the meat strips on a large baking sheet, and place in a warm oven (about 175°F) for 24 hours, turning the pieces every 4 to 6 hours. If the pieces start to crisp and blacken, lower the oven temperature. When done, the pieces should be light and completely dried. They will keep indefinitely without refrigeration if stored in a sealed container or plastic bag.

▲▲▲▲▲▲▲▲▲▲▲▲▲▲▲▲▲▲▲▲▲▲▲

Use as a lightweight meat source on camping trips as is,
or add to soups or stews.

TIBET:
BUTTER, CHEESE,
AND YOGURT

Like the people of the Indian subcontinent, Tibetans have traditionally eaten milk products of many kinds. But cattle don't thrive at high altitudes. The alternative, apart from relying on sheep and goats, which produce milk for only three or four months in a year, is milk from dzi, female yaks. Dzi are tough, can survive cold and high altitude, and produce a reasonable quantity of milk year-round. The Tibetans make butter, cheese, and yogurt from the milk.

The butter is churned in a long narrow cylindrical wooden butter churn with a pole down the middle, which is thumped rhythmically up and down until the butter thickens. The butter is used in tea and, like whey, for a skin and hair softener and protector in the cold winter months. Once made, it is usually stored in a sheep stomach, looking like a leather pouch, in which it can be easily transported or stored for long periods. Over time, the butter sours or ferments; for most Tibetans the soured butter, rather than the fresh or sweet product we are familiar with, is preferred. One of the features of the Barkhor market in Lhasa is the row of butter vendors, their great pungent blocks of butter sliced open, quite cheesy in look and aroma.

In Tibet, cheese, like butter, is made for long keeping. Once the cheese has been made, it is cut into small squares, threaded on a string, and dried in the rafters of a house or suspended above the fire in a nomad tent. The resulting hard, dry, and very lightweight chunks are often left on the string for easy carrying. This cheese is an efficient traveling food that can be rehydrated by long soaking or boiling. As you might expect from its long exposure to dry air near the family cooking fire, the cheese has a distinctively smoky taste, not at all unpleasant.

Yogurt is made whenever fresh milk is available, and can sometimes be found for sale in larger villages and towns. One summer, near the village of Burang in the far western corner of Tibet, we were delighted to find dzi milk yogurt for sale at a small farm. Every day for the next two weeks we ate large quantities of yogurt, it never ceasing to feel like a special treat. Shortly before we left, I discovered in my bicycle panniers a clean white silk undersock, so into the sock we spooned a quart of yogurt. We suspended the sock above a bowl (to catch the drips of whey, a refreshing drink) for about three hours. After a few coaxing squeezes to hurry the process along, what remained in the sock was a rich, smooth cream cheese!

It's funny about that cheese; I don't think either of us will ever forget just how good it tasted.

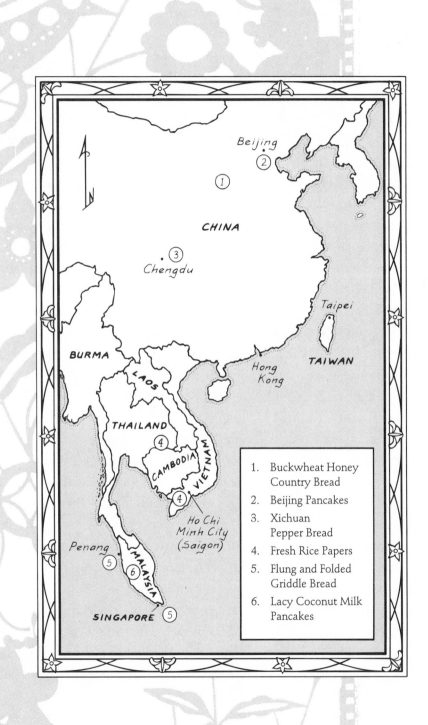

1. Buckwheat Honey
   Country Bread
2. Beijing Pancakes
3. Xichuan
   Pepper Bread
4. Fresh Rice Papers
5. Flung and Folded
   Griddle Bread
6. Lacy Coconut Milk
   Pancakes

China, Vietnam, and Malaysia

Flatbreads from Central Asia moved east to northern China, becoming
transformed along the way into distinctive and delicious local specialties.

In many parts of northern China—with its continental climate of cold winters and hot summers—wheat grows well, much as it does in the plains of North America. Consequently, wheat, not rice, is the staple grain. It is made into breads and noodles and eaten with a wide variety of foods.

As in Central Asia, flatbreads in northern China are cooked either on the walls of tandoor-style ovens or on a skillet or griddle over a flame. There is a wider variety of foods available than in the Central Asian grasslands, and so breads are not as central to the diet and do not need to be consumed in such quantity. Consequently, Chinese flatbreads are usually smaller than Central Asian breads and are often flavored with sesame seeds or chopped scallions or spices like Xichuan pepper. (Strongly flavored breads are difficult to eat in the same quantity as more "neutral" breads.)

Halong Bay, Vietnam: Fishing junks

Alongside the staples of bread and noodles, in the northern plains as well as in the mountains and fertile valleys of Xichuan Province, dried and preserved vegetables, and meat when available, are prepared in a variety of ways. Tofu is an important food throughout China, used in stir-fries for texture and for its nutritional content. The principal meat is pork, which is usually finely chopped or sliced and added to soups and stir-fries for its flavor, rather than served as the main event.

Farther south, in the subtropical and tropical climates of Vietnam and Malaysia, rice is the primary grain. A generous climate and ample water resources give these regions a wide variety of foods, which are generally eaten with plain rice. Some rice is

Vietnamese rice wrappers drying

ground into flour and combined with water or coconut milk to make thin flatbread wrappers, distant tropical cousins of Central Asian flatbreads. These are eaten wrapped around combinations of meat, herbs, vegetables, and fruits.

Wheat-flour breads, made from imported flour, are also found in Malaysia and other parts of Southeast Asia, wherever there are transplanted populations from India. Thus Indian flatbreads and other foods have become part of the culinary tradition in the cities of Malaysia and in Singapore.

Chengdu, Xichuan: Xichuan pepper breads

Buckwheat Honey Country Bread

shaobing tienda • China

Wheat, not rice, is the staple food in many parts of China, although much of the wheat is eaten in the form of noodles rather than bread. Bread making, especially of oven-baked breads, is almost certainly an art that was imported into China from Central Asia. Historical accounts document the baking of breads in ovens—slapping the bread against the oven walls—as early as the T'ang Dynasty, around 600 A.D. But bread was still considered very exotic fare. Now, in small shops and street stalls in most large cities and towns, breads of various shapes and flavors are sold in great quantity.

Shaobing, or "roasted cake," is probably the most common flatbread throughout China. There are a great many varieties of shaobing, all of which fall into one of two categories: *tienda,* sweet, and *xienda,* salty or savory. The savory shaobing most familiar to people outside China is a rectangular, somewhat flaky bread covered with sesame seeds. It pulls apart into different layers created by a lard-flour mixture around which the dough has been repeatedly folded, rolled out, and folded again. Most of the shaobings we've tasted in villages and small towns in China are, however, not at all rich and refined.

This particular sweet country-style shaobing is made with buckwheat honey. If buckwheat honey is not available where you live, substitute whatever honey you prefer. Buckwheat honey does, however, have a very distinctive taste that holds up well in baking.

2½ cups soft whole wheat flour

1 teaspoon salt

1 tablespoon sunflower or peanut oil

Approximately 1¼ cups lukewarm water

2 to 3 tablespoons buckwheat honey

You will need a medium-sized bowl, unglazed quarry tiles (see page 20) to fit on a rack in your oven, and a rolling pin.

Mix the flour and salt together in a medium bowl. Stir in the oil. Make a well in the center of the mixture, pour in the warm water, and stir from the center out to incorporate the flour; add a tablespoon or so more water if the dough is too dry to be easily kneaded. Turn out onto a lightly floured bread board and knead for 3 to 5 minutes. Clean out the bowl, oil lightly, and return the dough to the bowl. Cover with plastic wrap, and let stand for at least 30 minutes. (We often leave shaobing dough overnight at room temperature, covered with plastic wrap. In the morning it is slightly soured and just as easy to work.)

Line the bottom rack of the oven with quarry tiles, leaving a 1-inch gap between the tiles and the oven walls. Preheat the oven to 450°F.

Divide the dough into 4 pieces. Flatten each piece between floured hands. Then, with a rolling pin, continue to flatten each bread to an 8-inch square. Spread 1 to 2 teaspoons buckwheat honey over one half of each square. (If the honey is thick and too sticky, causing the dough to tear while spreading, dilute with a little hot water.) Fold over the other half of each bread to make a 4- by 8-inch rectangle. Roll gently to seal the two sides firmly together.

Bake the breads on quarry tiles for 6 to 8 minutes, until the tops have begun to brown. Cool on a rack momentarily before serving.

▲▲▲▲▲▲▲▲▲▲▲▲▲▲▲▲▲▲▲▲▲▲

Makes 4 rectangular flatbreads, approximately 4 inches by 8 inches.

Serve on their own for breakfast or as a snack, or serve with
Savory Hot Soy Milk (page 81).

Savory Hot Soy Milk

do jiang • Taiwan and North China

Taipei is one of the world's great cities in which to eat. It excels in its street food, market food, and in its hundreds of little noodle and snack shops scattered in back alleys all across the city.

In the district of Yung Ho, just across the Chung-cheng Bridge, there are many tiny restaurants, each with an enormous steaming vat of soybean milk and a red-hot charcoal oven baking around the clock. On a cold winter morning, or almost any time for that matter, there is nothing better than a bowl of hot soybean milk. *Do jiang,* as it is called, can be ordered either sweet, with the addition of sugar, or salty (our favorite), served with bits of scallions, dried shrimp, ginger, coriander leaf, and a few drops of chile oil.

Our version of *do jiang* is tart with a dash of vinegar, spiced with scallions and chile oil, and fragrant with coriander. The texture and flavor come from a combination of chopped dried shrimp and dried pork. You can eat it with a spoon, like soup, or dip a fresh Buckwheat Honey Country Bread into it for a moist, chewy mouthful.

2 cups unsweetened soy milk

1 teaspoon cider vinegar

1 teaspoon dried shrimp (see page 413), finely chopped

1 tablespoon finely shredded dried pork (see page 413)

¼ cup small croutons or bread cubes

2 scallions, finely chopped

1 teaspoon coarsely chopped fresh coriander

¼ teaspoon chile oil (see page 411), or to taste

You will need a saucepan.

Heat the soy milk over medium-high heat until boiling. Reduce the heat to low and stir in the vinegar. Pour into one large or two small soup bowls. Add the shrimp, pork shreds, croutons, scallions, and coriander. Drizzle the chile oil on top and serve.

▲▲▲▲▲▲●▲●▲▲●●▲▲●▲▲▲●▲▲

Makes 1 large traditional-sized serving or 2 smaller servings.

Serve hot with Buckwheat Honey Country Bread (page 79) or
Xichuan Pepper Bread (page 93) for dipping.

Spicy Peanut Sauce

Xichuan, China

This sauce is one of the best all-around accompaniments for flatbreads that we know of. It is traditionally served over cold wheat flour noodles, and is a great dip for uncooked vegetables like broccoli, cauliflower, and carrot sticks. It's excellent for parties, and for kids; it keeps well in the refrigerator, and it is very simple to prepare.

When you make the sauce, it will be thin, but as it sits (especially if kept in the refrigerator), it will again become almost as thick as the peanut butter you began with—a reminder of just how much oil is in the peanut butter.

½ cup unsweetened peanut butter

½ cup warm water

1 teaspoon cayenne, or more to taste

¼ cup cider vinegar

2 tablespoons soy sauce

1 large clove garlic, finely chopped

3 to 4 scallions, finely chopped

You will need a medium-sized bowl.

In a medium-sized bowl, combine the peanut butter and warm water, and whisk until well blended and smooth. Stir in the cayenne, then stir in the vinegar and soy sauce. Stir in the garlic and scallions.

If you are serving over noodles (Xichuan-style), you might want to thin the sauce even more, and add a little more cayenne. But if you are using it as dip for bread, you won't want it any thinner than this. The sauce gets thicker as it sits, much thicker if refrigerated. You may need to thin it by blending in a little warm water when you take it from the refrigerator. This is a good keeper in the refrigerator, but if you plan to make it ahead, don't add the garlic and scallions until just before you serve the sauce.

Note: This recipe can be doubled or tripled, but increase the garlic and scallions by a lesser proportion.

▲▲▲▲▲▲▲▲▲▲▲▲▲▲▲▲▲▲▲▲▲▲

Makes 1¼ cups of sauce.

Serve as a dip for Xichuan Pepper Bread (page 93) or other savory breads, and steamed vegetables. This sauce is traditionally served over cold noodles; and it's very good with soba noodles, hot or cold.

WINTER IN NORTH CHINA

Late one cold February night I went to catch a train to go from Zhejiang in Henan Province to Xian in Shaanxi Province. I'd been in China many times before, and had been on many Chinese trains, but I'd never travelled across northern China in the middle of the winter. So the railway station came as something of a shock. It was very large and for some reason absolutely packed with people, thousands of people, at one o'clock in the morning. Lighting in the cold concrete building was so dim as to be almost nonexistent, and the cold night air seemed frozen with the breath of so many people huddled close together. The restrooms had long since reached their capacity, and the enormous long lines in front of ticket booths were at the point of absurdity, even for China.

I had a ticket, but not a seat, so to get on the train I had to line up for hours. When the time for my train came close, the line I was in was first led out in front of the enormous station, and then taken back like a snake through the terminal, in order to control the crowd, to keep people from being pushed to the floor and trampled. Just as the train came in, the crowd surged forward, and like everyone else, I ran and pushed and jumped. Somehow I got onto the train; most people weren't so lucky. The train was already immensely overcrowded. Just outside a w.c., I found a

Chengdu, Xichuan: Street scene in winter

small place on the floor to sit with my knees tucked up under my chin. It was an excruciatingly long night, one of the longest of my life. At one point I caught a look out a window just as another train came speeding by in the other direction. It was as overcrowded as the train I was on. The windows were all filled—completely filled—with expressionless faces, people waiting, just like me, for the time to pass.

I arrived in Xian, the ancient imperial capital of the Middle Kingdom, around midday and fortunately found a hotel room not far from the station. The heat wasn't working, nor was the water, but it would be by evening, I was told. So I left my bag in my room and headed out. I poked my head into a few shops, all of which seemed even colder than the street. The shopkeepers were dressed in heavy cotton padded coats, hats, and gloves with the fingers cut off at the knuckles. The tips of their fingers were reddish blue and swollen with cold.

I strolled along a little farther and found a small outdoor market. The only food for sale was meat and flatbread. Some of the meat was dried, but most had already been boiled or roasted and was for sale in small portions. The market had a very Central Asian feel to it. I bought a few ounces of meat and some breads, and continued on my way. "Shaobing," the vendor had called the flatbreads, but they had nothing in common with shaobing. They were tough, stale, and plain, tasting more like a cardboard box than bread: winter in north China.

Beijing Pancakes

bao bing • North China

Bao bing are soft, fine, round breads, ideal for wrapping strong-tasting morsels such as Mushu Pork or Four-Thread Salad. The unyeasted dough is made with boiling water. The water's heat transforms the texture of the flour, giving the dough a characteristic soft earlobe feel, ideal for wrappers. It can be mixed up and kneaded just fifteen minutes before you cook the breads, or it can be left to stand for several hours.

Bao bing are easy and forgiving to make and yet so pretty that the cook usually feels a warm glow of self-congratulation, at least in our household! Perhaps it comes from knowing that all they are made from is flour and water and a dab of sesame oil. Perhaps it is the miraculous pulling apart of each pair of little breads as they come off the griddle, one side pale and steam-cooked, the other brown-speckled from the heat of the skillet.

We like to serve an array of dishes (see the suggestions on page 86) with a stack of bao bing so that each diner can sample different combinations.

2 cups unbleached all-purpose flour, plus about ½ cup flour for rolling out

1 cup boiling water

About 2 tablespoons roasted sesame oil (see page 417)

Vegetable oil

You will need a mixing bowl, a rolling pin, a round cutter or a glass to cut out 3-inch circles, a pastry brush, and a cast-iron or other heavy skillet or griddle.

Sift the 2 cups flour into a mixing bowl. Pour in the boiling water and stir with a wooden spoon until all the flour is incorporated and a dough has formed.

Dust your kneading surface lightly with flour and turn out the dough. Knead for 10 minutes, or until the dough is smooth and soft to the touch.

Rinse out the mixing bowl. Place the dough in the bowl, cover with plastic wrap, and let stand for at least 15 minutes, or as long as 3 hours.

Place a small dish of sesame oil near your work surface. Cut a piece off the dough, about a third of the total, and leave the rest covered. Working on a lightly floured surface, roll the dough out to a thin sheet, no more than ⅛ inch thick. Work from the center outward as you roll, turning the dough over and dusting lightly with flour if it begins to stick to the rolling pin.

continued

Using a 3-inch round cutter or a glass (we use a plastic glass), cut an even number of circles out of the rolled-out dough (you should get 6 or 8). Gather together the scraps and place them with the covered dough.

With a pastry brush, paint the top surface of half the dough circles with sesame oil. Place an unoiled dough circle on top of each oiled round.

Before you roll out these paired circles again, place a heavy skillet or griddle over high heat. Pour a little vegetable oil into the pan once it is hot, then remove from the heat. Wipe the oil from the pan with a paper towel.

Roll out one double circle of dough until a uniform 1/16 inch thick. As you work, roll from the center out, and lift and turn the dough a quarter-turn or less after each stroke of the rolling pin. This way you can keep a circular shape as you gradually make the circle larger and thinner. Don't worry if a little oil leaks out the side as you work. Roll out the remaining pairs of dough; before you start on your last pair, return the skillet to medium-high heat.

Place a dough circle in the heated skillet and let it cook for 1 minute. You should see a slight bubbling in the top surface as steam builds up between the layers: If this hasn't happened after 1 minute, raise the heat slightly and let cook a little longer; the first side should be speckled with brown spots. Turn over, and cook for 45 seconds to 1 minute longer. Remove from the pan with a spatula. Split apart the two layers (they may already have started to separate near the end of their cooking), and wrap in a towel. Repeat with the remaining double circles.

As you cook them, you will get more confident about the timing and will be able to start rolling out the rest of the dough while you cook. Roll out and cook the remaining dough, including the scraps, keeping the cooked pancakes well wrapped in a cloth. Serve warm immediately after cooking. (Alternatively, reheat cooled pancakes by steaming: Place a stack of bao bing on a plate and put the plate in a bamboo steamer over boiling water for 5 to 10 minutes.)

▲▲▲▲▲▲▲▲▲▲▲▲▲▲▲▲▲▲▲▲▲▲▲

Makes approximately 20 thin, supple bread wrappers.

Try wrapping Mushu Pork (page 87) in bao bing, or just wrap them around the satisfying crunch and flavor of Four-Thread Salad (page 88). For a more elaborate meal, begin with Spicy Pork and Tofu (page 95) and Xichuan Eggplant (page 96), served with stacks of bao bing, and follow with the pork. Guests can make up their own flavor combinations as they taste the various dishes.

Mushu Pork

Mushu pork, like many well-loved Chinese dishes, is a pleasure as much for its combination of textures as for its blend of flavors. Marinated shreds of pork are stir-fried with slivered Chinese mushrooms, then stirred together with soft-cooked scrambled eggs and subtly flavored with rice wine. This soft-textured dish is usually then wrapped in Beijing Pancakes; you can also, less traditionally, serve it with steamed rice.

½ pound lean boneless pork loin, trimmed of all fat

m a r i n a d e

1 tablespoon soy sauce

1 tablespoon Chinese rice wine or dry sherry (see Note)

1 tablespoon water

1 teaspoon sugar

1 teaspoon cornstarch

¼ cup (approximately 20) dried lily buds (see page 416)

10 dried black "flower" mushrooms (see page 413)

4 large eggs

1 teaspoon salt (see Note)

4 scallions, quartered lengthwise and cut into 1-inch lengths

2 tablespoons vegetable or peanut oil

2 tablespoons Chinese rice wine (see Note) or dry sherry

1 teaspoon soy sauce

You will need three bowls, a plate, and a wok and spatula.

Slice the pork across the grain into paper-thin slices, then cut into narrow shreds 1½ to 2 inches long.

In a bowl, mix together the marinade ingredients. Add the shredded pork, turning and stirring to coat well. Set aside for 30 minutes, stirring once or twice.

Rinse the dried lily buds and dried mushrooms, then place in a bowl and soak in hot water for 20 minutes; drain.

Cut the hard ends off the lily buds and cut each bud crosswise in half. Cut the stems off the mushrooms and discard, then slice the caps into narrow slices. Set aside.

When ready to begin cooking, beat the eggs in a bowl until frothy. Add the salt, and place the bowl by the stove, along with the other ingredients, as well as a medium-sized plate and a deep serving platter.

Heat a wok over high heat. When hot, add 1 tablespoon of the oil and swirl to coat the wok. Pour the beaten eggs into the wok and lower the heat to medium-high. Gently lift and pull back the edges of the egg mixture as it cooks, allowing the uncooked portion to flow into contact with the hot wok (similar to cooking an omelette). When the egg is no longer runny, but still soft and not firmly set, transfer to the plate. Using your spatula, break the egg into small bite-sized pieces, then set aside.

Wipe out the wok and place over high heat. When hot, add the remaining 1 tablespoon oil and swirl to coat the wok. Toss in the scallions and stir-fry for 10 seconds. Add the shredded pork, lower the heat to medium-high, and stir-fry, tossing and pressing the meat against the hot surface of the wok until the meat is no longer pink, 2 to 3 minutes. Add the rice wine, lily buds, and mushrooms and stir-fry for another minute. Add the eggs and stir in gently. Add the soy sauce, cook for 30 seconds, then turn out onto the serving platter. Serve at once.

Note: Rice wine for cooking often can be found in Chinese grocery stores. Check the label to see whether salt has been added. If so, omit the salt, but taste the mushu just before serving (after the soy sauce has been added), and add if necessary.

▲▲▲▲▲▲•▲▲▲▲▲▲▲▲▲••▲▲▲

Serves 4.

Serve with Beijing Pancakes (page 85), accompanied by Four-Thread Salad (below).

Four-Thread Salad

Xichuan, China

The name of this recipe illustrates the importance of presentation in Chinese cuisine. Actually, the "threads" are traditionally three: slivers of carrot and cucumber and short lengths of softened cellophane noodles (mung bean threads). We like to add a fourth—fine lengths of scallion—for taste and texture. The threads are tossed in a soy and rice vinegar dressing, with a hint of Xichuan from the combination of Xichuan peppercorns, chile flakes, and garlic. The salad can be prepared ahead and refrigerated, covered, for an hour or two before being served. This gives the dressing time to penetrate the vegetables. But you can also toss the salad and serve immediately.

2 ounces mung bean threads
(see page 416)

2 cups boiling water

½ pound carrots, scraped and cut into
2-inch julienne (fine matchsticks)

1 teaspoon salt

½ teaspoon sugar

½ pound English cucumber
(1 small or ½ large)

2 to 3 scallions

d r e s s i n g

1 large clove garlic, minced

¼ teaspoon salt

¼ teaspoon Xichuan peppercorns (see
page 419), dry-roasted (see page 154)
and ground

3 tablespoons soy sauce

1 tablespoon rice vinegar

½ teaspoon roasted sesame oil
(see page 417)

½ teaspoon dried chile pepper flakes,
dry-roasted (see page 154)

You will need a medium-sized bowl, a colander, and a small bowl.

Soak the bean threads in the boiling water for 1 minute, or just until softened but not mushy; drain. Using sharp scissors, cut into 2-inch lengths. Set aside.

Place the carrots in a medium-sized serving bowl. Sprinkle with ½ teaspoon of the salt and the sugar, and let stand for 15 minutes.

Wash the cucumber, trim off the ends, and slice in half lengthwise. Scrape out the seeds and discard. Slice the flesh into slivers the same size as the carrots. Place in a colander, sprinkle with the remaining ½ teaspoon salt, and toss. Let stand for 15 minutes.

Slice the scallions (both the white and the tender green part), into long narrow ribbons about 2 inches long. Add them to the carrots.

Rinse the cucumber briefly under cold water, then squeeze gently to drain excess moisture. Add to the carrots. Stir in the bean threads.

In a small bowl, combine the dressing ingredients and stir well. Pour over the salad and toss gently to coat well. Serve at room temperature. This salad tastes best an hour or two after it has been dressed, when the flavors of the dressing have had a chance to blend and to penetrate the vegetables.

▲▲▲▲▲▲▲▲▲▲▲▲▲▲▲▲▲▲▲▲▲▲

Serves 4 to 6.

*Serve as one of the dishes in a Beijing Pancake (page 85) meal or as a refreshing crisp salad
to set off spicier soft-textured dishes such as Spicy Pork and Tofu (page 95)
or Xichuan Eggplant (page 96).*

Hot-and-Sour Soup

Xichuan, China

Permission for independent travelers to enter Tibet was first granted by the Chinese government in late 1984, provided that the travelers entered Tibet by air. We had both always dreamed of going to Tibet, so when the opportunity arose, we each quickly made our way there. Over the next two years, we returned to Tibet three more times. Because the flight to Lhasa originated in Chengdu, one of the two principal cities in the province of Xichuan, we ended up spending a lot of time there exploring the city's back streets, markets, and restaurants while we waited for space on the plane.

On our first visit, Chengdu felt much like other large Chinese cities. There were state-run hotels, state-run restaurants, state-run markets, long, colorless Soviet-style boulevards, and not much action even in the back streets. But in the period from 1985 to 1987, Chengdu transformed itself into a thriving free-market city, bustling with private enterprise to a degree unparalleled in China at that time. Tiny restaurants and garden-plot markets sprang up everywhere; all you had to do was to turn off a large boulevard, head down a lane, and there would be a steamy little shop, the proprietors as eager to please as the employees of the state-run restaurants had long been consistently rude and inhospitable. The food varied from place to place; it was luck of the draw. But when the food was good, it was really good. Humble foods, family foods—ma po dofu, hot-and-sour soup, dondon noodles, warm savory flatbreads—the restaurants were little more than household kitchens putting out a menu. We haven't been back to Chengdu since the late eighties, but we have a feeling it must be just the same: a great place to eat.

▲▲▲▲▲▲▲▲▲▲▲▲▲▲▲▲▲▲▲▲▲▲▲

This classic soup appears on many restaurant menus, but it is rarely made with attention to the balance of the flavors. The recipe is straightforward but yields a complex-tasting soup, a satisfying meal-in-one when served with bao bing or flatbreads. The mix of textures—slippery, crunchy tree ears, soft, dense black mushrooms, smooth squares of tofu, tender marinated shredded pork—is a delight and almost as memorable as the double punch of vinegar sour married to black pepper hot.

¼ cup tree ears (see page 419)

¼ cup (20 to 25) dried lily buds
    (see page 416)

8 dried black mushrooms
    (see page 413)

½ pound lean boneless pork loin,
    trimmed of all fat

marinade

1 tablespoon soy sauce

1 tablespoon rice vinegar

1 teaspoon cornstarch

1 tablespoon water

Freshly ground black pepper

soup

3 cups chicken stock plus 2 cups water
    or 5 cups water

2 large blocks (about 4 inches by 4
    inches) firm tofu, cut into ½-inch cubes

3 scallions, finely chopped

2 tablespoons cornstarch

¼ cup cold water

2 tablespoons soy sauce

6 tablespoons rice vinegar

¼ teaspoon freshly ground black pepper

1 large egg, well beaten

1 teaspoon roasted sesame oil
    (see page 417)

You will need two medium-sized bowls, a large saucepan with a lid, and a small bowl.

Place the tree ears, lily buds, and mushrooms in a medium-sized bowl. Rinse with cold water, then pour over about 3 cups hot water. Let soak for 20 minutes.

Meanwhile, slice the pork and cut into slivers as thin as you can make them. (This is easier if the meat is cold and therefore firmer.)

In a medium bowl, mix together all the marinade ingredients, and stir until smooth. Set aside 3 tablespoons of the shredded meat, then add the rest to the marinade and toss to coat well.

In a large saucepan, bring the water or stock and water to a boil. Add the reserved shredded pork, reduce the heat, and let simmer, partially covered, for 15 minutes.

Meanwhile, drain the soaking dried ingredients. Cut any hard bits off the tree ears and discard. Cut the hard ends off the lily buds and discard. Cut each lily bud in half, then pull apart to shred slightly. Cut the stems off the black mushrooms and discard, then slice the caps thinly.

Add the tree ears, lily buds, and black mushrooms to the simmering soup base and bring to a boil. Add the marinated meat, lower the heat, and add the tofu and half the chopped scallions. Simmer for 5 minutes over medium-low heat, covered.

In a small bowl, stir together the cornstarch and cold water, then stir in the soy sauce, and stir until smooth. Stir into the soup, raise the heat, and bring back to a boil. Boil for 1 to 2 minutes, until thickened slightly. Add the rice vinegar and pepper, and lower the heat to a simmer. Add the beaten egg, then immediately remove from the heat, and stir gently to break the egg into fine strands as it cooks. Gently stir in the sesame oil. Serve in one large bowl or ladled into individual bowls, garnished with the remaining chopped scallions.

▲▲▲▲▲▲▲▲▲▲▲▲▲▲▲▲▲▲▲▲ ▲▲▲

Serves 4.

We like to serve this as a warming meal-in-one, since the soup tends to knock out the competition! Have plenty of Beijing Pancakes (page 85) or Xichuan Pepper Bread (page 93) on hand. For a more ambitious meal, you could begin with Spicy Peanut Sauce (page 82) with more pepper breads, and then serve Four-Thread Salad (page 88) after the soup to refresh your guests' palates. Finish the meal with fresh tangerines or snow apples.

Xichuan Pepper Bread

guo kua • Xichuan, China

These breads are a Xichuan breakfast specialty. There is usually a choice between "sweet" and "salty"; the sweet version is made the same way as the savory version, but crude brown cane sugar is substituted for the basic seasoning of Xichuan peppercorns and finely chopped scallions. The savory breads are sometimes made elaborate with chopped pork, a variation that is also very good.

Xichuan pepper, also known as *fagara,* has been used in Chinese medicine and cooking for longer than almost any other spice. Before making these breads, try to find good fresh pepper, with a strong fragrant aroma; a Chinese grocery is a better bet than a spice store.

The dough is made with both boiling water (which cooks the starches in the flour and makes a very soft dough) and cold water (which yields a stronger dough). The mix produces a soft, pliable dough, which is also elastic enough to take rolling out.

dough
3 cups unbleached all-purpose flour
2 teaspoons baking powder
1 teaspoon salt
½ cup boiling water
½ cup plus 2 tablespoons cold water

filling
1 tablespoon plus 1 teaspoon peanut oil
1 teaspoon Xichuan peppercorns (see page 419), dry-roasted (see page 154) and finely ground
1 cup finely chopped scallions (white and tender green parts) or 1 cup finely chopped garlic chives (see page 415)

You will need a food processor, a rolling pin, and one or two heavy skillets at least 8 inches in diameter.

Place the flour, baking powder, and salt in a food processor and pulse to mix well. With the motor running, pour the boiling water in a thin stream through the feed tube, then add the cold water and process until the mixture forms a ball. Process for 1 minute longer, then turn the dough out onto a lightly floured surface. Knead briefly, then cover with plastic wrap and let sit for 15 minutes.

Divide the dough into 8 equal pieces. Working with one piece at a time, leaving the others covered, roll out the dough on a lightly floured surface to a circle 8 inches in diameter. Spread ½ teaspoon of the oil over the top of the bread, then sprinkle on ⅛ teaspoon of the Xichuan pepper. Spread 2 tablespoons of the chopped scallions or garlic chives evenly over the bread. Then, roll the bread up like a jelly roll, as tightly as possible. Anchoring one end of the resulting tube on your work surface, coil the bread as tightly as possible, and pinch the other end against the coil to make a smooth round. Flatten gently with the palm of your hand. Roll the bread out again gently with a rolling pin until it is about ¼ inch thick and 6 inches across. (Do not worry if the odd piece of scallion or garlic chive leaks out; you can patch any small holes in the dough.)

Before you begin rolling out and filling a second bread, place a heavy skillet over medium heat. When the skillet is hot, rub it thoroughly with a lightly oiled cloth or paper towel. Lower the heat to medium-low and place the first bread in the skillet. Cook for 3 minutes, or until the bottom is flecked with light brown spots. Turn over and cook for 3 minutes longer, or until both sides are flecked with light brown. Transfer the bread to a rack to cool slightly, then wrap in a towel to keep soft.

Meanwhile, continue rolling out and shaping the remaining breads while the first one bakes, then cook them in the same manner. If you are feeling comfortable about cooking times, heat another skillet so that you can have two breads cooking at once. Serve warm.

▲▲▲▲▲▲·▲·▲▲▲▲·▲▲·▲·▲▲▲

Makes 8 round breads, about 7 inches across and ¼ inch thick.

Serve with Spicy Pork and Tofu (page 95), Spicy Peanut Sauce (page 82),
or Xichuan Eggplant (page 96).

Spicy Pork and Tofu

mapo dofu • Xichuan, China

Mapo dofu, *a Xichuan specialty, is great winter food—nothing fancy, just* spicy and good. This version is flavored with pork, but a vegetarian version is also tasty.

Kunming, China: Tofu vendor

Although the instructions and list of ingredients look quite long, this is a simple dish to make. As with any stir-fried dish, all the ingredients must be prepared before you start cooking. Then total cooking time is only about twelve minutes. Furthermore, the blended flavors of its ingredients seem to intensify as the dish cools, so we often like to prepare it ahead to eat at room temperature, and we make enough for leftovers. It can be stored, covered, in the refrigerator for up to 3 days and then reheated.

¼ cup tree ears (see page 419)

1 cup boiling water

2 tablespoons finely chopped fresh ginger (one 2-inch piece)

1 tablespoon minced garlic

2 tablespoons dried chile pepper flakes

½ teaspoon salt

1 teaspoon vegetable oil

1 teaspoon rice vinegar

2 tablespoons peanut or vegetable oil

¼ pound lean ground pork or beef

3 scallions, finely chopped

3 large squares (about 4 inches by 4 inches) firm tofu, cut into ¾-inch cubes

2 tablespoons soy sauce, diluted with ¼ cup water

½ teaspoon sugar

1 teaspoon cornstarch, dissolved in ¼ cup cold water

½ teaspoon Xichuan peppercorns (see page 419), dry-roasted (see page 154) and finely ground

1 teaspoon roasted sesame oil

You will need several small bowls, a heavy skillet, a mortar and pestle or spice grinder, and a wok or large skillet and a spatula.

Soak the tree ears in the boiling water for 20 minutes.

In a small bowl, mash the ginger and garlic together into a fine paste. Set aside.

Roast the chile flakes in a dry skillet over medium heat for 3 to 4 minutes, or until fragrant. Transfer to a mortar or spice grinder, add the salt, and pound or grind together. Turn out into a small bowl. Stir in the oil and vinegar to make a paste, and set aside.

Drain the tree ears and chop into small pieces, discarding any hard bits.

Before starting to cook the mapo dofu, place all your ingredients next to the stove. Place a shallow serving dish nearby.

Heat a wok or large skillet over high heat. When hot, pour in the oil and swirl around to coat. When the oil is hot, toss in the garlic and ginger mixture and stir-fry over medium-high heat for 30 seconds, tossing and scooping with a spatula to ensure even cooking.

Add the chile paste and tree ears and stir-fry for another 30 seconds or so. Toss in the meat and cook for 2 to 3 minutes, stirring constantly to ensure even cooking, until the meat has changed color. Toss in the scallions and stir-fry for 30 seconds. Carefully add the tofu and then mix gently, running the spatula along the wok's surface to keep the food from sticking, trying not to break up the tofu squares. Add the soy and water mixture and the sugar. Raise the heat, and then add the dissolved cornstarch and bring to a boil. Lower the heat to medium, and let simmer for 2 to 3 minutes, until the sauce thickens. Add the Xichuan pepper and sesame oil and stir well, then remove from the heat and turn out into the serving dish. Serve hot or at room temperature.

▲▲▲▲▲▲▲▲▪▲▲▪▪▲▲▲▲▲▪▪▲▲▲

Serves 4.

The sauce in mapo dofu is so delicious that you must be sure to have stacks of Xichuan Pepper Bread (page 93) to mop it up with. Mapo dofu makes a great meal-in-one or goes well paired with Xichuan Eggplant (below). It's also very good with plain rice.

✳

Xichuan Eggplant
yu xiang qiezi • Xichuan, China

Don't be surprised by the amount of garlic in this recipe. Ginger, garlic, and peppers are used in great abundance in Xichuan cuisine, but Xichuan restaurants outside China usually prepare only a tame relative of the real thing. According to nutritional studies, Thais and Koreans eat more garlic than anyone else in the world—an average of a little more than two pounds of garlic per person each year. We don't know whether or not the people of Xichuan were included in any of these studies, but surely they must also rank right up there.

In this quickly prepared stir-fry, eggplant and mushrooms are flavored by a classic Xichuan combination of ginger, scallions, and hot peppers, as well as garlic. The dish is succulent and almost meaty in texture—a great treat for vegetarians and nonvegetarians alike.

6 dried black mushrooms
  (see page 414)

1 cup hot water

2 tablespoons peanut oil

8 to 10 garlic cloves, finely chopped

4 scallions, chopped

One 1-inch piece fresh ginger, peeled
  and finely chopped

4 to 6 Chinese or Japanese eggplants
  (see page 414) or 3 to 4 medium
  Italian eggplants (see Note), cut into
  strips approximately 2 inches long
  by ½ inch thick

1 tablespoon hot pepper paste (see
  page 415) or 1 tablespoon finely
  chopped and seeded jalapeño
  (see page 410)

2 tablespoons rice vinegar or
  apple cider vinegar

1 tablespoon soy sauce

1 tablespoon sugar

You will need a small bowl and a wok or large skillet and a spatula.

Wash the dried mushrooms well in cold water. Place in a small bowl with the hot water, and let soak for at least 30 minutes.

When the mushrooms are soft, remove from the water, reserving the soaking liquid. Cut them into narrow strips, discarding the woody stems.

Heat a wok or large skillet over high heat. Add the oil, swirling to coat. When the oil is hot, add the garlic. Stir-fry, stirring occasionally, until it is just starting to brown, about 20 seconds. Then immediately add the scallions and ginger. Stir-fry for 30 seconds, then add the eggplant and mushrooms. Stir-fry for 2 to 3 minutes, until the eggplant begins to soften slightly. Stir in the hot pepper paste or jalapeño, add the vinegar, soy sauce, and sugar, and mix well. Pour in the reserved mushroom water and bring to a boil. Reduce the heat and simmer for 10 to 15 minutes. Serve hot or at room temperature.

Note: If using Italian eggplants, salt the eggplant strips liberally and let stand in a colander in the sink to drain for 30 minutes. Then rinse well, squeeze out excess moisture, pat dry, and proceed with the recipe.

▲▲▲▲▲·▲·▲▲▲·▲▲·▲·▲▲

Serves 4.

Serve with Beijing Pancakes (page 85) and Four-Thread Salad (page 88).

NEW YEAR IN VIETNAM

At dusk on our first day in Ho Chi Minh City, in early 1990, we traveled by cyclo through the city and out to a distant suburb to have dinner with friends. It was the third day of Tet, the Lunar New Year. The gentle warm evening air purred with the sounds of life, a measured amount of chaos: people laughing, firecrackers exploding, street hawkers exclaiming loudly in praise of their wares.

A Saigon-style cyclo, or bicycle rickshaw, is unique in design. The driver sits high up on a seat behind his passengers, an arrangement that makes the rickshaw faster, easier to pedal, and incredibly well balanced in sharp turns. It also gives the riders a tremendous view, riding along the street as if gliding in a comfortable armchair. The only disadvantage to the cyclos is that they have terrible brakes—but everyone else on the road has long since learned to give way to them.

We were with our two-year-old son, Dominic, and Anwei, an old friend. Anwei was born in Saigon. At age fourteen, after the end of the American war, he tried to leave the country by boat but was caught and put in jail. A few years later he and his parents were permitted to leave; they settled in Hong Kong, where we met him. Anwei had since returned to Vietnam to live.

In the one month we had in Vietnam, we would drive the entire country, south to north. We would have a Russian car, a driver, a guide, a false police permit, all arranged by Anwei. We would pay for hotel rooms in stacks of money that were measured, not counted. We would stay in a brothel in Cholon, a sleazy nightclub in downtown Saigon, a beautiful beach resort in Danang, a grand old French colonial mansion in Hue. We would have one of the most intense and vividly clear months of our lives, all thanks to Anwei. And we would eat and eat and eat.

Saigon cyclo

After almost an hour's ride through Ho Chi Minh City, our cyclos at last arrived at the small restaurant where we were to have our New Year's meal. The neighborhood was quiet, the restaurant peaceful. The fragrance of night-flowering jasmine blended with the smell of incense slowly burning at a household altar. We were twelve at dinner, including childhood friends of Anwei, some who had left the country and now returned, some who had never left.

Food arrived: grilled chicken, grilled beef, pounded shrimp on sugarcane, piles of fresh herbs, steamed squid with a ginger dressing, tiny white vermicelli noodles, bowls of *nuoc cham* (dipping sauce), plates stacked with fresh rice papers, and bowls piled high with fresh mint, leaf lettuce, *rau ram* (Vietnamese coriander), fresh coriander, and crisp white bean sprouts. We were shown how to wrap little bits of meat and fresh herbs with leaf lettuce or with fresh rice paper wrappers. We wrapped vermicelli noodles and bean sprouts with a sprig of mint and a morsel of grilled chicken, and then dipped it all into nuoc cham—salty, hot, sour. The combinations were endless, the tastes fresh, fabulous, uncomplicated. We drank bottled beer (Chinese mainland beer) or Coca-Cola, one can being more expensive than a plate of food.

"Hey, Joe," called out the cyclo driver in a heavy American G.I. accent as Dominic climbed back into the rickshaw to begin our long ride home. "How 'bout a candy?" he continued, handing over a candy sucker and getting a smile. Like many cyclo drivers, ours had been a soldier in the war. Now he had a baby daughter, just about the same age as Dominic. As we rode along through the night, we asked questions and he told stories. And then we rode along quietly, trying to imagine.

Fresh Rice Papers

banh uot • Vietnam

More so than in any other cuisine we know, much of the preparation of any given meal in Vietnam takes place at the table, whether wrapping foods, grilling meats, assembling hot soups, or even putting together sauces. The people dining, not just the cook, make choices about what goes well with what and about how something might best be eaten.

Vietnamese cuisine has a particular genius when it comes to wrapping foods. With fresh rice papers, called *banh uot,* or dried wrappers (which are rehydrated at the table by soaking them momentarily in water), many meals are put together as each person wraps bits of food with other bits of food and then dips the wrapped foods into different sauces. Unlike a Central Asian flatbread meal, where substantial amounts of hearty breads are eaten, the rice wrappers are paperthin and anything but substantial. However, frequently wrapped inside are rice noodles—more carbohydrates—and bean sprouts, a complementary protein. Meat is almost always served, but generally as a condiment, to add another flavor, not as the centerpiece of the meal.

Like fresh pasta, freshly made banh uot are quite different from their dried counterparts. Stacks of fresh rice papers are sold in markets in Vietnam, but elsewhere, you'll generally have to make them yourself. They're easy to prepare, and you'll enjoy their soft silkiness. But in truth, we usually use dried rice papers (*banh trang);* they are incredibly convenient and very inexpensive, and they can be kept almost indefinitely in the cupboard. Serve them with a wide, shallow bowl full of lukewarm water for moistening them. To moisten a wrapper, place it in the water for fifteen to thirty seconds—long enough for it to become moistened through and supple. Transfer to your plate or work surface and use immediately for wrapping.

1 cup rice flour	2 tablespoons vegetable oil
½ cup cornstarch	Vegetable oil for cooking and coating wrappers
½ cup tapioca flour or potato starch	
2½ cups water	

You will need a large bowl, a sieve, one or two 8-inch nonstick skillets or well-tempered crêpe or omelet pans with tight-fitting lids, a baking sheet, a large plate, and a wooden spatula.

In a large bowl, combine all the ingredients and whisk until smooth. Strain the batter through a sieve to remove any lumps, and let stand for 15 to 30 minutes. It will be very runny, like a very thin crêpe batter.

Place an 8-inch skillet, with a tight-fitting lid, over medium-low heat. Place a baking sheet beside the stove and spread 2 to 3 tablespoons vegetable oil on it, which you will use to coat the wrappers as they cool. (Keep the oil container handy so you can add more oil to the baking sheet when needed, probably when half the sheets are cooked.) Lightly oil a large plate and set it nearby.

After the frying pan has heated for 5 minutes, add a few drops of oil to the pan, then rub the bottom and sides with a paper towel to distribute the oil. Wipe off any excess. Stir or whisk the batter well. Using a ladle, measure 2 tablespoons of batter, pour it into the pan, and swirl it around to coat the surface. Immediately cover with the lid and let cook for 1 minute. (Steam will build up and cook the top surface while the bottom surface is heated by the pan.) Lift the lid to see if the top of the rice sheet looks shiny, with small bubbles (do not let any moisture from the underside of the lid drip onto the rice sheet); if not, wipe the underside of the lid dry, replace the lid, and let cook for another 20 to 30 seconds. When the rice sheet is shiny, lift out of the pan with a wooden spatula and place, shiny side up, on the oiled baking sheet.

Reheat the pan and dry off the underside of the lid. Whisk the batter well, and continue making rice sheets (you don't need to oil the pan each time, just for every second or third sheet). As each cooked rice sheet cools slightly, flip it over on the baking sheet to coat the other side well with oil; then, once completely cool, transfer to the large plate. Until the sheets are cool, they are sticky and may, even with the oil, stick together.

Once you get the temperature and procedure under control, you may want to speed up your production by using two pans in tandem. Make sure the baking sheet stays well oiled.

Once they have cooled, store the rice sheets on a plate wrapped in plastic wrap in the refrigerator. They will keep for 48 hours, but are at their best the day they are made.

TROUBLESHOOTING

Like crêpes, fresh rice papers sometimes take a while to master. Use the first one or two as test samples and adjust the pan temperature, batter thickness, and quantity as necessary.

continued

If the batter immediately sticks to the pan when you pour it in, before you can swirl it around, lower the temperature slightly. If there is still a problem, whisk a little more water into the batter.

If the batter does not reach the edges of your pan, thus giving an irregular rather then a round shape, increase the quantity used each time to 2½ or 3 tablespoons. The smaller your pan, the easier the rice papers are to handle. We often make 6-inch rice sheets in a 6-inch crêpe or omelet pan (using slightly less than 2 tablespoons of batter for each).

▲▲▲▲▲▲·ı▲▲ıı▲▲ıı▲▲·ıı▲▲▲

Makes 18 to 22 thin round rice papers, 7 to 8 inches across.

Use them to wrap Shrimp Roll-ups with Fresh Herbs (page 107) or Grilled Lemon Grass Beef (page 103) or for other combinations as you like. Be sure to have a dipping sauce, such as Vietnamese Dipping Sauce (page 109) or Peanut Dipping Sauce (page 105), on the table to round out the flavor combinations.

Grilled Lemon Grass Beef

thit bo nuong • Vietnam

One of our most extraordinary meals in Vietnam—and that is saying quite a lot—was a dinner at a Bo Bay Mon ("Beef in Seven Ways") restaurant in Saigon. We're not particularly big on meat-based meals, so when an acquaintance asked us if we would join him, it was not with great enthusiasm that we accepted. The meal that came to the table was exactly as advertised—beef prepared in seven different ways, seven different courses. It was a meal full of creativity, variety, and great flavors. We were kept busy wrapping foods, combining flavors, and dipping foods in tasty sauces. Each of the seven beef dishes had a distinctly different taste, so with each new dish there were new choices, new decisions to be made about what would go well with what.

By now we've almost agreed upon a favorite, lemon grass beef, but we could easily have chosen all seven.

marinade

2 stalks fresh lemon grass or 2 tablespoons dried lemon grass (see page 415), soaked for 20 minutes in 1 to 2 tablespoons water

2 to 3 cloves garlic, finely chopped

2 shallots, finely chopped

1 bird chile or serrano chile (see page 410), finely chopped

2 tablespoons fish sauce (nuoc mam, see page 414)

1 tablespoon fresh lime juice

1 tablespoon water

1 tablespoon roasted sesame oil (see page 417)

1 pound rump roast or eye of round, trimmed of all fat

2 tablespoons dry-roasted sesame seeds (see page 154)

accompaniments

20 Fresh Rice Papers (see page 100) or dried store-bought rice papers (banh trang)

1 cup diced cucumber

2 cups shredded or finely chopped lettuce

¼ cup fresh coriander leaves

¼ cup fresh mint leaves

¼ cup roasted unsalted peanuts, finely chopped

1 cup Peanut Dipping Sauce (page 105)

2 bird chiles or serrano chiles (see page 410), finely chopped

You will need a large mortar and pestle or a food processor, a small bowl, a large shallow bowl, and small wooden or metal skewers.

continued

To prepare the marinade: If using fresh lemon grass, trim off the outer leaves, then finely chop the bottom quarter of each stalk. Combine the fresh or dried lemon grass, the garlic, shallots, and chile in a mortar and pound to a paste. Alternatively, combine in a food processor and process to a paste.

Transfer the paste to a small bowl. Add the fish sauce, lime juice, and water and blend well. Add the sesame oil and stir. Set aside.

Cut the meat into very thin slices (less than ⅛ inch) against the grain. (This is easier if the meat is cold.) Then cut the slices into 1½-inch lengths. Place the meat in a shallow bowl, add the marinade, and mix well to coat. Cover and marinate for 1 hour at room temperature or up to 8 hours in the refrigerator.

If using wooden skewers, soak them in water for 30 minutes before using.

Prepare a charcoal or gas grill or preheat the broiler.

Wipe the marinade from the meat. Thread the pieces of meat onto wooden or fine metal skewers and sprinkle with sesame seeds. Cook on a lightly oiled grill rack or broiler pan approximately 3 to 4 inches from the heat for about 1 minute on each side for medium rare. Remove from the heat.

Cut the rice papers in half or in quarters and place on a plate on the table. If using dried papers, put out a large bowl of water for moistening them. Prepare a platter with skewers of beef and piles of cucumber, lettuce, coriander, mint leaves, and peanuts. Set out individual bowls of peanut sauce, and set out a small dish of chopped chiles. Your guests can then prepare their own rolls, starting with a leaf of lettuce, then laying on it the rice paper and an assortment of the other ingredients.

If you want to serve prewrapped rolls, let the meat cool and then prepare the rolls as follows: Cut each rice paper in half. If using dried rice papers, dip in warm water to soften. Lay a slice of beef on each wrapper half, and top with some cucumber, coriander and mint. Roll up into cylinders, and trim any ragged edges. Serve stacked on a bed of lettuce, with individual bowls of peanut sauce.

▲▲▲▲▲▲▲▲◄◄▲▲◄◄▲▲▲◄◄◄▲▲◄◄ ▲▲▲

Serves 4.

Serve as a main course, preceded by a clear soup and followed by jasmine tea.

Peanut Dipping Sauce

nuoc leo • Vietnam

*Nuoc leo is a traditional sauce from central Vietnam, although it is now **found*** practically all over the country. There are many versions of it; this one is rich with peanut butter, spicy with garlic and chile, lightly salted with fish sauce, and slightly sweetened. A bottled sauce called tuong, made of fermented soy beans, sugar, and salt, gives it body. Nuoc leo is usually served as a dip for strong-tasting beef and pork dishes. We also enjoy it with Chinese flatbreads, such as Xichuan Pepper Bread.

12 to 15 unsalted raw peanuts or unsalted dry-roasted peanuts

1½ tablespoons sesame seeds

1 tablespoon peanut oil

3 cloves garlic, finely chopped

2 tablespoons lean ground pork (if tuong is unavailable)

1 tablespoon tomato paste

1 teaspoon hot pepper paste (see page 415), or to taste, or ½ teaspoon minced fresh bird chiles or serrano chiles (see page 410), to taste

¼ cup tuong (or the ground pork and appropriate amounts of fish sauce and water)

1 tablespoon fish sauce (nuoc mam, see page 414) (¼ cup if using pork rather than tuong)

1 tablespoon unsalted peanut butter

1 cup warm water (½ cup if using pork rather than tuong)

1 teaspoon sugar

You will need a small heavy skillet, a mortar and pestle or a food processor, a heavy saucepan, and a small bowl.

Heat a dry skillet until very hot. Add the peanuts, and roast, stirring constantly, until you see the peanut skins blacken or the nuts are lightly browned, about 3 minutes. Let cool. Then rub off the skins, if any, and pound the peanuts in a mortar and pestle, or process briefly in a food processor, until coarsely chopped.

In a similar fashion, roast the sesame seeds in a heavy skillet over medium heat, stirring constantly, until the seeds begin to brown, 2 to 3 minutes. Remove from the heat and continue stirring for 1 minute, then set aside.

Heat the oil in a heavy saucepan over medium-high heat until hot. Add the garlic and cook until lightly browned, about 1 minute. If using pork, add and stir well. Lower the heat, add the tomato paste and chile paste or minced chiles, and stir. Add the tuong, if using, and fish sauce and stir well. (If your tuong contains whole rather than mashed soy beans, mash the beans against the side of the saucepan to obtain a smoother texture.)

Combine the peanut butter and warm water in a small bowl, and add to the sauce. Stir, then add the sugar. Bring to a boil, reduce the heat, and simmer for 2 minutes, stirring constantly.

Pour the sauce into small individual serving bowls. Sprinkle the chopped roasted peanuts and roasted sesame seeds on top as a garnish.

▲▲▲▲▲▲▲▲▲▲▲▲▲▲▲▲▲▲

Makes 1 generous cup dipping sauce.

Serve in individual sauce bowls as a dip or condiment for Grilled Lemon Grass Beef (page 103) or for other grilled beef or pork dishes. Less traditionally, serve as a dip for Xichuan Pepper Bread (page 93) or Buckwheat Honey Country Bread (page 79).

Sauces for sale in market in Hanoi

Shrimp Roll-ups with Fresh Herbs

cuon tom • Vietnam

The main road south out of Saigon passes through agricultural areas and small villages, then reaches a wide river, where there is always a long queue of rack-

ety old buses and trucks, loaded bicycles, and straw-hatted women, waiting for the next ferry. This must be the Mekong, we thought when we first approached it, and it is, but only one of many branches of the river. Once off the ferry on the other side, we found ourselves in the Mekong Delta—flat, fertile rice-growing country—the landscape traversed with little streams, big streams, little rivers, and big rivers—water every-where—and rice paddies, fruit trees, and villages.

Mekong Delta: Rural market and boats

At one point, around lunchtime, we stopped at a small rural market. Most shoppers had poled their way here in small shallow boats along narrow streams and canals, a much more convenient way to travel in the Delta than by road. Our driver, Lum, and guide, Lam, had arranged to meet a friend here, and before long the friend showed up. Then onto a boat we stepped and away we went.

For lunch at the friend's home we sat in a shaded garden sipping Chinese bottled beer (brought in the trunk of our car from the big city) and talking about the state of the world. The conversation was in Vietnamese and Lam would translate to Naomi in Mandarin. Plates of lightly steamed shrimp, fresh rice wrappers, chopped pineapple, tomato slices, fresh herbs, and leaf lettuce appeared, together with bowls of nuoc cham. "Shrimp should be eaten with a sweet acid for balance," our host explained, wrapping a chunk of pineapple, a slice of tomato, a sprig each of fresh coriander and mint, and a small shrimp together in a rice wrapper. "You can also eat shrimp with strawberries or kiwi," he continued, instructing us in the fine art of wrapping and combining foods, as he dipped his little flavor package into fish sauce laced with tiny bird chiles and made sour with fresh lime.

After lunch we strolled through his small pomelo plantation, our host pick-ing several of these enormous grapefruit-like fruits to send with us in the car. Dominic, our two-year-old son, finding his own way through the thorny trees, came across a four-foot-square wooden box set up on stilts. He climbed the small ladder, looked inside, and there sat an old monk lost in meditation.

continued

Soon we were again in the boat, back to the market, and off on our way. Delta life had a little more meaning, and a little more mystery.

▲▲▲▲▲▲·▲▲·▲▲▲▲▲▲▲·▲▲·▲▲▲

This is a version of the shrimp roll-ups we ate that day. They are very easy and please even finicky eaters who are not accustomed to trying new flavors. You can also assemble the roll-ups ahead of time and serve as an appetizer. They are always a big hit with guests.

1 pound medium shrimp, fresh or frozen, in the shell

1 large head Boston, Bibb, or other tender leaf lettuce

1 cup mung bean sprouts

2 large tomatoes, thinly sliced

½ small pineapple, peeled, halved lengthwise, and thinly sliced (or 4 kiwifruits, peeled and thinly sliced)

½ cup fresh coriander leaves

½ cup fresh mint leaves

20 Fresh Rice Papers or dried rice papers (banh trang, see page 100)

1 cup Vietnamese Dipping Sauce (page 109) with optional carrot

You will need a large pot, a colander or strainer, and a medium pot.

Cook the shrimp in a large pot of boiling salted water for 3 minutes (if the shrimp are frozen, time the cooking from the moment the water returns to the boil), or until pink and firm to the touch. Drain and let cool. Traditionally the shrimp are served in the shell and each diner peels his or her own; however, you may wish to peel and devein the shrimp before serving.

Clean the lettuce, removing tough stem ends from the leaves. Place the leaves in a serving bowl.

Blanch the bean sprouts by placing them in a colander or strainer and dipping them into a pot of boiling water for 1 minute.

Arrange the tomato slices, pineapple slices, mounds of the coriander and mint, and the bean sprouts on a serving platter.

Stack the rice wrappers on a plate so that guests can help themselves. If using dried wrappers, provide one or more large bowls filled with warm water for moistening them.

Place the shrimp on a serving plate.

Place a small bowl of the dipping sauce, with fine shreds of carrot floating in it, by each diner.

To eat, peel several shrimp. Take a fresh rice paper or a dried rice paper briefly moistened in warm water until soft, and place it on a lettuce leaf. Place 1 or 2 shrimp, some mint and/or coriander leaves, a piece of pineapple, and a tomato slice or two on the paper. Roll up the bundle, and dip in the dipping sauce.

▲▲▲▲▲▲◦▲▲◦▲▲▲◦▲▲▲◦▲◦▲▲▲

Serves 4 as a main course or 8 as an appetizer.

If you prefer, assemble the shrimp roll-ups up to 2 hours ahead of time, and cover with a damp tea towel. Serve stacked on a platter with a small bowl of dipping sauce for each guest.

Vietnamese Dipping Sauce
nuoc cham • Vietnam

Nuoc cham is the classic dipping sauce that accompanies many Vietnamese meals. Every Vietnamese seems to have a clear idea of the balance of spices and flavors he or she likes in the sauce. This recipe is therefore a guide. It makes a light yet tasty nuoc cham that we prefer. Feel free to vary the proportions according to your own taste.

3 cloves garlic

1 small bird chile or serrano chile (see page 410)

6 tablespoons fish sauce (nuoc mam, see page 414)

3 to 4 tablespoons fresh lemon or lime juice

5 to 6 tablespoons cold water

2 tablespoons sugar

1 small carrot, julienned (optional)

You will need a large mortar and pestle or a small bowl.

If you are using the traditional mortar and pestle method, chop the garlic and chile coarsely, then pound them to a fine paste with the mortar and pestle. Add the fish sauce, lemon or lime juice, and water and stir. Stir in the sugar. Alternatively, mince the garlic and chile, then place in a bowl, and mash together. Add the remaining ingredients and stir well.

Place in small individual sauce bowls for dipping. If you wish, place a few strands of carrot in each bowl.

Nuoc cham keeps if sealed well and stored in the refrigerator. However, after more than a week, the garlic and chile lose some of their punch.

▲▲▲▲▲◦▲◦▲▲◦▲▲▲◦▲▲▲◦▲◦▲▲▲

Makes approximately 1 cup dipping sauce.

Use as a condiment and flavor enhancer with Vietnamese meals.

PORTRAIT OF VARUSAI

Varusai makes rolling chapattis into aerobic exercise. He starts at dusk every night from his four-wheeled food stand set off to one side of King Street in the town of Georgetown on the island of Penang. He starts and he doesn't stop: rolling out the flatbreads, cooking them on two different griddles, stoking the charcoal fires underneath the griddles, serving curries, taking money, making change, and all the while talking, laughing, listening. He finds his rhythm and off he goes. There is nothing

Varusai rolling chapattis in Penang

calm about the way Varusai works; there's no time for letting a piece of dough rest, let alone for Varusai to rest. He attacks each bread, rolling furiously with an eight-inch rolling pin which has two small handles. Roll them out, cook them, roll them out, cook them. These are not the fine, pliable, very thin chapattis served in homes all across the north of India; Varusai's are street food chapattis: heavy, a little tough, nutritious, cheap. Eat them with a bowl of spicy split mung bean stew, or a goat-head curry. The curries come served in plastic bowls, the chapattis on plastic plates. There are three or four rickety tables, each with three or four rickety stools, set up in the street, where people can sit for dinner.

Penang, an island just off the northwest corner of peninsular Malaysia, is an extraordinary place to eat. With equal populations of Chinese, Indian, and Malay—all with access to an incredibly rich tropical harvest—the island is a culinary paradise. For dinner you can choose Hokkein food, Hakka food, Teochiu, Cantonese, Nyonya, Tamil, Tamil vegetarian, Thai, Malay, Sinhalese; the variety of food, as well as the quality, is dizzying. And yet there is no place in Penang I would rather eat than at Varusai's chapatti and curry stand.

I first met Varusai in 1979, staying in Penang for several weeks and going to eat chapattis every night. We were both single fellows with an interest in chapattis, and we hit it off immediately. But then twelve years went by, and when I returned I wondered if Varusai would still be on the street.

"Of course I'm here," laughed Varusai, still standing in the same place still furiously rolling. "I'm a father, what to do?"

Varusai first came to Penang from south India as an orphan, six years old. His grandfather lived here, and he took Varusai in. His grandfather owned a "beede" stand, a tiny kiosk on the sidewalk where he sold "beedes," little cigarettes hand-rolled in a leaf. At night his grandfather would close the shutters of the kiosk and they would sleep; Varusai could stretch out but his grandfather slept sitting up or stretched out outside on the sidewalk. Varusai's grandfather is dead now, but Varusai's chapatti stand is set up right in front of the old kiosk.

"Grandfather is my god," Varusai told me one night. "Every Friday the imam from the mosque comes by and says a prayer for my grandfather. In exchange I feed him dinner." Varusai's grandfather not only looked after Varusai but he took care of other street kids as well. "My brothers," Varusai says proudly with a smile, holding his arms out to the three men who work with him—washing dishes and serving food—whom he has known since he was six.

Varusai works most nights until well past midnight, rolling out two hundred to two hundred and fifty chapattis. In the morning he goes to the market, and through the day he prepares his curries and chapatti dough. His margin of profit is small, and he never turns away someone who hasn't the money for chapattis. Now in his late thirties, he still has the energy of a young man, but not without cost. Two years ago he got sick with a recurring fever and inflamed joints, an illness that lasted almost a year, and in that time he had to spend all the money he had ever saved. And as he says, he's now a father. Varusai married a woman who was born Hindu, but who married an abusive man and then divorced him, taking with her her daughter and an element of social stigma. She certainly had no dowry, but neither did Varusai, and now she's a Muslim.

The way Varusai sees it, his chapatti stand serves a certain social function: "It is okay to eat murtabaks and oily Chinese noodles in the daytime, but in the evening it is important to eat healthy foods like chapattis." I agree, and from the look of it, so do many other people in Penang. I never know, when I go down to eat, who I will be sitting with: an old yogi who walks slowly up on wooden shoes, a wealthy merchant who has parked his Mercedes just across the street, a drug-dealing rickshaw driver, a middle-class family of four. Varusai has a dedicated clientele, and with good reason (though I've never tried the goat-head curry).

Flung and Folded Griddle Breads
murtabak • Malaysia

Murtabak is one of those good foods that have traveled far and wide. It is a bread of Indian origin, now a popular street food served throughout much of Southeast Asia, in a variety of different ways. To start, a simple pliable unyeasted

Penang: Making murtabak

bread dough is stretched thin, then lightly brushed with oil, folded into a square, and quickly fried on a hot griddle. In Thailand it is spread with sweetened condensed milk, rolled up, and eaten as an evening snack. In Indonesia it is often stuffed with meat and served as a light meal.

What makes murtabak so distinctive is the way in which the dough is flung through the air to make it paperthin and transparent. A murtabak maker holds onto one side of a piece of dough with both hands, then, with a quick and agile flick of the wrists—like the gesture used to fling open a folded bedsheet—flings the other side of the dough through the air. The technique varies from person to person, and place to place, but the effect is the same, holding onto one edge of a sheet of dough while flinging or twisting it through the air to increase its size. A masterful murtabak maker can begin with a ball of dough and have a paperthin dough two feet in diameter in less than a minute.

When we first began experimenting with murtabak at home, we did so out of curiosity, not really believing that we could turn out acceptable murtabaks. But much to our surprise, it isn't hard at all. Perfection takes practice, of course, but less-than-perfect murtabaks are just as good—if not better—with their somewhat uneven texture. Make up a dough and experiment with a few breads to find your own particular flick of the wrist.

2 cups hard unbleached white flour	¾ to 1 cup hot water
½ teaspoon salt	Peanut oil for coating and for frying

You will need a mixing bowl or a food processor, a rolling pin, and a 10-inch cast-iron or other heavy skillet or electric frying pan.

In a mixing bowl, combine the flour and salt. Stir in hot water slowly until all the flour is moistened. Form into a ball, turn out onto a lightly floured surface, and knead until smooth and elastic, about 5 minutes. Alternatively, combine the flour and salt in a food processor. Then pour hot water in a steady trickle through the feeder tube, pulsing regularly until a ball of dough forms. Process for 15 seconds, then turn out onto a floured surface and knead 1 or 2 minutes more. Let the dough rest for 10 minutes.

Cut the dough into 4 pieces of equal size and shape each into a ball. Coat your palms with oil and rub oil over each dough ball. Let rest for 15 to 30 minutes, covered with plastic wrap or a damp cloth.

Working with one ball at a time, on a smooth unfloured work surface, flatten the dough out with the palm of your hand. Once it is about 6 inches in diameter, start rolling it out thinner with a rolling pin. When it gets to about 12 inches across, start stretching it by hand: Your goal is a rectangular piece of dough about 18 inches by 14 inches and so thin that it is translucent. The simplest and least dramatic stretching technique is to pick up the dough and work your way around the rim, stretching as you go. You can also try picking up just one edge and then flinging out the dough, as described above. The flinging will stretch part of the dough; rotate it and try flinging again.

Once the dough is stretched, lay it down flat (any creases will tend to stick to each other) and brush the top surface lightly with oil. Fold the longer sides over to the middle so their edges just touch, then fold the other two sides over, so their edges just meet at the center. You now have a rectangular package about 8 inches by 6 inches. Set aside, covered with a cloth or plastic wrap, while you stretch and fold the remaining breads. You will find they get easier and more fun as you go along; just remember to treat the dough with the same caution as plastic wrap, as it does tend to stick to itself quite tenaciously.

Heat a 10-inch cast-iron skillet over medium-high heat, or heat an electric frying pan to 400°F. When hot, add 2 tablespoons peanut oil and heat. Then lower the heat to medium. Transfer the first bread to the skillet and fry, moving it around to avoid scorching, until golden and crisp, about 2 to 3 minutes. Turn over; if there are any burned patches, lower the heat slightly. Fry until golden and crisp on both sides, 2 minutes longer. Turn out onto a plate and cover to keep warm while you cook the remaining breads. Before you place each bread in the skillet, add 1 teaspoon oil and wait until it has had time to heat.

▲▲▲▲▲▲▲▲▲▲▲▲▲▲▲▲▲▲▲▲▲▲

Makes 4 rectangular folded flatbreads, about 8 inches by 6 inches.

Serve these warm for breakfast or as a snack, with honey or jam or on their own. Use fresh or the next day in Dal and Bread Fry (page 114), a wonderful breakfast or late-night snack. Murtabak also make a great accompaniment to many Indian dishes, such as Gujarati Mango Curry (page 144) or Egg Curry with Tomato (page 165).

Dal and Bread Fry

Penang

A friend recently observed that this dish has the feel of Mexican home cooking, and we agree. It is full of complex carbohydrates and complementary proteins, and it's a pleasure to eat with so many satisfying textures and comforting flavors. The bread gives body, the egg binds it together, and the soupy dal stew moistens and adds subtle spicing.

We prefer to make this dish with plain dal, such as Lentils with Onion, Garlic, and Tomato or Five-Lentil Stew, rather than the traditional channa dal. We give amounts for making one serving; simply multiply the ingredients as necessary to serve two or more. Once you have the breads and the lentil stew on hand, the dish takes less than five minutes to cook and assemble. With a large skillet you could make two servings at once.

1 Flung and Folded Griddle Bread
   (page 112)

1 teaspoon peanut or corn oil

1 large egg

1 tablespoon warm water

Generous pinch of salt

Freshly ground white pepper

½ cup Lentils with Onion, Garlic, and
   Tomato (page 127) or Five-Lentil Stew
   (page 126), heated

You will need a 6- to 8-inch cast-iron or other heavy skillet and a small bowl.

Cut the bread lengthwise into strips a scant ½ inch wide. Cut each strip in half crosswise.

Heat a 6- to 8-inch heavy skillet over medium-high heat. Then add the oil and spread over the skillet. When hot, add the bread strips and fry until warm, a minute or so, stirring occasionally.

Meanwhile, in a small bowl, whisk the egg. Add the warm water, salt, and pepper to taste and whisk until well mixed.

Pour the egg mixture over the murtabak strips and lower the heat to medium-low. Cook until the egg has set almost completely, 1 to 2 minutes, then flip over and cook briefly on the other side.

Transfer to a plate, top with the hot dal, and serve.

▲▲▲▲▲▲▲▪▪▪▲▲▪▪▪▲▲▲▪▪▲▲▲

Serves 1.

Serve on its own for breakfast or for a light meal at any time. We like a side order of chutney to spice things up a little more: Try Spicy Tomato Chutney (page 139) or Nepali Green Chile Chutney (page 141).

Lacy Coconut Milk Pancakes

roti jala • Penang

"Pancakes" is too heavy a word for these pretty and very easy-to-make breads. The dough is unyeasted and pourable, like a slightly thick crêpe batter. To get the lacy effect, you need a roti jala pourer: Take a small tin can open at one end, punch six holes in the other end, punching them out from the inside (use an ice pick, or a large drill bit and a hammer), and you have your newest kitchen implement. The dough is poured from the can onto the hot pan in a slow swirling motion, creating a lacy layer-upon-layer pancake.

1 cup unbleached all-purpose flour	1 teaspoon vegetable oil
½ teaspoon salt	1 large egg
10 ounces canned coconut milk (see page 411), stirred well	Oil for greasing the skillet

You will need a mixing bowl, a large ladle, a 10-inch cast-iron or other heavy skillet, a roti jala pourer (see above), and a wide spatula.

Sift together the flour and salt into a mixing bowl. Make a well in the center, and add the coconut milk, vegetable oil, and egg. Stir well until a smooth dough forms. Let stand, covered, for 30 minutes.

Heat a 10-inch cast-iron or other heavy skillet until hot. Pour about a teaspoon of oil on the skillet, then wipe off with a paper towel. Lower the heat to medium.

Test the consistency of the batter. It should be pourable but not watery; add a little water to thin it out if necessary.

Using a ladle, stir the batter. Then pour a scant ½ cup batter into the roti jala pourer, holding it over the skillet, and immediately start moving the pourer in a continuous circular motion over the skillet to create overlapping layers in the pan, keeping the pourer 3 to 4 inches above the skillet. (If too far above the skillet, the batter will break up into droplets by the time it hits the surface, rather than arriving in a smooth continuous stream.) Then cook 30 seconds or so, until you see the roti starting to lift slightly at the edges. Using a spatula, flip it over and cook the other side 30 seconds to 1 minute, until slightly golden. Then lift out of the pan and place in a basket or on a plate, wrapped in a cloth. Cook the remaining batter in the same way. Serve warm.

continued

TROUBLESHOOTING

We have concluded, after experimenting with batter thickness and hole size, that as long as the batter pours slowly but continuously through the holes, the roti are easy to make. If the holes seem too small and the batter isn't coming through, you can either enlarge them, or make the dough thinner by adding a bit more water. Be careful: If the dough is really watery, it may flood out through the holes and make "puddles" on the skillet (same taste, but not as decorative) rather than coming out in a thin steady stream.

▲▲▲▲▲▲▲·▴▴▴▴▴▴▴▴▴·▴▴▴

Makes approximately 20 round crêpe-like breads, 6 to 8 inches in diameter.

Serve the classic way, with Coconut Milk Chicken Curry (page 117) and a refreshing side dish of thinly sliced cucumbers, or eat plain as a snack with tea or coffee.

Coconut Milk Chicken Curry
gulai ayam • Penang

The Nyonya culinary tradition began in the nineteenth century, evolving out of intermarriages between immigrant Chinese men, who had come to work in Malaysia, and Malay women. The men were (and still are) referred to as Babas, and the women, Nyonyas—and hence, Nyonya cooking and Nyonya/Baba culture. Nyonya cuisine borrowed ingredients and methods of cooking from Chinese cookery, but came out tasting and looking more Thai or Malay than Chinese. Nyonya dishes tend to be very hot and wonderfully complex aromatically. Gulai ayam is one of many remarkable recipes that have been handed down through generations of Nyonya cooks in Malaysia.

For a visitor in Malaysia, it is increasingly difficult to sample Nyonya foods. The cooking has never been well established in restaurants, and with so many Nyonyas now working outside the home, even the home cooking tradition is suffering, as many of the dishes require long and elaborate preparation. Whether a simplified version of Nyonya cuisine will emerge or the cuisine will die a gradual death, is at issue now in Nyonya/Baba families.

This recipe for gulai ayam gives an idea of what Nyonya food is all about. The meat is coated in a blended spice paste, called a *rempeh*, then coconut milk is added to make a rich sauce that softens the edge of the spices and bathes the chicken as it cooks. Serve gulai ayam with Lacy Coconut Milk Pancakes.

Much to our regret, coconut milk is loaded with saturated fats. We love coconut milk curries and serve them for a special treat.

rempeh (curry paste)

4 dried red chiles

One 2-inch cinnamon stick

4 cloves

2 tablespoons coriander seed

1 tablespoon cumin seed

1 teaspoon fennel seed

½ teaspoon turmeric

½ pound shallots, peeled

One 1-inch piece fresh ginger, peeled and finely chopped

2 large cloves garlic, finely chopped

6 candlenuts or macadamia nuts

curry

2 pounds chicken breasts, thighs, and legs (see Note)

1 tablespoon vegetable oil

2 stalks fresh lemon grass, cut into 2-inch lengths and flattened with the side of a heavy knife

1¾ cups (14 ounces) canned or fresh coconut milk (see page 411)

1 cup water

2 teaspoons salt

continued

You will need a bowl, a small cast-iron or other heavy skillet, a mortar and pestle or a spice grinder, a food processor or large mortar and pestle, and a large heavy-bottomed saucepan with a lid.

Soak the chiles in warm water for 10 to 15 minutes. Drain, and remove the hard stems.

Remove the skin from the chicken and discard. Rinse off the chicken. Chop with a heavy cleaver into roughly 2-inch chunks.

Nyonya cake vendor in Penang

In a small heavy skillet, dry-roast the cinnamon, cloves, coriander seed, cumin, and fennel over medium heat, stirring constantly, until fragrant, 2 to 3 minutes. Remove from the heat and pound until very fine using a mortar and pestle, or grind very fine in a spice mill. (Be sure to grind the spices very fine to ensure that the sauce is smooth.) Add the turmeric and set aside.

Place the drained chiles, shallots, ginger, garlic, and nuts in a food processor and grind to a paste. Alternatively, chop them coarsely, then pound to a paste using a large mortar and pestle.

Heat the oil in a large heavy saucepan over medium-high heat. Add the chile paste and fry for 4 minutes, stirring constantly. Add the dried spice mixture and fry for another minute, stirring constantly. Add the chicken pieces and turn until the chicken is well coated with the curry paste. Add the lemon grass, then add 1 cup of the coconut milk and the water. Bring to a boil, then cover and simmer over medium heat until the chicken is tender, approximately 40 minutes, stirring occasionally.

Add salt and stir in the remaining ¾ cup coconut milk. Cook 5 minutes longer. Serve hot.

Alternatives: Gulai ayam is occasionally made with the addition of 1 pound potatoes or okra. Potatoes are cut into ½-inch cubes; okra are left whole. Add when adding coconut milk and water.

Note: If you prefer to have the curry boneless, start with 1¼ pounds skinless boneless chicken; we prefer the flavor of the meat on the bone. Boneless chicken will cook in approximately 30 minutes.

▲▲▲▲▲▲▲▲▲▲▲▲▲▲▲▲▲▲▲▲▲▲

Serves 4.

Accompany with plenty of Lacy Coconut Milk Pancakes (page 115) and a cooling salad such as Four-Thread Salad (page 88), or simply sliced cucumbers.

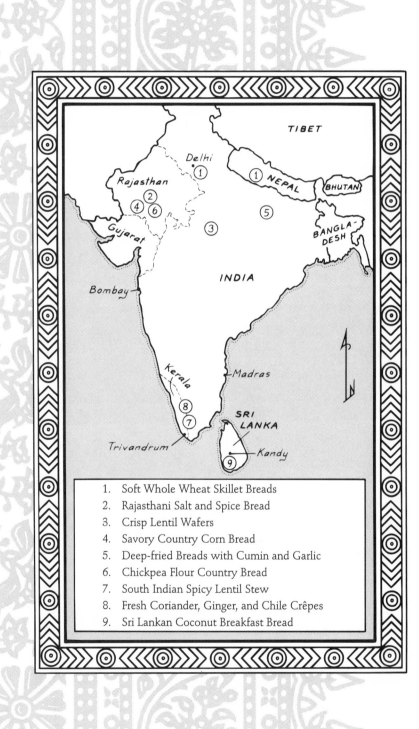

1. Soft Whole Wheat Skillet Breads
2. Rajasthani Salt and Spice Bread
3. Crisp Lentil Wafers
4. Savory Country Corn Bread
5. Deep-fried Breads with Cumin and Garlic
6. Chickpea Flour Country Bread
7. South Indian Spicy Lentil Stew
8. Fresh Coriander, Ginger, and Chile Crêpes
9. Sri Lankan Coconut Breakfast Bread

India, Nepal, and Sri Lanka

The Indian subcontinent is vast and varied, difficult to sum up in a few
words. It extends from the Himalayan peaks through the hot dry deserts and plains
of northern India to the lush mountains and tropical rice-growing regions of southern India and Sri Lanka. Despite India's many large cities, the population is largely
rural and agricultural. As a result, there are many distinctive regional cuisines.

Wheat is grown in India's northern plains and in Nepal, as are corn, millet,
and sorghum. In the south, rice is the dominant grain crop. Wheat-flour breads, such
as chapatti and puri, dominate in the north, while in the south, breads are more
commonly made from soured ground rice and lentils or from rice flour.

The northern parts of
India have seen waves of
invaders, from Alexander the
Great to the Moghuls from
Central Asia, who brought
Islam, lamb dishes, and a tandoor tradition. The south has
retained its long-standing vegetarian cuisine with less inter-

Agra: Taj Mahal in early morning

ruption, though it has adopted many of the new ingredients, such as chiles and
tomatoes, brought by the Portuguese from the New World.

Vegetarianism, rooted in age-old Hindu beliefs, is central to much of the subcontinent's culinary practices. Consequently, pulses such as lentils are an important element in the cuisine, as are dairy products. Intricate and subtle spice combinations, such as garam masala and other "curry powders," characterize the cuisines of most regions; these permit an extraordinary and delicious variety of dishes from a relatively small number of basic

Khajuraho: Sowing wheat

ingredients. In the valleys and southern parts of Nepal, the population is largely Hindu, and the influence of the Indian culinary tradition is strong: Chapattis, lentil stews (dal), vegetable dishes, and chutneys are the basis of the diet. In the Himalayan valleys and uplands, the climate, vegetation, and culture are more like those in parts of Tibet; people depend on corn, potatoes, barley, and herds of yak.

Sri Lanka is a large teardrop-shaped island lying off the southern tip of India. A paradise of tropical fruits and vegetables, Sri Lanka also produces tea, rice, and coconuts. These days many Sri Lankan breads are made from imported wheat flour.

Woman winnowing wheat

Soft Whole Wheat Skillet Breads
chapatti • North India and Nepal

Early one November morning I walked across the border from Pakistan into India. I was exhausted, having traveled across Pakistan by train overnight from Peshawar to Lahore. In the middle of the night two policemen—on a routine search of foreigners traveling second class—had gone through my bag as I slept, scattering my belongings out across the crowded compartment. They had then shaken me roughly from my sleep. It hadn't been the best of nights.

But the scene at the Indian border was the opposite. Everyone was relaxed and friendly, and though the process took time, by midmorning I was on my way to Amritsar, the site of the Golden Temple and the center of the Sikh religion. Little did I know that more than a million other people had also come to Amritsar on this day, which marked the four hundredth birthday of Guru Nanak, the founder of the Sikh religion.

I was shown to one of many tent camps set up for visitors; finding a room in the city would have been impossible. Huge crowds of people milled about everywhere, so for the time being I simply sat in the tent camp watching in a daze as people passed by. "Will you come to the Golden Temple?" a man from Chandigarh asked warmly, catching me by surprise. "Yes," I said, and off we went.

As we entered the Temple, I took off my shoes and left them by the entrance with several thousand other pairs of shoes. We followed the crowd, which formed itself into a long line, and then we waited. People were happy and at ease, as everyone waited.

Eventually we made our way around the temple and through a sacred smaller temple in the center of the larger one, where we were given a little ball of honey and wheat berries, food from the Sikh god. We then left the temple, finding an area just outside where people were again lined up, and there we waited again with everyone else. This time, when it came our turn, we moved into a large open-air compound together with several hundred other people. We all sat down cross-legged on the ground, forming long rows with aisles in between.

People soon came along with huge baskets of chapattis, quickly distributing four breads to each person on the ground. And then came more people carrying buckets full of dal, whole green mung dal. We were each given dal, holding out two of our chapattis in our left hand, making a cup in the breads to hold the soupy stew. To eat we simply (or not so simply) took chapattis from the bottom of the stack with our right hands and used them as a spoon to scoop out the dal. As soon as we were finished, we all stood up and left, and two or three hundred more people came and sat down. Twenty-four hours a day, people came and went, eating chapattis and dal.

After eating, I watched the cooking: men and women working together, stirring dal, making dough, rolling out chapattis, cooking chapattis. The smell and crackle from the wood fires blended with perfume, voices, and laughter.

▲▲▲▲▲▲▲▲▲▲▲▲▲▲▲▲▲▲▲▲▲▲

Making chapattis can be very relaxing. In quite a short time you can produce eight or ten breads, each one turning out a little bit different from the others, but all of them attractive, nutritious, and good. We've grown so accustomed to making chapattis that they now feel almost like a convenience food, a household staple of the best kind.

Chapattis are traditionally baked on a cast-iron plate called a *tava*. If you have a tava, use it; otherwise use a cast-iron griddle or skillet.

Chapatti making can be an ongoing, ever-changing process. Each griddle is different. Flours are different. What works well one day doesn't seem to work as perfectly the next. But whatever happens, your chapattis, ballooned or not, will be good to eat and satisfying and quick to make.

2 cups atta flour (or 2 cups whole wheat flour, sifted; see page 409) or more as needed

1 teaspoon salt

1 cup warm water, or more as needed

You will need a medium-sized bowl, a rolling pin, and a tava or a 9- to 10-inch cast-iron griddle or heavy skillet.

In a medium-sized bowl, mix together the flour and salt. Make a well in the center and add the warm water. Mix with your hand or with a spoon until you can gather it together into a dough (depending on your flour, you may need a little extra water or a little extra flour to make a kneadable dough). Turn out onto a lightly floured bread board and knead for 8 to 10 minutes. Cover with plastic wrap and let stand for 30 minutes or up to 2 hours.

Divide the dough into 8 pieces and flatten each with lightly floured fingers. Then roll each piece out with a rolling pin to an 8-inch round. Roll out each bread without flipping it over; lightly flour the bread board as necessary to keep the bread from sticking. Cover the finished breads with plastic wrap as you roll out the rest (do not stack the rolled-out breads; if you don't have enough counter space, roll out just a few at a time and begin cooking, then roll out the rest as the breads cook).

Heat a tava or a cast-iron griddle or skillet over medium-high heat. When the griddle is hot, place a chapatti on the griddle, top side down. Cook for only 10 seconds, and then gently flip over. Cook on the second side until small bubbles begin to form, approximately 1 minute. Turn the chapatti back to the first side and cook about 1 minute longer; at this stage, a perfectly made chapatti should start to balloon. This process can be helped along by gently pressing on the bread (we find the easiest method is to use a small cotton cloth or a paper towel, wadded up, to protect your fingertips from the hot bread): Gently press down on a large bubble in the bread, forcing the bubble to expand. If the bread starts to burn on the bottom before it has ballooned, move the chapatti (with the cloth or paper towel) in the griddle, dislodging it from the point at which it is beginning to burn.

Remove the finished chapatti from the griddle and wrap in a clean towel to keep warm and soft. Cook the remaining breads, stacking the breads on top of one another.

▲▲▲▲▲▲▲▲▲▲▲▲▲▲▲▲▲▲▲▲▲▲▲

Makes 8 thin round breads, 7 to 8 inches across.

Chapattis are great with almost any curry, lentil dish, yogurt dish, or chutney. With three or four chapattis and a bowl of Lentils with Garlic, Onion, and Tomato (page 127) or Five-Lentil Stew (page 126), you have a tasty, simple grain-based meal. Chapattis are also a satisfying snack eaten on their own.

Five-Lentil Stew

panch dal • North India

There are over sixty different varieties of dal (dal means "split peas" or "legumes"), but the five included here are the most common. The method of preparation used here is also quite common: The dal is first boiled with turmeric, then

Lentils for sale

tempered with an onion and spice mixture (called a *chaunce* in North India). The chaunce is what gives the dish its depth of flavor, and it's what makes dal a food that can be eaten day in and day out with great pleasure.

Panch dal is an easy and nutritious dish to serve with any one of several different Central or South Asian flatbreads—and an excellent way of getting acquainted with many varieties of dal as well. We find that it's useful to get to know the different dals by their Hindi names, as that is the way they are labeled in Indian groceries in North America.

dal	spice blend
¼ cup channa dal (see page 412)	1 tablespoon vegetable oil or ghee (see page 129)
¼ cup urad dal (see page 412)	1 large onion, finely chopped
¼ cup masur dal (see page 412)	1 tablespoon finely chopped garlic
¼ cup toovar dal (see page 412)	1 teaspoon cumin seed
¼ cup mung dal (see page 412)	1 teaspoon Hot Spice Powder (page 134) or store-bought garam masala
5 cups water	2 large tomatoes, chopped
½ teaspoon turmeric	1 teaspoon salt, or more to taste
½ teaspoon cayenne	

You will need a large pot with a lid, and a heavy skillet or saucepan.

Rinse the dals.

In a large pot, bring the water to a boil. Add the dals, stir, and bring back to a boil. Then remove from the heat, cover, and let sit for 2 hours.

Add the turmeric and cayenne to the dal and bring the water to a boil. Reduce the heat slightly and simmer until the dal is tender, approximately 35 minutes.

Ten to 15 minutes before the dal is ready, begin cooking the spice mixture:

Heat the oil or ghee in a heavy skillet or saucepan over medium-high heat. When hot, add the onion and garlic and fry for 2 to 3 minutes, stirring frequently. Add the cumin and garam masala and cook another minute. Add the tomatoes and salt, and cook until the tomatoes have been reduced, approximately 10 minutes.

Add the onion mixture to the dal, stir well, and cook for 2 to 3 minutes more to blend the flavors. Taste for salt and adjust the seasoning if you wish. Serve hot in one large bowl or in individual-sized bowls.

▲▲▲▲▲▴▵▴▴▵▴▴▴▴▴▵▵▴▴▵

Serves 4.

Serve with Soft Whole Wheat Skillet Breads (page 123) or a Central Asian naan for a simple, delicious meal (and a classic grain/legume combination). This dal is also very good as part of a larger Indian meal.

Lentils with Garlic, Onion, and Tomato
dal, dal fry • North India

With the exception of the odd expensive restaurant that can be found in the big cities, most restaurants in India serve a clientele of men, young and old, who can't get home for their meal or who don't have a home to go to for their meal. The food that is prepared tends to be limited in its range and has little of the wonderful regional variety that makes Indian cooking so extraordinary.

All that said, we love hanging out in little restaurants in India. They make for instant social contact, whether with the rickshaw driver eating beside you or with the cooks in the kitchen. If we go to the same restaurant three or four days in a row, then we're regulars and it's all the better. We

Chapattis and dal at a roadside restaurant

can sit with a cup of tea and watch the world go by, never a dull thing to do in India. The food may not be as good as in-home cooking, but it can still be very good.

▲▲▲▲▲▲·▲·▲▲··▲▲▲·▲▲··▲▲▲

Dal fry, a standby across North India, is as simple as can be, and absolutely delicious. A helping of plain cooked dal is fried with a little garlic and onion, and comes to the table piping hot, served with fresh whole wheat chapattis and perhaps a cup of yogurt or raita.

1 cup mung dal (see page 412) or 2½ cups cooked mung dal

4 cups water

½ teaspoon turmeric

1 bay leaf

One 1-inch cinnamon stick

½ teaspoon salt

1 tablespoon vegetable oil

2 to 3 cloves garlic, finely chopped

1 medium onion, finely chopped

2 medium tomatoes, chopped

You will need a medium-sized saucepan and a large deep skillet or saucepan.

Rinse the mung dal, and place in a saucepan with the water, turmeric, bay leaf, and cinnamon. Bring to a boil, then reduce the heat and simmer until tender, approximately 20 to 25 minutes. Stir in the salt. Discard the cinnamon stick, and set aside.

In a large skillet or saucepan, heat the oil over high heat. Toss in the garlic and onion and cook for 2 minutes. Add the chopped tomatoes and cook for 1 minute longer, stirring constantly. Add the cooked dal (watch out for spattering as the dal first hits the oil), and cook, stirring, for 2 to 3 minutes, or until heated through. Serve immediately in individual bowls or in one large bowl.

▲▲▲▲▲▲·▲·▲▲··▲▲▲·▲▲··▲▲▲

Makes approximately 3 cups dal. Serves 2 to 3.

Serve with Soft Whole Wheat Skillet Breads (page 123), Nepali Green Chile Chutney (page 141), and Ginger and Tomato Salad (page 131).

Clarified Butter

ghee • India and Sri Lanka

*Long ago a friend and I were preparing for a month-long trek into the moun-*tains in northern India, buying food and other supplies to be loaded on pack horses. "We must buy some ghee, too," said the guide. "But do we really need it? Won't it go bad during the trip?" I asked. He looked at me, surprised: Clearly I had no idea how wonderful ghee was. We found some for sale in the market; the guide spooned it into a clean container and carefully sealed it.

By the time our trek ended, we'd used ghee in lentils, rice, and thugpa, a kind of Tibetan stew. As we sorted through our remaining supplies, all scattered across the beds of an extremely dreary hotel room (though any room would have seemed oppressive after camping out for so long), the guide remembered our ear-lier exchange. Holding out the almost-empty ghee container, he said, "Still smells good, see." And it did.

▲▲▲▲▲▲▲▲▲▲▲▲▲▲▲▲▲▲▲▲

Clarified butter is sold in South Asian stores, but you can easily make a sup-ply for yourself. Clarifying removes the milk solids (which can go bad over time), leaving only the butterfat. Ghee adds a distinctive and enticing flavor to foods and keeps well as long as it is stored in a cool spot in a clean, well-sealed container.

1 pound unsalted butter

You will need a medium-sized heavy-bottomed saucepan, a glass or ce-ramic jug, cheesecloth, and a sterilized jar with a lid.

Melt the butter in a heavy-bottomed pan over medium-low heat. Once it has melted, continue cooking, without letting it boil, for about 30 minutes. The moisture in the butter will crackle as it evaporates, white foam will form on the sur-face, and the milk solids will sink to the bottom of the pan. When these solids start to turn brown, pour off the clear clarified butter into a clean jug, then pour it through several layers of cheesecloth into a sterilized glass jar. The cheesecloth will filter out any impurities, leaving a clear, pale yellow liquid. Let cool completely, then seal well. When it cools, ghee thickens into a soft yellow paste. It will keep for months.

▲▲▲▲▲▲▲▲▲▲▲▲▲▲▲▲▲▲▲▲

Makes approximately 1½ cups ghee.

Rajasthani Salt and Spice Bread

batia roti • Rajasthan, India

These breads are delectable, a real delight for those of us who like salty treats and the bite of pepper and cumin. They are unyeasted, filled with salt, cumin, pepper, and fresh coriander, all smoothed with ghee, and quickly cooked on a lightly oiled griddle.

2 cups unbleached bread flour

1 cup water

2 teaspoons cumin seed

1½ teaspoons black peppercorns

1 teaspoon salt

¼ cup chopped fresh coriander

Approximately 2 tablespoons ghee (see page 129) or unsalted butter, at room temperature

You will need a medium-sized bowl, a small cast-iron or other heavy skillet, a spice grinder or mortar and pestle, four small bowls, a rolling pin, and a medium cast-iron or other heavy skillet or griddle.

Place the flour in a medium bowl. Make a well in the center, and add the water, stirring it into the flour, until a soft but not sticky dough forms. Turn out onto a lightly floured surface and knead until smooth.

Rinse out the bowl, set the dough back in the bowl, and cover with plastic wrap. Let stand for 30 minutes to 1 hour.

While the dough is resting, dry-roast the cumin seeds in a small heavy skillet, stirring constantly, until they just start to change color. Transfer to a spice grinder or mortar and grind to a powder. Set aside in a small dish. Dry-roast the peppercorns in the same fashion, grind, and set aside in another small bowl. Place the salt in another dish and the coriander in another.

Place a cast-iron skillet or griddle over medium heat to preheat.

Divide the dough into 8 equal pieces. With the palm of your hand, flatten each piece on a lightly floured surface, and set aside. (Do not stack.) Cover the dough with a cloth or plastic wrap to prevent drying out.

On a lightly floured surface, roll out one piece of dough into a 5- to 6-inch circle. Smear ½ teaspoon ghee onto the dough, then sprinkle ¼ teaspoon cumin, a scant ¼ teaspoon ground pepper, ⅛ teaspoon salt, and 1 teaspoon chopped coriander onto the dough. (At first you will want to use a measuring spoon; as you assemble subsequent breads, you will learn to judge the quantities by eye and feel, and the process will become smoother.)

Roll the dough up fairly tightly as you would a jelly roll, to give you a long cigar shape. Anchoring one end on your work surface, shape the bread into a flat coil, pressing the other end into the coil to make an even round. Flatten gently with the palm of your hand, then roll out to a circle about 5 to 6 inches across and less than ¼ inch thick.

Rub the heated griddle lightly with an oiled cloth or paper towel. Cook the bread for 1½ to 2 minutes on the first side, or until lightly golden. Then turn and cook for 1 minute longer, until golden. Assemble and shape another bread while the first is cooking. Transfer the cooked bread to a cotton cloth and wrap to keep warm while you cook the remaining breads. Serve warm or at room temperature.

▲▲▲▲▲▲·▲·▲▲▲▲·▲▲·▲·▲▲▲

Makes 8 filled round flatbreads, 5 to 6 inches in diameter.

Serve with Fresh Corn and Yogurt (page 146) and Gujarati Mango Curry (page 144) for a meal of savory contrasts. Or enjoy simply with plain yogurt as a snack or light meal.

Ginger and Tomato Salad
adrak aur tamatur salat • North India

With so many other foods on the table, Indian salads don't get the recognition that they deserve. Particularly in the north of India, however, there is seldom a meal served without at least a plate of freshly sliced cucumber, white radish, or tomato, and a wedge or two of fresh lime. Salads are rarely complicated; it's their simplicity that makes them such an ideal complement to the other foods.

This ginger and tomato salad is exquisite. It is a great addition to a larger Indian meal, as its fresh taste brings out the full flavors of other dishes. It's also a terrific match with kebabs and other grilled meats, as well as very good served simply with fresh hot naan. If you can avoid the temptation, wait until good fresh tomatoes are in season.

One 2- to 3-inch piece fresh ginger, peeled and cut into paperthin slices (approximately ⅓ cup)

1 medium banana chile (see page 410), seeded and cut into paperthin slices (approximately ⅓ cup)

¼ cup fresh lime juice

½ teaspoon salt

1¼ pounds (about 4 medium) fresh ripe tomatoes

Sprinkling of freshly ground black pepper

1 tablespoon finely chopped fresh mint

continued

You will need a small nonreactive bowl.

Place the ginger and chiles in a small nonreactive bowl. Add the lime juice and ¼ teaspoon of the salt. Let stand, tossing once or twice, for 20 minutes.

Slice the tomatoes and arrange on a serving plate. Sprinkle on the remaining ¼ teaspoon salt, the pepper, and mint. Turn gently to distribute the mint and seasonings. Add the ginger-chile mixture, arranging the ginger slices decoratively over the tomatoes.

Serve slightly chilled.

▲▲▲▲▲▲▲◆▲▲▲▲▲▲▲▲◆◆▲▲▲

Serves 4 as a side salad.

Serve alongside almost any combination of curry and flatbread. This salad is particularly good with Fried Cheese and Vegetable Curry (page 150), Five-Lentil Stew (page 126), or Gujarati Mango Curry (page 144).

Crisp Lentil Wafers
papad, pappadum • India

Pappadum are crisp, paperthin flatbreads made from mung or urad dal, and are usually sold in dried form, then roasted, grilled, or fried at home. There was a time when each family would prepare its own dough at home, roll out the thin round discs with a special grooved rolling pin, and then dry them in the sun. The dried discs would then be gathered and stored, ready for use whenever needed. Today, cottage industries turn out good-quality, inexpensive pappadum by the thousands, so much so that certain towns have become famous for them.

Indian groceries generally feature a wide variety of pappadum. Some are made with cayenne pepper, black pepper, or garlic. Some are brittle and so thin as to be almost translucent; others are relatively thick, made perhaps from a different kind of dal. We suggest buying a couple of different packages as they do differ quite a lot (and anyway, they are incredibly cheap and keep forever).

If you've never bought a package of pappadum and cooked them at home, then you have a wonderful surprise to look forward to. A common method of cooking pappadum is to deep-fry them, dropping them into a skillet or wok filled with a few inches of hot oil. The pappadum will instantly start to expand and change color. With a pair of tongs try to hold each under the surface of the oil until the whole pappadum has cooked (it may expand, as well as change color and texture), a process that should take no more than ten seconds. Pull the pappadum out with the tongs, shake gently to remove excess oil, then stand them on edge to drain further (a toast rack is ideal, or just lean them against each other), while they cool and crisp.

We prefer the taste and texture of pappadum that have been roasted or grilled, two methods that are much easier, not to mention fat-free. Pappadum can be cooked in your oven broiler or toaster oven, directly over a gas flame or electric burner, even over a campfire (a little bit like roasting marshmallows over a fire). With a little trial and error you will quickly discover a method that works well given the particular kind of pappadum you have and heat source you are working with. If you are holding a pappadum with a pair of tongs over a gas flame on your stove top, for example, start by holding it five or six inches away, and then bring it closer if you can. As it starts to cook, it will bubble and begin to turn color. Move it around until gradually the entire pappadum has come into contact with heat and has changed color, being careful not to let it burn. At this point the pappadum may not be quite crisp, but as it cools it will become very crisp, ready for serving.

No matter how you prepare your pappadum, cooking them is fast, easy, and fun. They can be served before a meal with drinks, as they sometimes are in North India, or with a meal. As part of a South Indian rice meal, pappadum are often crumbled over and into a great mound of rice. In several different South Indian vegetarian combinations, pappadum are eaten as a legume that complements the protein of the grain. Fried pappadum can also be sprinkled with grated coconut (see page 411), chopped coriander leaves, or cayenne.

Hot Spice Powder

garam masala • India

*Long before I ever went to India, I loved cooking Indian food. I'd get cook-*books out of the library and fill small jars with spices whenever I came across new ones I'd never tried before. I felt like a chemist, or an artist, whenever I heated a tablespoon of oil in my heavy black skillet, then watched as cumin seeds, turmeric, ground coriander, and black mustard seeds hit the oil and began to blend. The kitchen would instantly come alive with a complexity of smells and sizzles and pops.

And then I read about garam masalas, about all the different local and regional variations, about different masalas for chicken and fish and certain types of vegetables. Ah, the chemistry, the artistry. . . .

I think it was around that time that I bought an airplane ticket.

½ cup black peppercorns

½ cup coriander seed (see page 412)

½ cup cumin seed

2 tablespoons cloves

1 tablespoon green cardamom seeds (see page 409)

One 2-inch cinnamon stick, broken into pieces

You will need a large cast-iron or other heavy skillet, a wooden spoon, a bowl, and a spice grinder.

Heat a large skillet over medium-high heat. Add all the ingredients and dry-roast, stirring constantly with a wooden spoon, for 3 to 4 minutes, or until the spices start to give off an aroma. Keep stirring for 2 minutes more, then remove from the heat and transfer to a bowl. Let cool.

In a spice grinder, grind the roasted spices to a powder. Let cool completely. Store in a glass jar. Well-sealed in a glass jar, garam masala keeps indefinitely, though the vigor of the flavors will decline after several months.

▲▲▲▲▲▲▲▲▲▲▲▲▲▲▲▲▲▲▲▲▲

Makes about 1½ cups spice powder.

Use in recipes as directed; can also be sprinkled on deep-fried Crisp Lentil Wafers (page 132), on fresh corn-on-the-cob (together with a squeeze of fresh lemon juice), or on hot popcorn.

Fruit and Yogurt Curry with Nine Tastes
navratna • North India

We first tasted navratna in a tiny restaurant in Hong Kong's infamous Chungking Mansions. Chungking is a seventeen-story building complex in the heart of Kowloon, just next door to the Holiday Inn. On most floors there are several different guest houses, restaurants, apartments, or little businesses—all on the low-rent end. The people who live here, work here, sleep here, come from all around the world, a microcosm of the old British Empire and more. If Chungking were all you ever saw of Hong Kong, you'd have no idea where in the world you were. There are people from Afghanistan, Nigeria, Lebanon, Philippines, Trinidad. . . . So it goes without saying that Chungking is a wonderful place to eat in and explore. Restaurants with names like Nanak Mess and The Madras Club offer menus of regional Indian dishes that are seldom seen outside India.

Navratna, meaning "nine tastes," is a curry served all across North India but made in different ways. This particular version is considered nutritious comfort food and it isn't overly spicy. We like its unusual blend of tastes: Carrots, green beans, mango, and grapes are bathed in a mild yogurt-based curry sauce. It is a great dish for people who don't want chile heat, but do want to try an Indian curry.

1 cup carrots cut into bite-sized chunks (approximately ¼ pound)

1 cup peeled potatoes cut into bite-sized chunks (approximately mately ¼ pound)

1 cup yard-long or tender string beans cut into 1-inch lengths (approximately ¼ pound)

1½ cups water

1 tablespoon vegetable oil

½ cup chopped onion

2 cloves garlic, minced

½ teaspoon finely chopped fresh ginger

1 ripe medium mango, peeled and cut into bite-sized chunks

1 cup seedless red or green grapes

1 jalapeño, seeded and finely chopped

2 cups plain whole-milk or 2% yogurt

1 teaspoon sugar

½ teaspoon salt

1 teaspoon Hot Spice Powder (page 134) or store-bought garam masala

¼ cup finely chopped fresh coriander

You will need a large deep saucepan and a large heavy saucepan.

Place the carrots, potatoes, and beans in a large saucepan with the water, cover, and bring to a boil. Cook until tender but not mushy, about 8 minutes. Drain, reserving 1 cup of the cooking liquid. Set the vegetables aside. (The vegetables can be prepared several hours ahead, covered, and set aside at room temperature.)

In a large heavy saucepan, heat the oil. Add the onion and cook over medium-high heat, stirring constantly, until golden brown. Add the garlic and ginger and cook, stirring constantly, until the garlic begins to color. Add the mango, grapes, and jalapeño and cook, stirring constantly, for 1 minute. Add the reserved cooking liquid and bring to a boil. Lower the heat to medium-low, and add the cooked vegetables. Then stir in the yogurt, sugar, and salt and heat through. Do not allow the yogurt to boil. Stir in the spice powder and coriander. Remove from the heat, and serve immediately in a shallow serving dish.

▲▲▲▲▲▲▲▲▲▲▲▲▲▲▲▲▲▲▲▲▲

Serves 4.

Serve with plenty of Soft Whole Wheat Skillet Breads (page 123) or a Central Asian bread, such as Afghan Snowshoe Naan (page 40) or Afghan Home-style Naan (page 38), for an easy "comfort food" meal. This curry is also very good as part of a larger Indian menu.

Savory Country Corn Bread
tikkar • Rajasthan, India

This thick savory flatbread is characteristic of many breads in the western part of India. The dough is laden with chiles, fresh coriander, ginger, onion, and tomato, and it comes out, as you might expect, like a wonderfully savory meal in itself. It doesn't rise or puff up; instead, just at the end of the cooking, ghee or oil is brushed on both sides of the bread so that it ends up tasting almost as if it has been fried. There is nothing fine or delicate about this bread; it is simply very good.

2½ cups atta flour (or 2½ cups whole wheat flour, sifted; see page 409)

1 cup corn flour

1½ teaspoons salt

1 small onion, finely chopped

One 1-inch piece fresh ginger, peeled and finely chopped

2 large cloves garlic, finely chopped

1 jalapeño, seeded and finely chopped

1 medium tomato, finely chopped

2 to 3 tablespoons fresh coriander leaves

1½ cups lukewarm water, or more as needed

Approximately 6 to 8 tablespoons vegetable oil or ghee (see page 129)

You will need a medium-sized bowl, a rolling pin, and one or two cast-iron or other heavy skillets or griddles.

Combine the wheat flour, corn flour, and salt in a bowl and mix well. Add the chopped onion, ginger, garlic, jalapeño, tomato, and fresh coriander, and mix well. Make a well in the center and pour in 1½ cups lukewarm water, stirring it into the flour. The amount of water you need will vary; add more if necessary to form a kneadable dough. If the dough is too sticky, add a little more atta or wheat flour. Turn the dough out onto a lightly floured surface and knead for 4 to 5 minutes.

Wash, dry, and lightly oil the bowl. Return the dough to the bowl, cover with plastic, and let rest for 30 minutes.

Divide the dough into 8 equal pieces. On a generously floured surface, flatten each piece into a disc, flouring both sides. Cover 6 discs with plastic wrap (do not stack), and set aside.

On a lightly floured surface, with a rolling pin, roll out the 2 remaining discs to circles approximately 7 inches in diameter and roughly ¼ inch thick.

To cook, heat one or two heavy skillets (two are preferable as the breads take 15 minutes each to cook) over medium heat until hot. Transfer a rolled-out bread to a skillet. Cook for 7 minutes or until the bottom is covered with brown speckles. Turn and cook on the other side for approximately the same length of time. Brush about a teaspoon of oil or ghee on the top of the bread, turn the bread over, and fry for 1 minute, or until golden brown. Brush the second side with oil or ghee, flip the bread, and fry for 1 more minute. Transfer the bread to a plate. If possible, serve at once, while you continue to make the other breads; alternatively, wrap in a cloth to keep warm.

▲▲▲▲▲▲▲▲▲▲▲▲▲▲▲▲▲▲▲▲

Makes 8 round breads, 7 inches in diameter and ¼ to ½ inch thick.

Serve as a simple meal with plain yogurt and Spicy Tomato Chutney (page 139)
or Five-Lentil Stew (page 126).

Deep-Fried Lentil Patties

dal vadai • South India

Vadai are deep-fried lentil patties, similar in appearance to falafel but with a a different set of seasonings. They're eaten at any time of the day, most often served with a fresh coconut chutney.

Dal vadai are also prepared as street food. If they are fresh and hot, they are a temptation we never pass by. In fact, in India we eat deep-fried foods on a daily basis, whereas at home we seldom eat anything deep-fried. But in India we still consume far fewer fats: Eliminate meat and cheese, and there is plenty of room for other fat-laden calories . . .

1 cup channa dal (see page 412), soaked in water for 6 to 8 hours or overnight

2 teaspoons salt

1 tablespoon water

1 tablespoon finely chopped fresh ginger

1 small onion, finely chopped

1 to 2 jalapeños or cayenne chiles (see page 410), seeded and finely chopped

¼ cup fresh coriander leaves, roughly chopped

¼ cup fresh curry leaves (see page 412), roughly chopped (optional)

Oil for deep-frying

You will need a food processor, a medium-sized bowl, a wok or other deep pot for deep-frying, a slotted spoon, and a sieve or strainer.

Drain the dal, rinse, and drain again. Place the dal and 1 teaspoon of the salt in a food processor and process until uniformly ground and almost pureed, adding the water as the dal is ground.

Transfer the mixture into a medium-sized bowl. Add the ginger, onion, chile(s), coriander, and optional curry leaves. Stir to mix well. Cover and let sit for 1 hour.

To form the vadai, pull a ball the size of a walnut (approximately 1 tablespoon) off the dal mixture. Working with wet hands, form into a smooth ball and then flatten into a disc approximately 3 inches in diameter. Place on a plate while you form the remaining vadai.

In a wok or deep pot, heat oil for deep-frying to 350°F. To check the temperature of the oil, drop in a small piece of the dal mixture. If the piece immediately turns dark brown, the oil is too hot; if the piece does not almost immediately sizzle and fry, the oil is not hot enough.

Add 4 to 5 vadai to the hot oil and cook for about 4 minutes, or until a rich golden brown. Carefully remove the vadai with a slotted spoon and drain first in a sieve or strainer, and then on paper towels. Wait a minute or so before deep-frying each batch to allow the oil to regain sufficient temperature. Serve hot or at room temperature.

▲▲▲▲▲▲▲▲▲▲▲▲▲▲▲▲▲▲▲▲

Makes approximately 16 small deep-fried patties, about 3 inches indiameter.

These are traditionally served with Coconut Chutney (page 156), South Indian Spicy Lentil Stew (page 154), and Rice and Black Lentil Crêpes (page 151). As a snack, serve with Coconut Chutney (page 156) or Avocado Chutney (page 164).

Spicy Tomato Chutney

tomato achar • Nepal

Less than half the population of Nepal speaks Nepalese. In this mountainous country, roughly the size of Iowa or Illinois, there are Tamangs, Gurkhas, Sherpas, Nuwaris, Thakalis, Chetris, and Magars, to name just a few. Each population group has its own language, its own customs and culture, its own food.

We think of trekking in Nepal as one of life's truly wonderful experiences. In a single day of walking we can see different styles of architecture and different systems of agriculture, and we can taste a great variety of different foods—all the while in one of the most beautiful countries on earth.

Winnowing in Bhaktapur, Nepal

continued

There are hundreds of different fresh chutneys, all depending on what is in season and what particular tastes a cook wants to put together. This particular one we had trekking; after a long day of walking, nothing could have tasted better than a bowl full of dal, a pile of chapattis made from freshly ground wheat, and a tiny plate of fiery hot tomato chutney.

1 tablespoon vegetable oil

1½ tablespoons minced garlic (approximately 4 medium cloves)

1 medium onion, finely chopped

1 tablespoon finely chopped fresh ginger

3 fresh green chiles (see page 410), chopped

½ teaspoon fenugreek seed (see page 414), dry-roasted (see page 154) and ground

½ teaspoon cumin seed, dry-roasted (see page 154) and ground

2 large tomatoes (about 1 pound), coarsely chopped

½ teaspoon salt

1 cup loosely packed fresh coriander leaves, coarsely chopped

You will need a heavy saucepan or deep skillet with a lid.

Heat the oil in a heavy saucepan or deep skillet over medium-high heat. Add the garlic, onion, ginger, and chiles and fry for 1 minute. Add the fenugreek and cumin and cook 1 minute more, stirring. Add the tomatoes and salt, and bring to a boil. Lower the heat, partially cover, and cook for another 15 minutes, or until thickened almost to a paste.

Turn out into a bowl and stir in the coriander leaves. Serve as a condiment and dipping sauce for bread. Stored in the refrigerator, well sealed in a glass container. It will keep for a week.

▲▲▲▲▲·▲·▲▲·▲▲·▲▲▲▲·▲▲▲

Makes approximately 1½ cups sauce.

Serve to accompany Five-Lentil Stew (page 126) and a flatbread such as Rajasthani Salt and Spice Bread (page 130) or Chickpea Flour Country Bread (page 147).

Nepali Green Chile Chutney

haryo khursaniko achar • Nepal

This is another Nepalese chutney, also on the fiery side of things and very
quick to make. If you wish, cut back on the chiles. We have included in this book a
number of chutneys and salsas that combine fresh coriander and chiles. Each is quite
different from the next, but all are good accompaniments to meals based on bread.

½ teaspoon cumin seed, dry-roasted
(see page 154)

1 cup loosely packed fresh coriander
leaves, finely chopped

½ cup loosely packed fresh mint leaves,
finely chopped

4 green chiles (see page 410),
finely chopped

¼ teaspoon salt

Pinch of asafoetida (see page 409;
optional)

2 tablespoons fresh lemon juice

You will need a large mortar and pestle or a food processor.

In a large mortar, pound the cumin to a powder. Add all the remaining ingredients except the lemon juice and pound well to mash.
Add the lemon juice and continue to pound until a
slightly dry paste forms. Alternatively, combine all the
ingredients in a food processor and process briefly to
blend; you want a slightly rough paste, not a uniform texture. Turn out into a bowl and serve with bread as a dip.
This is best eaten immediately, or within 2 to 3 hours,
while the fresh herbs still have good flavor.

Jaipur: Chiles and limes to hang by the doorway

▲▲▲▲▲▲▲▲▲▲▲▲▲▲▲▲▲▲▲▲▲▲

Makes about 1 cup chutney.

*Serve with Savory Country Corn Bread (page 136) as a snack or light meal, or
as part of a larger South Asian menu.*

Deep-Fried Whole Wheat Breads with Cumin

puri • North India

There are better puris to be had in India than those served first thing in the morning from railway platforms, but there are few places so pleasurable to eat them. If you've been on the train all night, or all day and all night, or all night and all day and all night . . . well, fresh hot puris served with a chutney or spiced fried potatoes taste like nothing less than luxury. Fellow passengers stretch their arms and legs on the platform, or sip hot milk tea—*chai*—from little clay cups. "Chai, chai," hawkers yell out as they work quickly up and down the platform. "Chai, chai; puri, puri": the sounds of an Indian morning.

▲▲▲▲▲▲▲▲▲▲▲▲▲▲▲▲▲▲▲▲

When we make puris, we generally plan to have guests on hand to share the pleasure of eating the breads. We make up a cool yogurt dish and a curry before we get started with deep-frying the puris; that way we can serve the puris hot and at their best.

2 cups atta flour (or 2 cups whole wheat flour, sifted; see page 410)	1 teaspoon salt
1 cup unbleached white flour	1 tablespoon vegetable oil or ghee (see page 129)
1 teaspoon freshly ground black pepper	1½ cups plain yogurt, or more as necessary
1 teaspoon cumin seed, finely ground	
½ teaspoon turmeric	Oil for deep-frying

You will need a medium-sized bowl, a rolling pin, a large wok or deep pot for deep-frying, and a wooden spoon or slotted spoon.

In a medium-sized bowl, mix together the atta or whole wheat flour, white flour, pepper, cumin, turmeric, and salt. Sprinkle the oil over the dry ingredients and rub in with your fingers. Add the yogurt a little bit at a time, until a kneadable dough forms. The dough should be on the stiff side, but still easily kneadable; use less yogurt or more yogurt as necessary. Turn the dough out onto a lightly floured surface and knead for 8 to 10 minutes.

Rinse out, dry, and lightly oil the bowl. Return the bread to the bowl, cover, and let rest for 30 minutes or as long as 2 hours.

Divide the dough into 16 balls of equal size. Flatten each ball between your lightly floured palms and set aside; do not stack. Cover with plastic wrap.

You can either heat the oil and then roll out the puris as you cook them or roll out all the puris first and then cook them. We prefer the latter, as it gives us time to concentrate on the deep-frying. Roll out each puri into a circle approximately 6 inches in diameter. Set aside (do not stack them), and cover with plastic wrap.

Heat oil for deep-frying in a large wok or deep pot over medium-high heat until the temperature reaches approximately 375°F. If you don't have a thermometer, test the oil by frying a dried bread cube: If the oil is hot enough, the cube should brown in less than 1 minute, but it shouldn't brown instantly. Adjust your heat accordingly.

Set out a wooden bowl or platter lined with paper towels.

Start by frying one puri: Lay it gently in the oil. The puri will sink at first, and then will rise to the surface. (If the puri browns or blackens in less than 15 seconds, the oil is too hot; adjust the heat as necessary.) After the bread has risen to the surface, touch it gently with a wooden spoon or slotted stainless steel spoon, forcing it with a quick motion downward. At this point the puri should puff up into a balloon. Turn it over and continue to cook for 10 to 15 seconds. Remove to the paper-lined platter to drain. Continue cooking the rest of the puris, 2 or 3 at a time depending upon the size of your wok. Serve hot.

▲▲▲▲▲▲▲▲▲▲▲▲▲▲▲▲▲▲▲▲▲

Makes 16 puffed flatbreads.

Serve with any curry or lentil dish. Puris are particularly good with Gujarati Mango Curry (page 144) or Egg Curry with Tomato (page 165). We find that these deep-fried breads are more successful when served with only one curry and perhaps a fresh chutney. When the meal includes several curries and side dishes, we generally prefer Soft Whole Wheat Skillet Breads (page 123).

Gujarati Mango Curry

pukki keri nu shak • Gujarat, India

*We now enjoy mango season in Toronto. It's not like mango season in Cen-*tral America, or in India, but it's a mango season, and we love it. It's all due to the Global Supermarket, about which we have very mixed feelings, but we sure do like mangoes. For us mangoes are the best, especially the large yellow mangoes from India shaped like a fava bean the size of a cantaloupe. We put them in the refrigerator until they are well chilled, and then we peel them before cutting tidy slices: Buy them, chill them, and eat them, and back to the market for more. Mango season is never long enough, global supermarket or no.

Several times we've enjoyed the real thing. I mean, we've been in a place where mangoes grow and where they are ripe and in season. Mangoes are never expensive in season, because mango trees are huge and the mangoes tend to ripen all at once. The only drawback to mango season is that mangoes ripen when it is hot, really hot. Maybe that's what makes them so good eaten cold. . . .

We once had a layover in Karachi airport, an all-night layover that we were dreading. When we arrived it was very hot and muggy, and we were tired and hungry. We were directed to a little dormitory just outside the terminal where we'd been told that we would find a bed and a bite to eat. But when we arrived we found a bed but nothing to eat; the kitchen in the all-night café had already closed. So we sat down under a ceiling fan and drank a cup of tea, somewhat the worse for wear.

After a little while a man came over to our table, apologizing for there not being any food. "But would you like some mangoes?" he asked. "We have some in the refrigerator. . . ." Nothing could have tasted better.

▲▲▲▲▲▲▲▲▲▲▲▲▲▲▲▲▲▲▲▲▲▲▲

If you ever have more than enough ripe mangoes around, try this curry, medium hot, pale yellow, and full of the rich taste of the fruit. It's easy and it's great.

1 tablespoon tamarind paste or pulp
  (see page 419)
½ cup hot water
½ teaspoon cumin seed, dry-roasted
  (see page 154)
1 large clove garlic, coarsely chopped
1 small onion, coarsely chopped
½ teaspoon salt
1 tablespoon jaggery (see palm sugar,
  page 417) or brown sugar

1 cup warm water
1 tablespoon vegetable oil
½ teaspoon black mustard seed
  (see page 419)
3 ripe medium mangoes, peeled and
  cut into ¾-inch cubes
2 green or red chiles (see page 410),
  finely chopped
½ teaspoon turmeric

You will need two or three small bowls, a fine-meshed sieve, a large mortar and pestle or a spice grinder and a food processor, and a heavy skillet with a lid.

In a small bowl, dissolve the tamarind paste or pulp in the hot water and stir well. If using pulp, press the seeds to detach the flesh, and strain through a sieve into another bowl, pressing the pulp against the mesh with a spoon to extract the maximum from the tamarind; discard the pulp. Set the syrupy tamarind water aside.

In a large mortar, pound the cumin seed to a powder. Add the garlic, onion, and salt and pound to a paste. Alternatively, use a spice grinder to grind the cumin. Then combine the cumin, garlic, onion, and salt in a food processor and process to a paste.

Dissolve the sugar in the warm water in a small bowl, and stir in the reserved tamarind water.

In a heavy skillet, heat the oil. Add the mustard seeds and cook over medium heat until they pop (cover with the lid as they begin to pop). Add the cumin paste and cook, stirring constantly, until it begins to brown slightly. Add the tamarind mixture, together with the mangoes, chiles, and turmeric. Raise the heat and bring to a boil, then lower the heat to medium and simmer for 10 to 15 minutes, until thickened.

Serve hot with plenty of fresh bread for mopping up the sauce.

▲▲▲▲▲▲▲▲▲▲▲▲▲▲▲▲▲▲▲▲

Serves 2 to 3.

Serve accompanied by stacks of warm Soft Whole Wheat Skillet Breads (page 123) or Deep-Fried Whole Wheat Breads with Cumin (page 142). For a larger meal, add Ginger and Tomato Salad (page 131), Crisp Lentil Wafers (page 132), and Fried Cheese and Vegetable Curry (page 150).

Fresh Corn and Yogurt

raita • North India

In India, yogurt is often made from buffalo milk, which has a relatively high fat content. It is rich and delectable, and an important source of protein for a vegetarian population. We seldom prepare a North Indian meal without serving yogurt or a raita, a yogurt-based accompaniment.

This particular raita uses fresh yellow sweet corn, an import to India from the Americas that now grows all across North India and Nepal. Like most raitas, it goes well with almost any curry or dal and chapatti meal.

1 teaspoon vegetable oil

1 teaspoon cumin seed

2 tablespoons minced green or red chiles
or 1 jalapeño, seeds and ribs
removed (see page 410)

1 teaspoon grated fresh ginger

1 cup fresh corn, removed from the cob
and steamed until tender
(about 2 ears)

1½ cups plain yogurt

½ cup milk

1 teaspoon sugar

1 teaspoon coriander seed, dry-roasted
(see page 412) and ground

½ teaspoon salt

2 tablespoons coarsely chopped fresh
coriander

You will need a small skillet.

In a small skillet, heat the oil. Add the cumin seed and fry for 1 to 2 minutes, until brown.

Combine with all the remaining ingredients in a serving bowl and stir well. Serve chilled or at room temperature.

▲▲▲▲▲▲▲▲▲▲▲▲▲▲▲▲▲▲▲▲▲▲▲

Makes about 3 cups yogurt. Serves 6 as an accompaniment.

Serve on its own as a snack or light meal with a savory bread like Savory Country Corn Bread (page 136), Rajasthani Salt and Spice Bread (page 130), or Chickpea Flour Country Bread (page 147). This is always a welcome addition to a larger Indian meal or South Asian feast.

Chickpea Flour Country Bread

besan roti • Northwestern India

This thin, pale-yellow bread, flavored with chopped onion and cumin seed, is at its best when served with a curry and a cool raita. As with many cornmeal and other non–wheat-flour breads, be sure to let the chickpea batter sit for fifteen to twenty minutes before adding the wheat flour and beginning to work the batter into a dough. In this way, the chickpea flour can fully absorb the water.

This dough is best made in a food processor.

1 small onion, roughly chopped

1 teaspoon cumin seed

1 cup chickpea flour (see page 409)

½ teaspoon salt

2 tablespoons vegetable oil

½ cup water

1 cup atta flour (see page 410) or whole wheat flour, plus extra for kneading and rolling out

You will need a food processor, unglazed quarry tiles (see page 20) to fit on a rack in your oven or one large or two smaller baking sheets that fit side by side in your oven, and a rolling pin.

Combine the onion and cumin seed in a food processor and process until the onion is very finely chopped. Add the chickpea flour, salt, and vegetable oil and process for 25 to 30 seconds. With the motor running, add the water, a little at a time. Let the batter rest for 15 minutes (leaving it in the processor).

Add the whole wheat flour and process until a dough has formed. Process for another 45 seconds, and turn the hard, sticky dough out onto a lightly floured surface. Knead briefly until smooth.

Divide the dough into 8 equal pieces. Pat each piece between well-floured palms to a disc 3 to 4 inches in diameter. Set aside; do not stack. Cover with plastic wrap and let rest for 20 to 30 minutes.

Place quarry tiles on the bottom rack of your oven, leaving a 1-inch gap between the tiles and the oven walls. If using a baking sheet or sheets, place on the bottom rack. Preheat the oven to 450°F.

Begin rolling out the breads: Roll each one into a thin round approximately 8 inches in diameter. Roll firmly but carefully, as the dough tears easily; flour your rolling pin as needed.

continued

Roll out as many breads as you can fit in your oven at one time. Place the breads on the hot tiles or baking sheets. Bake for about 2 minutes, or until tiny bubbles rise across the entire surface of the bread and it is pale yellow in color; the bottom should be flecked with brown. Remove the breads and wrap in a towel to keep warm while you bake the remaining breads.

These breads are best served warm.

▲▲▲▲▲▲·▲·▲·▲▲▲·▲▲·▲·▲▲·▲▲

Makes 8 thin round breads, about 8 inches in diameter.

Serve with Fresh Corn and Yogurt (page 146) and Egg Curry with Tomato (page 165), or with almost any curry or savory legume.

Fresh North Indian Cheese
paneer chenna, paneer tikki • N o r t h   I n d i a

Paneer is fresh cheese made by souring hot milk with a little lemon juice and then pressing out the liquid until it becomes a firm mass. The process is simple and quick. The soft cheese produced after the whey has drained is called *paneer chenna.* It is used in desserts, and it is an ingredient in a number of savory dishes. When paneer chenna is pressed under a heavy weight for an hour or two, it firms up and becomes *paneer tikki,* or wedge cheese, used commonly in north Indian dishes, such as paneer kari (page 150). Paneer tikki has little taste of its own, but it has a delightful texture. Unlike most cheeses, it keeps its firmness even when heated, rather than melting.

2 quarts 2% or whole milk
3 to 6 tablespoons fresh lemon juice

You will need a colander, cheesecloth, a deep heavy, nonreactive saucepan, a wooden spoon, a large bowl, and a heavy weight.

Place a colander lined with three or four layers of cheesecloth over a large bowl.

In a heavy nonreactive saucepan, heat the milk gradually to boiling, stirring occasionally with a wooden spoon to keep it from scorching or from forming a skin. Then lower the heat to medium and add lemon juice 1 tablespoon at a time, stirring gently with a wooden spoon for 15 to 20 seconds after you add each tablespoon. The milk may turn with as little as 2 tablespoons lemon juice, but it may take more, so be patient; when it turns, the whiter curds will separate from the pale green whey, so both the color and texture of the milk will change. As soon as the milk starts to turn, remove it from the heat. Stir for another few seconds, and then pour into the cloth-lined colander.

Rinse briefly under slow-running cold water to remove the lemon taste. Gather the edges of the cheesecloth together, squeeze out the water, then knot together the cheesecloth (or loop a rubber band around it) to create a bag you can hang from a hook. Rinse out the bowl and place under the cheesecloth bag to catch the drips of whey.

After only 20 minutes you will have a soft cheese, paneer chenna.

To make paneer tikki, take the bag down, but don't untie it, and flatten the lump of chenna into an approximately 4-inch square. Leaving it covered with the cheesecloth, place it on a plate or on a countertop and flatten it with a heavy weight to compress it into the dense-textured cheese; we find it simplest to weight it with a bread board with a water-filled saucepan on top. Press the cheese for 2 hours. Remove from the cheesecloth and use immediately, or store in plastic wrap in the refrigerator.

▲▲▲▲▲▲▲▲▲▲▲▲▲▲▲▲▲▲▲▲▲

Makes about 1 cup soft fresh cheese or 8 ounces firm fresh cheese.

Use soft cheese as a spread for savory breads such as Savory Country Corn Bread (page 136). Use firm cheese in North Indian dishes such as Fried Cheese and Vegetable Curry (page 150).

Fried Cheese and Vegetable Curry
paneer kari • North India

Paneer is a very versatile food to have around. In Persian cuisine, where it may have originated, paneer is often served uncooked as a side dish, along with fresh herbs. In India it is always fried or grilled before being added to a dish at the last moment—as in this flavorful curry enriched with almonds and a little coconut.

masala (curry paste)

1 teaspoon minced fresh ginger

1 teaspoon poppy seeds

1 tablespoon coriander seed, dry-roasted (see page 412) and ground

1 tablespoon coarsely chopped almonds

2 cloves

Seeds from 1 green cardamom pod (see page 409), dry-roasted (see page 154) and ground

curry

1½ tablespoons vegetable oil

½ recipe Fresh North Indian Cheese (page 148), cut into ¼-inch squares

1 medium onion, finely chopped

½ teaspoon minced fresh ginger

1 clove garlic, minced

½ teaspoon salt

3 tablespoons fresh or frozen unsweetened shredded coconut (see page 411)

1 teaspoon cayenne

1 cup plain yogurt

Approximately ½ cup water

2 tablespoons finely chopped fresh mint, for garnish

You will need a mortar and pestle or a spice grinder and a food processor, a slotted spoon, and a large skillet.

Combine all the masala ingredients in a mortar or spice grinder and grind to a paste. Set aside.

Heat the oil in a large skillet, and fry the cheese cubes over medium-high heat until golden, approximately 10 minutes. Remove with a slotted spoon and set aside.

In the oil remaining in the pan, cook the onion over medium-high heat until golden, about 10 minutes.

Meanwhile, in a mortar, pound together the ginger, garlic, and salt until a paste forms. Alternatively, process to a paste in a food processor.

Add the garlic paste to the onions, then stir in the coconut, cayenne, and the masala paste. Cook for 5 minutes, stirring frequently. Lower the heat slightly, and stir in the yogurt; depending on how thick or runny your yogurt is, add up to ½ cup water, stirring until the sauce is smooth and creamy but not thick. Bring almost to a boil, then lower the heat.

Add the fried cheese and cook over low heat for 3 to 5 minutes, until heated through. Serve hot, garnished with the mint.

▲▲▲▲▲▲▲▲·▪▪▲▲▲▲▲▪▪▲▲▲·▲▲▲

Serves 4 as part of a bread-based meal.

Soft Whole Wheat Skillet Breads (page 123) or Chickpea Flour Country Bread (page 147)
go very well with this curry, along with Ginger and Tomato Salad (page 131) and
Sesame-Tamarind Chutney Powder (page 167) made up into a paste, or
Hot Peanut Chutney (page 161).

Rice and Black Lentil Crêpes
dosa • S o u t h   I n d i a

There are as many different kinds of dosas as there are kitchens in the south of India, but a basic dosa is prepared with a batter made from rice and urad dal. The batter is left to ferment, and then poured out onto a griddle to make anything from an eight-inch pancake to an enormous thin crêpe. Unlike the North Indian chapattis, which are used as a spoon to pick up other foods, moist and absorbent dosas are wonderful dipped into a curry or eaten with a coconut chutney—finger food par excellence.

Dosas, like other traditional breads and grain preparations from South Indian vegetarian cooking, have been made for centuries. Not only are they delicious and wonderfully creative from a cooking point of view, but they also combine complementary amino acids (from the legume and the grain) to create a full protein.

¾ cup urad dal (see page 413), soaked
    overnight in water to cover

Approximately 3½ cups water

2 cups rice flour

1 teaspoon salt

1 tablespoon vegetable oil

You will need a blender, a small saucepan, a large bowl, a 10-inch or larger griddle or cast-iron skillet, a rubber spatula, and a metal spatula.

continued

Drain the dal and place in a blender. Add 1 cup cold water and blend until smooth. (This may require giving the dal a stir manually at intervals.)

In a small saucepan, heat ½ cup water over low heat. Stir in 1 tablespoon of the rice flour, and cook, stirring until it begins to thicken. Remove from the heat and set aside.

In a large bowl, mix together the ground dal, salt, the remaining rice flour, and 2 cups water. Stir well to make a thin batter. Add the thickened rice paste and stir again to mix well. Cover the bowl and let stand for at least 5 to 6 hours at room temperature. (You can let the batter stand for up to 12 hours if necessary.)

Heat a large griddle or cast-iron skillet over medium-high heat. With a paper towel, lightly oil the griddle. The batter should be the thickness of a thin crêpe batter; add a bit more water to thin if necessary. Pour ½ cup batter onto the hot griddle, starting at the center and moving out. Use a spatula to help spread the batter as far as possible to the edges of the griddle; the dosa should be as thin as possible. Cook for approximately 2 minutes on the first side, then turn and cook for about 1 minute longer, or until cooked through.

Remove the dosa from the griddle, place on a plate, and cover with a clean cloth to keep warm.

Repeat with remaining batter, stacking the dosas as you finish them and covering to keep warm.

▲▲▲▲▲▲▲▲▲▲▲▲▲▲▲▲▲▲▲▲▲

Makes 15 to 20 thin, soft, crêpe-like breads, 8 to 10 inches in diameter.

Serve with South Indian Spicy Lentil Stew (page 154) and Coconut Chutney (page 156) for a very traditional South Indian meal. For a lighter, simpler meal, serve with Sesame-Tamarind Chutney Powder (page 167), mixed up into a paste for dipping.

South Indian Spice Powder

sambhar masala • S O U T H   I n d i a

I have no idea where my old friend Balu is now, or what he is doing. But fif-teen years ago, for six months we were the best of buddies, palling around our neighborhood in the city of Trivandrum like two long-lost peers, yet cultures apart. I was often a guest at family meals. Balu's mother even gave me permission to be in the kitchen, something generally unheard of in a South Indian Brahmin family. I was shown how to make sambhar masala, how to grate a coconut, how to grind rice in a large stone mortar and pestle. I would ask stupid questions, Balu would translate from English to Malaylam, and everyone would laugh.

"Balu," I asked one day, "what if I make a meal? A Western meal?" Balu looked interested and translated the idea. "No, thank you," said his mother and father. "No, thank you," said his brothers and sisters. "I'll come," said Balu.

I thought and thought about the meal. What could I prepare that Balu would like? It would have to be strictly vegetarian, and I was limited to some extent by what I could purchase in the market. A vegetarian spaghetti, I at last decided. That would be good.

The day of the meal came, and so did Balu. I served the meal and we sat down to eat, but Balu looked reluctant. I started eating; he took a bite. After a long, uncomfortable pause, I finally asked: "What's wrong, Balu, does it taste bad?"

"No, no," Balu replied as politely and apologetically as he could. "It is just that it doesn't have any taste."

▲▲▲▲▲▲▲·▲▲▲▲···▲▲·▲▲

This particular spice blend is essential for making South Indian Spicy Lentil Stew (page 154), but it can be used in other dishes as well. If you want to add a pinch of turmeric for color, be sure to add it after the other ingredients have been dry-roasted and ground (see Note).

1 teaspoon urad dal (see page 412)

1 teaspoon channa dal (see page 412)

2 tablespoons coriander seed
  (see page 412)

1 teaspoon cumin seed

2 teaspoons black peppercorns

1 teaspoon fenugreek seed
  (see page 414)

10 dried red chiles (see page 410),
  stemmed

Pinch of turmeric (optional)

You will need a heavy skillet and a spice grinder or large mortar and pestle.

continued

In a heavy dry skillet, roast the dals over medium-high heat, stirring constantly, for 5 to 8 minutes, until golden. Set aside.

In the same skillet, dry-roast the spices (except the turmeric) over medium-high heat, stirring constantly, until aromatic, about 3 minutes. Set aside.

In a spice grinder or large mortar, grind the dals to a powder. Grind the roasted spices to a powder, then grind the dried chiles to a powder.

Combine the dal, ground spices, and chiles. Add the turmeric if you wish. Store in a tightly sealed glass jar. This keeps well, but it does lose flavor over time, so it's best to make up a new batch after 6 months.

Note: Most seeds or pods benefit from dry-roasting before grinding in a spice grinder or mortar and pestle. Use the method described here to release the fragrant aromas of peppercorns and dried chile pepper flakes; spices such as cumin, fenugreek, cardamom, coriander, and black mustard seed; and nuts and sesame and poppy seeds.

▲▲▲▲▲▲▲▲▲▲▲▲▲▲▲▲▲▲▲▲

Makes approximately ⅔ cup spice powder.

Use as a spice mix in southern Indian recipes as directed.

South Indian Spicy Lentil Stew
sambhar • South India

This unique and satisfying hot lentil stew is served with most traditional South Indian meals. It can be thick with vegetables and tangy with the taste of tamarind, as this version is, or it can be thin and almost bland, but it is always on hand. Sambhar is poured over rice as part of the standard rice-based meal, or it is served in a small bowl to accompany dosas. The lentils are a complementary protein to rice, the mainstay of the South Indian vegetarian diet.

4 cups water

1 cup masur dal or mung dal
  (see page 412)

2 tomatoes, cut into large chunks

5 to 6 large okra, halved lengthwise

2 carrots, cut into large chunks

2 potatoes, cut into large chunks

1 tablespoon turmeric

2 teaspoons salt

2 teaspoons tamarind paste (see page
  419) or 1 tablespoon fresh lemon
  juice

1 tablespoon vegetable oil

1 tablespoon coriander seed
  (see page 412), ground

1 teaspoon cumin seed, ground

1 tablespoon black mustard seed
  (see page 417)

1 to 2 jalapeños, seeded and chopped

6 to 8 dried curry leaves (see page 412;
  optional)

1 tablespoon South Indian Spice Powder
  (page 153) or store-bought sambhar
  masala

You will need a large deep pot and a heavy skillet with a lid.

In a large pot, bring the water to a boil over high heat. Add the dal, tomatoes, okra, carrots, potatoes, turmeric, salt, and tamarind paste or lemon juice. Stir and bring back to a boil. Reduce the heat slightly and cook until the dal is tender, approximately 30 minutes; add more water if necessary.

Meanwhile, in a heavy skillet, heat the oil, and lightly fry the ground coriander and cumin seeds over medium heat. Add the mustard seeds, jalapeño, and optional curry leaves and fry for 2 minutes, covering the skillet as the seeds pop.

Add the fried spices to the cooked dal and vegetables. Add the sambhar masala and mix well. (The stew can be prepared up to 2 hours in advance, covered, and set aside at room temperature.) Just before serving, bring to a boil and simmer for 2 to 3 minutes, until thickened slightly.

▲▲▲▲▲▲▲▲▲▲▲▲▲▲▲▲▲▲▲▲▲

Serves 6 as an accompaniment to breads.

*Sambhar is served traditionally with Rice and Black Lentil Crêpes (page 151) and
Coconut Chutney (page 156); it is also served with Fresh Coriander, Ginger, and
Chile Crêpes (page 157).*

Coconut Chutney

South India

This southern Indian chutney is traditionally eaten with dosas and sambhar, although it is an excellent condiment with any curry and rice meal. For a smooth texture, the ingredients should be chopped as finely as possible. The chutney tastes best at room temperature, but it can spoil if kept unrefrigerated. If you make it ahead of time, refrigerate it, then bring to room temperature before serving.

1 cup fresh or frozen grated unsweetened coconut (see page 411)

1 to 2 jalapeños, seeded and finely chopped

½ teaspoon finely chopped fresh ginger

½ teaspoon finely chopped garlic

¼ teaspoon salt

¼ cup water

f r i e d   i n g r e d i e n t s

1 teaspoon vegetable oil

½ teaspoon black mustard seed (see page 417)

2 shallots, very finely chopped

3 to 4 fresh or dried curry leaves (see page 412); if using dried curry leaves, soak for 10 minutes in water, then drain

½ teaspoon hulled urad dal (see page 412)

¼ cup plain yogurt

You will need a large mortar and pestle or a food processor and a heavy skillet.

Using a large mortar and pestle, pound together the coconut, jalapeños, ginger, garlic, and salt. Add the water and pound until a past forms. Alternatively, place the coconut, chile, ginger, garlic, and salt in a food processor and process until finely ground. Add the water and process to form a thick paste.

In a heavy skillet, heat the oil. Add the mustard seed, stir, then cover and fry over medium-high heat until the seeds pop. Add the remaining fried ingredients, and cook, stirring constantly, for 2 to 3 minutes. Remove from the heat. Stir in the coconut paste and spoon out into a serving bowl. Blend in the yogurt, and serve.

▲▲▲▲▲▲▲▲▲▲▲▲▲▲▲▲▲▲▲▲▲

Makes about 1½ cups chutney.

Serve with Rice and Black Lentil Crêpes (page 151) or Fresh Coriander, Ginger, and Chile Crêpes (page 157) and South Indian Spicy Lentil Stew (page 154). This chutney is also traditionally served with Deep-Fried Lentil Patties (page 138).

Fresh Coriander, Ginger, and Chile Crêpes
rava dosa • South India

We're not usually big breakfast people. Yet in India we never miss breakfast, and we find ourselves over a period of time waking earlier and earlier each day to taste all the breakfasttime foods that are available in the market or in restaurants, but disappear completely by six or seven o'clock. Indian breakfasts are generally grain-based, creative, sometimes spicy, and always very tasty.

Breakfast seems to be the one meal of the day for which travelers often find it difficult to accept new or different foods. Ironically, in India, where breakfasts are so good, wherever you find a cluster of hotels with foreign guests, inevitably there is a thriving little shop nearby serving fried eggs and terrible toast, or porridge, or cornflakes.

Rava dosas are thin crêpe-like breads spiked with chiles, ginger, curry, and coriander leaves. They are made from wheat, not rice, but are served like ordinary dosas with coconut chutney and sambhar. They make a great start to a day.

2 cups semolina flour

1 cup plain yogurt

1 red chile pepper or jalapeño (see page 410), seeded, veins removed, and finely chopped

1 tablespoon finely chopped fresh ginger

1 tablespoon fresh or dried curry leaves (see page 412); if using dried, soak in water for 10 minutes before using

2 tablespoons fresh coriander leaves, roughly chopped

½ teaspoon salt

2 cups warm water

You will need a medium-sized bowl, a large cast-iron or other heavy griddle, a flat wooden spoon or a rubber spatula, and a metal spatula.

In a medium-sized bowl, mix together the semolina flour, yogurt, chile, ginger, curry leaves, coriander leaves, and salt. Stir in the water a little bit at a time until you have a smooth batter. Cover the bowl and let the batter rest for approximately 1 hour.

Heat a large cast-iron or other heavy griddle over medium-high heat. Using a paper towel, lightly oil the surface of the griddle, and reserve the towel for use between each dosa. When the griddle is hot, pour on ½ cup of the batter. As you pour, move in a circle out from the middle, distributing the batter in as large a circle as possible; then use the back of a wooden spoon or a rubber spatula to spread the batter to cover the gaps, again increasing the diameter of the dosa, to at least 9 or 10 inches. (Don't worry about making it too thin; the thinner the better.) Cook the dosa for 1½ minutes; after cooking for 1 minute, begin to loosen it from the griddle with a metal spatula. Coax the dosa, don't force it, as it will come off easily when it is golden brown and ready. Flip to the other side and cook for 1½ to 2 minutes, or until lightly browned in spots. Remove to a plate.

Rub the surface of the griddle with the oiled paper towel or, if it's particularly dry, add a little more oil. Continue cooking until all the dosas have been made. They can be stacked one on top of the other as they are cooked, or served immediately as they are made.

▲▲▲▲▲▲▲▲◦◦▲▲▲▲▲▲▲▲▲◦◦▲▲▲

Makes 8 thin crêpe-like breads, about 9 to 10 inches in diameter.

These are traditionally served for breakfast or in the late afternoon or evening with South Indian Spicy Lentil Stew (page 154) and Fresh Coconut Chutney (page 156). They are also good with Sesame-Tamarind Chutney Powder (page 167), mixed with water into a paste for dipping.

Shrimp and Tomato Curry with Coconut Milk

South India

If you are traveling around India and not in a rush, it is impossible not to make friends. I was once on a bus in the state of Karnataka, traveling between Mysore and Mangalore. The man sitting beside me asked me where I was from, and from there we got into conversation. At the time I'd been in India only a few weeks, and it was my first visit to a tropical country. I asked if he could please point out which tree was a mango, a papaya, a banana. To him, this was a little bit like asking the difference between a stop sign, a yield sign, and a sign for a sharp curve. But he was incredibly patient, as it took me a while to get to know the difference.

When we reached Mangalore, he asked if I would like to return with him to his village, to get a feel for village life. With no definite plans, I was delighted and off we went. "Do you have a dhoti?" he asked as we boarded a second bus. "No?" he asked again, seeing the uncomprehending look on my face, "then we must stop by a shop on the way home."

By late afternoon we were in Prakash's village, or on his farm to be precise. I was wearing a new white dhoti, a garment, traditionally worn by men in South India, which resembles an ankle-length wrap-around skirt. I had tied it according to instructions, in place of my trousers. Together we walked around the farm, balancing on narrow pathways between flooded rice paddies. In one field a man was up to his thighs in water and mud, guiding a plow behind a water buffalo making its way slowly across the field.

"Would you like to try?" asked Prakash, a twinkle in his eye. And before I knew it I was out in the water, my toes and feet sinking deep into the soft mud. The man handed me the plow and away we went, but what had looked quite easy was just the opposite. The plow was heavy, the ground was stubborn, and the buffalo kept on moving. I was halfway out into the field, clinging to the plow with all my might, and suddenly my new dhoti decided to come undone!

That night we ate a shrimp and tomato curry, one of the best meals I have ever had.

▲▲▲▲▲▲▲▲▲▲▲▲▲▲▲▲▲▲▲▲▲

In this quickly assembled curry, tomatoes and fresh coriander leaves blend with chiles, ginger, onion, and garlic, smoothed and enriched with coconut milk, to make a complex-tasting sauce for fresh shrimp. A delightful crowd-pleaser to be saved for special occasions because of all the saturated fat in the coconut milk.

continued

2 tablespoons peanut oil

1 medium yellow onion, chopped

2 cloves garlic, minced

2 teaspoons minced fresh ginger

2 green chiles or 1 jalapeño
(see page 410), chopped

4 fresh curry leaves, or 6 to 8 dried curry
leaves (see page 412) soaked in water
for 10 minutes before using

1 pound tomatoes, finely chopped

1 teaspoon Hot Spice Powder (page 134)
or store-bought garam masala

½ pound small shrimp, shelled and
deveined

1 teaspoon salt

2 tablespoons fresh coriander leaves,
chopped

Juice of 1 lime

¾ cup coconut milk (see page 411)

You will need a large, heavy nonreactive skillet.

Heat a large, nonreactive skillet over medium-high heat, and add the oil. When the oil is hot, toss in the onion, garlic, ginger, chiles, and curry leaves. Fry for 4 to 5 minutes, until the onion starts to brown. Add the tomatoes and spice powder, and continue cooking, stirring occasionally, until the tomatoes are softened, approximately 3 minutes.

Add the shrimp, salt, and coriander leaves, and stir well. Stir in the lime juice, then add the coconut milk and stir well. Simmer for 4 to 5 minutes, until the shrimp are cooked and the sauce has thickened somewhat. Serve hot.

▲▲▲▲▲▲••▲▲▲••▲▲▲•▲▲

Serves 4.

*Serve with Soft Whole Wheat Skillet Breads (page 123), steamed rice, and
Papaya and Peanut Salad (page 169).*

Hot Peanut Chutney

Nepal

Peanuts—called groundnuts in South Asia—have become the world's most abundant snack food, or at least the most common snack food of the Lesser Developed Countries (LDCs). Extremely rich in vitamin B_5 and high in protein, peanuts are in many ways an ideal dietary supplement in countries with widespread malnutrition. But peanuts (which are actually legumes, not nuts) are prey to an aflatoxin, aspergillus flavus, a fungus that has been proven to be carcinogenic in animals. Groundnut meal, which is fed to cattle and other domestic animals, and peanut butters are now routinely tested for aflatoxin, but local supplies of roasted peanuts in the LDCs often go untested. We love peanuts, and often depend on them when traveling as a good nutritious food, but we now keep a watchful eye out for the moldy ones.

All that aside, it's just a matter of time before someone in North America begins to market a chile peanut butter. Peanuts and chiles naturally call out for each other, as in this Nepalese chutney. Living in Sri Lanka and far from a jar of peanut butter, I used to buy roasted peanuts in the market and grind them at home. With a mortar and pestle a good four feet tall, I could grind them with very little effort— first throwing in a few dried chiles to give the peanut butter a little punch.

▲▲▲▲▲▲·▲·▲▲▲▲·▲▲▲··▲▲▲

In this peanut chutney, the roasted nuts are ground to a coarse powder and combined with dried chiles, spices, and lime juice. The chutney has a dry paste-like texture and a pleasant zip from the combination of salt, sweet, and hot; it makes an excellent condiment for flatbreads.

⅔ cup (about 4 ounces) roasted or raw unsalted peanuts

3 to 5 dried red chiles (see page 410)

One 1-inch piece fresh ginger, peeled and grated (about 1 tablespoon)

1 teaspoon cumin seed, dry-roasted (see page 154) and ground

¼ cup fresh lime juice

1 teaspoon sugar

½ teaspoon salt

You will need a heavy skillet if your peanuts are unroasted and a mortar and pestle or food processor.

If your peanuts are raw, dry-roast them in a cast-iron or other heavy skillet over medium heat until lightly golden.

continued

If using a mortar, coarsely chop the peanuts. Transfer to the mortar and pound fine. Break or chop dried chiles into very small pieces, discarding the stems, and add to the peanuts. Pound until finely ground. Add ginger and cumin and pound. Add the lime juice and blend well. The mixture should now have the consistency of a dryish paste.

Alternatively, if using a processor, transfer the peanuts to a processor and pulse to finely chop. Break up the chiles into small pieces, discarding the stems, and add to the processor together with the ginger, cumin, and lime juice. Pulse 4 or 5 times to blend.

Stir the sugar and salt into the chutney and blend well. Turn out into a bowl and serve with fresh breads.

▲▲▲▲▲▲▲▲▲▲▲▲▲▲▲▲▲▲▲▲

Makes approximately 1 cup chutney.

Serve with a Central Asian naan such as Pebbled Persian Bread (page 55) or Tibetan Barley Skillet Bread (page 71) as a light meal, or with almost any savory bread as a delicious quick snack. This is very good as a hot contrast to Fruit and Yogurt Curry with Nine Tastes (page 135) or Shrimp and Tomato Curry with Coconut Milk (page 159).

Sri Lankan Coconut Breakfast Bread
roti • S r i   L a n k a

Wheat flour and wheat breads are commonplace in Sri Lanka, a small tropi-cal country that, to the best of our knowledge, doesn't grow a grain of wheat. Coconut rotis are made early each morning in almost every neighborhood restaurant, and served throughout the day as a tasty snack with tea, coffee, or fresh juice.

It was only after I'd become quite addicted to coconut rotis that I began to wonder how on earth what appeared to be a traditional recipe had evolved out of an entirely foreign food. Tracing the flour to the wholesale market, I found fifty- and one-hundred pound bags labeled "American Flour." It didn't make sense. Sri Lanka is a poor nation. How, and why, should it import so much flour when it is easily self-sufficient in its production of rice?

American flour, I later discovered, pops up in the oddest places throughout the Third World. As a result of Public Law 480 (the so-called Food for Freedom Law), American grain is sold at reduced rates to Third World nations that line up politically in one way or another with the United States. What in government circles is put forth as "humanitarian aid" has been, in fact, a rather convenient way of finding markets for chronic U.S. grain surpluses. The problem with the program (though it is perhaps by design) is that in many poor nations it has created a greater dependence on a food resource that can increase in price or completely disappear overnight.

In Sri Lanka these rotis are made with white flour (the only kind available) and Third World coconuts. We prefer the whole-wheat version.

1½ cups fresh or frozen grated coconut
   (see page 411)
2 cups whole wheat flour

1 teaspoon salt
1½ cups warm water
1 teaspoon oil

You will need a medium-sized bowl, a large cast-iron or other heavy skillet or griddle, and a metal spatula.

In a medium-sized bowl, combine the coconut, flour, and salt. Make a well in the center, add the water, and mix gently. The consistency will be somewhere between that of batter and bread dough.

Heat a large cast-iron skillet or griddle over medium-high heat. Add the oil and spread it evenly with a paper towel. (Reserve the paper towel to wipe the skillet between batches.) Drop 4 or 5 heaping tablespoonfuls of the batter onto the hot skillet, leaving adequate space between them. Flatten each roti with a spatula so that they are no more than ¼ inch thick, and cook until browned on the bottom, about 3 to 4 minutes. Flip over. Cook 3 to 4 minutes longer. Remove and cool on a rack. Repeat with the remaining batter.

▲▲▲▲▲▲▲▲▲▲▲▲▲▲▲▲▲▲▲▲▲▲▲

Makes 8 to 10 small flatbreads, about 3 inches in diameter and ¼ inch thick.

These are traditionally served with soupy lentil dishes, like Five-Lentil Stew (page 126), Lentils with Garlic, Onion, and Tomato (page 127), or South Indian Spicy Lentil Stew (page 157) for lunch or a light meal. They are also good on their own for breakfast or a snack with coffee or tea.

Avocado Chutney

Sri Lanka

From April through June of 1978 I stayed with the Munasinghe family in the town of Kandy, Sri Lanka. They had a spare room for rent, and I was pleased to live in a home rather than a hotel. Shortly after moving in, I asked Ms. Munasinghe if I could help out in the kitchen. I explained that I was interested in Singhalese cuisine. She said nothing and for a while I wondered if I had made an inappropriate request, but a few days later I was taken into the kitchen and shown to a corner where there was a table, a gas burner, a coconut scraper, a few clay pots, and two or three knives. This was to be my own personal kitchen for the next three months, and the site of one of the most intensive cooking courses I have ever had.

Like everyone else in Kandy, I went to the market daily, and was soon a familiar face. I was in Sri Lanka as the hot season gave way to the rains, the peak season for fruit in this tropical country. During my stay I made a point of trying a new fruit every day; when I left, there were still many I'd never tasted.

Avocados are big, cheap, and delicious in Sri Lanka. This avocado chutney— a close relative of guacamole—was one of my few contributions to the family table. The Munasinghes approved and began to make it on their own.

1 large or 2 small ripe avocados, peeled and pitted

¼ cup shredded fresh or frozen unsweetened coconut (see page 411)

1 small tomato, finely chopped

2 tablespoons fresh lime juice

2 cloves garlic, unpeeled

2 tablespoons finely chopped shallots

½ teaspoon salt

¼ cup finely chopped fresh coriander

1 serrano chile, finely chopped

2 tablespoons dry-roasted shredded coconut (see Note)

You will need a medium-sized bowl, a small cast-iron or other heavy skillet, and a large mortar and pestle or a blender.

In a medium bowl, mash the avocado. Add the ¼ cup coconut, the tomato, and lime juice and mix well. Set aside.

In a small dry skillet, dry-roast the garlic cloves over medium-high heat for about 5 minutes, until the skins start to turn brown. Remove the skins and place the garlic in a mortar. Add the shallots and salt and pound to a paste. Alternatively, combine the garlic, shallots, and salt in a blender and chop to a paste.

Add the garlic mixture, coriander leaves, and chile to the chutney and stir well. Garnish with the roasted coconut and serve.

Note: To dry-roast coconut, place shredded fresh or frozen coconut in a dry heavy skillet over medium-high heat and toast, stirring constantly to avoid scorching as the coconut dries out. It will start to turn a golden brown and to give off a wonderful scent after 5 minutes or so. Remove the pan from the heat, and continue stirring for another minute as the coconut becomes golden all over. Then remove from the pan and let cool.

▲▲▲▲▲▲·▲·▲▲·▲▲▲·▲·▲▲··▲▲▲

Makes approximately 3 cups dip.

This is great as an appetizer served with Crisp Lentil Wafers (page 132). A welcome addition to almost any larger Indian meal, it is also good served simply with Sri Lankan Coconut Breakfast Bread (page 162) or Deep-Fried Whole Wheat Breads with Cumin (page 142).

✳

Egg Curry with Tomato
anda curry • Gujarat, India

*I once lived in a small yoga ashram in South India. One of the few require-*ments of the ashram was that everyone maintain a vegetarian diet. For the most part, this took no effort whatsoever, as almost all the local restaurants were strictly vegetarian and the food they served was some of the best I have ever tasted.

Even so, I must admit that I wasn't always faithful to the rule (yet never without guilt). Miles away—I can't remember how I first stumbled in—a little restaurant called The Gujarati specialized in serving the regional cuisine of the state of Gujarat. With whole wheat puris and northern-style dal, the food was completely different from anything served in South India. My favorite dish was the egg and tomato curry, a nonvegetarian dish.

It's not always easy to know in India whether or not a restaurant is vegetarian, but if you see eggs upon entering you know immediately that it is not. There is ongoing debate in the country about whether unfertilized eggs should or should not be eaten by vegetarians, but I have never encountered a restaurant that claims to serve only the unfertilized sort.

▲▲▲▲▲▲·▲▲·▲▲·▲▲▲▲··▲·▲▲▲

Anda curry is easy to make and a very pretty dish to serve, with eggs poached and floating in a bed of spicy stewed tomatoes.

1 tablespoon vegetable oil

2 to 3 cloves garlic, finely chopped

1 medium onion, diced

2 teaspoons coriander seed (see page 412), ground

1 teaspoon cumin seed, ground

1 teaspoon turmeric

1 teaspoon cayenne

2 pounds tomatoes, chopped

1 teaspoon salt

¼ cup fresh coriander leaves

½ teaspoon Hot Spice Powder (page 134) or store-bought garam masala

6 to 8 large eggs

You will need a large nonreactive saucepan with a lid.

In a large nonreactive saucepan, heat the oil over medium-high heat. Add the garlic and onion and fry until the onion is soft and translucent. Add the ground coriander, cumin, and turmeric and cook for another minute. Add the cayenne, tomatoes, and salt and bring to a boil, then reduce the heat and simmer for 10 minutes. Lower the heat and stir in the fresh coriander and spice powder.

Gently break the eggs into the sauce without breaking the yolks. Cover the saucepan with a lid and cook for approximately 3 to 4 minutes for soft yolks, or longer to the desired consistency. Serve hot.

▲▲▲▲▲▲·▲▲·▲▲▲▲▲▲·▲▲··▲·▲▲

Serves 4 to 6.

Serve with Deep-Fried Whole Wheat Breads with Cumin (page 142) and Avocado Chutney (page 164) for a meal full of flavor. This is an easy-to-prepare curry that can be served alongside any number of different dishes, but avoid serving with another tomato-based dish.

Sesame-Tamarind Chutney Powder

Kerala, South India

During my stay in Trivandrum, at least once a day for five months—on most days more than once a day—I made a visit to a little restaurant known locally as the Hole in the Wall. It was just a stone's throw away from where I was living, and though the restaurant served only mediocre meals, it did offer excellent "chai"—tea with milk—and home-style dosas served with sesame-tamarind chutney paste. I often went there for breakfast, but I always stopped by in midafternoon, around four o'clock, when I knew that the dosas would be hot and ready. They would come on a small banana leaf, and then a waiter would come along with a spoonful of chutney paste. Most people would eat their dosa and then order "chai"; breaking custom, I would order my "chai" to have along with my dosa. Together they were a perfect snack, and a perfect way to make it through the long hot afternoon until dinner, still hours away.

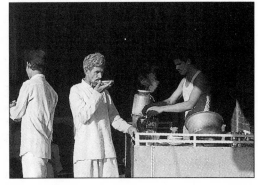

Tea stand

▲▲▲▲▲▲▲▲▲▲▲▲▲▲▲▲▲▲▲▲▲▲

The following recipe makes a powder that stores well. To use, just sprinkle the powder over bread or rice or, in more orthodox fashion, mix it with vegetable oil or water to make a paste, and serve in condiment dishes as you might a hot mustard.

8 dried red chiles (see page 410)

¼ cup white sesame seeds

¼ cup urad dal (see page 412)

⅛ teaspoon asafoetida (see page 409)

½ teaspoon tamarind paste (see page 412)

½ teaspoon salt

You will need a heavy skillet, a spice grinder, a mortar and pestle, and a small bowl.

In a dry heavy skillet roast the chiles over medium heat, stirring them constantly to prevent scorching, for 3 to 5 minutes. Set aside.

Using the same skillet, dry-roast the sesame seeds until they begin to turn slightly golden. Remove from the heat and keep stirring for a minute or so; they will go on roasting in the retained heat of the pan, and it is important not to let them overcook, as they can lose their sweet nuttiness and become bitter. Remove from the pan and set aside.

Using the same technique, dry-roast the dal, stirring constantly, until roasted and golden, 5 to 8 minutes. Remove from the pan and set aside.

In a spice grinder, grind the chiles and then, separately, the dal, and place in a bowl. Then grind the sesame seeds; you can grind them in the spice grinder, but they quickly turn into a paste and start to release their oils, so we prefer to use a mortar to pulverize them.

Add the sesame seeds to the other ground ingredients, together with the asafoetida, and mix well. Transfer 2 to 3 tablespoons of the ground powder to the spice grinder, add the tamarind paste and salt, and blend well. Return this mixture to the remaining powder and mix well. Let dry completely, stirring every now and again, before storing in a well-sealed glass container.

▲▲▲▲▲▲▲◦▴◦▴▴▴◦◦▴▴◦◦▴▴◦◦▴▴▴

Makes 1 scant cup powder.

Use as a condiment with bread: Dip bread into the powder or sprinkle a little powder on top. Alternatively, mix up with a little oil to make a paste, and place on the table to accompany Rice and Black Lentil Crêpes (page 151) or Fresh Coriander, Ginger, and Chile Crêpes (page 157).

Papaya and Peanut Salad

Kerala, South India

If we were making up a list of "super foods"—broccoli, garlic, almonds, beets, guavas, and other foods that are absolutely loaded with nutrients—then papaya would not only be on the list, it might be at the top. Papayas are extremely high in vitamins A and C. They are natural diuretics. The little black seeds, horribly foul-tasting as they are, are eaten in many parts of tropical Asia as a remedy for various kinds of intestinal worms, a remedy we can vouch for. And the skin is loaded with papein, which can be used for tenderizing meat. A papaya tree is almost as remarkable as its fruit, growing twenty to thirty feet tall in the space of a couple of years, then producing fruit in great abundance. Public health programs in Malaysia and in India have long tried to encourage people to eat more papaya because it is so nutritious, abundant, and inexpensive. But in places like India and China, where foods are believed to be either hot or cold and where good health is maintained by a proper balance of hot and cold in the body, papaya is seen as an extremely "hot" food. As a result, it is a food often avoided during pregnancy, a time when hot foods are considered harmful. The habit of squeezing lime onto a slice of ripe papaya comes out of this belief as well; the lime works to neutralize the "hot."

This recipe uses green or semiripe papaya more as a vegetable than as a fruit. Green papayas can be purchased year-round at Thai and Southeast Asian groceries.

In this recipe, grated papaya is tossed with chopped peanuts, fresh coriander, chopped jalapeño, and roasted coconut, then moistened with fresh lime juice, to make a refreshing, tangy, and power-packed salad. It is very easy to assemble, even if you are starting from scratch and roasting the peanuts and shredded coconut.

2 cups packed grated green or semi-ripe papaya (see Note)

½ cup unsalted peanuts, dry-roasted (see Note) and roughly chopped

Juice of 2 limes

3 tablespoons shredded unsweetened fresh coconut (see page 411), dry-roasted (see Note)

2 tablespoons finely chopped fresh coriander

1 jalapeño, seeded and finely chopped

½ teaspoon salt

Leaf lettuce for serving

You will need a medium-sized saucepan and a large bowl.

Bring 2 cups of water to a boil in a medium saucepan. Toss in the grated papaya, and bring back to the boil. Turn off the heat and let sit for 2 minutes. Then drain.

In a large bowl, combine the peanuts, papaya, lime juice, and coconut. Mix in the coriander leaves, chile, and salt. Chill in the refrigerator for 30 minutes.

To serve, mound the salad on a plate lined with lettuce leaves.

Harvesting chiles in Rajasthan

Note: Green papaya is quite hard and grates easily. Just peel, cut in half, scoop out the seeds, and grate on a grater.

To dry-roast coconut and peanuts: use a dry cast-iron or other heavy skillet set over medium-high heat.

To roast coconut: Place fresh or frozen grated coconut in the skillet and toast, stirring constantly to prevent burning. Once the coconut begins to color and to give off a wonderful scent, keep close watch; after about 30 seconds, it should suddenly look evenly golden or pale brown. Remove from the heat and keep stirring for 30 seconds, then turn out into a bowl. Store, once cooled, in a well-sealed container.

To roast peanuts: Place them in the hot skillet and stir frequently as they toast. After 4 or 5 minutes you will see some begin to change color and this is a signal to be very attentive. Within a minute, all the nuts should look as if they have browned patches. Remove from the heat and keep stirring for a short time before turning out into a bowl. Store in a well-sealed container.

Serves 4 as a side dish or 2 to 4 as a snack.

Serve as a side dish to accompany a larger Indian meal, or serve as a snack or light meal with a hearty savory flatbread such as Chickpea Flour Country Bread (page 147) or Rajasthani Salt and Spice Bread (page 130).

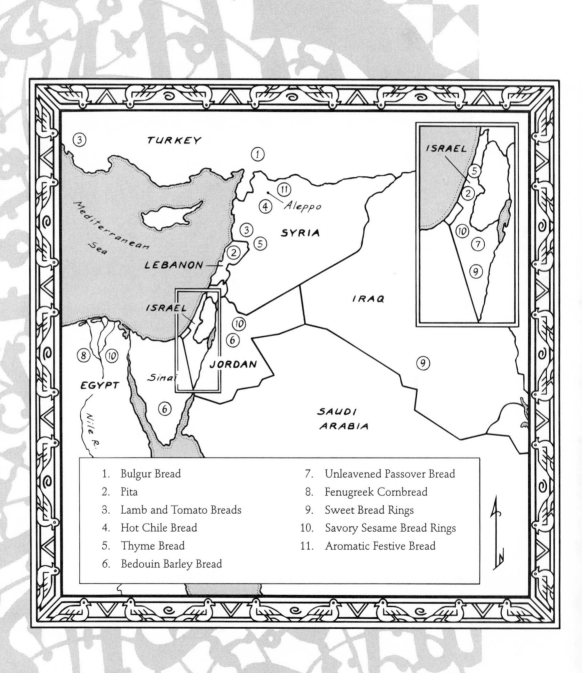

1. Bulgur Bread	7. Unleavened Passover Bread
2. Pita	8. Fenugreek Cornbread
3. Lamb and Tomato Breads	9. Sweet Bread Rings
4. Hot Chile Bread	10. Savory Sesame Bread Rings
5. Thyme Bread	11. Aromatic Festive Bread
6. Bedouin Barley Bread	

Eastern Mediterranean

We have included Turkey, Syria, Lebanon, Israel, Egypt, Yemen, Iraq, and Jordan in this chapter. Though Yemen and Iraq do not border the Mediterranean, from a culinary and cultural point of view they have a great deal in common with the countries of the Eastern Mediterranean.

Diyarbakir, Turkey: Carrying ka'kat

The climate of the Eastern Mediterranean is dry, with hot summers and moderate winters, which are colder in the mountains and areas farther from the coast. The climate in Yemen is temperate in the high-altitude uplands and hot and steamy along the coast of the Red Sea. In the dry heat, wheat thrives, as long as there is sufficient water; in more marginal areas, barley or sorghum is the principal grain.

The earliest wheats and the first breads are generally believed by archaeologists to have originated in this region: Wheat was first cultivated in the fertile crescent between the Tigris and Euphrates in what is now Iraq, while the earliest traces of grain cooked into flatbreads are in Egypt. Wild wheats, early relatives of our modern domesticated bread wheats, still grow in the valleys and plateaus of southern Turkey and Anatolia.

Flatbread traditions remain vigorous, from classic pita to the simple unleavened breads of the Kurdish and Bedouin nomads. Most are made with wheat, while some are a blend of wheat with a locally available grain such as corn, sorghum, or barley. Breads are used not just on their own as daily food, but also—dried or flavored—as an ingredient in soups, casseroles, and salads. Wheat is also transformed into bulgur (coarsely ground parboiled wheat) for easy storage; bulgur can be used for breads or pilafs, or kneaded with meat to make *kibbeh*.

Nile Delta: Baking in a traditional oven

Because of its agricultural fertility and its place on trade routes between Asia and Europe, between Arabia and the Mediterranean, the Eastern Mediterranean has seen waves of invaders and outside influences. Local cuisines are a blend of traditions, including Arab, Turkish, Kurdish, Ottoman, Persian, and others. As a result, many dishes from different countries in the area are close cousins and go well together. They make generous use of the lemons, olives, and herbs that flourish in the region and are pleasing for their strong, clean, fresh taste.

This is the region of the mezze tradition, where small dishes of salads, grilled meats, olives, and yogurt cheese are served with an array of flatbreads to make a meal. Mezze are a paradise for salad-eaters as well as for bread-lovers. Some dishes in the mezze tradition are elaborate, but most are simple combinations of fresh ingredients, often dressed with lemon juice, perhaps with a little olive oil and plenty of flat-leafed parsley or other herbs.

Yemen, near Manakha: Threshing with bullocks

Well-kneaded yeasted bread dough (above);
assorted flours (inset)

From the chapter Central Asia: *Afghan Snowshoe Naan, page 40, with hot tea*

Mount Kailash with Chiu Gompa in Tibet

Uzbek woman with melons in Tashkent

*Farsi woman
with tandoor in
Turkmenistan*

From the chapter China, Vietnam, and Malaysia: *Xichuan Pepper Bread, page 93, and Rice Wrappers* (bang trang),

*Rural market in
Dong Ha,
Vietnam*

In the rice fields in Dali, Yunnan

*Baking large
griddle breads
in Shanghai*

From the chapter India, Sri Lanka, and Nepal: *Stacked Pappadum (top), page 132, and Chapattis (bottom),*

Making chapattis

Rice and lentils for sale

Fields near Jaipur in Rajasthan

page 123; and corn dal

From the chapter Eastern Mediterranean: *Bulgur Bread, page 175, and Cutting-Board Salsa, page 178*

Kurdish women on the move in southern Turkey

Plowing the fields with a camel in Yemen

A baker in Cairo

From the chapter **Morocco, Tunisia, and Ethiopia:** *Moroccan Anise Bread, page 242, with North African Chile Paste*

A traditional village, Anti-Atlas, Morocco

A nomad family baking bread in the sand, Douz, Tunisia

Oranges and clementines in southern Morocco

page 245

From the chapter **Armenia, Georgia, and Azerbaijan:** *Paperthin Lavash, page 283*

Azeri vegetable seller in Tbilisi, Georgia

A local market in Baku, Azerbaijan

Pomegranates for sale from the trunk of a car in Kuba, Azerbaijan

From the chapter Europe: *Olive Ladder Bread, page 323*

At the market in Mulhouse, France

First snowfall in Chandolin, Switzerland

Cherry trees in autumn in Provence

*Cleaning dried corn
in Tlacolula, Oaxaca*

From the chapter North America: *Blue Corn Tortillas, page 364;
Tomatillo Salsa, page 397; and High-Tech Crackers, page 392*

Bulgur Bread

nane casoki • Kurdistan

Three Kurdish men sat with me one afternoon in a small shop in Dyarbakir, Turkey, and described in great detail all the Kurdish flatbreads they could think of. It took them an entire afternoon. They went on and on about *nane casoki,* their favorite. "It must be eaten hot!" they said, as one man closed his eyes and gently squeezed his lips together. I came home determined to try nane casoki, and on the first attempt we became instant converts.

2 cups bulgur	2 cups boiling water
1 teaspoon salt	Approximately 2 cups hard unbleached white flour
½ cup minced onion	

You will need a medium-sized bowl, a food processor, unglazed quarry tiles (see page 20) to fit on a rack of your oven or one large or two small baking sheets, a rolling pin, and a baker's peel or baking sheet (optional).

In a medium-sized bowl, combine the bulgur, salt, and onion. Pour the boiling water over and let stand for 30 minutes. Transfer to a food processor fitted with a standard metal blade and process briefly, about 20 seconds. Add 1 cup flour and process to a smooth texture. Turn the mixture out onto a generously floured surface, and knead, incorporating flour as necessary to keep dough from sticking, for 3 to 4 minutes. (Although a processor makes the job easier, you can also incorporate the flour into the bulgar by hand, then turn out onto a well-floured surface and

Southern Turkey: Kurdish nomads and their tents

knead for 10 minutes.) Cover the dough and let stand until you are ready to proceed further, from 15 minutes to 3 hours.

Line the bottom rack of your oven with quarry tiles, leaving a 1-inch gap between the tiles and the oven walls. Preheat the oven to 450°F.

continued

Divide the dough into 8 pieces, and flatten each on the well-floured surface. With a rolling pin, roll out one or two breads to very thin rounds, about 8 to 10 inches in diameter. (Work with only as many as will fit in your oven at one time.) Handling the breads gently, place on the hot tiles (you can also dust a baker's peel or the back of a baking sheet with flour and use the peel or sheet to transfer the breads to the hot tiles). Bake for 1½ to 2 minutes, then turn over and bake for another minute, or until the breads begin to brown around the edges. (We sometimes bake this bread for nearly twice as long, or until both sides are spotted with brown all over. These breads are very attractive, but crisper. Try both ways.)

Keep the baked breads warm by stacking them and wrapping them in a clean kitchen towel while you roll out and bake the remaining breads. Serve warm or at room temperature.

·· ▲▲▲▲▲··▲▲▲▲▲▲▲▲··▲

Makes 8 thin, supple, and slightly chewy flatbreads, between 8 and 10 inches in diameter.

Serve with Cutting-Board Salsa (page 178), Armenian Tomato and Eggplant Salsa (page 287), Okra and Chicken Stew (page 286), or grilled meats such as Marinated Lamb Kebabs (below). This is an excellent bread for the mezze table (see page 203).

Marinated Lamb Kebabs
kebab • Turkey

Tradition has it that the method of grilling meat on skewers was brought to Turkey and the Eastern Mediterranean by Mongol invaders, nomadic herdsmen from the steppes of Central Asia who cooked their fresh-killed sheep on their swords or spears over open fires. Whether or not the legend is true, kebab, or shashlik as it is also known, is found as far east as the Caucasus Mountains and beyond to Tajikistan and Uzbekistan, Mongolia, and Chinese Central Asia, as well as west to Morocco (where it is now known by the French word *brochette*).

This traditional kebab takes large chunks of lamb and keeps them tender and moist on the grill. The secret? In classic Turkish style, a method that spread far and wide with the Ottoman Empire, the marinade has an onion juice base and the meat is grilled on its own, without pieces of tomato or pepper, since many cooks in the region believe that juices from the vegetables toughen the meat during grilling.

1 pound onions, peeled

1 tablespoon salt

½ cup olive oil

3 tablespoons fresh lemon juice

2 teaspoons freshly ground black pepper

3 pounds boneless leg of lamb trimmed of fat and sinew and cut into 1-inch cubes

You will need a food processor, a fine-meshed sieve, a medium-sized bowl, a large shallow nonreactive bowl, a charcoal or gas grill, and 12 metal skewers.

Grate or mince the onions in the food processor. Place in a fine-meshed sieve over a bowl, add the salt, and stir well. The onion will shed its juice into the bowl. You should get approximately ½ cup onion juice; discard the onions.

Transfer the juice to a large shallow bowl. Add the oil, lemon juice, and pepper. Place the meat chunks in the marinade, and stir to coat. Cover, refrigerate, and let marinate for 6 to 8 hours.

About 1 hour before you want to serve the meal, remove the meat from the refrigerator. Prepare a charcoal or gas grill.

Thread the meat onto 12 metal skewers so that the pieces are just touching, not tightly squeezed together. Grill the

Street vendor grilling lamb kebabs

meat on a rack about 5 inches from the heat for 15 to 20 minutes, until only slightly pink inside. (Because the marinade adds flavor and succulence, even meat that is cooked through or slightly charred will still be moist and full of flavor.) Serve hot.

.·▲▲▲▲▲▲▲·▲▲▲··▲▲▲··▲

Serves 8.

Offer Pita (page 181), Afghan Snowshoe Naan (page 40), Paperthin Lavash (page 283), or Bedouin Barley Bread (page 212), for wrapping chunks of lamb as they are pulled from the skewers. Serve with Cutting-Board Salsa (page 178), Olive Salad (page 180), a plate of fresh herbs, and Mint and Yogurt Sauce (page 43) or Herb and Pepper Relish (page 301).

Cutting-Board Salsa

mezair • Kurdistan

Our household name for mezair is "cutting-board salsa," because all the in-gredients can be chopped together into one large pile on a cutting board—an excellent way to blend the different flavors, and it's fun. I first tasted this salsa in the town of Van in eastern Turkey, where it was served alongside pieces of grilled chicken and a bulgur pilaf; the combination was absolutely delicious. The amount of chiles in this recipe produces a salsa that is mildly hot; adjust according to your own taste.

1 large clove garlic

2 to 3 jalapeños, seeded

½ cup lightly packed chopped
 flat-leafed parsley

3 to 4 tablespoons chopped fresh
 mint

1 pound ripe tomatoes

¼ teaspoon salt

Juice of 1 lemon

You will need a large cutting board.

On a large cutting board, mince the garlic and then the chiles. Add the parsley and mint and chop. Slice and then chop the tomatoes, adding them to the other ingredients. Mix as you continue to chop by turning the salsa with the flat of your knife or cleaver. Mix in the salt. Transfer the salsa to a small serving bowl and blend in the lemon juice. The salsa will be quite runny, making it ideal for being spooned generously over bulgur or rice or for being sopped up with flatbreads.

Makes approximately 2 cups salsa.

Serve with Bulgur Bread (page 175), Pita (page 181), or Paperthin Lavash (page 283). This salsa makes a colorful addition to the mezze table (see page 203).

Bulgur Pilaf

plof • Kurdistan

Bulgur pilafs are so easy, delicious, and versatile that they can become a household staple. We like to prepare this Kurdish recipe as part of a Thanksgiving dinner; in its way, it almost becomes the centerpiece of the meal. Tomato and sweet pepper are lightly stir-fried, then cooked with the bulgur in a chicken broth. The bulgur absorbs the liquid as it cooks, and as it simmers in the stock, it absorbs flavor from the vegetables. The dish is ready in less than twenty minutes—light fluffy grains punctuated with colorful pieces of tomato, basil, and pepper.

1 tablespoon olive oil

2 scallions, finely chopped

½ cup finely chopped red bell pepper

1 large tomato, chopped

½ cup loosely packed fresh basil
    leaves

1 cup medium or coarse bulgur

2½ cups boiling chicken stock or
    water

½ teaspoon salt

You will need a large heavy saucepan.

Heat the oil in a large saucepan over medium-high heat. Add the scallions and bell pepper and stir-fry for 30 seconds. Add the tomato and basil and continue to stir-fry for 2 minutes. Add the bulgur and mix well. Pour in the boiling stock or water, add the salt, and mix well. Bring the liquid to a boil, and then reduce the heat to low. Simmer uncovered until all the liquid has been absorbed, about 15 minutes. Serve hot.

··▲▲▲▲▲▲·▲··▲▲▲·▲▲▲·▲▲

Serves 4 to 6 as part of a meal.

Serve with Pita (page 181) or Georgian Cheese-Filled Quick Breads (page 292),
accompanied by Cutting-Board Salsa (page 178) and Grilled Marinated
Chicken (page 222) or Olive Salad (page 180).

Olive Salad

*Olives of every kind—hard green, splotchy purple-mauve, small and wrink-*led black—are on display in markets all around the Mediterranean. Their flavors vary from tart to fruity with all shades between—a far cry from tasteless lye-cured "California-style" olives. Olive salads around the Mediterranean are equally varied. In Morocco, they are usually spiced with cumin and a little harissa, which gives a hot tang to each mouthful. We like this milder salad, similar to those we've eaten in Turkey and Syria. The contrasting crunch of the onion is a pleasure, as is the bright green of the parsley. The salad is wonderful as an hors d'oeuvre or a side dish, scooped up with pieces of fresh bread. Note that the recipe is not precise about salt; salt-cured olives are somewhat salty already, but to varying degrees.

½ cup fresh lemon juice

1 tablespoon extra-virgin olive oil

2 cups Kalamata or other large purple olives, pitted and coarsely chopped

1 medium red onion, finely chopped

1 cup packed flat-leafed parsley, finely chopped

Salt to taste

You will need a small bowl.

Whisk together the lemon juice and oil.

Place the olives, onion, and parsley in a bowl. Pour over the lemon and oil mixture, and stir well. Taste for salt, and season accordingly.

The salad can be served immediately, or prepared ahead and refrigerated, covered, for up to 6 hours. Serve at room temperature.

· · · ▲ ▲ ▲ ▲ ▲ ▲ ▲ · ▲ · ▲ ▲ ▲ ▲ ▲ ▲ ▲ · ▲

Serves 4 to 6 as an hors d'oeuvre or side salad or 8 to 10 as part of a mezze table (see page 203).

Serve with plenty of breads: Hot Chile Bread (page 201), Thyme Bread (page 207), Bulgur Bread (page 175), or Pita (page 181) are all good matches for the olives.

Pita

Pita, commonly referred to in Arabic as khubz ("bread"), is the most widely available bread throughout the Eastern Mediterranean. Unfortunately, in these days of mass production, even there the khubz that makes its way to restaurant tables is often the same ubiquitous too-quick-to-go-stale white pita served in restaurants in North America. This is not true in Egypt, however, where the local pita—called *baladi*—is made from 100 percent whole wheat flour and freshly baked several times a day in neighborhood bakeries. To a visitor, bread can seem unbelievably cheap, because it is subsidized by the government. The quality of the baladi, as well as its price, is strictly controlled by the government; bread is an important political issue, just as it is in many other places all around the world.

As for homemade pita, cast away any thought of those white cardboard-like supermarket breads. Fresh homemade whole wheat pitas, or those made with half white, half whole wheat, are quick and delicious. They are most easily made on quarry tiles or baking sheets in the oven, but they can also be baked on a griddle or in a cast-iron skillet on the stove.

2 teaspoons dry yeast	1 tablespoon salt
2½ cups lukewarm water	1 tablespoon olive oil
5 to 6 cups hard whole wheat flour, or 3 cups each hard whole wheat flour and hard unbleached white flour, or unbleached all-purpose flour	

You will need a large bread bowl, unglazed quarry tiles (see page 20) to fit on a rack in your oven or several baking sheets, or a cast-iron or other heavy griddle or skillet at least 9 inches in diameter, and a rolling pin.

In a large bread bowl, sprinkle the yeast over the warm water. Stir to dissolve. Stir in 3 cups flour, a cup at a time, and then stir 100 times, about 1 minute, in the same direction to activate the gluten. Let this sponge rest for at least 10 minutes, or as long as 2 hours.

Sprinkle the salt over the sponge and stir in the olive oil. Mix well. Add more flour, a cup at a time, until the dough is too stiff to stir. Turn it out onto a lightly floured surface and knead for 8 to 10 minutes, until smooth and elastic. Rinse out the bowl, dry, and lightly oil. Return the dough to the bowl and cover with plastic wrap. Let rise until at least doubled in size, approximately 1½ hours. (The dough can be made ahead to this point and stored, covered, in the refrigerator for up to 7 days.

To save the dough in the refrigerator for baking later, gently punch it down. Wrap it in a plastic bag that is at least three times as large as the dough, and secure it just at the opening of the bag; this will give the dough room to expand while it is in the refrigerator. Then, from day to day, simply cut off the amount of dough you need and keep the rest in the refrigerator. After a few days, the dough will smell increasingly fermented, but the fermentation actually improves the taste of the bread, especially if baked on quarry tiles. The dough should always be brought to room temperature before baking.)

If baking the breads: Place unglazed quarry tiles, or two small baking sheets, on the bottom rack of your oven, leaving a 1-inch gap all around between the tiles or sheets and the oven walls to allow heat to circulate. Preheat the oven to 450°F.

Gently punch down the dough. Divide the dough in half, then set half aside, covered, while you work with the rest. Divide the other half into 8 equal pieces and flatten each piece with lightly floured hands. Roll out each piece to a circle 8 to 9 inches in diameter and less than ¼ inch thick. Keep the rolled-out breads covered until ready to bake, but do not stack.

Place 2 breads, or more if your oven is large enough, on the quarry tiles or baking sheets, and bake for 2 to 3 minutes, or until each bread has gone into a full "balloon." If there are seams or dry bits of dough, or for a variety of other reasons—e.g., your quarry tiles are not sufficiently preheated—the breads may not balloon properly. But don't worry, they will still taste great. The more you bake pitas, the more you will become familiar with all the little tricks and possible pitfalls, and your breads will more consistently balloon. Wrap the baked breads together in a large kitchen towel to keep them warm and soft while you bake the remaining rolled-out breads. Then repeat with the rest of the dough.

To cook the pitas on top of the stove: Preheat a 9-inch or larger griddle or cast-iron skillet over medium-high heat. When hot, lightly grease the surface of the griddle with a little oil.

Meanwhile, gently punch down the dough and divide it in half. Cover one half and divide the other half into 8 pieces. Flatten each piece with well-floured hands, then roll out one at a time into circles less than ¼ inch thick and 8 to 9 inches in diameter.

Gently put one bread onto the griddle. Cook for 15 to 20 seconds, then gently turn over. Cook for about 1 minute, until big bubbles begin to appear. Turn the bread again to the first side, and cook until the bread balloons fully. To help the process along, you can press gently with a towel on those areas where bubbles have already formed, trying to push the air bubble into areas that are still flat. (This is a technique that will quickly improve with practice). The breads should take no more than 3 minutes to cook, and, likewise, they shouldn't cook so fast that they begin to burn; adjust the heat until you find a workable temperature. Wrap the cooked breads in a large kitchen towel to keep them warm and soft while you cook and roll out the rest of the dough in the same way. There is no need to oil the griddle between each bread, but after 4 or 5 breads, you might want to lightly oil the surface again.

Alternatives: You can, of course, make smaller breads by dividing the dough into smaller pieces. The rolling out and cooking method and times remain the same. Children particularly love smaller pocket breads.

·٠٠▲▲▲▲▲▲▲▲٠٠▲▲▲▲▲▲▲▲٠٠▲

Makes approximately 16 pocket breads, 8 to 9 inches in diameter.

Serve with any Central Asian or western Asian meal. Always have stacks of fresh pita on the mezze table (see page 203), whole or cut in wedges, and wrapped to keep soft and warm.
Use to make Toasted Pita (page 184).

Toasted Pita

fattah • Eastern Mediterranean

Toasted breads, or Mediterranean croutons, as we like to call them, are a great way to use slightly tired or dried-out flatbreads. Pita or any other predominantly wheat-flour flatbread will work well; an eight-inch pita yields approximately one loosely packed cup of toasted triangles. They can be prepared ahead, then stored in a plastic bag.

4 fresh or dried-out pita or other pocket-style or thin flatbreads
3 to 4 tablespoons olive oil

You will need two baking sheets.

Preheat the oven to 300°F.

Brush the breads with the oil. Cut each bread into 8 wedges, then split each wedge apart. Spread on two baking sheets. Place in the center of the oven and bake for 15 minutes, turning the breads over after 8 to 10 minutes. Remove from the oven and let cool. The triangles will crisp up as they cool and can then be stored in tightly sealed plastic bags.

··▲▲▲▲▲▲▲·▲▲▲▲▲▲▲▲·▲▲

Makes approximately 4 cups toasted bread triangles.

Use in Bread Salad (page 186) and Layered Chicken and Yogurt Casserole (page 187), and for Yemeni Yogurt Soup (page 185), or use as you would croutons, to enhance and garnish a broth or other soup.

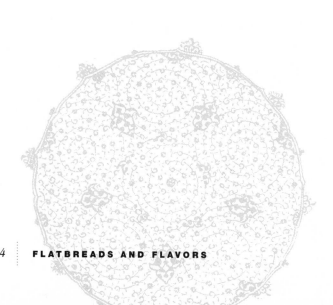

Yemeni Yogurt Soup

chefout • Yemen

Yogurt-based soups are popular throughout western Asia. Served with bread, they make for simple and nutritious meals. In this Yemeni version, toasted bread adds both flavor and a wonderful contrast in texture. Serve it cold, with fresh breads.

2 cups plain 2% or whole-milk yogurt, chilled

1 cup 2% or whole milk

1 cup fresh coriander leaves, finely chopped

2 medium cloves garlic, minced

1 to 2 jalapeños, seeded and finely chopped

2 cups Toasted Pita (page 184), crumbled into bite-sized pieces

Sprigs of fresh coriander for garnish

You will need a blender or food processor.

Combine all the ingredients except the toasted pita in a blender or food processor and blend well. Place a handful of toasted pita in the bottom of each soup plate and pour the soup over. Serve immediately, garnished with sprigs of fresh coriander.

··▲▲▲▲▲▲·▲▲·▲▲▲▲▲▲·▲

Serves 4.

Serve accompanied by a salad such as Lentil and Sweet Pepper Salad (page 199) or Chickpea Salad with Spearmint (page 200) and plenty of San'a Sorghum Bread (page 189), Bedouin Barley Bread (page 212), or Pita (page 181).

Bread Salad

fattoush • Israel, Jordan, Lebanon, and Syria

The root word for all the dishes in the Arab world using toasted flatbread is fatta—hence fatteh, fattoush, etc. As with most home-cooked dishes, there are a great many versions of fattoush, especially in Syria and Lebanon. This one uses crisp flatbreads to enhance the taste and texture of a fresh tomato and cucumber salad.

Our all-time favorite cucumbers, tender and very sweet, are not often available in North America—even as seeds for planting. They are generally referred to as Middle Eastern cucumbers and look like smaller, finer versions of an English cucumber. They are so good that it is worth asking your local produce market if they can be stocked.

Even without that wonderful variety of cucumber, however, fattoush is a simple, refreshing dish that can be served as part of a mezze meal or as a salad on a hot day, to be scooped up with fresh pita. It should be dressed ahead and allowed to stand for twenty minutes. Then, at the last minute, the toasted pitas are crumbled and stirred in; their slightly crunchy texture is a wonderful contrast to the wet softness of the tomatoes and cucumbers.

2 cups chopped plum tomatoes

1 cup sliced peeled English or Middle Eastern cucumber (quartered lengthwise and thinly sliced)

1 cup chopped scallions

1 cup finely chopped flat-leafed parsley

1½ cups Toasted Pita (page 184)

dressing

1 small clove garlic, crushed

¼ cup extra-virgin olive oil

¼ cup fresh lemon juice

½ teaspoon ground sumac (see page 418) or 1 tablespoon additional lemon juice, or to taste

½ teaspoon salt

¼ teaspoon freshly ground black pepper

You will need a small bowl.

Place all the salad ingredients except the toasted pita in a serving bowl.

Whisk together the garlic, oil, and lemon juice in a small bowl. Pour over the salad and toss well. Let stand for 20 to 30 minutes.

Just before serving, crumble the toasted bread into bite-sized pieces and add to the salad, together with the sumac, salt, and pepper. Toss well. Serve with plenty of soft flatbreads, which can be used to scoop up the salad.

Serves 4 to 6 as part of a meal or a mezze table (see page 203).

Serve with fresh warm Pita (page 181) or Thyme Bread (page 207) to accompany grilled meats, such as Grilled Marinated Chicken (page 222), or with a filled bread such as Lamb and Tomato Breads (page 197) for a simple lunch, perhaps accompanied by Yemeni Yogurt Soup (page 185).

Layered Chicken and Yogurt Casserole
fatteh djaj • Lebanon and Syria

Not only is this casserole a wonderful invention for using leftover pitas, but it is also a spectacular-looking dish guaranteed to dazzle guests. It is easy to prepare, and not nearly so time-consuming as the length of the recipe might suggest. This recipe is inspired by a dish in Mary Laird Hamady's wonderful cookbook *Lebanese Mountain Cookery*. In this particular interpretation of chicken fatteh, the chicken is poached and then both the meat and the cooking broth are combined with rice, yogurt, and toasted bread in a casserole that needs no further other cooking. The chicken and broth can be cooked ahead, then taken from the refrigerator or freezer just before you begin to cook the rice; the last steps take thirty minutes at most.

During the final assembly stage, you may find that you want to arrange the ingredients slightly differently. What is important is that the bread pieces be toasted so they can absorb moisture and flavor, and that some combination of yogurt, herbs, and pine nuts tops things off.

One 3-pound roasting chicken (makes 3 to 4 cups meat) 2½ quarts water

1 tablespoon black peppercorns

One 2-inch cinnamon stick

¼ teaspoon cloves

1 medium onion, coarsely chopped

1 to 2 large sprigs fresh thyme

2 cups plain yogurt

1 cup long-grain white rice

4 cloves garlic, finely chopped or crushed

Juice of 1 lemon

1½ teaspoons salt

4 cups Toasted Pita (page 184)

¾ cup mixed finely chopped flat-leafed parsley and fresh mint

3 tablespoons pine nuts, dry-roasted until golden (see page 154)

2 tablespoons unsalted pistachios, coarsely chopped

continued

You will need a large pot with a lid, a sieve, cheesecloth, a medium-sized bowl, a pot with a tight-fitting lid, and a small saucepan.

Wash the chicken. Pull off the skin and trim off excess fat.

Place the cold water and chicken in a large soup pot. Add the peppercorns, cinnamon, cloves, onion, and thyme and bring to a boil over medium-high heat. Lower the heat and simmer gently, partially covered, for 1 hour. Remove from the heat.

Meanwhile, place the yogurt in a sieve or colander lined with cheesecloth (see Yogurt Cheese balls, page 206, for details) and let drain over a bowl for 1 hour to thicken.

Remove the chicken from the broth with tongs, and place the chicken on a work surface. Let cool somewhat, then pull the chicken meat off the bones, shredding it into bite-sized pieces. Discard the bones. Strain the broth and discard the solids. Pour 4½ cups of broth into a container and place the broth in the refrigerator to cool. (If you are in a rush, you can skip this step and use the broth without defatting it.) Set aside the remainder of the broth in the refrigerator or freezer for another use. (The recipe can be prepared ahead to this point and the chicken, broth, and yogurt stored, covered, in the refrigerator for up to 48 hours.) Skim the fat off the surface of the cooled broth.

Rinse the rice thoroughly in cold water until the water runs clear, then drain well. Place in a saucepan with a tight-fitting lid and add 2¼ cups of the defatted broth. Bring to a vigorous boil, then cover, reduce the heat to very low, and cook for 20 minutes. Remove from the heat.

Meantime, combine the remainder of the defatted broth, the chopped garlic, and lemon juice in a small saucepan and bring to a gentle boil. Add 1 teaspoon of the salt and simmer for 5 minutes. (If you have refrigerated the chicken pieces, place them in the broth to rewarm.) You are now ready to assemble the fatteh.

Assemble the fatteh on a large shallow serving dish (we use one that is about 8 inches across the bottom with gently sloping sides about 4 inches high) or a platter: Leave 1 cup of the toasted pita in triangle-shaped pieces and break up the rest into bite-sized pieces. Spread the broken pieces over the bottom of the dish and lean the triangles up against the sides or, if using a platter, place around the edge. Pour two thirds of the garlic broth over the crumpled bread. Spoon on the rice, spreading it evenly, then distribute the chicken pieces evenly over the rice. Pour the remainder of the broth over the chicken.

Mix together the yogurt and the remaining ½ teaspoon salt and spread over the chicken. Scatter the chopped herbs over the yogurt, then sprinkle on the pine nuts and chopped pistachios. Alternatively, you can mix the chopped mint into the yogurt, leaving only the parsley and nuts as top dressing; we prefer the dense mixture of both herbs on top—try it both ways. Serve immediately.

..▲▲▲▲▲▲▲▲▲▲▲▲▲▲▲▲▲▲

Serves 6 to 8 as a one-dish meal.

Serve accompanied by Pita (page 181) and a salad such as Herbed Carrot Salad (page 248).

✳

San'a Sorghum Breads
kutma • Yemen

Sorghum is one of the world's most commonly eaten grains. The plant is gen-erally resistant to drought and can grow well in hot climates and where the growing season is short. It is Africa's most important food grain, and is also widely cultivated in India and China. Several varieties grow up to ten feet tall; the stalks are used as a building material as well as a valuable source of fuel.

Sorghum breads can be found wherever sorghum is an important part of the food supply. Sorghum flour is often mixed with wheat flour when both are available. In several different instances in Turkmenistan, in Central Asia, we were told that a small amount of sorghum flour should be added to any wheat flour dough to help improve the taste and texture of the bread, much as rye or buckwheat flour is sometimes added to bread doughs in France. With collective farming imposed on Turkmenistan, people lament that few farms now bother to grow the sorghum

needed to supply local bakers: "You should have tasted the bread here in the old days!"

Sorghum growing in Yemen

Despite its worldwide use, sorghum flour can be hard to find in North America. (The United States is, ironically, the world's major producer of sorghum, but the grain is used almost entirely as animal food.) We've recently been able to find sorghum flour in a well-stocked Indian grocery under its Hindi name, *juwar,* although the first time we took it up to the cashier, he shook his head and told us that we didn't want to buy it: "It's poor people's food," he said, "you won't like it." But we do like it, and wish only that we could find a fresher supply.

continued

These sorghum breads come from Yemen, where sorghum is the major cereal crop. The breads are large soft rolls with a good crust and pleasing mixed-grain flavor. In the highlands of Yemen, sorghum is grown on centuries-old stone-walled terraces that follow the contours of the hillsides. As the young shoots grow, the terraces are filled with their rich bright green—hardly the usual image westerners have of the Arabian Peninsula.

2½ cups lukewarm water	2 teaspoons salt
2 teaspoons dry yeast	2 to 3 cups sorghum flour
3 cups hard unbleached white flour	

You will need a large bread bowl and a large baking sheet.

Put the warm water in a large bread bowl and sprinkle the yeast on top. Gently stir to dissolve the yeast. Then, stir in the unbleached flour, a cup at a time. Stir the batter 100 times in the same direction, about 1 minute, to help develop the gluten. Cover this sponge with plastic wrap and let stand for 30 minutes to 1 hour.

Sprinkle the salt over the sponge, then sprinkle on 1 cup sorghum flour, and stir to mix. Add more sorghum flour, ½ cup at a time, until the dough is too stiff to stir. Turn it out onto a floured surface, and knead for approximately 8 minutes, until smooth and elastic. Use additional sorghum flour as needed to prevent the dough from sticking to your work surface. Rinse and dry your bread bowl, lightly oil, and place the dough in the bowl. Cover with plastic wrap and let rise for 1½ to 2 hours, until approximately doubled.

Gently punch down the dough and let rest five minutes.

Lightly oil a 12- by 18-inch baking sheet.

Knead the dough for 1 to 2 minutes on a lightly floured surface. Divide the dough in half, and put one half aside, covered with plastic wrap. Roll out the other half into a rectangle approximately 8 inches by 14 inches. Starting at a narrow end of the rectangle, roll up the dough, keeping it fairly tight, into a jelly-roll shape. Using a sharp knife, slice the roll into 8 equal pieces. Lay one of the slices about 4½ inches from one end of the baking sheet and arrange the others around it, like petals on a flower, leaving ½ inch between each bread. Repeat the process with the remaining dough. (As the breads bake, the pieces will bake into each other.)

Cover with plastic wrap and let rise for 30 minutes.

Preheat the oven to 375°F. Place the baking sheet in the center of the oven and bake for 30 minutes, or until the breads are slightly brown on top and hollow-sounding when tapped on the bottom. Cool on a rack before serving.

Makes 16 round sorghum breads.

Sorghum breads make a great traditional meal served with Yemeni Stew (page 194) or with Spicy Yemeni Salsa (below). Break up into rolls and serve in a cloth-lined basket. These breads have a very easy good flavor; they are delicious eaten on their own or as part of virtually any bread and soup combination.

Spicy Yemeni Salsa

zhoug • Israel

This distinctive sauce of fresh green herbs, chiles, and spices comes from the Yemeni community in Israel. Mention Yemeni food to an Israeli and he or she will immediately think of zhoug—a hot dip for breads that is a staple in the community. There is green zhoug and red zhoug; we tasted several versions of each in Israel and then developed this recipe for the herb-laden green version. (Oddly enough, we never ran across zhoug in Yemen, but there was a closely related sauce called hilbeh, made with fenugreek and plenty of fresh coriander.)

¾ pound Anaheim chiles (see page 410), stemmed

1 jalapeño, stemmed

1 cup loosely packed fresh coriander leaves

1 cup loosely packed flat-leafed parsley

1 tablespoon finely chopped garlic

1 teaspoon salt

1 teaspoon ground cumin seed from 4 to 5 green cardamom pods (see page 409), ground to a powder

You will need a blender or food processor.

Place all the ingredients in a blender or food processor and process until smooth.

Serve in a small bowl as a dipping sauce for bread. The salsa can be stored in a well-sealed glass container in the refrigerator for 4 to 5 days.

Makes approximately 2 cups salsa.

Serve as a dipping sauce for San'a Sorghum Bread (page 189) or any soft flatbread. This makes an excellent condiment with grilled meats and a pretty, bright green dipping sauce for the mezze table (see page 203).

CULTURAL CHANGE

Ed Keale, an archaeologist and the curator of the West Asian Department of the Royal Ontario Museum in Toronto, told us the following story as we were preparing for a visit to Yemen. When we explained the purpose of the trip—that is, to learn more about flatbreads—Dr. Keale smiled. He is a West Asian specialist: Consequently, a good portion of his life's work has been in small, out-of-the-way places in western Asia where flatbreads can be, for the most part, the only food available. Dr. Keale may not study flatbreads, but he knows a lot about them.

"I learned an important lesson in archaeology," Dr. Keale explained with a laugh, "all because of flatbreads. In the 1960s I worked for several years on a project in the western part of Iran, just near the Iraq border. In the small village where I lived, the staple food was lavash. It was made very thin and baked in a tannur oven. It would immediately dry out; the way people ate the dried bread was to sprinkle it with water and wrap it in a towel. But I never really liked it. You know how bread goes when you try to bring it back to life in a microwave? Well, it was a little bit like that: Eat it quickly or suffer.

"We had a person we hired to help cook. One day I asked him if he could make a different kind of bread. We went to the market together to buy flour, and we discussed the problem at length. The kind of bread I had in mind was something like sanguake, the Iranian bread baked in an oven on hot pebbles. I liked sanguake because it was thicker and soft inside. Our cook had no idea how to make sanguake, but he agreed to try. So he tried, but it was a dismal failure. His bread came out gooey and just awful, really inedible. We went back to eating lavash.

"My project was discontinued soon after but I had an opportunity to go back to Iraq as part of a study group nearly ten years later. One of my first surprises arriving back was seeing people in the village eating a bread I'd never seen before. It was round and a little bit thick, like the sorghum breads in Yemen. Everyone was eating it; it had become the staple food of the village. Lavash was still around, as it was used in religious ceremonies, but this new bread was definitely the staple.

"When I ran into our old cook, I asked him where the new bread had come from, what its origins were. Maybe it was from a different region of the country?

" 'No,' he told me, looking very bewildered. 'Don't you remember the bread you asked me to make? This is the bread. . . .' "

Dr. Keale laughed once more: "I will never forget it. As an archaeologist I think always of things changing slowly over a long period of time. And food, food is so specific to a culture. It makes you wonder about certain theories. . . ."

Yogurt and Pomegranate Dip

akeel • Yemen

*One afternoon in San'a, the capital of Yemen, I was browsing through a sta-*tionery store, looking for a new pen. When I'd picked one out and stepped up to the counter to pay, the man behind the cash register asked me in fluent English where I was from and whether I'd had a chance to visit one of the great old houses in the center of the city. If I hadn't, he went on, I was welcome to come see his. Dying to go, I said that I'd be delighted.

San'a: Traditional houses

I waited around for fifteen or twenty minutes, and then he locked up the shop and away we went. On the way home we stopped in the market to buy a neatly packed bunch of *qat* leaves, which in Yemen are chewed for a mild sort of high. When we at last got to his house, we climbed up a white-washed winding staircase, eight or nine stories high. Only at the top, as we emerged into a room lit on three sides by double-paned stained glass windows, could I make out where I was. This small beautiful room, called a *mafraj,* was white-washed like the staircase and strewn with old, colorful carpets and large cushions. I was delighted to discover that the interiors of San'a's towering old houses are as incredible as the exteriors. They are, without a doubt, some of the most extraordinary homes in the world.

For the next two or three hours we chewed qat (he taught me how), smoked tobacco (not my favorite pastime) from a huge waterpipe in the middle of the room, and watched Egyptian soap operas on television. At one point my host disappeared, then returned with two bowls of akeel. Colorful, unique, and refreshing, it was a great surprise—like so much else in Yemen.

·· ▲ ▲ ▲ ▲ ▲ · ▲ · ▲ ▲ ▲ ▲ ▲ ▲ ▲ ▲ ·· ▲

Akeel takes only minutes to put together. The preparation is simply a matter of stirring fresh coriander, pomegranate seeds, and chopped scallions into chilled yogurt. Akeel is beautiful served in glass bowls.

1 ripe pomegranate

2 cups plain yogurt, chilled

2 scallions, finely chopped (white and
    tender green parts)

¼ cup chopped fresh coriander

Sprigs of fresh mint for garnish
    (optional)

continued

You will need a small bowl.

Cut the pomegranate in half across its equator, then gently lift out the seeds, section by section, and set aside in a bowl, discarding any discolored parts. You don't want the seeds to "bleed" their juices into the yogurt, so try not to bruise or break them.

Place the yogurt in a glass or other decorative serving bowl. Stir in the scallions, coriander, and all but a small handful of the pomegranate seeds. Garnish with mint sprigs and sprinkle the remaining pomegranate seeds on top. Serve slightly chilled.

·· ▲ ▲ ▲ ▲ ▲ · ▲ · ▲ ▲ ▲ ▲ ▲ ▲ ▲ · ▲ ▲ · ▲

Makes 2½ cups dip.

Serve akeel to guests on a warm autumn afternoon (when pomegranates are in season) as a refreshing snack on its own or with Sweet Persian Bread (page 62). Alternatively, include it on a mezze table (see page 203) or in other meals as a dip or sauce for bread, grilled meats, or steamed vegetables.

Yemeni Stew

saltah bi hulba • Yemen

In the practice of Buddhism there is something referred to as "beginner's mind." Like the mind of a young child, a beginner's mind is open and sees every-

Yemen: "Truckstop" selling Yemeni lamb stew

thing as if for the first time. We sometimes like to think of travel from the perspective of a beginner's mind, as there is nothing quite like plopping yourself down into a place about which you know very little, a place where even the simplest of things cannot be taken for granted.

My beginner's mind was ready and alert as my plane landed in San'a. Without a single sentence in Yemeni, and not having spent much time in any Arab country, I was at a complete loss when it came to almost everything.

In those first few days, exploring villages and towns outside San'a, I'd go looking for something to eat in the afternoon or evening but would often come up emptyhanded. I couldn't figure out meal patterns, or even where to find bread. One lucky afternoon I stumbled into a dark little restaurant at lunchtime. There was great activity as people devoured a hot, soupy stew with chunks of sorghum flat-breads. All I had to do was to sit down, and instantly an earthenware pot of stew and a plate of breads arrived. And when I tasted . . . oh, I was hooked: hulba and saltah, the national dish of the Yemen highlands.

1½ teaspoons vegetable oil	½ pound potatoes, cut into ½-inch cubes
2 medium yellow onions, diced	1 tablespoon salt
1¼ pounds boneless chicken or lamb, trimmed of fat	2 tablespoons fresh coriander leaves
8 cups water	1 recipe Spicy Fenugreek Sauce (page 196)
½ cup mung dal (see page 412)	

You will need a large pot with a lid.

Heat the oil in a large pot, and gently sauté the onions over medium heat for 2 minutes. Add the chicken or lamb and sauté until lightly browned on all sides. Add the water, turn the heat to high, and bring to a boil. Add the dal and bring back to a boil, skimming off any foam that comes to the surface. Lower the heat, partially cover, and let simmer for 1 hour, or until the meat is tender and the dal is cooked.

Add the potatoes, increase the heat to high, and bring to a boil. Then lower the heat and simmer until the potatoes are tender, about 10 minutes. Remove from the heat.

Remove the chicken or lamb from the broth. Shred into small pieces, and return to the broth. Add the salt and coriander leaves. Bring to a boil. Whisk the Spicy Fenugreek Sauce to a froth, and add to the stew. Serve immediately.

.‚‚▲▲▲▲▲‚‚‚▲▲‚‚‚▲▲‚‚▲

Serves 4 as a one-dish meal.

Serve with San'a Sorghum Breads (page 189), Bedouin Barley Bread (page 212), or Pita (page 181).

Spicy Fenugreek Sauce

hulbah • Yemen

This is the enticing sauce I tasted in Yemeni Stew.

¼ cup fenugreek (see page 414)

1 cup boiling water

3 cloves garlic, finely chopped

¼ cup finely chopped onion

2 large tomatoes, chopped

½ teaspoon cayenne

½ teaspoon salt

Freshly ground black pepper to taste

You will need a spice grinder and a small bowl.

In a spice grinder, grind the fenugreek to a powder. Transfer to a small bowl, and cover with boiling water. Let sit for 2 to 3 hours.

Add all the remaining ingredients and stir until well blended. This keeps well sealed and refrigerated, for 4 to 5 days.

·∙▲▲▲▲▲▴∙▴▴▲▲▴▴▴▴▴∙▴

Makes approximately 1 cup sauce.

Use as an ingredient in Yemeni Stew (page 194).

Lamb and Tomato Breads
lachmanjan, lachma bi ajun
Syria, Lebanon, Israel, and Turkey

*These savory breads are pretty as well as full of flavor. We like our lach-*manjan small, with a thin, almost crisp, crust; here the topping is a blend of tomato and lamb, lightly seasoned with allspice and cinnamon and sprinkled with pine nuts. These pizza-like breads make an excellent snack or appetizer. For a vegetarian version, omit the lamb, increase the amount of tomatoes and shallots, and scatter a little goat cheese on top, if you wish.

dough

1 cup lukewarm water

½ teaspoon honey

1 teaspoon dry yeast

1 cup hard unbleached white flour

½ teaspoon salt

1 tablespoon olive oil

Approximately 1½ cups hard whole wheat flour

filling

1 teaspoon olive oil

¼ cup finely chopped shallots

3 cloves garlic, finely chopped

¼ pound finely ground lean lamb

8 ripe plum tomatoes, chopped, or chopped canned plum tomatoes, well drained

⅛ teaspoon ground cinnamon

⅛ teaspoon allspice

½ teaspoon salt

¼ teaspoon freshly ground black pepper

1 to 2 tablespoons pine nuts

You will need a large bread bowl, a heavy skillet, several baking sheets and a small rolling pin.

In a large bowl, dissolve the honey in the lukewarm water. Stir in the yeast. Stir in the white flour, then stir in the salt, oil, and 1 cup of the whole wheat flour. Then stir 100 times in the same direction, about 1 minute, to develop the gluten. Stir in more whole wheat flour until the dough is too stiff to stir. Turn out onto a lightly floured work surface and knead for 8 to 10 minutes. Clean out the bowl, wipe dry, and lightly oil. Return the dough to the bowl, cover with plastic wrap, and let rise for 1½ to 2 hours, until more than doubled in volume.

While the dough is rising, prepare the filling: In a heavy skillet, heat the olive oil. Add the shallots and garlic and cook over medium heat until soft, 2 to 3 minutes, stirring occasionally. Add the lamb and cook for 2 to 3 minutes, or until the meat changes color. Add the tomatoes and cook over medium-low heat for 2 to 3 minutes until soft. Drain off any excess liquid; the filling should be moist but not watery. Stir in the cinnamon, allspice, salt, and pepper and set aside.

Gently punch the dough down, and turn out onto a lightly floured surface. With a sharp knife, cut into 12 pieces. Let rest, covered, for 5 to 10 minutes.

Preheat the oven to 450°F. Lightly oil two or three baking sheets.

Work with one piece of dough at a time, keeping the rest of the dough covered. With the lightly floured palm of your hand, flatten the dough. With a small rolling pin, roll out to a circle approximately 4 inches in diameter. Place 1½ to 2 tablespoons of the filling in the center of the bread, leaving a ½-inch border around the edge. Sprinkle a few pine nuts on top. Place the bread on a lightly oiled baking sheet, and continue to prepare breads in the same fashion. When the baking sheet is full, bake in the lower third of the oven until the crust is lightly browned, approximately 7 minutes. Set on a rack to cool slightly, then wrap in a cotton cloth to keep warm while you repeat with the remaining breads. Serve hot.

Alternatives: You can also serve lachmanjan as we've eaten them in Turkey, topped with a generous sprinkling of fresh mint and rolled up.

Makes 12 small round thin flatbreads, approximately 4 inches in diameter.
Serves 6 to 12 as a snack or part of a mezze table and 4 as part of a meal.

Serve as a snack or hors d'oeuvre or part of a mezze table (see page 203). Can also be served as a meal on its own, accompanied by Lentil and Sweet Pepper Salad (page 199) and Olive Salad (page 180).

Lentil and Sweet Pepper Salad

Eastern Mediterranean

You can sop up this easy lentil salad with flatbreads or, as our children do, spoon it up by the bowlful. For us it falls into the category of comfort food, fresh and nourishing but never overpowering. We always make a large quantity—as it tends to disappear quickly.

The lentils can be prepared ahead and stored, covered, in the refrigerator. You can also use half French-style green (Le Puy) lentils and half brown. Cook them separately, since green lentils tend to cook more quickly than brown lentils. The chopped peppers and other ingredients should be added just before serving.

1 cup brown or green lentils, washed, soaked for 30 minutes in 2 cups boiling water, and drained

3 cups water

2 cloves garlic, cut in half

1 medium to large red bell pepper, cored, seeds and membranes removed, and diced

2 tablespoons extra-virgin olive oil

½ teaspoon coriander seed (see page 412), dry-roasted (see page 154) and finely ground

½ teaspoon salt

½ teaspoon freshly ground black pepper

3 tablespoons fresh lemon juice

¼ cup packed fresh coriander leaves, finely chopped

You will need a saucepan with a lid and a small bowl.

Place the soaked lentils in a saucepan with the water and garlic cloves. Bring to a boil, then reduce the heat and simmer, partially covered, until lentils are tender but not mushy (30 to 45 minutes for brown lentils, 10 to 15 minutes for green). Drain, and discard the garlic. (The recipe can be prepared ahead to this point and the lentils stored in a well-sealed container in the refrigerator for up to 48 hours.)

Place the lentils in a shallow serving bowl. Add the peppers.

Place the olive oil in a small bowl. Add the ground coriander, salt, pepper, and lemon juice, and whisk to blend well. Stir in the coriander leaves. Pour the dressing over the lentils and peppers and mix gently. Serve at room temperature.

Serves 4 as a main dish or 8 to 10 as part of a mezze table.

Serve with Pita (page 181) or Lamb and Tomato Breads (page 197) as a simple yet satisfying lunch or light supper or place on the mezze table (see page 203).

Chickpea Salad with Spearmint

salatit bi humus • Lebanon, Syria, Israel

This quickly assembled chickpea salad uses dried spearmint and sumac, the classic flavors of Lebanon. The sumac gives extra zip to the lemon-based dressing. If you can't find ground sumac, you may want to increase the lemon juice by a tablespoon or so, or give the dressing a different emphasis by substituting a pinch of chile flakes. We prefer dried spearmint here; it has a more delicate taste and texture than all but the tenderest leaves of fresh mint. If you feel differently, substitute two tablespoons of finely chopped fresh mint for the spearmint.

2 cups cooked chickpeas (see Note) or
canned chickpeas, drained

1 teaspoon ground sumac (see page 418)

1 small clove garlic, crushed

2 tablespoons dried spearmint

2 tablespoons fresh lemon juice

1 tablespoon red wine vinegar

3 tablespoons olive oil

½ teaspoon salt, or more to taste

You will need a jar or small bowl.

Place the chickpeas in a serving bowl. In a jar or bowl, mix together all the remaining ingredients and shake or whisk well. Pour over the chickpeas, and stir to coat. Taste for seasoning and adjust as necessary. Let sit for at least 30 minutes before serving to give the flavors time to blend and to penetrate the chickpeas.

Note: Chickpeas (also known as garbanzos), like other legumes that require soaking and long cooking, are handy to have precooked in the freezer. To cook, soak overnight in three times their volume of water (they will almost double in volume), then drain and place in a large pot with twice their volume of water and, if you wish, a coarsely chopped onion. (Do not add salt; it will toughen the skin and prevent the chickpeas from cooking properly. Season, when using, after cooking.) Bring to a boil, then boil over medium heat until tender but not mushy, about 1½ hours. Check every so often to ensure that they do not run dry. When done, drain, reserving the water for vegetable stock, and freeze in pint containers. To use, just unfreeze in a little warm water over low heat.

·· ▲ ▲ ▲ ▲ ▲ · ▲ · ▲ ▲ · · ▲ ▲ ▲ · · · ▲

Serves 4.

Serve as part of a mezze table (see page 203) or as a salad, paired with Pita (page 181),
Hot Chile Bread (page 201), or Thyme Bread (page 207) and
Yemeni Yogurt Soup (page 185).

Hot Chile Bread

felaveri • Syria

Just around the block from the famous old Baron Hotel in Aleppo, Syria, there is a flatbread bakery that opens late in the afternoon and turns out a wonderful wide variety of breads until well into the night. You can't miss it—there is always a line of customers spilling out the door. All the breads are paperthin and soft, baked in a long, flat, wood-fired oven. Two breads come for the price of one; one has a topping and the other is plain. The plain one is placed on the savory one, and then the whole thing is rolled up into a big cigar that can be eaten as you walk along the street. I was so thrilled the first time I saw them that I bought one bread of every kind—enough food for an entire day.

It took us a long time and many failed attempts to successfully re-create the bakery's felaveri. No matter what we did, we couldn't keep the bread soft, until at last we devised this rather unorthodox way of using both the stovetop and the broiler. It may sound tedious, but you quickly get the hang of it and then it's very easy. If you wish to reproduce the bread-rolled-in-a-bread, make half the breads plain and half with topping.

d o u g h

2 teaspoons dry yeast

2½ cups warm water

5 to 6 cups hard unbleached white or all-purpose flour

2 teaspoons salt

t o p p i n g

¼ to ⅓ cup olive oil

1 tablespoon plus 1 teaspoon sesame seeds

2 to 4 teaspoons dried chile pepper flakes

You will need a medium-sized bread bowl, three small bowls, a rolling pin, and two cast-iron or other heavy skillets or griddles at least 10 inches in diameter.

In a bread bowl, dissolve the yeast in the warm water. Add 2 to 3 cups of flour, a cup at a time, stirring constantly in the same direction with a wooden spoon until a thick batter begins to form. Then stir 100 times in the same direction, about 1 minute, to help activate the gluten. Let rest for 10 minutes.

Sprinkle on the salt. Continue to stir in flour until the dough is too stiff to stir. Turn out onto a bread board and knead for 5 to 7 minutes, until the dough is smooth and elastic. Wipe out and lightly oil the bread bowl. Return the dough to the bowl and allow to rise until doubled in volume, approximately 1 hour.

Place each of the topping ingredients in a small bowl.

continued

Punch down the dough. Turn out onto a lightly floured surface, and divide into 16 equal pieces. Flatten each piece between floured palms. On a well-floured surface, begin rolling out the paperthin breads, keeping the remaining dough covered. Work with 2 pieces of dough at a time, rolling out each one as far as it can be easily rolled and then switching to the other. Continue rolling out until each round of dough is 7 to 9 inches in diameter. Brush each bread with 1 teaspoon of the olive oil, then sprinkle with ¼ teaspoon sesame seeds and ⅛ to ¼ teaspoon chile flakes, depending on how much heat you want.

Preheat the broiler and place the broiler rack approximately 3 inches from the heat source. Heat two lightly oiled cast-iron skillets or griddles over high heat. If using a gas stove, you will be able to work with two burners only, raising and lowering the heat as you need. If working with an electric stove, you will need to work with all four burners; turn two onto low heat. (Note: Use the back burners for the high heat and the front burners for low, so you can avoid having to reach over a very hot burner each time you transfer the skillets and breads to low heat.)

When the skillets are hot, if using a gas stove, turn the heat as low as possible just before you place each bread in a skillet; if using an electric stove, move the skillets to the low-heat burners just before you place the breads in the skillets. The dough will be very thin and quite flimsy, so work carefully when placing the breads in the skillets. Cook for 2 minutes over low heat. Then quickly place both skillets underneath the broiler, and broil for 1 minute. Transfer the breads to a rack to cool briefly. Place the skillets back on the stove over high heat, and continue shaping and baking the breads. Between batches, rub each skillet with a lightly oiled paper towel or cotton cloth.

Serve the breads after they have cooled briefly, or wrap in a towel to keep soft.

····▲▲▲▲▲▲▲▲·▲▲·▲▲▲▲▲··▲

Makes 16 thin round flatbreads, about 8 inches in diameter.

Serve these as a snack or light meal on their own or with Yogurt Cheese balls (see page 206) or plain yogurt to balance the heat of the chiles. Or if you'd like a strong flavor to meet the chiles halfway, try Olive Salad (page 180) or Spicy Yemeni Salsa (page 191).

MEZZE TABLE

Mezze, maza, meze, mezeler, mezedes, mezza, mezethakia, meza, al mezah:
There are as many different names for mezze as there are languages along the eastern rim of the Mediterranean, and there are as many different mezze dishes as there are cooks to invent them. Mezze is a way of eating; as with tapas or antipasti, almost anything that is small and tasty qualifies as a mezze dish, even main dishes if they can be served in small portions. Mezze dishes are often served as hors d'oeuvres to accompany drinks, or set out as a first course. But when served with plenty of fresh warm flatbreads, even the most humble array can instantly become a meal. And the mezze table is one of the all-time great ways of giving bread a central role in a meal, whether a simple home-style supper or a dazzling festive spread.

A basic mezze meal can be as simple as a basket of warm Pita, a plate of fresh herbs, another of feta cheese or Yogurt Cheese, a dish of olives, and a pitcher of iced water. Add a dip or a salsa, a salad or two, and a grill such as Grilled Marinated Chicken, and a simple light meal becomes a more elaborate dinner.

Keep in mind that whatever is served should be easy to pick up or to eat with flatbreads. Place all the breads and dishes on the table at the same time. There are no courses in a mezze meal, no rules about what must be eaten first and what later. Think of a long summer night on the Mediterranean with plenty of time to eat, to talk, and to eat some more. A mezze meal should be as informal and relaxing as it is delicious.

To give a mezze meal the status of a mezze feast, simply increase the number and variety of the dishes, including perhaps a few heartier choices like kebabs or one or two bean dishes. When making your selections about what to serve, think also about how the table will be arranged, about colors and shapes, contrasts and complements. Place a rich red salsa beside a pale cream-colored dip, a white feta next to the black olives, an orange or a carrot salad near a plate of fresh green herbs.

We often refer to the mezze table in the serving suggestions at the end of each recipe. Listed below are guidelines and possible mezze table choices, some better suited to a simple meal, others more elaborate, for festive occasions. Because the mezze table is a flexible way of eating, don't hesitate to try different combinations.

THE BASICS

Assume that you will always include, as basic elements on the table, most of the following: flatbreads such as Pita or Paperthin Lavash, whole or cut into wedges; a plate of black olives; some goat cheese or yogurt or both (Yogurt Cheese shaped into balls and rolled in herbs is a standby); and a dish of fresh herbs such as mint, coriander, tarragon, chervil, and dill.

FOR AN APPETIZER TABLE

For six to eight people, with other courses to follow, select at least two kinds of bread, three salads, and two or three dips and sauces, keeping in mind that you want contrasting colors and flavors on your table. For a more elaborate table, but still one to be followed by other courses, add Baked Bulgur Patties Stuffed with Lamb and Pine Nuts, or Walnut and Eggplant Roll-ups.

FOR A MEZZE FEAST

For eight to twelve people or more, increase the number of salads and dips, include at least one filled or flavored bread as well as two others for dipping and wrapping, and serve at least three choices from the "grills and other substantial dishes" category below.

Breads

Bulgur Bread (page 175); Pita (page 181); Paperthin Lavash (page 283); Bedouin Barley Bread (page 212); Fenugreek Corn Bread (page 223); Moroccan Anise Bread (page 242); Afghan Home-style Naan (page 38); Afghan Snowshoe Naan (page 40); Pebbled Persian Bread (page 55); Uighur Nan with Cumin and Onion (page 31); Georgian Cheese-Filled Quick Bread (page 292); Lamb and Tomato Breads (page 197); Hot Chile Bread (page 201); and Thyme Bread (page 207).

Salads

Twice-Cooked Eggplant Salad (page 246); Olive Salad (page 180); Bread Salad (page 186); Herbed Carrot Salad (page 248); Orange and Black Olive Salad (page 250); Lentil and Sweet Pepper Salad (page 199); Chickpea Salad with Spearmint (page 200); Two Reds Salad (page 249); Green Bean Salad with Walnut Vinaigrette (page 303); Sweet Onion Salad (page 65); and Grilled Vegetable Salad (page 265).

Sauces, Condiments, and Dips

Yogurt and Pomegranate Dip (page 193); Cutting-Board Salsa (page 178); Armenian Tomato and Eggplant Salsa (page 287); Berber Bean Puree (page 244); Mint and Yogurt Sauce (page 43); Spicy Yemeni Salsa (page 191); Eggplant Puree with Yogurt (page 217); Hazelnut Spice Blend (page 211); Thyme and Sesame Blend (page 208); Green Pepper Relish (page 274); Sour Plum Sauce (page 309); Herb and Pepper Relish (page 301); Pomegranate and Walnut Sauce (page 299); Bedouin Spice Blend (page 214); and Yogurt and Tahini Sauce (page 226).

Grills and Other Substantial Dishes

Grilled Marinated Chicken (page 222); Baked Bulgur Patties Stuffed with Lamb and Pine Nuts (page 219); Georgian Leek Pâté (page 305); Marinated Lamb Kebabs on small skewers (page 176); Chicken Street Kebabs (page 44); Georgian Walnut Sauce Casserole (page 311); Spicy Cumin Kebabs (page 33); Deep-Fried Patties (page 225); and Herbs and Greens Egg Pie (page 58).

Yogurt Cheese

labneh • Eastern Mediterranean

*Labneh is a fresh yogurt cheese, usually stored under olive oil. It is also a bril-*liantly simple way of preserving milk products. Yogurt is made and sold all over the Eastern Mediterranean. Traditionally, in the mountains of Lebanon, Syria, and Turkey, the yogurt is made of goat milk. The fuller the flavor of the yogurt, the more tasty the labneh you can make with it.

Once we began making these fresh cheese balls at home, we realized they were so easy that we could always manage to have some on hand. Find a convenient corner out of the sun to hang your cheese as it drains, and then the process is simple. Goat's milk yogurt is our favorite, but plain cow's milk yogurt also produces a very good and milder cheese. Two cups of yogurt will produce almost half a pound of creamy fresh cheese.

2 cups plain yogurt (goat's milk or cow's milk, low-fat or whole-milk)
1 teaspoon salt (optional)
Olive oil for storing (optional)

You will need a colander or large sieve, cheesecloth, and a medium-sized bowl.

Place a colander or large sieve over a bowl. Line the colander with a large piece of cheesecloth. Stir the salt, if using, into the yogurt, and then pour the yogurt into the colander. Gather together the edges of the cheesecloth, secure with string or a rubber band, and suspend your impromptu bag over the bowl. Let drain for 24 hours in a cool spot.

When you take the bag down, you will find a firm creamy mass of cheese inside. Using a tablespoon, scoop up lumps the size of a small walnut, shape them into balls (wet your hands for easier handling), and set them on a plate, without touching each other. Alternatively, pack the cheese into a bowl, and serve as a fresh creamy cheese (this will keep in the refrigerator, covered, for 3 to 4 days).

The labneh balls can be eaten fresh. However, to store them, place on the plate in the refrigerator, loosely covered with cheesecloth, for a day or two to get slightly drier and firmer. On the second or third day, sterilize a glass jar, then stack the labneh in it. Pour in olive oil to cover and seal well. Keep unrefrigerated in a cool, dark place. You can also add pieces of garlic or hot chile to the oil.

To serve, use a clean spoon to scoop out the labneh, allowing excess oil to drain off. Chop several tablespoons of fresh herbs—thyme, mint, basil, chervil, or tarragon—and roll the cheese in the herbs. Or, roll in caraway seeds or paprika, or in a dukka (see Hazelnut Spice Blend, page 211, and Thyme and Sesame Blend, page 208), or serve plain. Serve with plenty of bread.

Makes approximately ½ pound fresh yogurt cheese.

Serve on a mezze table (see page 203) or as an appetizer or snack with fresh flatbreads.

Thyme Bread

khubs zatar • Syria, Lebanon, Israel, and Egypt

There are many different versions of zatar bread. Most of those we have tasted, in Israel and Egypt, are chewy, pita-style breads. Sometimes the topping, especially in Lebanese-style zatar breads, is made of a blended thick paste of zatar and olive oil. However, we prefer the zatar lightly sprinkled on, and we like this less common version of the bread—paperthin and soft. It comes from the same Aleppo bakery as Hot Chile Bread. It is ideal as a light snack or party food.

d o u g h

2 teaspoons dried yeast

2½ cups warm water

5 to 6 cups hard unbleached white or
    unbleached all-purpose flour

2 teaspoons salt

t o p p i n g

¼ to ⅓ cup olive oil

Approximately ½ cup Thyme and
    Sesame Blend (page 208)

You will need a medium-sized bread bowl, a rolling pin, two small bowls, and two cast-iron or other heavy skillets or griddles at least 10 inches in diameter.

Make the dough and roll out the breads according to the directions for Hot Chile Bread (page 201). Once the breads are rolled out, brush each one with 1 teaspoon olive oil and sprinkle with 1 generous teaspoon thyme blend. Then bake in the same manner as for Hot Chile Bread. Wrap in a towel to keep soft. Serve warm or at room temperature.

Makes 16 thin supple breads, about 8 inches in diameter.

Serve alone or with soup and salad—try Yemeni Yogurt Soup (page 185) and Herbed Carrot Salad (page 248)—for a light meal.

Thyme and Sesame Blend

zatar • Lebanon and Israel

Zatar is the Arabic word for thyme and, somewhat confusingly, is also the name of this dukka, or herb blend, from the Eastern Mediterranean. Spice merchants in the Jewish Market (Menachne Yehuda) in Jerusalem and in Tel Aviv's Carmel market sell it; you can also find it in specialty import stores in North America, but, as with most spice and herb mixtures, it's better to make your own.

If you are serving zatar as a condiment or as part of a mezze course, place several small bowls on the table so guests have it within easy reach. You can also, as with other dukkas, put out small bowls of good olive oil: First dip your bread in the oil, then touch it to the zatar before each mouthful. Zatar is also used as a topping for breads (see Thyme Bread, page 207).

2 tablespoons sesame seeds	½ teaspoon salt
3 tablespoons fresh thyme leaves or 2 tablespoons dried thyme	½ to 1 teaspoon ground sumac (see page 418), to taste

You will need a heavy skillet and a spice grinder or mortar and pestle.

Place a small skillet over medium-high heat. Add the sesame seeds and toast, stirring constantly, until they start to change color and give off a slight roasted grain aroma. Remove from the heat, still stirring, then transfer to a bowl and set aside.

Grind the thyme leaves to a coarse powder in a spice or coffee grinder or a mortar. Add the sesame seeds and salt, and grind to a powder. Add the sumac. Store in a tightly sealed spice jar or other glass container.

Note: This recipe can also be made using hyssop rather than thyme, but we find it more bitter-tasting and less aromatic than thyme-based zatar.

·· ▲ ▲ ▲ ▲ ▲ ▲ ▲ · ▲ ▲ ▲ ▲ ▲ ▲ ▲ ▲ · · ▲

Makes approximately ¼ cup herb blend.

Serve with fresh Pita (page 181) or Savory Sesame Bread Rings (page 209) with, if you wish, a small bowl of extra-virgin olive oil for dipping. Zatar is an excellent addition to the mezze table (see page 203).

Savory Sesame Bread Rings

ka'kat • Israel

On a recent trip to Israel, we arrived by plane at Tel Aviv late one Friday afternoon. We drove to Jerusalem in the dark and had a much-needed night's sleep. Early the next morning, friends came by and we all went for a walk. It was a blustery, though sunny, late January morning, but already there were a great many other people out walking. Atop a hill we stopped to look out over the old city and the West Bank. Within our view there was so much history, and much to think about.

Nearby stood two Arabs selling large, wonderfully warm, soft, sesame-covered bread rings: ka'kat. With each ka'kat they served a little paper cone of ground thyme, into which we dipped our breads. We found a place nearby to sit outside with a cup of hot coffee. Then someone ran back for another ka'kat. And then another. And at last we'd eaten breakfast—in the sunshine, with a strong breeze and a timeless view.

1 teaspoon dry yeast

1½ cups warm water

3 to 4 cups hard flour, either half unbleached white and half whole wheat or all unbleached white

1 teaspoon salt

1 egg whisked with 1 tablespoon water, for egg wash

4 to 5 teaspoons sesame seeds

a c c o m p a n i m e n t s

Extra-virgin olive oil (optional)

Ground thyme, Thyme and Sesame Blend (page 208), or Hazelnut Spice Blend (page 211)

You will need a medium-sized bread bowl and two large baking sheets.

In a medium-sized bowl, dissolve the yeast in the warm water. Combine the flour and salt and add to the yeast, a cup at a time, stirring constantly in the same direction to help activate the gluten. When the dough will no longer take any more flour, turn it out onto a lightly floured surface and knead for 7 to 8 minutes, or until smooth and elastic. Clean out the bread bowl, lightly oil, place the dough in it, and cover with plastic wrap. Allow to rise until doubled in volume, approximately 1 hour.

Punch down the dough and divide it into 4 pieces. On your bread board, roll each piece under your palms (or hold it in the air between your palms and let it hang down as you make your rope) into a cigar-shaped rope 24 to 36 inches long, depending upon the size of the your baking sheets; if they are 18 inches long, you can make your "ropes" 36 inches long. Pinch together the ends of each rope to make a loop. Place the ka'kat rings on lightly oiled baking sheets, by shaping the loops into the traditional long oval shape and fitting 2 side by side on each sheet. Cover and let rise for 20 to 30 minutes.

Preheat the oven to 400°F.

Brush each bread liberally with egg wash. Sprinkle on the sesame seeds. Bake in the upper part of your oven for 15 to 17 minutes, until nicely browned; if the size of your oven and baking sheets permit, bake them side by side. If not, bake on 2 different racks and switch the sheets after 8 minutes. Cool slightly on a rack before serving.

Serve with olive oil if you like, and a bowl of one of the suggested accompaniments. Before taking each mouthful, guests dip their bread in the oil, then touch it to the herb—or, as we generally do, simply omit the oil and let the herb cling to the bread's moist crumb.

Makes 4 large oval breads, about 12 inches long.

Serve with one or more of the accompaniments listed, or with a salsa or dip such as Yogurt and Tahini Sauce (page 226) or Spicy Yemeni Salsa (page 191) as a snack.

Hazelnut Spice Blend

dukka • Eastern Mediterranean

Dukka are mixtures of finely chopped herbs, nuts, and/or spices traditionally eaten with bread: The bread is dipped in olive oil and then into the dukka mixture. This recipe makes a peppery aromatic blend that is delicious simply sprinkled on bread—it sticks very well without the oil. You may also want to place a small dish of olive oil on the table so your guests can try it both ways. As long as the hazelnuts are finely chopped and not reduced to a paste (which would release the volatile oils), the mixture can be made ahead and stored in an airtight container for several weeks.

½ teaspoon black peppercorns	1 teaspoon coarse salt
¼ cup fresh or dried thyme leaves	16 hazelnuts, finely chopped

You will need a large mortar and pestle or a spice grinder and a small bowl.

In a mortar, pound the peppercorns to a powder. Add the thyme and salt and pound to blend the flavors. Add the chopped nuts and pound until well blended. Alternatively, grind the peppercorns in a spice grinder and turn out into a bowl. Grind the nuts in the spice grinder, and add to the pepper. Add the thyme and salt and mash against the side of the bowl with a spoon to crush the thyme and blend the flavors.

Turn out into a small serving bowl and serve as a dip with fresh bread, with, if you'd like, a small bowl of extra-virgin olive oil. Store in a well-sealed glass container in the refrigerator for several weeks.

∙∙▲▲▲▲▲▲∙▲∙▲▲∙∙▲▲∙∙▲

Makes about ½ cup spice powder.

Serve with olive oil and Savory Sesame Bread Rings (page 209) or Bedouin Barley Bread (page 212); in fact, this is a delicious accompaniment to almost any flatbread.

Bedouin Barley Bread

fatir • Jordan, Israel, and Egypt

The Bedouin are Arabs who live in the desert and semidesert areas of Arabia, Jordan, Israel, Egypt, Libya, and Tunisia. They are traditionally nomadic, living in large tents, and moving with their herds of sheep, goats, and camels to find grazing and water, but nowadays many are settled in villages.

Aleppo, Syria: Making sajj on the street

There are three main breads made by the Bedouin communities in Israel. One is a modern bread, made with yeast and oil and baked in a standard oven. The other two are traditional breads designed for nomadic life. *Fatir* is large and thin, and baked on a sajj—a convex metal plate placed over an open fire or a gas stove. (A very similar bread, called *shrak,* is made in Jordan.) *Leba* is thicker and smaller in diameter, and baked in the coals of an open fire, like the sand-baked breads of southern Tunisia and Algeria.

One bright cold windy winter day, we stopped by a Bedouin village not far from the town of Beersheba, in Israel. When we asked around the village to find someone to talk with about baking and breads, a pleasant-looking mother of four came forward and invited us back to her home. In her kitchen she showed us her new modern oven and then, surprised that we were interested, pointed out her sajj hanging on the wall. Of course, she said, in the morning the sajj was the quickest and easiest way of baking. Its convex surface, usually made of hand-pounded aluminum or machine-spun steel, is placed like a small dome to heat over an open fire or a gas burner. The breads are rolled out thin and laid on top to cook.

Fatir takes very little time to prepare. Nomadic Bedouin store their grain whole, fresh-grinding flour for each batch of bread. Barley flour, mixed with a little wheat flour when available, is traditionally used. This recipe calls for equal amounts of wheat and barley flour.

2 cups barley flour

2 cups hard unbleached white flour, plus additional for dusting

2 teaspoons salt

1½ to 2 cups warm water

You will need a heavy skillet, a medium-sized bowl, a rolling pin, and a wok.

Place a heavy skillet over medium-high heat, and add the barley flour. Roast the flour, stirring constantly, until it has a roasted aroma and the color has changed to a light brown. Pour the flour into a medium-sized bowl, and allow to cool for a few minutes.

Add the wheat flour and salt to the barley flour. Make a well in the center, and pour in 1½ cups warm water. Stir from the center out, incorporating as much flour as possible. If the dough looks too dry to be kneadable, add a little more water.

When you can stir no longer, turn out the dough onto a lightly floured surface and knead for 5 to 7 minutes, adding white flour as necessary if the dough is too sticky. Cover and let stand for approximately 30 minutes.

Cut the dough into 8 equal pieces. Flatten each piece under the palm of your hand, dusting the pieces lightly with flour.

Roll out one bread at a time, keeping the remaining pieces covered. Roll each bread out until it is approximately 10 inches in diameter. The breads will be quite thin and easily torn, so handle with care.

Turn your wok upside down over a burner (see Paperthin Lavash, page 283, for a more elaborate description of this technique) and heat over high heat. When hot, oil lightly, using a paper towel. Reduce the heat slightly, and gently lay on a barley bread. Cook pressing down gently in different places momentarily to expose all parts of the bread to the hot cooking surface, for 1½ to 2 minutes, or until the underside of the bread has changed color. (Use a small piece of cotton cloth or a paper towel to protect your fingers as you press down on the hot bread.) Turn the bread over and cook again pressing down gently on different parts of the bread to hold it against the hot surface, for about 1 to 1½ minutes, until the bread has firmed up. Remove to a kitchen towel and wrap to keep warm. Roll out and cook the remaining breads in the same way. Serve warm.

··▲▲▲▲▲▲▲·▲·▲▲▲·▲··▲▲▲··▲

Makes 8 thin, supple breads, about 10 inches in diameter.

*The breads are delicious eaten with Yogurt Cheese balls (see page 206) or a dukka such as
Thyme and Sesame Blend (page 208), Hazelnut Spice Blend (page 211), or
Bedouin Spice Blend (page 214), the traditional Bedouin dukka.*

Bedouin Spice Blend

hawayij • Sinai and Negev Deserts and
the Arabian Peninsula

We have encountered hawayij in spice markets in many parts of the Arab world. Like the curry powders of India, it is used as an ingredient in other dishes. The Bedouin of the Sinai also eat it as a dukka, a spice blend into which fresh bread is dipped. You can buy hawayij ready-mixed in Middle Eastern groceries, but you might want to experiment with your own blend.

2 tablespoons black peppercorns

1 tablespoon caraway seed

½ teaspoon cardamom seed (from about
3 pods) (see page 409)

1 teaspoon saffron threads

1 teaspoon turmeric

You will need a heavy skillet, a spice grinder or mortar and pestle, and a small bowl.

Combine the peppercorns, caraway seeds, and cardamom seeds in a dry skillet and roast over high heat for 2 to 3 minutes, stirring constantly. Then pound to a powder in a mortar and pestle, or grind in a spice mill. Add the saffron threads and pound or grind. Transfer to a bowl, and add the turmeric, and mix well. Transfer to a well-sealed glass jar for storage. This keeps indefinitely, though with some loss of flavor after several months.

·‥▲▲▲▲▲▲▲‥‹▲▲‹‹‹▲▲‹‹▲

Makes approximately ¼ cup spice powder.

Serve as a dukka, or dip, with Bedouin Barley Bread (page 212) and a little olive oil,
or use as a spice in soups and stews.

Unleavened Passover Bread

matzoh • Israel and the Diaspora

Matzoh is unleavened bread made from flour and water with no salt, no oil, and—most important—no yeast. It is eaten during Passover to commemorate the haste with which the Jewish people fled Egypt. During Passover no yeast or yeasted products may be eaten. In religiously observant households, the house is thoroughly cleaned and swept, and all old flour, biscuits, and other leavened products are discarded.

Matzoh must be made quickly and with clean flour in order to prevent naturally occurring yeasts from making the breads rise. The Shulchan Aruch, a sixteenth-century codification of Jewish law, requires that from the time the flour is mixed with water to the moment the breads are cooked, no more than eighteen minutes should elapse. In order to get everything done within the time limit, many hands are needed to roll out the breads and get them cooked, and only small batches can be made at a time.

Historically, Jewish communities, whether in small villages in Italy or in the cities of Iraq or Morocco, turned the production of matzoh *shmura,* or "kosher for Passover" into a group effort. A special patch of wheat, blessed by a rabbi, was set aside to be harvested separately. The wheat was milled using specially cleaned (and blessed) millstones in order to ensure no contamination by leavening agents. Most communities decorated their homemade matzoh with small holes, using a metal comb or a fork to help prevent the bread from forming air pockets and rising during its short baking time. If any bread puffed up during cooking, it was pushed down firmly to force the air out.

Today, in Moscow, in Jerusalem, in New York, and in many other places in the world, the production of matzoh has been centralized and commercialized. We've come to think of it as a somewhat tasteless cracker that comes in a cardboard box. But homemade matzoh is a far more interesting and tasty bread.

We were asked to bake matzoh for a Passover seder held by friends in Toronto several years ago. Since then, making matzoh with friends just before Passover has become an annual ritual. And at the seder table each year, the breads are a reminder of just how good basic foods can taste.

We begin with wheat berries, grind them into flour, and sift out the coarsest bran before starting to make the dough. With the small dough this recipe makes, we can get all the breads into the oven (if not completely baked) in less than eighteen minutes from when we first add water to the flour. The recipe assumes that you wish to make matzoh within the time limit; without a large commercial oven, and several helping hands for the rolling out, you must begin with a small dough to get all breads done in time. To make more, make the recipe a second time. If you aren't worried about complying with the time limit, you can bake in larger batches.

Approximately 2 cups flour, preferably freshly ground and with the coarsest bran sifted out: either hard whole wheat flour, spelt flour (see page 404), or kamut flour (see page 403)

Approximately 1 cup spring water

You will need a medium-sized bowl, a rolling pin, a fork or metal comb or other utensil for making holes in the breads, and quarry tiles (see page 20) to fit on a rack in your oven or one large or two small baking sheets.

Place quarry tiles or baking sheet(s) on the bottom rack of your oven, and preheat the oven to 425°F.

When the oven is hot, place 2 cups flour in a medium-sized bowl and stir in water until a kneadable dough forms; you may have to add a little more flour or water, depending on your flour. Turn the dough out onto a lightly floured surface and knead quickly and vigorously until smooth, about 3 to 4 minutes. (Although you are trying to get the breads into the oven quickly, the time spent kneading is important, as it makes the dough easier to roll out very thin.) Cut the dough into 12 equal pieces and flatten each into a round with lightly floured hands.

Work with one piece of dough at a time, keeping the others covered with plastic wrap. On a lightly floured surface, roll out one piece of dough as thin as possible. Prick it all over with a fork or a sharp-toothed comb, and then try to stretch it slightly to widen the holes you have made. Transfer to the quarry tiles or baking sheet, placing it to one side to leave room for more breads and bake for 2½ to 3 minutes, until golden on the bottom and starting to crisp around the pricked holes.

Meanwhile, continue rolling out the dough, placing each bread in the oven as it is ready. If you are working with a partner, one should roll out the dough while the other pricks, stretches, and bakes the breads. This will make it easier to get all the breads baked in time. If your oven is small, you may not be able to fit in enough breads at once to get them done in time. If so, you can bake some of the breads on your stove top in a dry skillet, to get them all started baking within the 18-minute time limit.

For traditional crisp, dried matzoh, leave the breads out on a rack to cool completely and to dry.

Alternatives: If you prefer salted breads, stir 1 teaspoon salt into the flour, then add the water. You can also add a little olive oil to the dough if you wish. Matzoh made with salt and oil is still matzoh, but not matzoh appropriate for a Passover seder (there is no need to rush to bake these breads).

.. ▲▲▲▲▲▲ ▲.. ▲▲▲ ▲ ▲ ▲ ▲ ▲.. ▲

Makes 12 thin breads approximately 8 inches in diameter.

Serve in place of bread during Passover. At other times of the year, make the salted version and serve on a mezze table (see page 203) or as a snack to accompany Yogurt Cheese (page 206) or sauces such as Yogurt and Tahini Sauce (page 226).

Eggplant Puree with Yogurt
Eastern Mediterranean

The creamy texture of this puree comes from yogurt as well as the softness of baked eggplant. The yogurt also softens the bite of the other ingredients, making the dip a subtle treat. Be sure not to overdo either the salt or the garlic. If you want to increase the quantity, double the amounts of eggplant, yogurt, oil, and lemon, but increase the garlic and salt only by half as much again. This puree is very good served simply with flatbreads, but it's also delicious as a dip for steamed or raw vegetables.

1 medium eggplant (about ¾ pound)

1 clove garlic, crushed (see Note)

½ teaspoon fine sea salt

¼ teaspoon freshly ground black pepper

1 tablespoon olive oil

½ cup plain 2% or whole-milk yogurt

1 tablespoon fresh lemon juice

1 to 2 tablespoons finely chopped fresh mint or 1 tablespoon dried spearmint

You will need a baking sheet or ovenproof skillet, a medium-sized bowl or a blender or food processor, and a small bowl.

Preheat the oven to 425°F.

Wash and dry the eggplant and prick with a fork in about 8 to 10 places. Place on a baking sheet or in an ovenproof skillet and bake for 45 minutes to 1 hour.

continued

(Alternatively, you can grill the eggplant over a charcoal fire until the skin has changed color and the flesh is softened and sunken.) Let cool. Peel the eggplant, and squeeze out and discard any liquid. Finely chop, then transfer to a medium bowl and mash with a fork until smooth. Alternatively, puree in a blender or food processor, and transfer to a bowl.

Mash together the garlic and salt in a small bowl. Stir in the pepper and olive oil. Add to the eggplant and blend well. Stir in the yogurt and then the lemon juice. Stir in the mint and transfer to a serving dish. Let sit for at least 15 minutes before serving to give the flavors a chance to blend. This can be stored, covered, in the refrigerator for up to 3 days.

Note: In midwinter, when garlic tends to be old and very strong-tasting, we like to dry-roast it, whole and unpeeled, in a heavy skillet, before using it in this mild dip.

Makes 1 cup dip.

Serve with plenty of Pita (page 181), Bedouin Barley Bread (page 212), or Paperthin Lavash (page 283) as a dip or salad. It's also delicious as a dip for lightly steamed vegetables, and a good dish for the mezze table (see page 203).

Baked Bulgur Patties Stuffed with Lamb and Pine Nuts

kibbeh • Syria

Early one October morning, driving down from atop Nemrud Dag in south-
eastern Turkey, I passed through a small Kurdish village where several large groups
of people were out working. I couldn't see exactly

Kurds making bulgur in southern Turkey

what was going on, but at the center of each group
two men with enormous wooden mallets were
pounding away at something in a large stone mortar. I discovered that in the mortar was wheat, and
they were making bulgur. Parents, children, grandparents—everyone had a job. The wheat first had
to be parboiled, then partially sun-dried, then put
into the mortar to be pounded and cracked.
Enough bulgur would be made, I was told, to last
the entire winter.

We don't know when—or why—people first started making bulgur, but it
has been around for a very long time. The process is ingenious, for not only does
the parboiling dramatically reduce the amount of time and fuel needed to cook the
wheat, but it also has the effect of driving certain nutrients from the less digestible
outer layers into the center of the grain, making them more accessible.

Bulgur is much-loved in Armenia and Syria, as well as among the Kurds. It
is prepared in many ways, but reaches perhaps its most sophisticated form with
kibbeh (also called *koubbeh*), a paste made of ground meat kneaded together with
bulgur and moistened with a little water.

We have eaten kibbeh stuffed and plain, cooked and raw, in Istanbul and
Aleppo as well as in Jerusalem, that kaleidescope of Eastern Mediterranean cuisines.
Here it is used as the outer shell of small patties filled with a succulent mixture of
lamb and pine nuts. We have substituted a small quantity of olive oil for the mass
of butter usually used to moisten the kibbeh before baking. Kibbeh is traditionally
kneaded by hand, which takes a fair amount of time and effort. This recipe calls for
a food processor, which will give the necessary elasticity in a very short time. The
patties can be assembled and baked ahead, then stored in the refrigerator for up to
forty-eight hours or in the freezer for up to a month.

You can serve kibbeh as an hors d'oeuvre, as part of a mezze meal, or
accompanied by bread and a salad.

continued

stuffing

¼ cup pine nuts

1 teaspoon olive oil

1 large onion, finely chopped
    (about 1 cup)

⅓ pound lean boneless lamb, finely
    ground (see Note)

3 tablespoons fresh lemon juice

¼ teaspoon ground cinnamon

½ teaspoon salt

kibbeh

1 pound lean boneless lamb, cut
    into cubes

½ teaspoon salt

2 cups fine or medium bulgur

2 medium onions, finely chopped
    (about 2 cups)

¼ teaspoon dried chile pepper flakes or
    crumbled dried red chile

Approximately ½ cup water

Olive oil for brushing

Salad greens or several bunches of fresh
    herbs for serving

You will need a large heavy skillet, a spatula, a food processor, a medium bowl, two baking sheets, and a small bowl.

To *prepare the stuffing:* Heat a large heavy skillet over medium-high heat. Add the pine nuts and dry-roast for about 5 minutes, or until golden brown, stirring constantly. Remove from the skillet and set aside.

In the same skillet, heat the oil over high heat. When hot, add the onion, lower the heat to medium-high, and sauté until golden, stirring constantly. Add the ground lamb, and stir, using a spatula to keep it well separated and to prevent it from sticking, until the lamb has changed color. Lower the heat to medium, and add the lemon juice, cinnamon, and salt. Stir in the pine nuts, and cook for 30 seconds more. Remove from the skillet and set aside.

To *prepare the kibbeh:* Place the lamb and salt in a food processor and process to a paste. Add the bulgur, onions, and chile, and process for 30 seconds. Add ½ cup water and process for another 30 seconds. The dough should be moist and pasty; add a little more water if it seems very stiff. Process for 3 to 4 minutes (this replaces the traditional hand kneading and makes the dough somewhat elastic). If the dough still seems stiff, add a little more water and process briefly to mix. Turn out into a bowl.

Preheat the oven to 350°F. Lightly brush two baking sheets with oil.

Place a bowl of water for moistening your hands by your work area. To make the patties, first moisten your palms, then scoop out 1 heaping tablespoon of the kibbeh and flatten between your palms into a 2½- to 3-inch disc. Place 1 teaspoon of the filling on one side of the kibbeh, and fold over to enclose. Shape into a round or oval and place on a lightly oiled baking sheet. Form the rest of the patties in the same way. (You should have about 35 patties.)

Brush the top of each patty generously with olive oil. This will help seal in moisture and prevent the kibbeh from toughening during baking. Bake for 20 minutes, or until golden brown. Serve hot or at room temperature, stacked on a decorative plate or on a small platter lined with lettuce leaves or fresh herbs.

If making ahead, let cool, then store, well-covered, in the refrigerator or freezer. To serve, bring to room temperature, brush with a little olive oil, then heat on a baking sheet, covered with aluminum foil, in a warm (300°F) oven for about 20 minutes.

Note: Because it is difficult to obtain extremely lean ground lamb, we prefer to buy boneless leg of lamb and chop it ourselves; we chop it into cubes, then process it to a paste in the food processor, and then briefly chop the paste with a cleaver or knife to break it up more finely.

Makes approximately 35 meat-filled patties. Serves 6 to 8 with flatbread and several salads or 10 as part of a mezze table.

Olive Salad (page 180), Herbed Carrot Salad (page 248), and Twice-Cooked Eggplant Salad (page 246) would make a great combination with the kibbeh, or serve as part of a mezze table (see page 203).

Grilled Marinated Chicken

Eastern Mediterranean

*Early one chilly October morning I arrived in Munich, planning to travel over-*land to India as cheaply as possible. Near the central railway station, I approached a stranger to ask where I might change money. As we stood talking, a third person came up and asked if either of us was interested in driving a car to Iran. The other man laughed and said no; I quickly said yes. "All right," the third man said gruffly, "but we're leaving now." We walked out of the station and down the street, and there I was shown a new Chevy Blazer. He handed over the keys and some German money and told me to go buy food. Fifteen minutes later, we were on the road—fourteen Blazers altogether, all being delivered to Teheran—and for the next two weeks we stopped only for food and to sleep alongside the road at night.

My "employer" turned out to be more than a bit crooked, and driving on crazy two-lane dirt roads in Bulgaria and eastern Turkey was at time unsettling. Yet the trip was an adventure, and not without its pleasurable interludes. In Turkey we stopped at least twice a day at truck-stop restaurants, and filled up on salads, breads, and kebabs—kebabs of all kinds, hot off the grill.

·‥▲▲▲▲▲·‥▲▲▲▲·‥▲

As an appetizer, as one dish of many on a mezze table, or as part of a light lunch, this easy dish is always a success. Bite-sized pieces of chicken are coated in the familiar Mediterranean flavors of lemon juice and mint, then cooked briefly under the broiler. In summer you may prefer to thread them on small skewers and grill them on the barbecue.

2 pounds boneless skinless chicken breasts

¼ cup fresh lemon juice

1 tablespoon olive oil

2 cloves garlic, finely chopped

2 tablespoons dried spearmint

½ teaspoon freshly ground black pepper

1 to 2 teaspoons sea salt

Salad greens for serving

¼ cup chopped flat-leafed parsley, for garnish

You will need a shallow bowl, a small bowl, a roasting pan with a rack or small wood or metal skewers.

Rinse the chicken. Slice across the grain into ½-inch-wide slices, and place in a shallow bowl.

In a small bowl, whisk together the lemon juice, oil, garlic, and spearmint.

Pour this marinade over the chicken, and turn to coat. Cover and let marinate in the refrigerator for at least 1 hour, or up to 8 hours.

Preheat the broiler or prepare a charcoal or gas grill. If using wood skewers, soak in water at least 30 minutes.

If not using skewers, arrange the chicken pieces on a rack over a roasting pan and sprinkle with salt. Alternatively, thread the chicken onto the skewers, then sprinkle with salt. Broil or grill 4 to 5 inches from the heat for 5½ to 7 minutes, turning the pieces or skewers over after 3 minutes.

Arrange salad greens on a decorative platter to make a bed for the chicken. Lay chicken pieces or skewers on top, and garnish with parsley. Serve warm.

⋯⋅▴▴▴▴▴⋅⋅▴▴⋅⋅▴▴▴⋅⋅▴

Serves 10 as part of a mezze table or 6 as part of a bread and salad meal.

Serve with plenty of Pita (page 181), Afghan Snowshoe Naan (page 40), or Paperthin Lavash (page 283) for wrapping, accompanied by Herbed Carrot Salad (page 248) and Cutting-Board Salsa (page 178).

Fenugreek Corn Bread

E g y p t

In the Nile Delta, all the way from Cairo to Alexandria, in front of every vil-lage home you can see a beehive-shaped oven, simply built with mud and straw. A small fire of thatch and twigs burns in a lower chamber, heating the bottom of an upper chamber, where the flatbreads are baked. It requires relatively little fuel to heat the oven and to bake the breads, but the oven must be rebuilt every two years. The oven design is a very practical one in an area where fuel is scarce, but mud is always available.

This delicious bread comes from the Nile Delta: aromatic with freshly ground fenugreek and a blend of corn and wheat flours, and simple to prepare.

½ teaspoon fenugreek seed (see page 414)	2 to 3 cups hard unbleached white flour
1 teaspoon dry yeast	1 teaspoon salt
2 tablespoons brown sugar	1½ cups corn flour (see page 412)
1½ cups lukewarm water	

continued

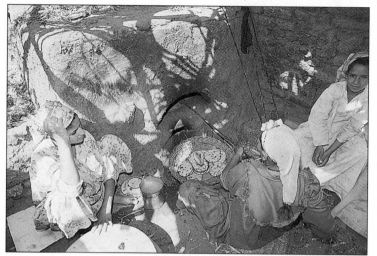

You will need a heavy skillet, a mortar and pestle or spice grinder, a medium-sized bread bowl, several large (12- by 18-inch) baking sheets, and a rolling pin.

In a heavy skillet, dry-roast the fenugreek seeds over medium-high heat until they begin to bounce around and to brown slightly, about 2 to 3 minutes; do not burn. Grind to a powder in a mortar or spice grinder, and set aside.

In a medium-sized bowl, sprinkle the yeast and sugar over the warm water, and stir to dissolve. Stir in 1½ cups white flour, and then stir 100 times in the same direction, about 1 minute, to develop the gluten.

Sprinkle the salt and ground fenugreek over the dough, and stir to mix well. Gradually stir in the corn flour. Then stir in more unbleached flour until your dough will not accommodate any more flour, and turn out onto a lightly floured surface. Knead for 5 to 6 minutes, adding additional flour only as needed. Rinse out the bread bowl, lightly oil it, and put the dough back into the bowl. Cover with plastic wrap and let rise until doubled in volume, approximately 1½ hours.

Punch down the dough and let rest for 5 minutes. Lightly oil several large baking sheets.

On a lightly floured surface, cut the dough into 8 equal pieces. Flatten each piece between floured palms. With a rolling pin, roll out each bread to a round approximately 6 inches in diameter. As you finish rolling out each bread, place it on a baking sheet. Cover the breads with plastic wrap and let rest for 20 minutes.

Position a rack in the center of your oven, and preheat the oven to 400°F.

Bake the breads, one sheet at a time, for 12 to 15 minutes, or until lightly browned on both top and bottom. Remove and cool on racks. Serve warm or at room temperature.

·˙· ▲ ▲ ▲ ▲ ▲ ˙ ▲ ˙ ▲ ▲ ▲ ▲ ▲ ▲ ▲ ▲ ˙ ▲ ▲

Makes 8 round flatbreads about 6 inches in diameter.

Serve these with several different salads or simply with a plate of Kalamata olives, slices of garden fresh tomatoes, and a hot sauce such as Spicy Yemeni Salsa (page 191).

Deep-Fried Patties

ta'amia • Egypt

*Fava beans and their close cousins, white broad beans, are used through-*out the Eastern Mediterranean and North Africa. Here they are stewed, flavored with herbs and spices, then mashed to make ta'amia, flavorful deep-fried patties that look like small hamburgers and fill a similar niche. Like falafel (deep-fried chick-pea-based patties) in Israel, Syria, and Jordan, they are a popular street food in Egypt; served with a pita and some freshly chopped onion or a tomato sauce, they make a great quick lunch. Traditional preparation involves a lot of pounding and grinding, but a food processor is ideal for the job and reduces both the time and effort required. Ta'amia can be prepared ahead, frozen, and then reheated before serving.

1 pound dried fava beans (see page 414) or dried white broad beans, soaked overnight in cold water to cover

1 teaspoon dry yeast

1 tablespoon warm water

1 large red onion, finely chopped

4 cloves garlic, finely chopped

1 bunch flat-leafed parsley, finely chopped

1 teaspoon salt

2 tablespoons ground cumin

1 tablespoon ground coriander

1 teaspoon cayenne

Peanut oil for deep-frying

You will need a food processor, a wok or other deep pan for deep-frying, and a slotted spoon.

Drain the beans, rinse under cold water, and drain again. Transfer to a food processor.

Dissolve the yeast in the warm water, and add to the processor along with all the remaining ingredients. Process until a thick pasty mass has formed. Cover and let rest for 30 minutes.

To make the ta'amia, pull off chunks of the mashed beans approximately the size of a ping-pong ball, or just a bit smaller (about 1 inch around), and flatten into round patties. As you form each patty, lay it on a tray or on a work surface by your stove top. Cover and let rest for 30 minutes.

Heat oil for deep-frying in a wok or other deep pot over moderately high heat until it reaches 375°F. (To test the temperature of the oil, take a small piece of ta'amia mixture and drop it in; it should begin to sizzle immediately, but shouldn't burn.) Using a long-handled spoon to avoid getting splashed with hot oil, carefully add in 4 or 5 ta'amia, or as many as will comfortably fit in the pan. Fry for 3 to 5 minutes, or until nicely browned. Lift the finished ta'amia out with a slotted spoon and drain on paper towels to absorb any excess oil. Repeat with the remaining patties, adjusting the temperature of the oil as you go along, since the oil will cool with each new batch. Serve warm. Or, alternatively, make ahead and freeze (once cooled) in plastic bags. To serve, reheat in a baking pan, covered with aluminum foil, in a 300°F oven for about 20 minutes.

Makes 40 to 45 small patties, 1½ to 2 inches across.

Serve warm with plenty of fresh Pita (page 181), Yogurt and Tahini Sauce (page 226), chopped onions, and tomato wedges. Let guests serve themselves so they can combine the ta'amia with the pita and other accompaniments as they wish.

Yogurt and Tahini Sauce

Egypt

This simple sauce from Egypt can be varied in an almost infinite number of ways; its creamy yogurt and tahini base can support a variety of fresh herbs and other strong tastes. It is made to be drizzled over Deep-Fried Patties.

3 tablespoons tahini (see page 418)

6 tablespoons plain yogurt

6 tablespoons fresh lemon juice

½ teaspoon salt

½ teaspoon dried chile pepper flakes (optional)

1 tablespoon finely chopped flat-leafed parsley (optional)

You will need a small mixing bowl.

Blend all the ingredients together in a bowl. Serve in small individual bowls as a dipping sauce. Store in the refrigerator in a sealed glass container for up to 1 week.

Makes about 1 cup dipping sauce.

Serve as a dip for Deep-Fried Patties (page 225) or steamed vegetables, accompanied by Pita (page 181).

Egyptian Brown Beans

ful medames • Egypt

A friend from Switzerland flew to the United States for a summer just after finishing university. He traveled all around the country, visiting small towns and out-of-the-way places. Now, many years later, the trip is still one of his fondest memories—and hamburgers are still one of his favorite foods. In that one summer, he ate more than one hundred hamburgers, and "that was not enough."

Humble foods and travelers have a way of finding each other. Bread and cheese in France, souvlaki in Greece, chapatti and dal in north India, fried rice in Thailand; affordable and easy to find, common foods are naturally the ones most accessible to travelers, and the foods most often eaten. But perhaps there is more to it than convenience. Traveling is all about trying to see from the inside out, and how else to begin in the United States but by eating a hamburger in a small-town café or a big-city greasy spoon?

As a first-time visitor to Egypt, without much Arabic, I had a hard time knowing where and what to eat. Early one morning at a street vendor's stall in Cairo's fabulous Khan el Khalili market, I discovered baladi and ful (whole wheat pita and brown beans). As I stood spooning my ful with a piece of bread, alongside at least a dozen other people, for a moment I was no longer a tourist. I never missed another morning in the market.

2 cups ful medames (see page 415) or other ful, such as dried fava beans (see page 414) or broad white beans, soaked overnight in water to cover, or 4 cups canned Egyptian brown beans

1 tablespoon olive oil

3 to 4 cloves garlic, finely chopped

½ teaspoon salt

¼ teaspoon freshly ground black pepper

garnish and accompaniments

Lemon wedges

Cumin seed or ground cumin

Paprika or cayenne (optional)

4 to 6 Hamine Eggs (page 229)

½ cup packed flat-leafed parsley or fresh coriander leaves, finely chopped

Salt and freshly ground black pepper

2 tomatoes, cut into small chunks (optional)

1 red or white onion, thinly sliced (optional)

You will need a large saucepan and a small skillet.

Drain the beans and place in a large saucepan. Add 8 cups cold water and bring to a boil. Cook until soft, 1½ to 2½ hours; drain. If using canned beans, place in a large saucepan and bring to a boil. Remove from the heat, and drain. Transfer the beans to a medium bowl.

Heat the oil in a small skillet, and fry the garlic until just beginning to brown. Add the garlic, salt, and black pepper to the beans.

Serve the beans hot or at room temperature in soup bowls. Squeeze some lemon juice over each serving, then sprinkle on a pinch of crushed cumin seed and optional paprika or cayenne. Top with a Hamine Egg and some parsley or coriander leaves. Place extra lemon wedges, chopped parsley or coriander, cumin, and paprika, along with salt and pepper, on the table, so that each person can adjust the seasonings to taste. Serve with the tomato chunks and sliced onion for garnishing the beans.

Alternatives: We tasted a similarly delicious combination called lebleb, in Tunisia, based on chickpeas rather than beans. An aromatic chickpea-laden broth was served in individual bowls, topped to taste with a pinch of cumin and paprika, a dash of capers, sprinklings of chopped herbs and chopped egg, and a dab of hot chile paste. A lemon wedge gave the option of fresh lemon juice drizzled over the broth.

Serves 4 to 6.

Serve with Pita (page 181) or Fenugreek Corn Bread (page 223), with chopped tomatoes and sliced onion as accompaniment, which each person can add to the beans or eat as a side salad. (We think that ful served with Hamine Eggs tastes best when, as you eat the dish, you mash the egg into the beans, thus blending it with all the other flavors.)

Hamine Eggs

beid hamine • Egypt

Hamine eggs are a unique and delicious take on the hard-boiled egg. The eggs are wrapped in onion skins and slow-cooked in water for anywhere from six to twelve hours (*hamine* refers to the slow-cooking method). The result is an egg creamy in texture with a beautiful light brown color. Hamine eggs are traditionally served with Egyptian Brown Beans, but they are also very good on their own with a soft fresh pita.

Outer skins from 3 to 4 onions

6 large eggs

1 tablespoon olive oil

You will need a deep saucepan with a lid.

Wrap the onion skins around the eggs and place the eggs in a deep saucepan; the eggs should fit somewhat snugly in the pan so that they don't rattle around and crack when cooking.

Add enough cold water to cover the eggs by 1 to 2 inches. Pour in the olive oil, which helps reduce the amount of water that evaporates during cooking.

Cover the saucepan, and cook over the lowest possible heat for at least 6 hours, or as long as overnight, checking occasionally to make sure there is sufficient water.

Serve warm or at room temperature. You can leave the eggs in their prettily dyed shells and have your guests peel them, or, if serving as part of another dish such as Egyptian Brown Beans, peel before serving. They will keep for several weeks in the refrigerator, but are best eaten, unrefrigerated, within a day of cooking.

Makes 6 creamy-textured eggs.

Serve with Egyptian Brown Beans (page 227), flatbreads such as Pita (page 181) or Bedouin Barley Bread (page 212), and a bowl of fresh herbs.

Sweet Bread Rings

ka'kat • Eastern Mediterranean

Fresh ka'kat can be found on busy street corners, in markets, and at bus stands all the way from Istanbul to Cairo. They are nourishing, inexpensive, tasty, and easy to eat on the run—everything an ideal street food needs to be. There are dozens of regional varieties of ka'kat: Some are sweet, some savory; some are large rings (see page 209), while others are made very small; some are dense and chewy, while others are crisp on the outside and soft and light inside.

We're not sure where ka'kat came from originally. Wherever we ask, the answer is always the same: "From here, of course."

This particular version is slightly sweet, aromatic with the addition of mahleb—the ground-up kernels of a species of black cherry that grows in the Eastern Mediterranean—and sprinkled with sesame seeds. You can find mahleb, whole or ground (whole is preferable, because it keeps its wonderful flavor and aroma better), in Middle Eastern groceries and well-stocked spice shops. Like almonds, it is best kept in the freezer to prevent it from becoming rancid.

2 teaspoons dry yeast

¼ cup sugar

2 cups warm water

4 to 5 cups hard unbleached white flour

1½ teaspoons salt

4 tablespoons unsalted butter, melted

¼ teaspoon mahleb (see page 416), ground

1 egg beaten with 1 tablespoon water, for egg wash

3 to 4 tablespoons sesame seeds

You will need a medium-sized bread bowl, two large baking sheets, and a pastry brush.

In a medium-sized bread bowl, dissolve the yeast and sugar in the warm water. Add 2 to 3 cups flour, a cup at a time, stirring constantly in the same direction to help activate the gluten, until a thick dough begins to form. Then stir 100 times in the same direction, about 1 minute. Let rest for 10 minutes.

Add the salt, butter, and mahleb, stir, and continue to add more flour, using a wooden spoon to stir it in. When the dough will no longer take any more flour, turn it out onto a lightly floured surface. Knead for 8 to 10 minutes, or until smooth and elastic, adding flour only when necessary. Rinse out the bread bowl, oil lightly, and return the dough to the bowl. Cover with plastic wrap and allow to rise until doubled in volume, approximately 1½ hours.

Punch down the dough and divide into 16 pieces. On a lightly floured surface, roll each piece under your palms into a cigar-shaped rope 6 to 7 inches long. (You can also roll them in the air between your palms, letting the bread hang down vertically from your hands.) Pinch together the ends of each rope to form an oval-shaped loop. Place the ka'kat on lightly oiled baking sheets, at least ½ inch apart. Cover and let rise for 30 minutes.

Place the racks in the upper part of the oven, and preheat the oven to 400°F.

Just before baking, brush the breads with egg wash and sprinkle on the sesame seeds. Bake for 20 minutes, or until nicely browned; switch the baking sheets after 10 minutes. Cool slightly on a rack, then wrap in a cloth to keep warm. Serve warm.

Makes 16 oval bread rings about 3½ inches across.

Serve for breakfast, or for a snack with tea or coffee—they are delicious anytime. Also a good pair with Yogurt and Pomegranate Dip (page 193).

Date-Bread Morsels

Dates and bread have a natural affinity. Whenever we make Date Syrup, we divide the date residue into two-cup portions, wrap them in plastic bags, and freeze them to use later in one of two breads described here.

This first date bread, leavened with yeast, can take on different forms: Roll the dough out into bread sticks, or shape it into rolls. The breads described here come out looking a little like dates, about two inches long and one inch wide, and they make a delicious snack. The dates almost disappear in the bread, conditioning the dough and giving it a wonderful sweet date flavor.

1 cup warm water

1 teaspoon dry yeast

2 cups date residue from Date Syrup (page 234)

2 cups hard unbleached white flour

1 teaspoon salt

2 to 3 cups hard whole wheat flour

You will need a medium-sized bread bowl and one large or two small baking sheets.

continued

In a bread bowl, mix together the warm water and yeast. Stir in the date residue and white flour, then stir 100 times in the same direction, about 1 minute, to develop the gluten. Let this sponge sit, covered, for at least 10 minutes, or as long as 1 hour.

Sprinkle the salt over the sponge, and then stir in the whole wheat flour, a cup at a time. When the dough is too stiff to add additional flour, turn out onto a lightly floured bread board. Knead for 8 to 10 minutes; the dough will feel somewhat stiff, but persevere. Clean the bread bowl and oil lightly, then return the dough to the bowl, cover with plastic wrap, and let rise for 2 to 3 hours.

Lightly oil one large or two small baking sheets.

Punch down the dough and let rest for 10 minutes.

To make the tiny breads, divide the dough into 8 pieces. On a lightly floured work surface, roll each piece out under your palms into a long rope approximately ½ inch in diameter. Using a sharp knife, cut each rope into 1½- to 2-inch segments. Place the segments on the baking sheet(s), making sure that they are far enough apart so that they won't bake into each other. Cover and let rise for 20 minutes. Preheat the oven to 425°F.

Bake on the top rack of the oven for 10 minutes, or until lightly golden and firm to the touch. Serve warm or at room temperature.

·····▲▲▲▲▲▲·▲·▲▲▲▲▲▲▲·▲·▲

Makes about 4 dozen little date-shaped breads.

*Serve for breakfast or as a snack with yogurt and tea or coffee or to accompany
Yogurt and Pomegranate Dip (page 193).*

Unyeasted Date Rounds

This unyeasted date bread is our own creation, inspired by stories about the Bedouin relying upon breads made from date "flour" when making long trips across the desert. We've asked about date "flour" on numerous occasions, only to be looked at rather blankly. Does it really exist? We don't know. But we've come to love the bread, which has all the wonderful qualities of a bread made with dates in a dough quickly made and baked.

This recipe is well suited to bread-making sessions with young children, as they can use a rolling pin and cut out crazy shapes. You can also make chewy date crackers with this dough: Roll it paperthin and bake it in a hot (500°F) oven on quarry tiles (see page 20). Once the crackers have cooled, store them in plastic bags to keep them soft, or leave them out to get a crunchy cracker texture.

1 cup warm water

1 tablespoon salt

4 cups date residue from Date Syrup (page 234)

6 to 7 cups hard whole wheat flour

Sesame seeds (optional)

You will need a medium-sized bread bowl, a dough scraper, a rolling pin, a round cookie cutter or equivalent (a thin-rimmed glass will do), and a large baking sheet.

In a medium-sized bowl, mix the warm water and salt. With a wooden spoon, stir in the date residue. Stir in the flour, a cup at a time, until the dough is too stiff to stir. Turn the dough out onto a floured surface and knead for 6 to 8 minutes, until relatively smooth and elastic, adding flour as necessary. Use a scraper to keep your work surface smooth and not too sticky. Clean out the bread bowl, oil it, and return the dough to the bowl. Cover with plastic wrap, and let rest for 30 minutes.

Place a rack in the center of the oven, and preheat to 425°F. Lightly grease a large baking sheet.

Divide the dough into 2 equal pieces. Roll each piece out with a rolling pin on a well-floured surface until less than ¼ inch thick. Using a cookie cutter or a thin-rimmed glass, cut out shapes. Place the shapes on the greased baking sheet; if using optional sesame seeds, sprinkle the seeds onto the baking sheet before putting down the breads.

Bake for 8 to 10 minutes. Place on racks to cool slightly, then wrap in a towel to keep warm; or alternatively, allow to cool completely and firm up.

Makes 2 to 2½ dozen small thin breads.

Serve as a snack as you would cookies or crackers. These are very good with yogurt or with Yogurt and Pomegranate Dip (page 193), or served to accompany a dessert such as Fruit Compote with Scented Waters (page 237).

Date Syrup

dibis • Iraq

*A friend whose father was from the Basra region, in the heart of Iraq's date-*growing area, remembers hearing stories about her grandmother's entire village engaged in making date syrup at the height of date season. The syrup is delicious as a dip for bread, either on its own or mixed with plain yogurt, and as a sweetener, just as it is traditionally used in Iraq. The residue left after the cooked dates have been pressed to make syrup is prized in our household as an essential ingredient in Date-Bread Morsels and Unyeasted Date Rounds.

5 pounds pitted dates
8 cups boiling water

You will need a large saucepan, a large sieve or wire mesh colander, a large bowl, a flat wooden spoon, and two or three 1-pint Mason jars.

Wash the dates. Place the dates and boiling water in a large saucepan, stir well, and let stand to soak, covered, for 1 hour.

Place the pan of dates over medium heat, and bring the water to a boil. Reduce the heat and simmer for 10 to 15 minutes. Remove from the heat and let cool.

Working with about 2 cups of the date mixture at a time, spoon the cooked dates into a large sieve or fine-mesh strainer placed over a large bowl, and gently mash and press them against the mesh with a wooden spoon. Once most of the syrup has drained through from each batch, empty the colander, and set aside the date residue.

Store the date syrup in sterilized Mason jars in the refrigerator, and use as a dip or as a sweetener; keeps well for up to 2 months.

······▲▲▲▲▲▲▲·▲▲▲▲▲▲▲·▲▲·▲

Makes approximately 5 cups syrup.

Serve plain or blended with an equal quantity of plain yogurt to accompany Date-Bread Morsels (page 231), Pebbled Persian Bread (page 55), or Sweet Persian Bread (page 62). It can be used as a dip or spread on the breads like jam.

Tahini and Date Syrup Dip
dibis w'rashi • Iraq

This dip combines Date Syrup with tahini, the sesame paste so often used in Middle Eastern cooking. Dibis w'rashi is delicious scooped up with fresh flat-breads—perfect with bread for lunch or for a quick afternoon snack for our children to tide them over until supper.

½ cup Date Syrup (page 234)
1 tablespoon tahini (see page 418)
1 tablespoon fresh lemon juice, or to taste (optional)

You will need a small bowl.

Blend all the ingredients together in a bowl. Serve as an accompaniment to bread.

·· ▲▲▲▲▲▲▲·▲·▲▲▲·▲▲▲▲▲·▲·▲

Makes ½ cup dipping sauce.

Serve for breakfast or a snack with plenty of Savory Sesame Bread Rings (page 209),
Unyeasted Date Rounds (page 232), or Bedouin Barley Bread (page 212).

Aromatic Festive Bread
madnakash, shooshma hatz • Syria

This sweet, aromatic bread comes from the Armenian community in Syria. It can be made with twice the amount of yeast to speed up the process, but we prefer a longer rising and fermentation. Like Sweet Bread Rings (page 230), madnakash is lightly flavored with mahleb, a spice used throughout the Middle East. Mahleb gives bread a warm, inviting aroma and a taste almost like fresh peaches; it is especially good in sweet and festive breads such as this one. Mahleb is available whole and ground in Middle Eastern grocery stores and from well-stocked spice shops. For the best flavor, buy it whole and grind it just before using.

continued

1½ cups milk

¼ cup honey

4 tablespoons unsalted butter, melted

1 teaspoon dry yeast

Approximately 4 cups hard unbleached
   white or unbleached all-purpose flour

1 teaspoon salt

1 teaspoon mahleb (see page 416),
   ground

1 egg beaten with 1 tablespoon milk,
   for egg glaze

2 tablespoons sesame seeds

You will need a small saucepan, a medium-sized bread bowl, a rolling pin, one or two baking sheets, and a pastry brush.

In a small saucepan, bring the milk just barely to a simmer. Pour into a medium-sized bowl, and add the honey and melted butter. Stir to dissolve the honey. Let cool to lukewarm (a splash or two feels just warm on your wrist).

Stir the yeast into the milk mixture and let sit for 2 to 3 minutes to dissolve the yeast. Then stir in 2 cups flour. Stir in the same direction 100 times, about 1 minute, to develop the gluten. Sprinkle the salt and mahleb over the dough, and stir in. Gradually stir in additional flour until a kneadable dough begins to form.

Turn out onto a lightly floured surface and knead for 5 to 6 minutes, or until smooth and elastic. Clean out the bread bowl, lightly oil it, and return the bread to the bowl. Cover with plastic wrap and let rise until about 2½ times its original size.

Gently punch down the dough. Divide it into 6 equal pieces. With the palm of your hand, flatten each piece on a well-floured surface. With a rolling pin, roll out each bread to around 6 inches in diameter. Arrange on one or two lightly oiled baking sheets, cover, and let rise for 30 minutes.

Preheat the oven to 350°F.

Just before placing the breads in the oven, use your middle and index fingers to make four "dimples" across each bread, then four more across these to form a cross. Make more dimples around the circumference of each bread, about ½ inch from the edge, to join the ends of the cross. Brush each bread with the egg glaze, and sprinkle 1 teaspoon of sesame seeds on each. Place in the center of the oven and bake for 15 minutes, or until lightly browned. (If your baking sheets do not fit side by side in your oven, place on two racks near the center of your oven and switch baking sheets after about 7 minutes.)

·· ▲ ▲ ▲ ▲ ▲ ▲ ▲ ▲ ▲ ·▲ ▲ ▲ ▲ ▲ ▲ ▲ · ▲

Makes 6 flat loaves about 6 inches in diameter.

Serve these breads on their own with tea or coffee, or with Fruit Compote with
Scented Waters (page 237) as a dessert.

Fruit Compote with Scented Waters

We haven't included many recipes for "sweets" in this book, but this is so easy, and so appropriate after a Middle Eastern or Central Asian meal, that we couldn't leave it out. It matches up well with nane sheer, the sweet Persian cookie-style bread, and its perfumed aroma and soft appealing texture make it a memorable dessert. The dried fruits are rich with flavor, so servings should be small. Serve with the sweet breads, which can be dipped in the aromatic juice, and for a touch of luxury, with a glass of Sauternes.

½ pound unsulfured dried apricots
  (about 2 cups)

¼ pound raisins (about ¾ cup)

¼ pound pitted prunes (about ¾ cup)

2 tablespoons sugar, or more to taste

1½ cups water

1 teaspoon rose water (see page 418)

1 teaspoon orange blossom water
  (see page 417)

1 tablespoon fresh lemon juice

You will need a large nonreactive bowl and a small bowl.

Rinse the fruit quickly, and place in a nonreactive bowl.

In a small bowl, mix the sugar, water, and rose and orange waters. Pour over the fruit. Let stand for at least 24 or up to 48 hours, covered, in a cool place or in the refrigerator.

Just before serving, stir in the lemon juice. Taste, and sprinkle on an extra tablespoon or more of sugar if you wish. Serve at room temperature, in a glass serving bowl.

·••▲▲▲▲▲•••▲▲•••••▲▲•••

Serves 8 to 10.

Serve with Sweet Persian Breads (page 62) or Unyeasted Date Rounds (page 232) or Aromatic Festive Bread (page 235). Fruit compote is the ideal dessert for the mezze table (see page 203); it is well complemented by a good Sauternes.

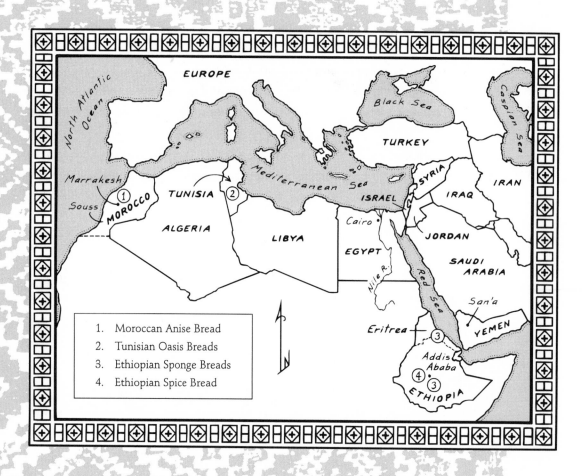

1. Moroccan Anise Bread
2. Tunisian Oasis Breads
3. Ethiopian Sponge Breads
4. Ethiopian Spice Bread

Morocco, Tunisia, and Ethiopia

In the parts of North Africa that border the Mediterranean, a mild climate favors agriculture. Olives and wheat historically grow well here, and a wide variety of fruits and vegetables like those in the Eastern Mediterranean also thrives.

The southern, noncoastal parts of Morocco, Algeria, and Tunisia, cut off by rugged mountains from this mild Mediterranean clime, are desert or near-desert regions. Oases in the mountains or desert historically were inhabited by settled groups of Berbers. They grew barley, olives, and some fruits and vegetables and also maintained herds of sheep and goats. The surrounding deserts were the preserve of nomadic and seminomadic groups of Arab origin, who moved with their herds of camel, sheep, and goats to find grazing. Now in Tunisia the two ways of life have merged to some extent, as the nomads have become settled in the oases, although meat and butter or lamb fat remain important in the diet. In the Atlas and Anti-Atlas Mountains of southern Mo-

Taroudant, Morocco: Carrying breads to the bakery

rocco, the Berber agricultural tradition remains strong.

Nomad flatbreads are made of wheat or barley flour and baked on a griddle over a fire or buried in the hot sand by a fire. Those of the settled villages are baked at home in a tandoor-like hole in the ground or on a clay surface over a fire. In the towns and cities, bakeries turn out commercial flatbreads, usually of wheat flour. The old tradition of taking a household bread to the bakery for baking is still alive and well in Morocco.

The mainstays of the diet in Morocco and Tunisia are wheat and barley, made into bread or couscous, together with olive oil or butter, hot red chiles (for *harissa,* the North African chile paste), cumin and garlic and legumes, vegetables, and meat from lamb or chicken, often slow-cooked in a *tagine,* or stew. Moroccan salads, with their bright colors and fresh tastes, make a great contribution to an Eastern Mediterranean–style mezze table.

Morocco: Flattening breads before baking

Ethiopia has a hot and humid Red Sea coast, but it is best known abroad for the cuisine of its more temperate central highlands. Here, the largely Amharic-speaking population lives at elevations of over three thousand feet. The predominant grain is teff, a small, millet-like grain, which is used for making the Ethiopian mainstay, *injera,* a large soured bread with a spongy texture. Wheat and barley are also grown.

The Coptic Christian Church in Ethiopia has many fasting days, on which no meat or animal products may be eaten. As a result, though it has an array of meat dishes cooked in butter, Ethiopian cuisine has also developed an extraordinary vegetarian repertoire, enlivened by herbs and spices. Like *berbere,* the national hot chile blend, the sauces, meat stews, and vegetarian dishes that make up an Ethiopian meal are flavored with chiles, cardamom, onion, holy basil, mint, fenugreek, ginger, and other spices, in unusual and pleasing combinations.

Tunisian desert: Woman leading donkey

Moroccan Anise Bread

ksra • Morocco

There is really no single Moroccan bread, but there are countless variations on a theme: Almost all are flat, round, and leavened. Some are made from unbleached white flour, others from whole wheat and white, and others from corn or barley and wheat. Most households prepare their own dough and take it daily to the local baker to have it baked. In the mid- and late morning, women or preschool children walk down the lane with the shaped loaves on a board, covered with a cloth. They carry the board balanced on their heads or slung on one hip. When you see the array of breads lined up for baking at a local bakery, large and small, thick and thin, each covered with a different piece of cloth so that each family will know its own bread when the time comes to pick it up, you realize that there are nearly as many different kinds of bread as there are households.

Household bread in Morocco was traditionally made with a sourdough starter—usually soured with vinegar and then left to stand for twenty-four hours— but that is now changing as commercial dry yeast becomes more widely available. This particular home-style bread, flavored with anise, is an excellent accompaniment to Ramadan Lamb and Legume Soup and to Berber Bean Puree.

2 teaspoons dry yeast

2½ cups warm water

3 cups hard unbleached white flour

2 teaspoons salt

1 tablespoon anise seed

¼ cup cornmeal, plus extra for dusting

2 to 2½ cups hard whole wheat flour, plus extra for kneading

You will need a bread bowl and one large or two small baking sheets.

In a bread bowl, dissolve the yeast in the warm water. Stir in the unbleached white flour a cup at a time, stirring in the same direction. Then stir approximately 100 times, about 1 minute, in the same direction to help the gluten develop. Let this sponge sit, covered, for 30 minutes to 2 hours.

Sprinkle the salt and anise seeds over the sponge. Add the cornmeal and stir to mix. Stir in the whole wheat flour, a cup at a time, until the dough becomes too stiff to stir. Turn out onto a lightly floured bread board, and knead for 8 to 10 minutes, until smooth and elastic. Clean and lightly oil the bread bowl. Transfer the dough to the bowl, cover with plastic wrap, and allow to rise until doubled in volume, approximately 1½ hours.

Gently punch down the dough. Divide the dough in half. Knead each piece for about 30 seconds, working it into a ball.

Lightly grease two small baking sheets (or one large sheet), and dust lightly with cornmeal. With your palms, flatten each piece of dough into a flat round loaf approximately 9 to 10 inches in diameter. Set the loaves on the baking sheets, cover, and let rise for 30 to 40 minutes.

Preheat the oven to 400°F.

Just before baking, prick the top surface of each bread decoratively 8 or 10 times with a fork. Place in the upper third of your oven, and bake for 25 to 30 minutes, until nicely browned on top. To test for doneness, tap with your knuckles on the bottom of each loaf: The bread should sound hollow. Cool on a rack for 10 minutes to allow bread to firm up. Ksra is most delicious when eaten warm.

Makes 2 round, slightly domed, flat loaves, about 10 inches in diameter and 1½ to 2½ inches thick.

Serve warm or at room temperature with Moroccan dishes, such as Chicken Tagine with Olives and Onions (page 261), Berber Bean Puree (page 244), or Ramadan Lamb and Legume Soup (page 251).

Berber Bean Puree

bessara • Morocco

Like tortillas and beans, or chapattis and dal, bessara and ksra (Moroccan Anise Breads) combine complementary proteins for a simple delicious meal. We once tasted a bessara in a small café in Tafraoute, a town in the Anti-Atlas Mountains of southern Morocco, served somewhat diluted as a soup to accompany bread, but we think it's best like this, a dip to be scooped up with flatbreads. Though bessara is most commonly made with dried fava beans, we prefer this version using red kidney beans or small red beans.

1 cup dried red kidney beans or small red beans, soaked overnight in 3 cups water and drained

3 cups cold water

3 cloves garlic, peeled

¼ teaspoon salt

½ teaspoon dried chile pepper flakes

½ teaspoon cumin seed, dry-roasted (see page 154) and ground, or ½ teaspoon ground cumin

½ cup flat-leafed parsley, chopped

¼ cup fresh lemon juice

garnish (optional)

Extra-virgin olive oil

½ to 1 teaspoon cayenne

You will need a large saucepan with a lid and a food processor.

Place the beans in a saucepan and add the water and garlic. Bring to a vigorous boil, reduce the heat, and simmer, partially covered, until the beans are tender, about 1 hour for small red beans, somewhat longer for kidney beans.

Transfer the beans and cooking liquid to a food processor and puree, in batches if necessary. Place in a serving bowl. The consistency should be like that of thick soup; stir in a little warm water if necessary.

Stir in the salt, chile flakes, cumin, parsley, and lemon juice. Let stand for 30 minutes to allow the flavors to blend. If you wish, sprinkle on a little olive oil and cayenne. Serve with plenty of bread for dipping.

·· ▲ ▲ ▲ ▲ ▲ ▴ ▴ ▴ ▴ ▴ ▴ ▴ ▴ ▴ ▴ ▲

Makes about 2½ cups puree. Serves 4 to 6 as an appetizer with bread.

Serve with wedges of Moroccan Anise Bread (page 242) as an appetizer, followed by Chicken Tagine with Olives and Onions (page 261), or, for a light supper, by Tunisian Tomato Stew with Poached Eggs (page 267).

North African Chile Paste

harissa • Morocco and Tunisia

Harissa is a chile-hot condiment and spice paste. It is generally thought to have originated in Tunisia, but is now found throughout North Africa. Commercial harissa is sold in Morocco and Tunisia, as well as in France. This recipe produces a thick chile-hot paste flavored with coriander seed, caraway, cumin, and garlic, much more flavorful than any commercial harissa we have tasted.

Vendor sampling his olive oil in Tafraoute, Morocco

In Morocco, harissa is often placed on the table as a condiment, while in southern Tunisia it is served as an appetizer, with a side dish of olives. We became addicted to the Tunisian style of harissa eating: Pour extra-virgin olive oil (Tunisian if you can get it, or Italian) over a small bowl of harissa, and stir to blend. Tear off bite-sized pieces of bread and dip in the chile-hot oil. It's a great way to work through a stack of breads.

1 ounce dried hot red chiles (approximately ¾ cup), stems removed

1 teaspoon coriander seed (see page 412), lightly dry-roasted (see page 154)

1½ teaspoons caraway seed, lightly dry-roasted (see page 154)

½ teaspoon cumin seed, lightly dry-roasted (see page 154)

4 to 6 cloves garlic, coarsely chopped

½ teaspoon salt, or to taste

Extra-virgin olive oil

You will need a small bowl and a mortar and pestle, or a spice grinder and a food processor or blender.

Soak the chiles in warm water to cover for about 1 hour, until they are soft. Drain and finely chop, discarding any hard bits.

In a mortar, pound together the coriander, caraway, and cumin seed to a powder, then add the garlic and salt and pound to a paste. Add the chiles, and pound until broken down into a coarse paste. Then add enough olive oil to make a smooth paste.

Alternatively, grind the coriander, caraway, and cumin to a powder in a spice grinder. Then place the chiles, garlic, spices, and salt in a food processor or blender and process well, adding oil as necessary to blend into a smooth paste.

continued

Serve as a condiment in a small dish, and use as a spice paste to season Tunisian and Moroccan dishes. Store, covered with olive oil, in a well-sealed glass jar in the refrigerator.

Alternatives: For less chile heat, discard the chile seeds before soaking. For a southern Tunisian variant, chop up 2 medium onions, salt well, and let drain in a colander. Rinse off the salt, then add to the other ingredients when pounding.

⸱⸱▲▲▲▲▲⸱⸱▲▲⸱⸱▲▲▲⸱⸱▲⸱

Makes a generous ½ cup chile paste.

Serve as a condiment with Couscous with Seven Vegetables (page 258) or Ramadan Lamb and Legume Soup (page 251), or with grilled meats such as Marinated Lamb Kebabs (page 176) or Spicy Cumin Kebabs (page 33). Harissa lovers enjoy eating it as a fiery dip for bread: In addition to Moroccan Anise Bread (page 242), it is also well matched by Fenugreek Corn Bread (page 223) or Bedouin Barley Bread (page 212).

Twice-Cooked Eggplant Salad
zelouch • Morocco

We first tasted this salad in the Atlas Mountains of Morocco, at the Hotel des Cascades just outside the small Berber village of Immouzer des Ida Outanane. Traditional recipes call for large amounts of oil in the initial cooking of the eggplant. We have substituted a dry-frying technique that produces the same end result—a dense, garlicky, almost meaty salad/dip, brightened by the intense color of small chunks of sweet red bell pepper. If you don't like any chile heat in your food, substitute cumin and coriander for the harissa and omit the chile flakes.

2 medium eggplants (1 pound), cut into ¼-inch slices

Salt

1 tablespoon olive oil

3 cloves garlic, crushed

1 teaspoon North African Chile Paste (page 245) or ½ teaspoon each ground cumin and coriander plus generous pinch of dried chile pepper flakes

¾ cup water

½ large red bell pepper, cored, seeds and veins removed, and cut into ¼-inch dice

¼ cup fresh lemon juice

Freshly ground black pepper to taste

½ cup loosely packed chopped flat-leafed parsley

You will need a colander, a large bowl, one or two cast-iron or other heavy skillets or one or two large baking sheets, and a heavy saucepan or skillet.

Sprinkle the eggplant generously with salt, place in a colander in the sink or over a bowl, and let drain for 30 minutes. Rinse thoroughly with cold water and squeeze gently.

Morocco: Table laid with salad buffet

Heat a dry heavy skillet over medium heat. Cook the eggplant slices in batches, turning them constantly to prevent sticking, until dried and slightly brown. (The process goes more quickly if you have two skillets going.) Alternatively, preheat the broiler. Place the eggplant slices on one or two lightly oiled baking sheets, and broil for about 6 to 8 minutes, turning once after 3 minutes. Chop the eggplant into coarse chunks.

In a heavy saucepan or skillet, heat the oil. Add the garlic and brown slightly, then stir in the chile paste or spices. Add the eggplant and water, and bring to a boil. Then reduce the heat to medium-low and simmer, stirring occasionally and checking to be sure the mixture is not sticking, for 20 minutes, or until the mixture has cooked down to a thick, somewhat lumpy puree. Transfer to a serving bowl.

Stir in the red pepper, then stir in the lemon juice, ¼ teaspoon salt, the black pepper, and parsley. This is best made 30 minutes to an hour ahead to give the flavors a chance to blend. Adjust the seasoning just before serving if necessary.

··▲▲▲▲▲▲▲··▲▲▲··▲▲··▲

Serves 4.

Serve as part of a mezze table (see page 203) or as a distinctive salad or vegetable dish to accompany Marinated Lamb Kebabs (page 176) or Chickpea Salad with Spearmint (page 200). The salad is best scooped up with a soft mild-tasting bread such as Pebbled Persian Bread (page 55) or Pita (page 181).

Herbed Carrot Salad

Morocco

We are always looking for new ways to work with carrots; their fresh taste and color become so important as winter drags on. We prefer organic carrots; like other root vegetables, carrots concentrate the nitrates used in chemical fertilizers, and nitrates can interfere with the absorption of oxygen in the body. A friend who is a pediatrician alerted us to this after she had treated several small children for what looked like circulatory problems causing a bluish tinge to the skin. The cause? Excessive consumption of nitrate-loaded carrots.

In this salad, the strong flavors in the dressing are even better when given several hours or more to blend, so make the dressing ahead and add it to the freshly steamed carrots shortly before serving.

1 teaspoon cumin seed

3 tablespoons chopped fresh coriander

2 tablespoons finely chopped fresh mint

¼ teaspoon salt

3 tablespoons olive oil

2 tablespoons red wine vinegar

Pinch of sugar

3 tablespoons plain yogurt

2 pounds carrots, thinly sliced and steamed just until tender (about 5 minutes)

Fresh ground black pepper

Leaf lettuce for serving

You will need a mortar and pestle or spice grinder, a bowl or glass jar with a lid, and a medium-sized bowl.

In a mortar, grind the cumin seed to a coarse powder. Add the coriander, mint, and salt, and pound and blend well. Transfer to a bowl or glass jar. Add the oil, vinegar, and sugar and mix well. Alternatively, using a spice grinder, grind the cumin seed. Transfer to a bowl or glass jar and stir in the herbs and salt, pressing the herbs with the back of a spoon to crush them. Add the oil, vinegar, and sugar and mix well. Let stand in a cool place, well sealed for up to 24 hours to allow the flavors to blend.

To prepare the salad, stir the yogurt into the dressing. Transfer to a medium-sized bowl, and add the carrots and pepper to taste. Toss to coat the carrots well. The salad can be served immediately or refrigerated for up to 2 hours; bring to room temperature before serving. To serve, make a bed of leaf lettuce on a medium-sized plate, and mound the carrots onto the lettuce.

Serves 6 as a salad or 8 as part of a mezze table.

Serve as a salad with Moroccan Anise Bread (page 242) or with Paperthin Lavash (page 283), following Prune-Stuffed Kufta Soup (page 316) or Ramadan Lamb and Legume Soup (page 251). Alternatively, serve as a colorful addition to a mezze table (see page 203).

Two Reds Salad
Morocco

In this "two shades of red salad," beets and tomatoes are an unexpected but successful pairing, set off by handfuls of fresh green herbs and chunks of red onion. We can never decide which dish to use for serving: a bright yellow plate, perhaps, or a deep green bowl.

1 pound (3 medium) beets, washed and trimmed

1 pound (4 medium) tomatoes, cut into ¼- to ½-inch cubes

½ medium red onion, finely chopped

1 clove garlic, minced

¼ cup chopped flat-leafed parsley

¼ cup chopped fresh coriander

2 tablespoons extra-virgin olive oil

½ cup fresh lemon juice

½ teaspoon salt

Freshly ground black pepper

You will need a large saucepan and a small nonreactive bowl or a jar.

Place the beets in a large saucepan, cover with water, and bring to a boil. Cook, partially covered, at a medium boil until cooked through (about 1 hour). Drain. (The beets can be cooked 1 to 2 days ahead, and stored in a well-sealed container in the refrigerator.)

Let cool, then peel and cut into ¼- to ½-inch cubes. Place in a medium-sized serving bowl. Add the chopped tomatoes, onion, garlic, parsley, and coriander.

In a small bowl or jar, whisk or shake together olive oil, lemon juice, and salt. Pour over the salad. Grind pepper over and toss to blend well. Serve at once, or chill in the refrigerator for 30 minutes to 1 hour before serving.

Serves 6 to 8.

This bright and strong-tasting salad pairs well with Moroccan Anise Bread (page 242) or Fenugreek Corn Bread (page 243). It also makes a splash on a salad version of a mezze table (see page 203), set out with Twice-Cooked Eggplant Salad (page 246), Herbed Carrot Salad (page 246), Lentil and Sweet Pepper Salad (page 199), Chickpea Salad with Spearmint (page 200), and Orange and Black Olive Salad (page 250).

Orange and Black Olive Salad

Morocco

Different styles of orange and black olive salad can be found all the way from Turkey to Israel to Morocco. This Moroccan version combines the flavor of fresh mint with freshly ground coriander seeds. The sweet-acid of the oranges paired with the olives' rich taste is as exciting on the tongue as the dazzling contrast of black on orange is to the eye. This is an excellent addition to a mezze table and a very successful match for grilled meat.

4 medium navel or other juicy oranges

½ cup small black salt-cured olives (Moroccan or Niçoise)

½ teaspoon coriander seed (see page 414), lightly dry-roasted (see page 154)

1 clove garlic, minced

¼ teaspoon salt

¼ cup chopped fresh mint

Pinch of crumbled dried red chile or dried chile pepper flakes

1 tablespoon olive oil

Pinch of sugar

You will need a plate, a mortar and pestle or spice grinder, and a bowl.

Peel the oranges, taking care to remove all the bitter white underskin. Working on a plate or other rimmed surface to catch the juice, slice thin. Separate the sections in each slice, cut off any tough white connecting tissue, and discard. Reserving the orange juice, transfer the orange pieces to a decorative bowl. Add the olives.

In a mortar, crush the coriander seed. Add the garlic and salt, and pound to a paste. Transfer to a small bowl. Alternatively, grind the coriander seed in a spice grinder, then turn into a small bowl, add the garlic and salt, and use the back of a spoon to mash together to a paste. Add the remaining ingredients and the reserved orange juice to the paste and blend well.

Pour the dressing over the olives and oranges, toss gently, and serve.

·· ▲ ▲ ▲ ▲ ▲ · ▲ · ▲ ▲ ▲ · ▲ ▲ · · ▲

Serves 6 as a salad course or 6 to 8 as part of a meeze table.

Serve this salad as a palate-refresher after a meaty or strong-tasting course such as Ramadan Lamb and Legume Soup (page 251) or Marinated Lamb Kebabs (page 176). Or place on the mezze table (see page 203) as a decorative and delicious salad.

Ramadan Lamb and Legume Soup
harira • Morocco

Harira is a thick hearty soup, made with lentils, chickpeas, lamb, and barley, and slow-cooked in a flavorful broth. Served with Moroccan Anise Bread, it is a staple throughout the country. We first tasted it in Marrakesh, on our first evening in Morocco. Later, when we stayed in the Anti-Atlas region in the southern part of the country, we came to rely on it for supper almost every evening. During the fasting month of Ramadan, harira is commonly served just after sunset as the start of the meal that breaks the dawn-to-dusk fast. Lusciously sweet dates or flaky pastries coated in honey are often served alongside the soup. The combination may sound odd, but the dates in particular are a delicious match.

The soup is easy to prepare, despite the long list of ingredients and instructions. Be sure to make plenty, as it tastes even better the next day.

1 tablespoon olive oil

1 large yellow onion, finely chopped

1 pound lean lamb, trimmed of any fat
    and cut into slices ¼ inch thick and
    1 inch long

12 cups water

¾ cup brown lentils, rinsed and drained

¾ cup chickpeas (see page 409), soaked
    overnight in 4 cups water and
    drained

1 teaspoon turmeric

One 1-inch cinnamon stick

½ teaspoon dried chile pepper flakes,
    or more to taste

½ teaspoon freshly ground black
    pepper

¾ cup barley

1 tablespoon sourdough starter or
    1 teaspoon dry yeast (see Note)

1 pound (3 medium) ripe tomatoes,
    or 6 canned plum tomatoes, finely
    chopped

2 large celery ribs, finely chopped

½ cup finely chopped flat-leafed parsley

½ cup finely chopped fresh coriander

2 teaspoons salt or to taste

accompaniments

½ pound dates (optional)

2 lemons, cut into wedges

You will need a large heavy pot with a lid, two medium-sized saucepans, and a bowl.

Heat a large pot over medium-high heat. Add the oil, then add the onion and sauté until translucent and beginning to change color. Add the lamb slices and cook until they begin to brown. Add 8 cups of the water and stir well. Add the lentils, chickpeas, turmeric, cinnamon stick, chile pepper flakes, and black pepper. Bring to a boil, skimming off the foam that rises to the surface. Reduce the heat, partially cover, and simmer for approximately 2 hours.

While the soup is cooking, place the barley in a medium saucepan and add the remaining 4 cups water. Bring to a vigorous boil, stirring to prevent sticking, lower heat to medium and boil, partially covered, until the barley is just tender, approximately 35 minutes; add more water if necessary. Drain, reserving the cooking water, and place the barley in a bowl. Set aside.

When the soup has cooked for approximately 1½ hours, prepare the *tedouira,* which will thicken the broth and bring out its full flavor: Dissolve the starter or yeast in ½ cup of the reserved barley water. Put into a medium saucepan, and add the tomatoes and celery. Bring to a boil over medium-high heat, and cook for 10 to 15 minutes, until the mixture has thickened.

Add the tomato mixture, barley, and the remaining barley water to the soup, and continue cooking for 10 minutes. Add the parsley, coriander, salt, and pepper, and cook for another 5 minutes. Taste for seasoning.

Serve the soup hot, with a side plate of dates if desired. Place the lemon wedges on the table, so your guests can squeeze a little fresh lemon juice into the soup.

Note: Traditionally, a part of the household's sourdough starter is used as a thickening agent; a teaspoon of dry yeast can be substituted.

•• ▲ ▲ ▲ ▲ ▲ ▲ • ▲ ▲ ▲ ▲ ▲ ▲ ▲ • • ▲

Serves 8 as a meal-in-one. Serve accompanied by wedges of
Moroccan Anise Bread (page 242).

PORTRAIT OF OUZA

*Ouza married at the age of twelve. Thirty years later, she runs a large house-*hold in the old quarter of Taroudant, a small walled city in the Souss region of southern Morocco. Her niece Latifa had told us that Ouza would be happy to talk to us about Moroccan bread.

One clear sunny January morning, I walk with Latifa through the eastern gate of the town. A donkey cart comes slowly toward us, headed out to the country after dropping off a load of produce in the market. The high Atlas Mountains frame the horizon to the east, their snow-covered peaks unreal in the warmth of the morning. We walk through an open square, then turn left down a narrow mud and plaster-lined lane. Women and children greet Latifa and smile as she introduces me. Some of the women are bareheaded, like Latifa; others have covered heads and faces veiled from the nose down—I "see" their smiles from the lift of cheeks under the veils and the crinkling at the corners of their eyes. We pass a small *épicerie* that sells dried couscous, yogurt, juices, candy, and other small items; otherwise, this part of town looks as it may well have looked for centuries. It's restful to have no cars to dodge, no asphalt or cement underfoot, and to walk at an easy pace through the light and shadow of the labyrinth of small lanes that leads to Ouza's house.

Ouza greets us at the door, then we follow her through a dark passage and come out into the courtyard, tiled in blue and white. Two of Ouza's daughters-in-law are doing the laundry, scrubbing it by hand and then hanging it in the sun. We climb a narrow flight of steps to the flat rooftop overlooking the courtyard: This is Ouza's domain. She cooks up here while supervising the running of the household below. When I ask Latifa whether we're making too much work for Ouza by disrupting her morning, Latifa laughs and shakes her head emphatically. "She enjoys company, and besides, this is a very traditional household. Her daughters-in-law do all the work!"

Ouza has already made a large batch of bread dough and divided it into smaller individual doughs. Now she lights the fire in her kanoon to heat it for baking. The kanoon is a portable stove like a miniature tandoor oven, lined with clay; a wood fire is made in the lower chamber to heat whatever pot or dish is placed on top.

Ouza speaks no English or French, so Latifa translates. I take out my camera and tell Ouza that I would very much like to photograph her as she works. Her long fine-boned face, framed in a head scarf, tries to look serious as Latifa translates, and then she answers with a smile and a shake of her head. "She says you shouldn't bother because she's too old and ugly for photographs. But actually," continues Latifa, "she's pleased."

Ouza bends to add more small branches to the fire in the bottom of the kanoon. She places a shallow clay dish, the bottom part of a tagine, on top of the kanoon to heat and then, sitting on a low three-legged stool like a tiny milking stool, she starts to prepare the loaves. The pieces of dough sit covered with a cloth on a traditional shallow basket, called a *t'boug,* lightly dusted with flour. Working on the t'boug she flattens each piece of dough with the palm of her hand. She lets it rest a minute, then picks it up and pats it between her palms, rotating it slightly as she works. With the skill that comes of long practice, she soon has a thin supple flat-bread. She places it on an inverted sieve, shaped like a tamborine without bells, and waits for the fire to develop.

Once the fire is well established, Ouza uses the sieve as a peel and deftly places the dough on the hot tagine. She then starts flattening and forming another bread. Soon the smell of baking drifts out from the kanoon, mingling with the wood smoke. After it has cooked about five minutes on the first side and two or three on the second, Ouza lifts the baked bread off the heat and into a waiting basket. Then she slides the next pale bread onto the tagine, and so she continues, tending the fire, patting and shaping, chatting to us as she works, yet never skipping a beat.

Soon there are only two or three left to bake. As she flattens out the next bread, Ouza says something to Latifa. This bread is oblong and thinner than the others. She lifts the tagine off the kanoon, and, wetting the bread with a little water, slaps it onto the inside surface of the kanoon. "She's using it like a tandoor oven," I say to Latifa, surprised. She nods. "This is the old, traditional way of baking on the kanoon. But it's very difficult—and time-consuming—so most women don't bother." Ouza smiles with pleasure as we exclaim at the wonderful taste—slightly smoky—and texture—crisp on the outside and tender in the center—of the tandoor breads.

One of the daughters-in-law brings tea, then brushes the ashes out of the kanoon and clears up. On the tea tray are two bowls of oil, one a greenish olive oil, the other reddish brown. Latifa points to it and asks if I've ever tasted argan oil. It is made from roasted kernels from the pits of the fruit of the argan tree. Argans are low scrubby trees that grow in the Souss region of southern Morocco and nowhere else. They are eye-catching for visitors, because goats love the fruit (which resembles olives) and so climb far up into the trees to reach it! The oil can sometimes be found in Paris, but we have as yet not found a North American source. "Ouza likes argan oil, especially in the winter," Latifa says. "It's warming, and also very good for the skin."

Ouza motions to me to copy her gestures as she tears a bread in half, then dips the open edge into the argan oil and eats it. The flavor is nutty, slightly roasted, and very, very good. But the olive oil, too, must be tried. It comes from a cousin's olive grove nearby and was recently pressed, using old-style donkey-powered presses. Again, wonderful. We all sit around chewing our bread and drinking mint tea. "This is how the day goes, traditionally," says Latifa. "The bread dough is made up early, then left to rise. Some of it is cooked, mid-morning, on the kanoon. The rest is taken to the bakery for baking. We stop for tea and bread around ten-thirty, as we're doing now. Then it's time to start cooking the noon meal: tagine or couscous."

Ouza breaks in to tell Latifa something in Arabic, gesturing toward me and smiling. "She's asking me to ask you about coming again tomorrow. It's Friday, so she will be making couscous. Would you and Jeffrey like to come to learn how? Ouza would love to meet your children. . . ."

COUSCOUS

Couscous began as a simple Berber dish, grain—originally barley—steamed over a stew. Over the centuries, and especially after the arrival of the Arabs in Morocco, very elaborate versions of couscous were developed, most often made of wheat, but its fundamentals remained the same. The basic ingenious idea was to cook the grain in the steam from the stew, stacking the container of grain on top of the stew so that only one burner or cooking fire was necessary. This not only saved on fuel, but also infused the grain with the flavors of the stew. Though this cooking method is still used in Tunisia as well as in Morocco to cook barley grits (the finished dish is called *methouth* in Tunisia), it is most widely known and used for preparing wheat couscous.

Ouza putting couscous grains into steamer

Traditional wheat couscous is hand-rolled: Small bits of semolina (wheat meal, made from a coarse grinding of the endosperm of wheat berries) are dampened and rolled in a little fine white flour, becoming more rounded in shape as the flour sticks to them. The grains are then moistened, lightly oiled, and left to dry before being stored. The only couscous grain we can buy in North America is machine-rolled. Some is labeled "instant"; it has been precooked, then dried, and it can be eaten after only a short soaking in hot water or broth.

The traditional method for cooking couscous involves wetting the grains, giving them time to swell with the moisture, then steaming them; each step is repeated several times, so cooking instructions look misleadingly complicated. The goal is to produce fluffy, tender couscous grains. Once you understand the "why" of each step in the process, it all makes sense—somewhat like bread making.

Couscous is traditionally, and most conveniently, cooked in a *couscousière,* a two-part pot with a large saucepan on the bottom and a steamer on top. The broth, meat, and vegetables are cooked below and provide the steam for cooking the grain in the steamer. You can improvise a couscouière by lining a large steamer with cheesecloth and placing it over a slightly smaller-diameter saucepan. To ensure that the gap between the saucepan and the steamer (or top and bottom of the cous-cousière) is well sealed, so that all the steam forced up through the couscous, the easiest way is the traditional Moroccan method: Dampen a towel or other cloth and then wrap it around the pot-steamer seam, and tuck the ends in to seal it each time you place the steamer over the saucepan.

Couscous with Seven Vegetables

couscous aux sept legumes • Morocco

Eating grains with grains—flatbreads with couscous, for example—might sound a bit strange, and excessive in the carbohydrate department. But people in Morocco and Tunisia often eat the two together, just as naan is commonly eaten with pilaf in Central Asia, or chapatti is served alongside biryani. And when you come to think about it, have you never eaten toast and hash-browned potatoes or sat down to a meal with both corn and bread?

This particular version of couscous, from the Souss Valley of southern Morocco, is one of our favorites, loaded with tender slow-cooked vegetables and bathed in a delightfully flavored broth, ideal for sopping up with bread. Although the directions look long, they are not difficult and do leave you time between steps. Total cooking time is less than one and a half hours, so begin preparations less than two hours before you want to serve the dish.

broth and stew

1 medium turnip (approximately ½ pound)

2 to 3 medium carrots (½ pound)

2 to 3 small eggplants (½ pound)

One ½-pound chunk of pumpkin (see page 417)

3 small zucchini (approximately ½ pound)

2 tablespoons olive oil

2 medium onions (approximately ½ pound)

3 medium tomatoes (approximately ¾ pound), cut into wedges

½ pound beef shank or chuck, trimmed and cut into 1-inch chunks

1 to 2 cloves garlic, chopped

1 cup loosely packed fresh coriander leaves, half coarsely chopped and half finely chopped

¼ teaspoon dried chile pepper flakes

½ teaspoon freshly ground black pepper

1 teaspoon cumin, dry-roasted (see page 154) and ground

1 teaspoon saffron threads, crumbled or ground to a powder

4 cups water

½ teaspoon salt

1 to 2 tablespoons North African Chile Paste (page 245; optional)

couscous

1 pound couscous

1¾ to 2 cups cold water

1 teaspoon salt

1 to 2 tablespoons olive oil

You will need a large bowl or pot, a large flat roasting pan, a couscousière or large heavy-bottomed pot with a steamer, a cotton cloth, and a dish towel.

Fill a large bowl or pot with cold water. Peel the turnip and cut into ½-inch slices approximately 1½ inches square. Peel the carrots and cut into 1½-inch lengths not more than ½-inch thick. (If your carrots are thick, slice them lengthwise, then cut into 1½-inch lengths.) Cut 3 lengthwise strips of peel from each eggplant, then cut them crosswise into ½-inch slices. (If your eggplants are large, cut each slice into 3 or 4 thick wedges.) Do not discard the stem end; it tastes especially good after slow-cooking. Peel and seed the pumpkin and cut into ½-inch slices approximately 1½ inches square. Cut the zucchini into similarly sized pieces. Put the zucchini, then the eggplant and pumpkin, and then the carrot and turnip pieces into the cold water, and set aside.

Spread the couscous grains over the bottom of a large roasting pan or other flat pan with sides. (*Note: If using instant couscous, refer to the instructions in parentheses throughout the recipe.*) Gradually add 1 cup cold water, stirring and separating the grains and rubbing them between your fingers to prevent them from sticking. Let stand for 10 minutes.

Heat the lower part of a couscousière or a large heavy-bottomed pot over medium heat. Add the 2 tablespoons oil. When the oil is hot, add the onions, half the tomatoes, the meat, garlic, coarsely chopped coriander leaves, chile flakes, black pepper, and cumin, and cook, stirring, until the meat is browned on all sides. Dissolve the saffron in a little of the 4 cups water, then add the saffron mixture and the remaining water to the pot. Bring the broth to a boil, lower the heat, and let simmer very gently. (If using instant couscous, let the broth simmer over low heat, partially covered, for 15 minutes.)

Passing the couscous grains between your fingers, sprinkle half the couscous into the couscousière steamer, or other steamer, and set over the simmering broth, sealing the joint between the top and bottom of the pot with a damp cloth. As soon as you see steam rising through the couscous, sprinkle the rest of the couscous on top. When steam again rises through the couscous, remove the steamer, and spread the grains out in the roasting pan. Cover with a dish cloth, and let sit for 5 minutes.

Add the turnips, carrots, and salt to the broth, and let simmer gently. (If using instant couscous, let the broth simmer gently, partially covered, for another 15 to 20 minutes.)

Stir the couscous grains with your fingers. Gradually add another ¾ to 1 cup cold water, rubbing the grains between your fingers to aerate them and prevent lumps from forming. Sprinkle on the 1 teaspoon salt and mix well.

Place the steamer back over the broth and seal the joint with the damp cloth. Sprinkle half the couscous into the steamer, wait until steam rises through the grains, and then add the rest of the couscous. Cook, uncovered, for 10 minutes. Then spread the couscous out in the roasting pan again, and cover with the dish cloth. Let sit for 10 minutes.

Add the eggplant and pumpkin to the broth and let simmer. (If using instant couscous, let the broth simmer for another 10 minutes.)

Meanwhile, work through the couscous grains with your hands, rubbing them between your fingers to eliminate lumps. Then oil your palms with olive oil and briskly rub the grains between them to give them flavor and get rid of any remaining lumps.

Add the zucchini, the finely chopped coriander, the parsley, and the rest of the tomatoes to the broth, and let simmer. (If using instant couscous, let the broth simmer for 20 to 30 minutes longer. Meanwhile, prepare the couscous.)

Place the steamer back over the broth. Again sprinkle the couscous back into the steamer, as described above, but start with one third of the grains, wait for steam, then add the next third, and so on. Then cook, uncovered, for 15 minutes longer.

To serve, mound the couscous in a ring on a large platter, leaving a hollow in the center. Using a slotted spoon, lift the vegetables and meat out of the pot and heap them in the middle of the platter, arranging for color and taking care to handle the vegetables gently so they keep their shape. Ladle a little of the broth over the platter, and serve. Place the remaining broth in a serving bowl so that your guests can help themselves to more as they wish. If you like, spice up this broth by stirring the chile paste into it.

Note: Soaking the vegetables in cold water as directed seems to help them keep their shape during the long slow-cooking of the broth.

········▲▲▲▲▲▲▲▲·▲▲▲▲▲▲▲▲··▲

Serves 6.

For a festive meal, begin with several Moroccan salads and wedges of warm Moroccan Anise Bread (page 242). Follow the couscous with Mint Tea (page 268) and Aromatic Festive Bread (page 235).

Chicken Tagine with Olives and Onions

*A tagine is a shallow clay pot with a conical lid, traditionally used for slow-*cooked stews in Morocco. *Tagine* is also the name given to dishes cooked in the pot. The essence of any tagine is its broth; the seductive blending of different flavors found in the broth of a good tagine is a hallmark of Moroccan cooking. Tagines are always eaten with bread, so that every last drop of the broth can be enjoyed.

This dish is our adaptation of a recipe given to us by a young woman in Taroudant, Morocco. It combines lemon-marinated chicken with olives and decorative onion slices, dyed yellow with saffron and turmeric. The region around Taroudant grows olives in great quantity. Many are pressed for olive oil, using donkey-powered stone presses, while others are cured, to be eaten in salads or tagines, or on their own with bread.

Once the chicken has marinated, total cooking time of this slow-cooked dish is less than forty minutes. It can also be prepared ahead and then finished just before serving.

3 pounds chicken legs and breasts, skinned, excess fat removed, and cut into large pieces (legs in two, breasts into two or three)

m a r i n a d e

½ cup lemon juice (2 to 3 lemons), diluted with ¼ cup water

2 cloves garlic, chopped

b r o t h

1 tablespoon olive oil

1 to 2 jalapeños, seeded and finely chopped

½ teaspoon freshly ground black pepper

1 cup coarsely chopped flat-leafed parsley

1 tablespoon fresh thyme leaves

3 cups water

1 teaspoon salt

½ teaspoon turmeric (1 teaspoon if not using saffron)

2 pinches saffron threads, crumbled to a powder (optional)

2 medium onions, cut into ¼-inch slices

¾ cup medium salt-cured black olives

You will need a large nonreactive bowl, a large cast-iron or other heavy pot with a lid, a medium-sized saucepan with a lid, a slotted spoon, and a plate.

Place the chicken pieces in a nonreactive bowl, add the lemon juice and garlic, and toss to coat. Let marinate for 1 hour, turning occasionally.

Heat the oil in a large pot. Add the chicken pieces, reserving the marinade, and brown over medium heat, turning frequently. Add the marinade, jalapeños, pepper, parsley, and thyme. Add the water, and bring to a gentle boil. Add the salt, lower the heat, cover, and let simmer for 20 minutes.

Meanwhile, prepare the onions: Dissolve the turmeric and optional saffron in ½ cup warm water. Place ½ inch of water in a medium-sized saucepan, add the saffron and turmeric mixture, and stir well. Add the onion slices and bring to a gentle boil. Lower the heat and simmer, covered, until the onions are barely softened and yellow, 4 to 5 minutes. Using a slotted spoon, gently lift the onion slices out of water and place on a plate so that they keep their shape. (Save the cooking liquid for another purpose—for example, to cook rice or legumes.) (The recipe can be prepared ahead to this point, and the chicken, broth, and onions refrigerated separately. Twenty minutes before serving, place the chicken and broth back in the pot over moderate heat, and proceed with the recipe.)

Add the olives to the chicken, and place the onion slices over the chicken. Partially cover and let simmer 5 to 10 minutes longer (15 minutes if previously refrigerated), or until the chicken is very tender and at the point of falling from the bone.

Transfer the tagine to a large shallow serving bowl, arranging the onion slices and olives over the chicken pieces, and ladling the broth over all. Serve hot, with plenty of fresh bread to sop up the sauce.

Note: If you wish to increase the recipe—for example, to double or triple the amount of chicken—increase the amount of water by a lesser proportion. As a guide, when you first place chicken and water in pot to cook, the water should not quite completely cover chicken pieces. The other flavoring ingredients should be increased in proportion to the increase in volume of water.

Serves 6.

*Serve with Moroccan Anise Bread (page 242) or Pebbled Persian Bread
(page 55). You could start the meal with Herbed Carrot Salad (page 248)
and Berber Bean Puree (page 244) and the same bread.*

Tunisian Oasis Breads

khubs m'tabga • Southern Tunisia

The palmeries of southern Tunisia are spring-fed date palm oases surrounded by beautiful stark landscapes. These days we can only imagine what a relief the sight of a dark line of date palms at the edge of an oasis was to an incoming camel caravan, after traveling days through the desert.

The palmeries are still a welcome and necessary refuge from the desert, even if camel caravans rarely pass by. The date palms give shade and shelter from drying desert winds, their roots help draw up the water table, and their crowns prevent evaporation. Beneath the trees, cycles of growth and harvest unroll all year round: In December, fresh barley shoots glow emerald green, jasmine blooms gleam in the shade, and the last of the hot red chiles so necessary for harissa wait to be picked. Tomatoes ripen in early spring, while parsley thrives most of the year. There are also pomegranate and fig trees, massive ancient grapevines, and sturdy, fruit-laden orange trees. The moist air and sense of plenty feel miraculous in the middle of the barren desert.

Kebili, Tunisia: Baking Tunisian Oasis Breads

Harvest time for dates is November through January. Kebili, one of the oasis towns, celebrates the harvest annually with a large festival. Unlike the weekly markets in the region, which are the preserve of men only, the Kebili festival also brings out women of all ages, who enjoy the chance to shop, browse, snack, and chat.

When I visited Kebili at festival time, a group of women had set up "shop" baking breads for the crowd—breads traditionally associated with the Kebili region. The breads were warm and supple, filled with a lightly spiced blend of cooked scallion, green pepper, and tomato. I was told they were called *khubs m'tabga,* or folded breads. Two women worked rolling out dough rounds, then filling and flattening them. Another woman tended the open fire and baked the breads, without oil, on a *hamas,* a shallow clay plate rather like a Mexican comal. As she lifted each cooked bread from the hamas, she folded the hot bread in half, then handed it to an eager buyer. I later tasted several other versions, but none to match these Kebili folded breads eaten hot from the pan as the late afternoon festival-goers milled around and Arabic pop songs undulated from the cassette vendor's stall nearby.

··▲▲▲▲▲▲·▮·▲▲▲▲▲▲▲·▮·▲

These delicious savory filled breads are made with unyeasted dough and filled with a chile- and tomato-flavored paste, loaded with chopped scallions.

3 cups unbleached all-purpose flour plus 1 cup soft unbleached white flour, plus extra for kneading

2 teaspoons salt

2 cups warm water

f i l l i n g

2 tablespoons olive oil

1 tablespoon minced garlic

½ cup finely chopped scallions (white and tender green parts)

1 small green bell pepper, cored, seeded, and finely chopped

1½ cups drained canned plum tomatoes, coarsely chopped

Generous pinch of ground caraway

⅛ teaspoon ground cumin

Pinch of ground coriander

½ teaspoon dried chile pepper flakes, or more to taste

½ teaspoon salt

½ cup loosely packed flat-leafed parsley

You will need two medium-sized bowls, a medium-sized skillet, and a large cast-iron skillet at least 10 inches in diameter.

In a medium bowl, mix together the flour and salt. Make a well in the center and slowly stir in the water until a dough forms. Turn out onto a lightly floured surface and knead for 10 minutes. Clean out the bowl, lightly oil, place the dough back in the bowl, and cover with plastic wrap. Set aside.

Heat the oil in a medium skillet. Add the garlic and cook over medium-high heat, stirring occasionally, until it starts to brown. Add the scallions and green pepper and cook, stirring, for 2 minutes, or until slightly softened. Add the tomatoes and bring to a simmer. Reduce the heat to medium and simmer, stirring occasionally, until the sauce thickens, about 15 minutes. Add the spices, chile flakes, and salt and simmer 1 minute. Stir in the parsley, and transfer to a bowl. Let cool.

Working on a lightly floured surface, divide the dough into 8 pieces. Work with one piece at a time, keeping the others covered with plastic wrap.

Heat a large cast-iron or other heavy skillet over medium heat.

Meanwhile, divide one piece of dough in half, and flatten each with lightly floured palms. Then roll out each piece to a circle approximately 6 inches in diameter. Place 1 heaping tablespoon of the filling on the center of one dough circle. Place the other circle on top and, with moistened fingers, pinch the edges together to seal well. Flatten gently, then stretch the bread out thinner by picking it up and stretching the edges, working all around the bread again to keep it round. Then hold the bread by two opposite edges, and pull your hands gently apart to stretch the bread further to a 9-inch diameter round.

Place in the hot skillet and cook for 1 minute, then turn over and bake for 2 to 2½ minutes, until lightly speckled with brown on the bottom. Then turn over again and bake for 1 minute longer, or until lightly browned. Remove from the skillet, fold in half, and wrap in a cotton cloth to keep warm and supple. Repeat with the remaining breads. As you become more accustomed to the process, you will be able to roll out and shape a new bread while the previous bread is cooking. Serve warm.

Makes 8 thin filled folded flatbreads about 9 inches across.

Serve as a snack or with Grilled Vegetable Salad (page 265) or Tunisian Tomato Stew
(page 267) for a Tunisian lunch. Alternatively, serve with dishes with contrasting tastes
and textures, such as Yemeni Yogurt Soup (page 185).

Grilled Vegetable Salad
salata mechouya • Tunisia

Lemon juice, cumin, and parsley—there's a real Eastern Mediterranean fla-vor to this salad of grilled tomatoes, peppers, garlic, and onion. But the French ruled Tunisia for almost a century, and so there are also versions of salata mechouya that are like first cousins to a salade niçoise, with tuna, capers, anchovies, and slices of hard-boiled egg.

Grilling is a quick and flavorful way to cook vegetables with minimal loss of nutrients. You can grill on a charcoal or gas grill or dry-roast in a cast-iron pan on your stove top. Of course charcoal gives an extra smoky flavor, but the other methods do very well, especially when, as here, the vegetables are dressed as a salad.

3 to 4 medium tomatoes	½ teaspoon salt, or more to taste
6 green chiles (see page 410)	2 tablespoons fresh lemon juice
3 cloves garlic, peeled	1 to 2 tablespoons extra-virgin olive oil
1 small onion, quartered	¼ cup finely chopped flat-leafed parsley
¼ teaspoon cumin seed	leaves, plus 3 to 5 sprigs for garnish
¼ teaspoon black peppercorns	

You will need a charcoal or gas grill, or a large cast-iron or other heavy skillet, and a mortar and pestle or spice grinder.

Prepare a charcoal or gas grill, or heat a large heavy skillet over medium-high heat. Grill the tomatoes, peppers, garlic cloves, and onion pieces, turning the ingredients frequently, until the vegetables have blackened patches all over. Remove from the heat.

Remove the stems and seeds from the peppers. If you wish, peel the peppers; we like to leave the skin on for extra flavor. Cut the peppers into strips.

Cut the tomatoes into 4 or 5 pieces each. Slice the onion quarters in half crosswise and break up into layers. Crush the garlic.

Pound the cumin and pepper in a mortar and pestle, or grind in a spice grinder.

In a small bowl, blend together the salt, cumin, pepper, grilled garlic, lemon juice, and oil. Place the vegetables in a serving bowl. Pour over the dressing and stir to coat. Let sit for 30 minutes to blend the flavors.

Just before serving, stir in the chopped parsley. Taste for salt and add more if necessary. Garnish with parsley sprigs.

··▲▲▲▲▲▲·▲▲▲▲▲▲▲▲·▲

Serves 4 as an appetizer or salad.

Serve as an appetizer with wedges of warm Pita (page 181) or Fenugreek Corn Bread (page 223) or as a salad to accompany Grilled Marinated Chicken (page 222) with Bedouin Barley Bread (page 212) or Pita (page 181). Or serve as a light lunch paired with Berber Bean Puree (page 244) and Moroccan Anise Bread (page 242).

Tunisian Tomato Stew with Poached Eggs
chakchouka • Tunisia and Israel

Chakchouka is a great Sunday brunch dish, brought to the table in a skillet and served with sliced cucumbers and fresh flatbreads. It has become popular throughout North Africa and the Middle East. We like to use several different kinds of peppers, combining, for example, a yellow wax pepper, a red bell pepper, an Anaheim, and a jalapeño; they give a slightly crunchy texture as well as bright color to set off the smooth texture and colors of the poached eggs. The dish takes less than twenty-five minutes to prepare and serve.

1 tablespoon olive oil

10 ounces green chiles (see page 410) or 1 banana chile, 1 small red bell pepper, and 1 small Anaheim chile (see page 410), seeded and cut into long strips

2 small yellow onions, thinly sliced

1½ pounds ripe tomatoes, cut into wedges, or 8 to 12 canned plum tomatoes, halved or quartered

½ teaspoon salt

Pinch of freshly ground black pepper

6 large eggs

Pinch of cayenne or paprika

You will need a large cast-iron or other attractive heavy skillet with a lid.

In a large skillet, heat the oil over medium heat. Add the peppers and onions, and cook, stirring occasionally, for 6 to 7 minutes. Add the tomatoes, salt, and pepper, and cook about 7 minutes more, until the tomatoes are soft. Gently crack open the eggs, one at a time, and slide onto the vegetables, keeping the yolks intact. Cover the skillet and cook until the eggs are set, 6 to 7 minutes; if you prefer firm yolks, cook for 2 to 3 minutes longer.

Sprinkle with cayenne or paprika, and serve directly from the skillet.

Alternatives: If you'd like a more chile-hot version, add 1 minced jalapeño to the peppers.

••▲▲▲▲▲▲•▲•▲▲▲▲▲▲▲▲••▲

Serves 4 to 6.

Serve for breakfast or brunch, or as a light supper, accompanied by Moroccan Anise Bread (page 242), Hot Chile Bread (page 201), or Thyme Bread (page 207), and followed by Olive Salad (page 180) and Yogurt and Pomegranate Dip (page 193).

Mint Tea

thé à la menthe • N o r t h   A f r i c a

*Tea is one of the world's most common accompaniments to bread. Hot, satis-*fying, and cheap, a big bowl or mug of tea can give life to a bread that has become too hard to chew. Sipping and dunking, there is great pleasure to be had in the simplest of meals. Moroccan mint tea, with a touch or two of sugar, is one of the best.

4 cups water

3 to 4 teaspoons black tea leaves

1 large bunch fresh mint (spearmint, not peppermint)

2 to 3 tablespoons sugar

You will need a large pot or kettle and a teapot.

Bring the water to a boil. Place the tea leaves in a teapot. Add a good splash of the boiling water, swirl it around, and pour out (without pouring out the leaves); this will wash and wet the tea.

Bring the water back to a boil. Add the mint to the teapot and then the boiling water. Let steep for 3 to 4 minutes. Stir in the sugar and let steep for a minute or so longer. Pour out one glass of tea, then pour it straight back into the pot; this will help mix the flavors.

Pour the tea into tea glasses. Try doing it the traditional way, pouring from at least a foot above the glasses to aerate the tea. Serve alone or with bread or cookies.

Serves 4.

Serve with Aromatic Festive Bread (page 235), Sweet Persian Bread (page 62), or Unyeasted Date Rounds (page 232).

Ethiopian Sponge Breads
injera • Ethiopia

Injera is the traditional daily bread in most parts of Ethiopia. It is closely related to *lakhoach,* a soured, spongey, wheat-flour flatbread made across the Red Sea in Yemen (and now also by the Yemenite community in Israel where it is known as *lahuhua*). It is also related, more distantly, to dosas, the soured batter breads of southern India.

Traditional injera is a thin spongy flatbread made by cooking a soured batter on a large ungreased shallow clay pan about eighteen inches across. The closest approximation to this cooking surface in most North American kitchens is a large nonstick pan, usually about twelve inches in diameter. Actually, many members of the Ethiopian communities in North America and Israel prefer to use a nonstick electric skillet to ensure even heat, producing square injera with rounded corners. Our nonstick pan is round, twelve inches across, and heavy, so that the heat is evenly distributed. The tight-fitting lid is glass, so we can watch to see how each bread is baking.

In Ethiopia, most injera is made of teff flour. Teff is a very small grain related to millet. When ground, it is fine and medium brown in color. Until recently, it was unavailable in North America, but teff is now being grown commercially and sold here; ask for it at an Ethiopian grocery or a health food store.

The traditional process for making injera from teff, described below, looks complex and long, but once you do it, it seems easy. Flour and water are mixed with a little yeast and left for several days to sour before the dough is made up. Souring batters takes time, but it gives an incomparable flavor and a light texture. On the other hand, if you want to speed things up and simplify, you can, by using wheat flour and a little extra yeast (see Quick Injera, page 270). You lose the soured taste and a little of the sponge-like texture, but the breads are on the table very quickly.

teff injera

2 cups finely ground teff flour
  (see page 419)

3 cups lukewarm water

1 teaspoon dry yeast

1 cup water

You will need a large bowl with a lid or cover, a small bowl, a saucepan, and a 10- to 12-inch heavy nonstick skillet or electric frying pan, with a tight-fitting lid.

Place the flour in a large bowl. Add 2½ cups of the warm water, using your fingers to mix and to break up any lumps. The batter should be smooth and almost runny.

Dissolve the yeast in the remaining ½ cup warm water, then stir into the batter. Cover and set aside for 2 to 3 days to sour.

When ready to proceed, drain off any water that has separated from the batter and settled on the surface.

Bring 1 cup water to a boil, and stir in ½ cup of the soured batter to blend well. Lower the heat to medium and heat, stirring, until thick and smooth. Remove from the heat and cool until just warm to the touch but not hot. Stir into soured batter. If necessary to make the batter runny, add a little more warm water, then let rise for 30 minutes to 1 hour.

Preheat a large skillet over medium heat; or heat an electric frying pan to 420°F. When hot, stir the batter, then scoop ½ cup batter, or slightly less if your pan is less than 12 inches in diameter, into a cup and, beginning near the outer edge of the pan, slowly pour it in a thin stream, moving in a spiral toward the center of the pan. Then tilt the pan so the batter can flow over and cover any gaps. Cover and let cook for 2 minutes, then check for doneness: when done, the edges of the injera will begin to curl away from the pan. If not yet done, wipe the lid dry, cover the pan, and cook for about 1 to 2 minutes longer. Use a wooden spatula to begin lifting the bread off the hot surface, then peel it off, lay on a towel, and wrap to keep moist and warm. Stir the batter well, then cook the remaining breads in the same way.

quick injera
2 teaspoons dry yeast
4 cups lukewarm water
2 cups unbleached all-purpose flour

You will need a small bowl, two medium-sized bowls, a large fine-meshed sieve, a wooden spatula, and a heavy nonstick skillet or electric frying pan, 10 to 12 inches in diameter, with a tight-fitting lid.

In a small bowl, dissolve the yeast in ½ cup of the warm water.

Sift the flour into a medium bowl. Stir in the remaining 3½ cups water, and blend well. Add the dissolved yeast and blend well. The batter will be quite runny.

Place the sieve over a second bowl, and pour the batter through the sieve. Use a spatula to mash any lumps against the mesh of the sieve. You should now have a completely smooth batter. Let stand, covered, for 2 to 3 hours, until it is bubbling well.

Place a large skillet over medium-high heat; if using an electric pan, heat to 420°F. When the pan is hot, stir the batter and, if necessary, add enough warm water to make it runny. Scoop ½ cup batter, or slightly less if your pan is less than 12 inches in diameter, into a cup, then pour onto the heated griddle in a thin stream, starting at the outside and gradually moving in a spiral toward the center. Tilt the pan to let batter flow over and cover any bare patches, then cover and let cook for 1½ minutes. Lift off the lid and wipe off any condensation, then cover again and cook for another 1½ minutes, or until the edges of the injera begin to lift away from the pan and the top is slightly shiny, with small air holes. Leaving the pan over the heat, use a wooden spatula to help lift the injera off the hot surface, and slowly peel it off the pan. Lay on a towel to cool, and continue making breads. Do not stack the breads until they have cooled. Then wrap in a cloth to keep them supple until needed. Makes 8 thin, sponge-like breads about 12 inches in diameter and less than ⅛ inch thick.

··▲▲▲▲▲▲··▲▲▲▲··▲▲··▲

Makes 7 to 8 thin supple sponge-like breads, 10 to 12 inches in diameter.

Injera are meant to be both an eating surface and a flavor sponge, as well as a wrapper for other foods. To serve a meal of several Ethiopian dishes, lay two injera overlapping on each dinner plate (don't worry if they hang over the edge), then spoon on one small mound each of Ethiopian Beef Tartare (page 277), Spicy Chicken Stew (page 276), and Spiced Curds (page 278). Have a small stack of extra injera on the table, wrapped in a towel for warmth and to prevent drying out. Set out a bowl of Green Pepper Relish (page 274) and a small dish of Ethiopian Chile and Spice Paste (page 275), so guests can spoon some as a condiment or sauce on the other foods. Guests should eat with their fingers, tearing off an edge of injera and then using it to pick up a mouthful of food. The flavors will soak into the bread beautifully.

Ethiopian Spice Bread

ambasha • Ethiopia

Despite a growing number of excellent Ethiopian restaurants in major North American cities, many people think of Ethiopian food as almost a contradiction in terms; the Horn of Africa (Ethiopia, as well as Somalia and Sudan) is now known more for its famines, civil wars, and starving populations than for its ancient and sophisticated cultural and culinary traditions.

We've never been in Ethiopia, but in our minds we're often there. We have cooked and had cooked for us a range of Ethiopian dishes. Many—both in their basic ingredients and combinations of spices—are quite unlike foods from any- where else in the world. Ambasha, from the Amharic-inhabited central highlands, is one of a number of distinctive Ethiopian breads, and one of the few made with yeast and wheat flour.

Fenugreek, used commonly in many parts of the world as a spice (as in this recipe), is in fact a legume. In many parts of Ethiopia, it is boiled to make a gruel or soup for infants and young children. It grows wild in Ethiopia, has a high crude pro- tein content (over 30 percent), and is, like cardamom and coriander, widely traded in local markets. The blend of the three in ambasha is aromatic and provides a sub- tle backdrop to the honey it is often served with.

2 teaspoons dry yeast

2½ cups lukewarm water

3 cups hard unbleached white flour

1 tablespoon salt

Seeds from 1 green cardamom pod (see page 409), finely ground

½ teaspoon fenugreek seed (see page 414), dry-roasted (see page 154) and finely ground

1 teaspoon coriander seed (see page 412), finely ground

2 to 3 cups hard whole wheat flour

You will need a large bread bowl, one large or two small (10- by 14-inch) baking sheets, and a serrated knife.

In a bread bowl, dissolve the yeast in the warm water. Stir in the white flour. Stir 100 times in the same direction, about 1 minute, to develop the gluten. Sprinkle on the salt and spices. Gradually stir in the whole wheat flour until you can stir no longer. Turn the dough out onto a lightly floured bread board and knead for 8 to 10 minutes, until smooth and elastic. Clean out the bread bowl, oil lightly, and return the dough to the bowl. Cover with plastic wrap, and let rise for 1½ to 2 hours, until approximately doubled in volume.

Gently punch down the dough. Let rest for 10 minutes.

Preheat the oven to 400°F.

Divide the dough into 6 equal pieces. Form each piece into a small ball, then gently flatten to approximately 2 inches thick with the palm of your hand. Place on a large lightly greased baking sheet, or two small sheets, cover, and let rise until almost doubled in volume, about 30 minutes.

Just before baking, with a serrated knife, slash an X about ¼ inch deep on the top of each small bread. Bake in the center of the oven for approximately 25 minutes. To test for doneness, tap the bottom of a loaf—it should sound hollow. Remove and cool on a rack before serving.

Makes 6 small rounded loaves.

Serve with wild honey and strong Ethiopian coffee. Ambasha also makes a good accompaniment to Spiced Curds (page 278).

Green Pepper Relish

karya • Ethiopia

We first tasted this simple and attractive sauce in the small house of a newly arrived Jewish Ethiopian family outside Beersheba in Israel. It tasted so fresh that we thought there must be lemon or lime juice in it, but no, we were told, only sweet pepper, garlic, and salt. Back home we tested it and there it was, a simple refreshing dip for injera or other breads or a condiment for grilled meat. You can use a mortar and pestle, as we were instructed to do by our hosts, but a food processor is even quicker. For a slightly hot version, add a diced jalapeño to the relish.

1 very fresh, flawless large green bell pepper

1 medium clove garlic, peeled and coarsely chopped

⅛ teaspoon salt, or more to taste

You will need a large mortar and pestle or a food processor.

Wash the green pepper and chop coarsely, discarding the seeds, membranes, and core. Pound the garlic and salt in a mortar with a pestle. Add the pepper and pound to a pulp. Alternatively, combine the pepper, garlic, and salt in a food processor and process to a paste.

Serve at room temperature in a small bowl, with injera for dipping.

Makes about 1 cup sauce.

Serve as a snack or as an appetizer, with Ethiopian Sponge Breads (page 269) or Pita (page 181). If serving an Ethiopian meal, serve at the same time as Spicy Chicken Stew (page 276) and Ethiopian Beef Tartare (page 277) with injera. It is also a pleasant and refreshing accompaniment to grilled chicken, lamb, or beef.

Stack of dried chiles

Ethiopian Chile and Spice Paste
berbere • Ethiopia

Classic berbere is a powdered spice mix used as an ingredient in other dishes. In Ethiopia, with no refrigeration, a dried powder is necessary for storing many of the spices and herbs that go into berbere. The powder is often moistened to make a paste and served as a condiment or dip.

Seeds from 2 green cardamom pods (see page 409)

¼ teaspoon fenugreek seed (see page 414)

½ teaspoon black peppercorns

¼ teaspoon coriander seed

2 ounces dried red chiles (see page 410) (2 loosely packed cups), rinsed, soaked for 1 hour in hot water, and drained

⅛ teaspoon ground cinnamon

1 teaspoon salt

1 tablespoon minced fresh ginger

2 tablespoons minced garlic

2 tablespoons chopped onion

½ cup water

½ cup holy basil or ordinary basil leaves, finely chopped

½ cup fresh mint leaves, finely chopped

You will need a cast-iron or other heavy skillet, a mortar and pestle or spice grinder, a food processor, a medium-sized saucepan, and a sterilized glass jar.

In a heavy skillet over high heat, dry-roast the cardamom seeds, fenugreek, peppercorns, and coriander seed together for 2 to 3 minutes, stirring constantly. Place in a mortar or spice grinder and grind to a powder.

Place the soaked chiles in a food processor and process to a paste. Add the ground spices, the cinnamon, and salt. Process to blend. (Leave in the processor.)

Combine the ginger, garlic, onion, and water in a medium-sized saucepan and bring to a boil. Cook for 5 minutes, then add to the processor and process until pulverised. Add the basil and mint and process until well blended.

Spoon the paste into a sterilized glass jar. Seal well, and refrigerate.

Alternatives: To produce the powder of classic berbere, spread paste in a thin layer on a baking sheet and place in a 200°F oven until dried out, turning occasionally.

··▲▲▲▲▲▲▲··▲▲▲·▲▲▲▲··▲

Makes approximately 2 cups chile paste.

Use in Ethiopian recipes, diluted with a little water or oil, or as a dip for Ethiopian Sponge Breads (page 269) or other flatbreads.

Spicy Chicken Stew

yedoro minchet abish • Ethiopia

Ethiopian cuisine has plenty of chicken and meat in it, for feast days and for those who can afford it. More unusual, from an outsider's perspective, is the amount of butter, often clarified butter, that goes into many of the traditional dishes. We have reduced the quantities of butter somewhat, without overly compromising traditional tastes and textures. In Ethiopia the ingredients of this stew would include a honey-based alcoholic mead called *tej,* for which we have substituted red wine. The aroma that fills the kitchen as this cooks is rich and promising and, oddly enough, reminiscent of the flavors of French cuisine.

Yedoro minchet abish is a medium-hot dish of spiced minced chicken, aromatic with ginger and cardamom and rich with butter, onion, and red wine. To make an *alicha* ("mild") version of the same dish, omit the spice paste.

2 cups chopped onions

4 tablespoons unsalted butter

3 to 4 tablespoons Ethiopian Chile and Spice Paste (page 275)

½ teaspoon salt

¾ cup red wine

½ teaspoon minced fresh ginger

1 pound skinless boneless chicken meat, finely chopped

½ teaspoon freshly ground black pepper

⅛ teaspoon green cardamom seed (see page 409), ground, or ground cardamom

1½ cups water

You will need a medium-sized heavy saucepan.

In a dry heavy saucepan, cook the onions over medium heat until lightly browned, stirring constantly to prevent burning. Add a dash of water if necessary if the onions are sticking to the pan.

Add the butter, spice paste, and salt, and cook over low heat for 15 minutes, stirring frequently. Add the wine and ginger, then add the chicken and cook over medium-low heat for 10 minutes, or until the chicken has changed color. Add the pepper, cardamom, and water, and bring to a gentle boil, stirring occasionally. Lower the heat and simmer for 10 to 15 minutes, uncovered, until the sauce has reduced and thickened. Serve hot, with bread.

··▲▲▲▲▲▲·▲·▲▲·▲▲▲▲▲·▲▲·▲

Serves 2 to 4.

Serve with Ethiopian Sponge Breads (page 269), accompanied by Green Pepper Relish (page 274) and Spiced Curds (page 278).

Ethiopian Beef Tartare

kitfo lebleb • Ethiopia

This is a slightly cooked (lebleb) *version of kitfo, a spicy hot Ethiopian spe-*cialty very much like steak tartare. Traditionally, the chile heat in the dish comes from *mitmitta,* a powder made of dried hot bird chiles combined with cardamom and salt, and pounded to a powder. Chile powder of this heat and flavor is not available commercially in North America, so we have substituted fresh hot chiles.

To prepare uncooked kitfo, just remove the skillet from the heat after you stir in the spices. Add the meat and chiles, blend well, and serve.

½ teaspoon black peppercorns

1 teaspoon brown cardamom seed
  (see page 409)

¼ teaspoon salt

½ teaspoon finely grated or chopped
  fresh ginger

1 teaspoon finely chopped fresh mint
  or holy basil

2 tablespoons unsalted butter

½ cup finely chopped onions

1 pound ground lean beef (see Note)

4 to 6 bird chiles or serrano chiles
  (see page 410) , very finely chopped

You will need a mortar and pestle or a spice grinder, a bowl, and a heavy-bottomed skillet.

In a mortar or a spice grinder, grind the peppercorns and cardamom seeds. Then combine with the salt, ginger, and fresh herb in a bowl or the mortar, and stir or pound to blend.

In a heavy-bottomed skillet, melt the butter over medium heat. Stir in the onions and cook for about 5 minutes, or until the onions are translucent.

Stir in the spice mixture, then stir in the meat and chopped chiles. Cook gently for 2 to 3 minutes over medium heat, until the meat is slightly browned but still quite rare. Remove from the heat. Serve hot or at room temperature, mounded on a plate.

Note: You can buy ground beef, or for a more traditional chopped beef texture, buy a lean cut such as flank steak or eye of round and chop it very fine by hand with a cleaver.

·· ▲ ▲ ▲ ▲ ▲ ·▲ ·▲ ·▲ ·▲ ·▲ ▲ ▲ ▲ ·· ▲

Serves 3 to 4.

Serve with Ethiopian Sponge Breads (page 269) and side dishes of Spiced Curds
(page 278) and Green Pepper Relish (page 274).

Spiced Curds

ayib bemit'mit'a • Ethiopia

This vegetarian dish is one of many in Ethiopia that have developed as a result of the almost two hundred days of fasting observed by followers of the Coptic Church, the faith of the majority in the country. Traditionally, spiced curds are made from scratch, using curds pressed from buttermilk, but we have shortened the process by substituting cottage cheese. The blend of cool curds and hot chiles is a great combination.

1 clove garlic

1 pound cottage cheese (or buttermilk curds)

¼ teaspoon very finely chopped fresh ginger

¼ teaspoon salt

¾ teaspoon freshly ground pepper

1 to 2 bird chiles or 4 jalapeños (see page 410), seeded and very finely chopped

You will need a large mortar and pestle.

Slice the garlic clove in half, and rub the inside of the serving bowl well with the cut sides. Discard the garlic.

Turn the cottage cheese into the bowl.

In a mortar, pound together the remaining ingredients. Stir into the cottage cheese and mix well. Serve at room temperature or chilled.

▲•••▲▲▲▲▲•▲▲▲••▲▲▲•▲

Makes about 2 cups curds. Serves 3 to 4.

Ayib bemit'mit'a can be served on its own with Ethiopian Sponge Breads (page 269) or Ethiopian Spice Bread (page 272), or included as part of a larger Ethiopian meal.

Spicy Vegetarian Spread

infirfir shiro • Ethiopia

If you have Ethiopian Chile and Spice Paste on hand, infirfir shiro can be quickly prepared. The spice paste gives it chile heat, but when it is eaten with bread, the warmth of this chickpea sauce is neutralized and leaves only a glowing aftertaste. Like so many of Ethiopia's wonderfully creative foods, this recipe comes out of the meatless fasting days of the Coptic Church.

Infirfir shiro is an excellent accompaniment to almost any savory flatbread.

¼ cup vegetable oil

1 cup chopped red onions (2 small)

2 tablespoons Ethiopian Chile and Spice Paste (page 275)

3 cups water

1 teaspoon minced garlic

1 teaspoon minced fresh ginger

Seeds from 3 green cardamom pods (see page 409), ground

Approximately 1 cup chickpea flour (see page 410)

1 teaspoon salt, or more to taste

You will need a heavy saucepan.

Heat a heavy saucepan over high heat. Add the oil. When it is hot, add the onions, and cook over medium-high heat, stirring occasionally, until lightly golden.

Blend the spice paste with 1 cup of the water, and add to the onions. Bring to a boil. Add the garlic, ginger, cardamom, and remaining 3 cups water, and bring back to a boil.

Lower the heat to medium, then sift the chickpea flour gradually into the boiling mixture, stirring constantly to prevent lumps. The mixture will become increasingly thick and should finally have a thick, paste-like texture; if it starts to thicken quickly, add less than 1 full cup of chickpea flour, or add a little extra water. Stir in the salt and continue to cook for 3 to 5 minutes over medium-low heat. Taste and adjust seasonings if necessary.

Turn out into a bowl. Serve hot or at room temperature.

∙∙▲▲▲▲▲▲∙∙▲▲▲▲∙∙▲▲∙∙▲

Makes approximately 3 cups pâté-like spread.

Serve with Ethiopian Sponge Breads (page 269), Ethiopian Spice Bread (page 272), or other savory flatbread—try Pita (page 181) or Bedouin Barley Bread (page 212)—and a fresh salad or a dip such as Green Pepper Relish (page 274).

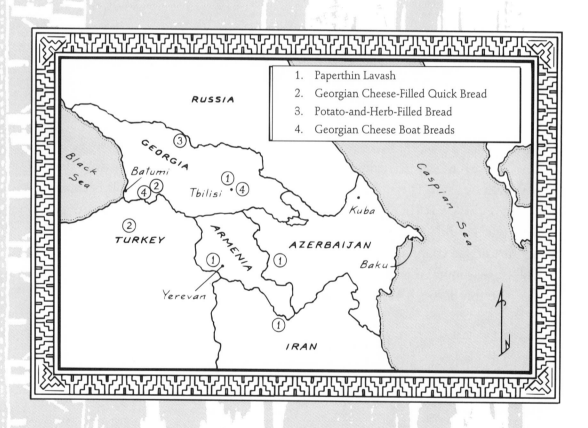

1. Paperthin Lavash
2. Georgian Cheese-Filled Quick Bread
3. Potato-and-Herb-Filled Bread
4. Georgian Cheese Boat Breads

RUSSIA

GEORGIA

Black
Sea

Batumi

Tbilisi

Caspian
Sea

Kuba

TURKEY

ARMENIA

AZERBAIJAN

Baku

Yerevan

IRAN

Armenia, Georgia, and Azerbaijan (the Caucasus)

Armenia, Georgia, and Azerbaijan are the three countries, formerly part of the Soviet Union, that make up the Caucasus. The region extends from the Black Sea to the Caspian Sea and Iran, and lies between the Lesser Caucasus mountains on Turkey's eastern border and the Greater Caucasus mountains to the west and north. With fish from the sea and fertile agricultural valleys, especially in Georgia and Azerbaijan, the region has traditionally been rich in food. In times of peace, it produces wine, olives, limes and lemons, cheeses, herbs and spices, and much more. But wars and conflicts, not just between Armenia and Azerbaijan, but also between Georgia's central government and several of the distinct and important populations (Abkhazians and Os-

Tbilisi, Georgia: Sifting corn flour

setians, for example) included within Georgia's borders, have meant frequent hardship recently, and serious shortages of food and fuel.

Flatbreads are an essential staple in the Caucasus, from the stove-top household version of Armenian lavash, to the cheese-filled khachapuri of Georgia and the tandoor-baked boomerang-shaped shotispuri turned out by Georgian bakeries. They are eaten in great quantities with every meal, paired with fresh herbs and cheese, or with a soup, stew, or grill. The large multidish feasts of all three Caucasus countries always include stacks of flatbread.

The Caucasus region lies on important historic trade routes between the Caspian and Black seas and has frequently been controlled by major powers: the Persians, the Ottomans, and, most recently, the Russians. Each has left a mark—subsequently adapted and modified—on the region's culinary traditions. From Persian cuisine comes the frequent use of pomegranates, fruit, and walnuts in savory dishes as well as the use of fresh herbs; from

Yerevan, Armenia: Large lavash hanging on a line

Ottoman tradition, grilled meats and slow-cooked meat and vegetable stews. The subtle spice blend *kmeli suneli,* which characterizes Georgian cooking, shows an Indian influence, perhaps brought by the Persians.

Flatbreads for sale in Yerevan

Paperthin Lavash

lavash • Armenia

Holding an Armenian lavash in my arms for the first time was one of the greatest bread moments in my life. I'd read about lavash, I'd heard stories about it, I'd tried to imagine the great paperthin breads, but nothing prepared me for the real thing! Arriving in Armenia by car from Georgia, all I could think about was finding lavash, but for two days I was unsuccessful. "People don't bake in their homes anymore, especially in the city," I was told sadly again and again in Yerevan, "but try in the market." So I tried in the market: "No, not today."

On the third day there they were at last, tucked away in a far corner. A gruff young man was selling the lavash. "No, you can't take a picture," he said. I wanted to buy some lavash, but I couldn't understand how much they cost. They were stacked in big bundles; I had no idea what size they were. Finally I gave the man ten roubles, what was then about thirty cents. He gave me a troubled look, but then proceeded to weigh out a few kilograms—yes, kilograms–of lavash. For ten roubles I walked away as if carrying a heavy sheep under my arm. By this time, word had spread around the market, and everyone was laughing. With my best I-know-just-what-I'm-doing look on my face, I quickly left the market and hurried back to my hotel. I untied the package, unfolded the lavash, and held a single paperthin bread up over my head: four feet wide, five feet long. Incredible lavash!

Lavash is a very old bread, and it's made by many people besides Armenians. In many parts of Iran it is the staple bread. In Lebanon, where it is called *khubz markouk,* it is thought of as mountain bread because it is the daily bread in many mountain villages. Because it is so thin, lavash dries out almost instantly, and in this way it's preserved. Whenever you need fresh bread, you simply sprinkle some water over it and wrap it in a towel, and immediately the bread is once again soft. Preserving bread in this way has traditionally been a way of putting up food for the winter, as well as conserving fuel resources. For nomadic or seminomadic peoples, lavash is a food that's easy to carry and needs no additional cooking.

The enormous paperthin lavash of Armenia are made in a tannur oven (see page 35), but in many other countries the breads are made on a sajj, a large concave iron plate placed over an open fire. At home we improvise with a large wok that we turn upside down over a gas flame. If you don't have a sajj, a tannur, a wok, or a gas stove, simply bake the lavash on baking sheets or unglazed quarry tiles in the oven.

continued

These lavash are much smaller than the great sheet I bought that day in Yerevan, more like the bread made in homes in parts of Lebanon, Georgia, Armenia, and Iran. They are very quick to bake and very thin and supple when fresh.

1 tablespoon mild honey (or brown sugar)

½ teaspoon dry yeast

1½ cups lukewarm water

2½ to 3 cups hard unbleached white flour

1 teaspoon salt

You will need a medium-sized bread bowl, a rolling pin, and a large wok for stove-top cooking, or quarry tiles (see page 20) to fit a rack in your oven or a large baking sheet for oven baking.

Stir the honey and yeast into the warm water in a medium-sized bread bowl until dissolved. Gradually add 2 cups flour, stirring continuously in the same direction. Then stir 100 times, about 1 minute, in the same direction to help develop the gluten in the flour. Sprinkle on the salt, and gradually add more flour until the dough is too stiff to mix. Turn the dough out onto a lightly floured surface and knead until smooth and elastic, 5 to 7 minutes, adding flour only as needed.

Clean and lightly oil your bread bowl, place the dough in the bowl, and cover with plastic wrap. Let rise for approximately 3 hours, or until doubled in volume. (You can also let the dough rise overnight in a cool place; the slower rise will give more flavor.)

Punch down the dough and let rest for 10 minutes.

Divide the dough into 8 equal pieces. Flatten each piece between floured palms. To roll out the lavash, work on two pieces at a time, leaving the remaining dough covered. Roll out one piece to a round 5 to 6 inches in diameter, and then switch to the other piece. (In rolling out yeasted doughs, it is important to roll them out only so far and then to let them rest before rolling out more; see page 17. The gluten is stretched as you roll it out, and once it gets accustomed to its new shape, it can be easily stretched some more.) Alternate between the two doughs until each is a very thin round approximately 13 to 14 inches in diameter.

***T**o cook the breads using a wok and a gas flame:* Turn the wok upside down over high heat. Lightly oil the top surface with a paper towel, and let it get hot before putting on a bread. The rolled-out bread is a little fragile at this point and may tear while being transferred to the wok. To carry it easily, roll it halfway up onto the rolling pin. Then lay one edge on the hot wok and gradually unroll the bread over the wok.

Cook for 15 seconds and then delicately turn the bread with a wooden spatula. Cook for 30 to 40 seconds, then turn over again and cook for 30 seconds. Remove the lavash and lay it on a clean kitchen towel. Fold the bread in half and wrap it in the towel to keep it warm. Cook the second bread, and then continue rolling out and cooking the remaining breads.

To bake the lavash: Position a rack in the lower third of the oven and arrange quarry tiles on the rack, leaving a 1-inch gap between the tiles and the oven walls. If you don't have quarry tiles, place a large baking sheet on the rack to preheat.

Preheat the oven to 450°F.

Bake the lavash on the tiles or baking sheet for 2 to 2½ minutes, until lightly brown.

Serve the breads warm. Breads left out to cool will quickly become dry and brittle. These can be eaten like crackers or broken up into soups and stews.

Makes 8 thin round flatbreads about 14 inches across.

Lavash is good with almost everything. Because it is thin and pliable, it is especially good with foods for which it can be used as a spoon, such as Okra and Chicken Stew (page 283), Red Beans with Sour Plum Sauce (page 308), and Armenian Tomato and Eggplant Salsa (page 287). Lavash also crosses cultures very well, and is ideal for an after-school snack, as it can wrap itself around almost anything.

Okra and Chicken Stew

bami shokeb • Armenia

Okra, gumbo, lady's fingers—we love it no matter what its name, and more or less no matter how it is prepared. If you like okra, try this Armenian home-style dish. Chicken is boiled, then boned and broken into pieces which float in an okra and tomato stew. Just before serving, the dish is tempered by the addition of a little lemon juice and dry white wine. Try it in the winter with Bulgur Pilaf and Paperthin Lavash.

One 2½-pound chicken or 2¼ pounds whole chicken legs and breasts

5 cups cold water

1 pound okra

¼ cup cider vinegar

1 tablespoon olive oil

3 to 4 cloves garlic, finely chopped

1 medium onion, finely diced

1 pound ripe tomatoes, cut into wedges, or one 16-ounce can plum tomatoes, drained and coarsely chopped

2 teaspoons salt

½ teaspoon cayenne

Freshly ground black pepper to taste

¼ cup fresh lemon juice

¼ cup dry white wine

You will need a large pot with a lid, a large bowl, and a large saucepan with a lid.

Place the chicken in a large pot and add the cold water. Bring to a boil, then gently boil, partly covered, until tender, about 45 minutes. To test for doneness, check to see if the meat near the bone of the drumsticks or thighs is no longer pink.

Lift the chicken pieces out of the pot and allow to cool. Place the broth in a container in the refrigerator to cool so that the fat can be skimmed off. (The recipe can be made ahead to this point and the chicken and stock stored in the refrigerator, well covered, for up to 48 hours.)

Wash the okra. Cut large okra in half, but leave medium and small ones whole. In a large bowl, soak the okra in the cider vinegar and 1 cup water for 20 minutes, giving the okra an occasional stir. Drain, discarding the soaking liquid.

Remove the skin from the chicken and separate the meat from the bones. Tear the meat into bite-sized pieces and set aside. Discard skin and bones.

Skim the fat off the chicken broth. Measure the broth. If necessary, add water to make 4 cups total.

Heat a large saucepan over medium-high heat, and add the oil. When the oil is hot, add the garlic and onion and sauté until the onion begins to look translucent.

Add the tomatoes and cook, stirring, for 2 to 3 minutes. Add the chicken and okra, then add the broth. Add the salt, cayenne, and black pepper, and stir gently to mix. Cover and bring to a gentle boil. Reduce the heat and simmer, partially covered, until the okra is just tender, about 10 minutes.

Add the lemon juice and wine, taste for seasoning, and simmer 4 to 5 minutes uncovered. Serve hot.

. ▲ ▲ ▲ ▲ ▲ . ▲ ▲ . ▲ ▲ ▲ ▲ ▲ . . ▲ ▲

Serves 4.

Serve accompanied by stacks of Paperthin Lavash (page 283) or Afghan Snowshoe Naan (page 40) and with Bulgur Pilaf (page 179) for a great meal.

Armenian Tomato and Eggplant Salsa

Armenia

In early October 1991, I arrived in Yerevan, the capital of Armenia, not knowing it was the last week of the first free election in Armenia since 1921. Sitting at the only empty chair for breakfast in a little restaurant on my first morning in town, I by chance sat next to a person of some authority in the main opposition party. We chatted over breakfast. Come that evening, I was in a small town several hours from Yerevan listening to the party's presidential candidate express his views before a crowd of several hundred people. Around about midnight, with the candidate and two dozen other party partisans, we sat down to a feast. It was a wild night, and a grand feast. With all the wonderful intensity of independence, free elections, and life-and-death issues, I felt almost ashamed inquiring in detail about the ingredients of this salsa. But the salsa was so good, and the ingredients such a mystery. . . .

The eggplant almost disappears in this salsa, yet it adds body and texture, as well as a delicious slightly smoky flavor. For a hotter version—this one is quite mild—simply increase the amount of chiles.

continued

2 small eggplants (about ½ pound)

1 pound ripe tomatoes or one 16-ounce can plum tomatoes, coarsely chopped

½ cup fresh coriander leaves

¼ teaspoon salt, or more to taste

3 large cloves garlic, finely chopped

1 jalapeño, seeded and coarsely chopped

3 scallions, finely chopped

You will need a baking sheet or a heavy skillet with a lid, and a food processor.

Preheat the oven to 425°F.

Prick the eggplants all over with a fork and place on a baking sheet. Roast in the oven for 30 minutes, or until the skin has changed color and the eggplant is soft and collapsed. Alternatively, place in a cast-iron frying pan with a lid and cook, covered, over medium heat, turning every 10 minutes, for 30 minutes. Set aside to cool.

Halve the eggplants and scrape out the flesh; discard the skin. Place the flesh in a food processor, and add all the remaining ingredients. Process until pureed. Taste for salt and chile heat, and adjust seasonings as necessary. Turn out into a serving bowl and serve at room temperature.

ᴵᴵ▲▲▲▲▲▲▲ᴵᴵ▲▲▲ᴵᴵ▲▲ᴵᴵ▲▲ᴵᴵ▲ᴵ

Makes approximately 3 cups salsa.

Serve with Paperthin Lavash (page 283) or Pita (page 181) for dipping, or as a sauce to accompany grilled lamb: Try Spicy Cumin Kebabs (page 33) or Marinated Lamb Kebabs (page 176).

Wheat Berry and Chicken Soup

herrisah • Armenia

Herrisah is an Armenian staple, a satisfying meal-in-a-bowl that is easy to make and unique in flavor. Chicken and wheat berries are boiled until they're tender, and then ground together to make a hearty pureed soup. This simple base is adorned with fresh tarragon, coriander, mint, pickled hot chiles, tomato wedges, a squeeze of lemon, a spoonful of caviar—whatever is tasty and in season. It is traditionally served with Paperthin Lavash and a plate of fresh herbs (as are most Armenian meals), together with a selection of different salad side dishes, a young goat cheese, and thin slices of basturma (dried meat).

The first time I tasted herrisah, I was in a tiny restaurant in the town of Kirovakan in central Armenia. The streets outside were lined with trees all in their autumn colors; winter was just around the corner. Herrisah felt like the ultimate in comfort food, yet at the same time I couldn't help but be reminded of faraway Vietnam. In both cuisines, fresh herbs are an essential part of almost every meal, and with so much of the meal assembled at the table, the final taste of most dishes is decided upon by each individual diner.

1½ cups wheat berries

12 cups cold water

2½ to 3 pounds chicken legs
  and breasts

1 onion, quartered

Sprig of fresh thyme

1 bay leaf

8 to 10 black peppercorns

2 teaspoons salt, or more to taste

Freshly ground black pepper

garnishes and
accompaniments

Herb Plate (see page 291)

lemon wedges

2 to 3 ripe tomatoes, finely chopped

2 cups plain yogurt

You will need two large pots with lids and a food processor, meat grinder, or blender.

Place the wheat berries in a large pot and add 4 cups of the cold water. Bring the water to a boil, and then remove from the heat. Cover and let stand for 2 hours.

Meanwhile, in another large pot, cover the chicken with the remaining 8 cups cold water and bring to a boil. Add the onion, thyme sprig, bay leaf, and peppercorns, and boil gently, partly covered, until the chicken is tender, about 45 minutes. Remove the chicken from the pot and strain the stock. Let the chicken cool, then remove and discard the skin. Remove the meat from the bones, and discard the bones.

Bring the pot of wheat berries back to a boil, and boil gently until the berries are soft to the bite, approximately 1 hour, adding more water if necessary. (The chicken, stock, and wheat berries can be prepared ahead and refrigerated in well-sealed containers for up to 48 hours.)

In a food processor, meat grinder, or blender, grind together the wheat berries and the chicken. Depending on which method you use, you may have to add some of the reserved chicken stock to help with the grinding; the wheat berries and chicken can be difficult to pulverize entirely, so do the best you can. (It makes no difference to the taste of the dish, and in fact we enjoy the slightly rough texture the berry pieces give to the soup.)

Transfer the chicken mixture to a large pot, and add the remaining chicken stock and salt. Bring to a simmer, stirring. Then taste for seasoning and add salt and black pepper to taste.

Serve in individual bowls, along with the garnishes and accompaniments, so each person can add to his or her own soup as desired.

·· ▲ ▲ ▲ ▲ ▲ · · ▲ ▲ ▲ · · ▲ ▲ · · ▲

Serves 6 to 8 as a one-dish meal.

Set out a basket of Georgian Cheese-Filled Quick Bread (page 292), cut into wedges, or Paperthin Lavash (page 283). An Olive Salad (page 180) and Provençal Sautéed Wild Mushrooms (page 325) served alongside, as well as the garnishes and accompaniments listed, can transform a simple meal into a special dinner.

HERB PLATE

Armenia

No meal in Armenia feels complete without a plate of fresh herbs—mint, coriander, tarragon, dill, basil, parsley, and chives—and a pile of lavash (see page 283). This approach to eating and assembling tastes came from Persia perhaps, or maybe the influence went the other way. In both cuisines, and often, too, in Georgia and Azerbaijan, the herbs are used by each person eating to finish off the balance of a dish in an individual way. They can be added to a cheese and bread combination, tossed into a bowl of soup, or just eaten wrapped in bread. An herb plate on the table has become an easy and pleasurable accompaniment to many of our meals.

If you grow fresh herbs in the winter, it is easier to maintain the herb plate habit through the cold months. Most major supermarkets as well as many produce markets now stock fresh herbs throughout the year. To assemble an herb plate, place washed and dried sprigs of fresh herbs on a plate. You can supplement the herbs with a small pile of trimmed scallions, some small radishes, and watercress.

BREAD STORY

Mkrtesh, a young Armenian living in Tbilisi, Georgia, took me to meet his mother. "She can tell you about traditional breads," he said. Speaking in careful primary-school-teacher Russian (she taught seven-year-olds) so I could understand every word, she told me the following story:

> In the 1920s the Armenian population in Turkey was being persecuted and massacred. A great number of Armenians fled to Georgia, including my grandparents and my great-uncle. They crossed through the mountains and settled in the western part of Georgia near the Turkish border. It's a poor part of the country and was even poorer then. There were no wheat-flour breads; all the breads in the nearby villages were hard and made of corn. My great-uncle, whose name was Rafik, was a baker. He began making wheat-flour flatbreads, small lavash-style breads, using sourdough. They were delicious. His secret was that he put a little honey in the dough. Soon people from all the villages in the area were buying their bread from him. And they didn't call the bread lavash, they called it *rafik*!

Georgian Cheese-Filled Quick Bread

emeruli khachapuri • Georgia

Khachapuri from Emereti are famous throughout Georgia; they are the cheese breads most commonly made at home, quick and delicious. One evening in Tbilisi I was taught how to make them by Lianna, a friendly woman in her early forties, originally from the region of Emereti.

As I stood by watching, Lianna quickly mixed yogurt with flour and baking powder, then divided the dough and began to form the breads. Onto each flattened round of soft-textured dough, she placed a mound of cheese mixed with egg, then deftly pleated the dough up over the filling, flattened it with the palm of her hand, and presto! Suddenly there was an innocuous-looking flat, round bread waiting to be cooked, giving no hint that it was filled with cheese. As she baked them in the oven, Lianna explained that traditionally these were baked on a clay griddle, called a ketsi, over an open fire, though ketsi are now found only in rural areas. While the first batch baked, she assembled the next, chatting as she worked.

··▲▲▲▲▲·▪▪▲▲▪▪▪▪▲▲▲▪▲·▲

Georgians eat khachapuri as a snack or for lunch as a light but satisfying meal; it is also a good complement to soups of all kinds. The breads are soft and surprisingly thin, about a quarter inch thick, so the cheese is a mild flavoring, not an overpowering taste. Once you are used to mixing and shaping the breads, they will take you only twenty minutes from start to warm-bread-on-the-table finish.

cheese filling

4 ounces mild Cheddar or mozzarella cheese, grated and then finely chopped (scant ½ cup)

2 ounces feta cheese, well crumbled (approximately 3 tablespoons)

2 tablespoons plain yogurt

1 large egg

dough

3 to 4 cups unbleached all-purpose flour

1½ teaspoons baking powder

½ teaspoon salt

2 cups plain yogurt

You will need two baking sheets, a medium-sized bowl, a large bread bowl, and a small rolling pin (optional).

Place an oven rack at the lowest position, and preheat the oven to 450°F. Lightly oil two baking sheets.

To prepare the cheese filling: Blend together all the ingredients in a bowl. Set aside.

In a large bowl, mix together 1 cup flour, the baking powder, and salt. Add the yogurt and stir well. Then continue stirring in flour until the dough has lost its stickiness and can be worked with your hands. Turn out onto a lightly floured surface and knead for 3 to 4 minutes, until soft and slightly elastic.

Divide the dough into 8 equal pieces. Keeping the remaining pieces covered with a cloth, work with one piece of dough at a time. Flatten the dough with the lightly floured palm of your hand. Then, either stretching the dough or using a small rolling pin, flatten it out to a round about 6 to 8 inches in diameter. Place 1 heaping tablespoon of the cheese filling in the center of the dough. Pinch an edge of the dough between your thumb and forefinger and stretch it halfway over the filling to the center of the dough round. Then pinch the edge an eighth of a turn along from the first position and bring it to the center. Continue all the way around the circle, stretching the dough as you do so, and pleating it over the filling, until you have a dough-covered mound. Pinch the pleats closed, and then, with the lightly floured palm of your hand, gently press down on the top of the mound to flatten it. Turn the bread over and gently press down again on the other side. This will push the filling out into the edges of the bread; it should be ¼ to ½ inch thick and 7 to 8 inches in diameter.

Place the bread on a prepared baking sheet and continue making breads until the first baking sheet is full. Bake the breads for 5 to 6 minutes, then remove from the oven, slide into a basket lined with a cloth, and cover to keep warm. Prepare the remainder of the breads while the first batch bakes, and then cook in the same fashion.

Alternatives: Another version of this bread uses cooked small red beans as a filling. When you have some on hand (perhaps extra from making Red Beans with Sour Plum Sauce, page 308), try substituting them for the cheese filling: Fry 1 chopped clove of garlic in a little olive oil, then add 1 cup cooked red beans and fry over medium heat, stirring, for 5 minutes. Let cool, season with salt and pepper and some chopped fresh coriander, then use as a filling, following the same method as for the cheese filling.

··▲▲▲▲·▲·▲▲▲·▲·▲▲▲·▲·▲

continued

Makes 8 filled flatbreads, about 8 inches in diameter and ¾ inch thick.

Serve warm for lunch or for a snack with a bowl of Sour Plum Sauce (page 309) or Herb and Pepper Relish (page 301), for dipping. Alternatively, serve as part of a larger meal. Traditionally the breads are served whole, stacked in a cloth-lined basket or on a plate. You can also cut them into wedges and serve on a platter.

Potato·and·Herb·Filled Bread
khachapuri ossetinski • Georgia

One evening, late in 1989, I was invited to a party in the old quarter of Tbilisi, where I met an array of young and middle-aged Georgians. All well-educated, fluent in either English or French as well as Russian and Georgian and, often, other

A potato vendor in Baku

European languages, they were a lively crew. The house we were in, now broken up into three apartments, had been built by the last king of Georgia after he abdicated in the 1820s. My hosts were direct descendants, now living through the end of the Soviet era. Like every other Georgian festive event I ever heard about or attended, the party revolved around good food and drink and conversation.

As I was introduced, and people learned that I was interested in finding out about traditional flatbreads, several people had stories to tell. One woman asked if I'd tasted the Ossetian khachapuri, "the one that's filled with potato and herbs." She then described how her friend's grandmother made it, with whole wheat flour and plenty of herbs.

⋅⋅▲▲▲▲▲⋅⋅⋅▲▲⋅⋅⋅⋅▲▲⋅⋅▲

This is a mountain or country version (whole wheat and slightly crusty) of Ossetian khachapuri, a potato-filled bread from the Ossetian region of Georgia, in the Caucasus Mountains. You can add a little crumbled goat cheese to the filling if you wish; we prefer the direct taste of the herbed potato filling. Try dipping the bread into a salsa, or eat it for a light lunch with a fresh tomato salad.

1 pound (3 medium) new potatoes, washed and cut into large chunks

2 cups water

2 sprigs fresh mint (optional)

1 teaspoon olive oil

1 small onion, finely chopped

1 teaspoon dry yeast

Pinch of sugar

½ cup warm water

1 cup plain yogurt

5 to 7 cups hard whole wheat flour

2 teaspoons salt

¼ cup coarsely chopped flat-leafed parsley

½ cup coarsely chopped fresh coriander

½ cup coarsely chopped fresh mint

¼ cup crumbled aged goat cheese (optional)

Freshly ground black pepper

You will need a heavy saucepan with a lid, a skillet, a cup, a large bread bowl, a medium-sized bowl, a rolling pin, and two or three large baking sheets.

Place the potatoes and water in a heavy saucepan with the optional mint sprigs, and bring to a boil. Lower the heat to medium, cover, and cook until the potatoes are done, about 15 minutes.

While the potatoes are cooking, heat the oil in a medium skillet, and sauté the onion until golden, 5 to 8 minutes. Remove from the skillet and set aside.

Drain the potatoes, reserving the potato water. Discard the mint.

In a small cup, dissolve the yeast and sugar in the warm water.

In a large bowl, combine the yogurt, 1 cup of the reserved potato water, and the yeast mixture. Stir well. Then add 2 cups flour, a cup at a time, stirring constantly in the same direction. Stir the dough 100 times in the same direction, about 1 minute, to develop the gluten. Sprinkle on 1 teaspoon salt. Continue adding flour and stirring until dough becomes too difficult to stir (at about the 4- to 5-cup mark).

Flour your kneading surface generously, then turn the dough out onto the surface and begin to knead. The dough will be soft and somewhat sticky to begin with, so keep your hands floured and renew the flour on your working surface as necessary to prevent the dough from sticking. Knead for 10 minutes; as you knead, the dough will begin to firm and will start to feel elastic and supple. You don't want it to become dry and stiff, just less sticky and more supple.

Wash, dry, and lightly oil the bread bowl, then place the dough back in the bowl and cover with plastic wrap. Let rise for 2 to 3 hours, or until almost doubled in bulk.

Gently push down the dough and turn out onto a lightly floured surface. Divide the dough into two equal parts, cover half, and set aside. Then divide the remaining dough into 8 equal pieces. Let rest, covered with a towel or plastic wrap, for 10 minutes.

continued

Preheat the oven to 375°F. Lightly oil two or three large baking sheets.

Combine the potatoes and onion in a medium bowl. Using a knife or the edge of a spoon, break the potato pieces into smaller bits, the size of coarse crumbs. Mix in the chopped fresh herbs, optional goat cheese, the remaining 1 teaspoon salt, and plenty of freshly ground black pepper.

Flatten 4 pieces of the dough out with the palm of your hand. Then roll or stretch one piece of dough out into a circle about 6 to 8 inches across. Place 2 mounded tablespoons of the potato mixture in the center of the round. Pinch an edge of dough between your thumb and forefinger and stretch it halfway over the filling to the center of the circle. Then pinch the edge a little farther along and pull it over to join the first, making a pleat in it as you do so. Continue all around the circle so that the filling is completely enclosed. Gently press down on the pleats with the palm of your hand to cover the filling completely and seal it, then turn the bread over and flatten gently on the other side. You should have a flattened bread about 4 to 6 inches across and almost ½ inch thick. If the filling mixture pokes any holes in the dough, patch with a scrap of dough, moistening and pressing down to stick patch in place.

Place the bread on a prepared baking sheet. Roll out and fill the next three pieces of dough and place them on the baking sheet. Bake in the center of the oven for about 20 minutes, until golden brown and firm on the bottom, and lightly brown and still tender on top. While the first breads are baking, prepare the remaining 12 in the same fashion, putting a second tray of breads in the oven when ready.

Let the breads cool on a rack for 10 minutes, then serve warm. Once completely cooled, the breads can be frozen, stored in well-sealed plastic bags. To serve, defrost, and preheat the oven to 350°F. Place several breads side by side (not stacked) in a brown paper bag, sprinkle the bag generously with water, and place in the oven for 10 to 15 minutes.

··▲▲▲▲▲▲··▲▲··▲▲▲··▲▲

Makes 16 round filled flatbreads, 5 to 6 inches across.

Serve on their own as a snack, or serve as a centerpiece for a warming lunch or supper with Herb and Pepper Relish (page 301), Provençal Sautéed Wild Mushrooms (page 325), and a fresh tomato salad or Green Bean Salad with Walnut Vinaigrette (page 303).

Georgian Cheese Boat Breads

adjaruli khachapuri • G e o r g i a

*Although this khachapuri comes from the Black Sea coast, it is also very pop-*ular in the capital, Tbilisi. I first tasted it in a basement khachapuri parlor just off Rustaveli Street in the center of the city, where nothing was served but these cheese boats and soft drinks. It was lunchtime, and the place was jam-packed. The khacha-puri was like an oval deep-dish cheese pie, served with an egg baked on top—wonderfully satisfying on a cool fall day. Like everyone else in the room, I drank Lagarditse, a local fruit-flavored soda water, to wash it down.

This version, which we prefer, is like the khachapuri we ate in Batumi, on the Black Sea coast; it has a more generous curve of crust and is less overpowered by masses of cheese.

2 cups warm water

Pinch of sugar

2 teaspoons dry yeast

5 to 6 cups hard unbleached white
flour or unbleached all-purpose flour

2 teaspoons salt

1 tablespoon olive oil

f i l l i n g

6 ounces soft young goat cheese, at
room temperature

2 ounces Gruyère, coarsely grated

¼ cup plain yogurt

You will need a large bread bowl, a medium-sized bowl, unglazed quarry tiles (see page 20) to fit on a rack in your oven, a baker's peel or two baking sheets, and a rolling pin (optional).

Place the warm water in a large bowl, stir in the sugar and yeast, and let stand for several minutes, until the yeast has dissolved. Then gradually add 2½ cups flour, stirring constantly in the same direction. Stir 100 times in the same direction, about 1 minute, to develop the gluten. Sprinkle on the salt, add the oil, and con-tinue adding flour and blending it into the dough until it is less sticky.

Turn the dough out onto a floured surface and knead for 10 minutes, until smooth and elastic, with a slight sheen. Form into a ball, and place in a lightly oiled clean bowl or on a lightly floured surface to rise, covered with plastic wrap, until doubled in volume, 1½ to 2 hours.

Preheat the oven to 450°F. If using quarry tiles, arrange on the bottom oven rack, leaving a 1-inch gap between the tiles and oven walls. If not, lightly oil two baking sheets.

continued

Gently push down the dough. On a lightly floured surface, using a sharp knife, cut the dough into 4 equal pieces. Flatten each piece out with the lightly floured palm of your hand, then cover with plastic wrap while you prepare the filling.

Place the cheeses and yogurt in a bowl, and blend together to a smooth consistency.

Work with one piece of dough at a time, leaving the remaining dough covered with plastic wrap. With your hands or a rolling pin, stretch and flatten the dough into a long oval 8 to 10 inches long, 5 to 6 inches wide, and no more than ¼ inch thick. Place a generous ¼ cup of filling in the center of the oval. Spread to within an inch of the edges. Roll the edges over to make a thick rim, pinching the sides together to form a point at the ends. (The bread should look boat-shaped.) Shape and fill a second bread. Slide the breads onto a peel and then onto the quarry tiles, or slide onto the baking sheets and place on the bottom oven rack. Bake until the crust is golden and the bottom is firm and crusty, about 12 to 15 minutes. Wrap in a towel to keep warm while you prepare and bake the remaining two breads the same way. Serve hot.

·· ▲▲▲▲▲·· ▲▲▲·· ▲ ▲·· ▲

Makes 4 open-faced filled breads, about 10 inches long and 6 inches wide.

Serve hot with a Salad of Tomatoes and Roasted Onions (page 329) for a simple yet very filling lunch or light supper.

Pomegranate Sauce and Pomegranate and Walnut Sauce

narshab • Georgia

Autumn is pomegranate season in the Caucasus, and the markets in Georgian cities and towns gleam with stacks of rosy fruit. The seeds are used for garnish, the juice as a souring flavor in cooking.

In North America it's difficult to find any but sweet pomegranates, and commercially available pomegranate juice, produced by only a few companies, is always sweet. In order to reproduce the tart tang of sour Georgian pomegranates in this sauce, we add fresh lemon juice. You can also use sour pomegranate syrup (for sale in Middle Eastern groceries). Heat gently and then add the remaining ingredients, omitting the lemon juice. The syrup

Pomegranates in Tbilisi

tends to have a slightly processed flavor as well as a less attractive brown color, but it is a reasonable substitute. A third, nontraditional, substitute is cranberry juice. Its red color and tart fruit taste give the balance needed for this sauce. Generally, cranberry juice is sweetened very little, so you can usually omit the lemon juice. Taste the sauce once it has cooled and add lemon juice if it lacks a sour tang.

In Georgia, narshab is used as a dip for bread or a condiment for grilled and roasted meats and for fish.

pomegranate sauce

3 cups fresh pomegranate juice or cranberry juice (see Note)

1½ tablespoons fresh lemon juice (omit if using tart pomegranates or unsweetened cranberry juice)

1 large or 2 small cloves garlic, minced

3 tablespoons finely chopped fresh coriander

Pinch of dried chile pepper flakes or hot paprika (optional)

Small handful of pomegranate seeds (optional)

pomegranate and walnut sauce

½ cup walnut halves or walnut pieces

¼ teaspoon salt, or to taste

You will need a nonreactive saucepan and, for pomegranate and walnut sauce, a mortar and pestle or a food processor.

To make pomegranate sauce: Bring the pomegranate or cranberry juice to a boil in a nonreactive saucepan, then lower the heat to medium-low and simmer for

10 to 15 minutes, until reduced to about 1½ cups. Remove from the heat, add the lemon juice, garlic, coriander leaves, and optional chile flakes, and stir well. Let stand until cool.

Store in a tightly sealed container in the refrigerator. Serve with a handful of fresh pomegranate seeds floating on the surface, if available.

To make pomegranate and walnut sauce: Place walnuts in a mortar or processor and pound or pulse until they have been broken down into a paste. Stir into pomegranate sauce. Let stand for 30 minutes to allow flavors to blend, then add salt to taste. Store and serve as described above.

Note: If you are squeezing your own pomegranate juice, cut the fruit around its equator, hold half in the palm of your hand, seed side down, and squeeze hard over a bowl. You will get a surprising amount of juice from each fruit, provided your pomegranates are fresh and firm

··▲▲▲▲▲▲·▲▲▲··▲▲▲··▲

Makes approximately 2 cups sauce.

Serve either sauce as a dipping sauce for Georgian Cheese-Filled Quick Bread (page 292) or Potato-and-Herb-Stuffed Bread (page 294) or as a condiment for grilled meats.

Herb and Pepper Relish

adjika • Georgia

It was day two on the Moscow-Tbilisi "express." We were already running eight hours late. I'd been playing an incomprehensible card game with a smoky compartmentful of Georgians all afternoon. As evening approached, a smiling conductor came by, conveying an invitation from someone in the next carriage.

Puzzled, I followed him along the corridor and across the drafty swaying platform to the next car. Imagine my surprise and pleasure to discover that I had been summoned to share an impromptu feast. My hostess was a plump, well-dressed Armenian woman, an English teacher, whose parents had fled to Georgia in 1922 from eastern Turkey. As we clattered along the Black Sea coast, the water dark blue-gray in the dusk, she told me, in perfect English, that she had been playing a marathon series of backgammon games with the conductor, a Georgian, since leaving Moscow. Now she had beaten him and his penalty for losing was to provide a meal. She had heard there was a foreign woman on the train who was interested in traditional foods, so she'd sent the conductor to invite me to join them.

Azeri selling herbs and peppers in Tbilisi

Out came the breads, the cheese, spiced sausage, sour plum sauce, a bottle of wine, all from Georgia. The conductor then produced a bottle of adjika, a cross between salsa and relish. My hostess explained that every Georgian household has its own version of this sauce, which is most commonly served as a relish with meats or as a dip for bread. Some Georgians also eat adjika drizzled over slices of fresh melon; the contrast of cool, wet sweet melon with spicy hot sauce is very successful.

·· ▲ ▲ ▲ ▲ ▲ ▲ · ▲ ▲ · ▲ ▲ · ▲ ▲ · ▲ ▲ ▲ · ▲ ▲

This version of adjika is milder-tasting than some, slightly runny—and with the same complexity of flavors that made me want to eat it like soup on the train, rather than dabbing it politely on my bread, cheese, and sausage, as the Georgians do. After experimenting with various combinations and proportions of herbs, I believe this recipe comes closest to the conductor's, still our favorite blend. A close second is the alternative version, made with a little ground meat, described on page 302; it is particularly delicious as a dip for bread.

continued

4 cloves garlic, finely chopped

2 jalapeños, finely chopped

1 green bell pepper, finely chopped

1 red bell pepper, finely chopped
(or another green bell pepper)

2 to 3 plum tomatoes, fresh or canned,
finely chopped

1 cup flat-leafed parsley, finely chopped

1½ cups fresh coriander leaves, finely
chopped

¼ cup fresh dill leaves, finely chopped

3 tablespoons red wine vinegar

Salt to taste

You will need a bowl or a food processor.

Mix all the ingredients thoroughly in a bowl, or, for a somewhat finer texture, process in a food processor for 10 seconds. Store in the refrigerator in a well-sealed nonreactive bowl or other container for at least 24 hours before using, to give all the strong flavors time to blend. Traditionally—at least in all the households I visited—adjika is stored in a clean wine bottle, and then poured out as needed.

Alternatives: For a variant that gives the sauce more body, add ¼ pound lean ground pork. Fry the meat in a little olive oil with half an onion, finely chopped. Let cool. Mix in with the other ingredients and refrigerate. Keeps for 4 to 5 days.

Makes about 3 cups sauce.

Serve with filled breads such as Georgian Cheese Boat Breads (page 297), Potato-and-Herb-Filled Bread (page 294), or Georgian Cheese-Filled Quick Bread (page 292) for a light lunch or satisfying snack. Place on the table as a condiment when serving grilled meats such as Marinated Lamb Kebabs (page 176) or as part of a mezze table (see page 203).

Green Bean Salad with Walnut Vinaigrette

lobio • Georgia

This is a fresh, simple, tasty dish. The dressing is a vinaigrette, with walnuts
pounded into it for richness and flavor. Extra walnuts are chopped fine and tossed
into the salad for texture and to please the eye as a contrast with the green beans.

d r e s s i n g

3 tablespoons walnut pieces, finely
chopped

¼ cup extra-virgin olive oil

1 tablespoon fresh lemon juice

2½ tablespoons red wine vinegar

2 large garlic cloves, minced or crushed

Pinch of salt

1 pound green beans, topped, tailed,
and sliced into 1-inch lengths, or, if
very small and tender, left whole

½ cup packed coarsely chopped fresh
coriander

Salt to taste

Freshly ground black pepper (optional)

You will need a large mortar and pestle or a food processor, a small bowl,
and a saucepan with a lid.

Pound half the walnuts to a paste in a mortar, or process in a food processor. Turn out into a bowl. Add the oil, lemon juice, vinegar, garlic, and pinch of salt, and whisk to blend. Let sit for at least 30 minutes, or up to 2 hours, to allow flavors to blend.

Cook the beans in an inch or so of water in a covered saucepan until crisp-tender, 5 to 7 minutes. Drain, and place in a serving bowl. Pour the dressing over, and toss well. Add all but a tablespoon or so of the coriander leaves, and toss again. Add salt and optional pepper to taste, and garnish with the remaining walnuts and coriander leaves. Serve warm or at room temperature.

··▲▲▲▲▲▲·▲·▲▲▲·▲▲▲··▲

Serves 4 as a side dish.

*This dish can be served as a salad, or as an appetizer before, for example, Herbed Red
Snapper with Pomegranate and Walnut Sauce (page 314) or Prune-Stuffed Kufta Soup
(page 316). It's also great as part of a light lunch with Georgian Cheese Boat Breads
(page 297) or Georgian Cheese-Filled Quick Bread (page 292).*

Georgian Spice Blend
khmeli suneli • Georgia

Spice vendors sell different blends of khmeli suneli in all the markets in Georgia, in the way different masalas are sold in India. As in India, every cook has his or her favorite blend or blends, and at least a pinch of khmeli suneli goes into most of the stews, vegetable pâtés, soups, and sauces in Georgia.

Selling spices in Tbilisi

This blend has evolved as we've experimented with traditional khmeli suneli, trying to reproduce the flavors that first seduced us in Georgian kitchens and markets. Feel free to experiment with the proportions given.

1 tablespoon coriander seed (see page 412)

¼ teaspoon fenugreek seed (see page 414), dry-roasted (see page 154) and ground, or ½ teaspoon ground fenugreek

2 teaspoons finely chopped flat-leafed parsley or 1½ teaspoons dried parsley

1 teaspoon finely chopped fresh mint or ½ teaspoon dried mint

½ teaspoon fennel seed or finely chopped fresh tarragon

1 teaspoon finely chopped fresh oregano or thyme or ½ teaspoon dried oregano or thyme

1 teaspoon dried calendula (pot marigold) petals or dried marigold petal, or 2 to 3 saffron threads, crumbled to a powder

You will need a mortar and pestle or a spice grinder.

Combine all the ingredients in a mortar and pound together to a fine powder or grind in a spice grinder. Store in a tightly sealed container. Like most spices and spice blends, this will keep for several months, with a loss of flavor and immediacy after the first month.

········▲▲▲▲▲▲▲·▲·▲▲▲▲·▲·▲▲·▲·▲

Makes approximately 3 tablespoons spice blend.

Use as directed in Georgian recipes; the blend is also great rubbed onto lamb, beef, or chicken before grilling or roasting.

Georgian Leek Pâté

prasi pkhali • G e o r g i a

Pkhali *are traditional Georgian vegetable pâtés; crushed walnuts and a won-*derful blend of spices and fresh herbs give them depth of flavor and firm texture. They are a great addition to the vegetarian repertoire and can be served in the same way as salads: as part of a large meal, or to accompany a light meal of bread and soup. This leek pâté is best made ahead and chilled overnight to allow the flavors to blend and the texture to firm up.

4 medium leeks (about 1 pound)

⅓ cup walnut pieces

¼ teaspoon salt, or to taste

½ teaspoon coriander seed (see page 412), dry-roasted (see page 154) and ground (see Note)

1 teaspoon finely chopped or crushed garlic

¼ teaspoon crumbled dried red chile, dried chile flakes, or hot paprika

2 tablespoons finely chopped fresh coriander, plus extra leaves for garnish

1 tablespoon finely chopped flat-leafed parsley

1 tablespoon finely chopped fresh mint or basil (see Note)

1 tablespoon fresh lemon juice

You will need a heavy saucepan with a lid, a colander, a large mortar and pestle or a food processor, and a small bowl.

Trim the root ends and the dark green parts from the leeks. Quarter the leeks lengthwise, then slice into ¼-inch slices. Rinse well in cold water to remove all sand and grit, then drain.

Place 2 inches of water in a heavy saucepan, add the leeks, cover, and bring to a boil. Reduce the heat to medium and cook until the leeks are tender, about 7 to 10 minutes. Drain in a colander, reserving the cooking water.

In a large mortar, pound or grind the walnuts, salt, coriander seed, garlic, and chile to a paste. Or process in a food processor. Add the leeks, chopped fresh herbs, and lemon juice, and pound and stir briefly, or pulse two or three times, to blend well. If the mixture seems dry and crumbly, blend in 1 to 2 tablespoons reserved cooking water from the leeks. Transfer to a small lightly oiled bowl and pack in well. Refrigerate for at least 6 hours, or overnight, well covered with plastic wrap, to let firm up.

Serve directly from the bowl or invert onto a plate, and garnish with a sprinkling of coriander leaves.

continued

Note: If you have Georgian Spice Blend (page 304) on hand, substitute 1 tablespoon of it for the coriander seed, and reduce the fresh mint or basil to 1 teaspoon.

·· ▲▲▲▲▲▲·▲▲▲ ▲▲·▲▲·▲ ▲

Makes approximately 2 cups pâté.

Serve with Paperthin Lavash (page 283), Georgian Cheese-Filled Quick Bread (page 292),
or Pita (page 181) for a snack or as an appetizer. This pâté is also a great addition to the
mezze table (see page 203), or served as a side dish in an Armenian or Georgian meal.

Walnut and Eggplant Roll-Ups
badrigiani • Georgia

I learned to make these elegant stuffed eggplant roll-ups, a Georgian spe-
cialty, in the town of Batumi on the Black Sea coast. Vaso, a man in his late seventies, took me step-by-step through the detailed preparation of the rolls. Vaso was pleased to have a chance to speak English, a language he had learned as a young man in Harbin in China. He loved Chinese food and was fluent in the Beijing dialect.

These roll-ups are a delicacy. Serve them as an hors d'oeuvre on a special occasion. The eggplant should be tender and meaty; it should cut as easily as the walnut paste that fills it.

5 long thin Japanese eggplants, about 12 inches by 1½ inches, (or ten 6- to 8-inch long eggplants)

Salt

f i l l i n g

¾ cup walnut pieces

2 to 3 cloves garlic

1 teaspoon coriander seed, dry-roasted (see page 154) and ground

¼ teaspoon fenugreek seed (see page 414), dry-roasted (see page 154) and ground, or ground fenugreek

½ teaspoon salt

Pinch of dried chile pepper flakes or crumbled dried red chile

½ cup coarsely chopped fresh coriander

½ cup packed fresh basil or mint leaves, finely chopped

¼ cup packed flat-leafed parsley, finely chopped

3 scallions, finely chopped

1 tablespoon fresh lemon juice

1 teaspoon balsamic vinegar

2 tablespoons olive oil

g a r n i s h

1 tomato, sliced

Small sprigs of flat-leafed parsley and fresh basil

You will need a food processor or large mortar and pestle, a bowl, and a large heavy skillet with a tight-fitting lid.

Cut the stems off the eggplants and slice in half lengthwise. Salt the cut sides liberally, place cut side down on a board or cookie sheet, and press flat: The easiest method is to place a cutting board or a baking sheet on top of the eggplants and then top it with a heavy cast-iron pan or a large saucepan filled with water. Let the eggplants stand under the weight for at least 1 hour or as long as 3 hours—you want them to be as flattened and supple as possible.

Meanwhile, prepare the filling: Combine the walnuts, garlic, coriander seed, fenugreek, salt, and chile pepper flakes in a food processor, and process until a thick paste forms or pound to a paste in a large mortar. Turn out into a bowl and stir in the rest of the filling ingredients. Let stand, covered, at room temperature for 15 to 30 minutes to allow the flavors to blend.

Rinse the salt from the eggplants, squeeze excess juices from the eggplant, and dry well. If using long eggplants, cut each piece in half crosswise.

Heat a large skillet over medium-high heat, and add 1 tablespoon of the oil. When the oil is hot, add half the eggplant slices. Reduce the heat to medium, cover, and steam-cook for about 15 minutes, until the skin is soft and easily pricked with a fork, and the flesh is moist and grayish all through. Cook the remaining eggplant in the same way.

Spread a thick layer of filling on the cut side of each slice, roll up, and place on a serving platter, seam side down. Refrigerate for 1 hour before serving, to allow the filling to firm up. Serve garnished with tomato slices and parsley and basil leaves.

··▲▲▲▲▲▲··▲▲▲··▲▲▲··▲

Makes 20 roll-ups. Serves 5 to 6 as an appetizer.

Serve as an appetizer or as part of a mezze table (see page 203). If you open a meal with these, you might continue with Herbed Red Snapper (page 314) and a Green Bean Salad with Walnut Vinaigrette (page 303), accompanied by Afghan Snowshoe Naan (page 40) or Paperthin Lavash (page 283).

Red Beans with Sour Plum Sauce

lobio tkemali • Georgia

Georgian cuisine does remarkable things with beans, combining them with distinctive and sometimes entirely unexpected flavors to produce wonderful additions to the legume repertoire. Lobio tkemali is a surprising combination of beans and tart spicy plum sauce. It is traditionally served cold, as an appetizer, with a bowl of extra plum sauce on the side. We also like to eat it warm as a bean stew, with Georgian Cheese-Filled Quick Bread—unbeatable.

1 cup dried small red beans or kidney beans, soaked overnight in 4 cups cold water

5 cups cold water

1 large yellow onion, quartered

¼ cup Sour Plum Sauce (page 309)

½ cup fresh coriander leaves, coarsely chopped

garnish and accompaniments

1 cup Sour Plum Sauce (page 309)

1 red onion, thinly sliced

4 to 6 pickled Balkan-style green peppers

½ pound cheese: sliced mozzarella or string cheese, or cubed feta, or a combination

½ cup Kalamata olives

You will need a large heavy saucepan with a lid.

Drain the beans and place in a heavy saucepan, add the 5 cups cold water and the onion, and bring to a boil. Skim off any foam, reduce the heat, partially cover, and simmer until the beans are tender but not reduced to mush, about 1 to 1½ hours (small red beans will take less time than kidneys). Remove the onion pieces and stir in salt. Set the beans aside to cool, and then stir the plum sauce into the cooled beans. Alternatively, if you are serving them warm, and immediately, stir the sour plum sauce into the hot cooked beans. (The beans can be made ahead and stored in a sealed container for 2 to 3 days in the refrigerator. Before serving, bring to room temperature, or if you wish, reheat the beans before serving.) Stir in all but a pinch or two of the coriander leaves, and garnish with the remaining leaves. Taste and adjust seasonings as necessary.

Serve with a bowl of the plum sauce, separate plates of the sliced red onion, pickled peppers, and cheeses, and a small bowl of olives, so guests can garnish and add to the beans as they wish.

Alternatives: We also like to add 2 to 3 cups of chicken or vegetable broth to the beans to make a hearty bean soup for 4.

· · ▲ ▲ ▲ ▲ ▲ ▲ · ▲ · ▲ ▲ ▲ · ▲ ▲ ▲ · ▲ · ▲

Makes about 3 cups beans. Serves 4 as an appetizer.

Serve with the garnishes and accompaniments listed above, along with Georgian Cheese-Filled Quick Bread (page 292).

Sour Plum Sauce
tkemali • Georgia

During my stay in Georgia, I tasted many versions of tkemali and loved every bite of its spicy fruitiness. I had it served alongside khachapuri and grilled lamb, and in red bean stew; its tart taste and deep red color were a perfect complement to a wide range of different foods. "What's this made of?" I asked time and time again, but always came the same reply: "Tkemali. It's a Georgian fruit, there is no Russian word."

My last day in Georgia, I was making one last stroll through the market in Tbilisi, and there they were finally, tkemali, the end of that year's crop. Tkemali are small sour plums, red or yellow in color. We now make "tkemali sauce" at home with ordinary not-yet-perfectly-ripe plums and add lime juice for sourness. If you're lucky enough to find damsons, an English sour plum, they are ideal. We have also made tkemali using sour cherries; the flavor is wonderful, though passing the cooked fruit through a colander to pick out the cherry pits takes a little time. Sour plum sauce should be made at least a day ahead, so that flavors have time to blend.

1 pound fresh plums, preferably damsons or other sour plums, or not fully ripe plums

Approximately 2 cups water

1 tablespoon minced or crushed garlic (2 to 3 cloves)

½ teaspoon coriander seed (see page 412), crushed, or ¼ teaspoon ground coriander (see Note)

½ teaspoon fenugreek seed (see page 414), dry-roasted (see page 154) and ground, or ½ teaspoon ground fenugreek (see Note)

½ to 1 teaspoon crushed dried red chile or dried chile pepper flakes

1 to 3 tablespoons fresh lime juice (depending on tartness of plums)

1 cup coarsely chopped fresh coriander

½ teaspoon salt, or to taste

continued

You will need a heavy nonreactive saucepan with a lid, a small bowl, a colander, and a medium-sized bowl.

Chop the plums coarsely and place, pits and all, in a heavy-bottomed nonreactive saucepan. Add water to just cover (about 2 cups). Bring to a boil, then lower the heat, cover, and simmer until the plums are softened to a mush, about 15 minutes, checking occasionally to make sure they are not sticking or burning.

Meanwhile, combine the garlic and spices in a small bowl.

Drain the plums in a colander placed over a medium bowl. Remove and discard the pits. Add the plums to the bowl, and mash with a fork until smooth. Blend in the spice mixture. Add the lime juice. If the plums are very tart, like damsons, you may not need to add lime juice. The sauce should have a definite tart taste. Stir in the coriander leaves and then salt to taste. Let cool. Store in a glass jar, well sealed, in the refrigerator. Plum sauce will keep for several months sealed and refrigerated.

Note: If you have Georgian Spice Blend (page 304) on hand, substitute 1 tablespoon of the powder for the coriander seed and fenugreek.

▲··▲▲▲▲▲▲·▲▲▲▲·▲▲▲·▲▲·▲

Makes about 2 cups sauce.

Use as a condiment and dipping sauce with any bread—this is particularly delicious with
Georgian Cheese-Filled Quick Bread (page 292) or Potato-and-Herb-Filled Breads
(page 294)—and as an ingredient in Red Beans with Sour Plum Sauce (page 308).
It also makes an interesting chutney-style accompaniment for grilled meats,
such as Marinated Lamb Kebabs (page 176).

Turkey Bathed in Georgian Walnut Sauce
satsivi • Georgia

In the western hills of Georgia, twenty miles or so from the Turkish border, there is a small spa town named Bojormi, famous for its waters. One mellow October day, I drove to Bojormi from Tbilisi with a Georgian friend named Nino and her father. En route we passed through Stalin's birthplace, still displaying a larger-than-life-size statue of him in the main square.

That evening in Bojormi we sat down to a feast with friends, a real Georgian feast. As at every Georgian festive meal, one person was appointed *tamada,* or master-of-ceremonies. The tamada proposes toasts and controls the flow of wine and good spirits. The toasts take place seemingly at any time in the meal. Often passionate, always heartfelt, they can be flowery and old-fashioned, romantic and patriotic, sentimental and chivalrous. The first toast was to Georgia. Nino translated as the long emotional sentences rolled off the tamada's tongue, then we drank, some men with tears in their eyes. Every so often throughout the meal, the tamada would stand to propose another toast: to friendship, to family, to Georgia again, to the dead. In between there was food, such food: tiny grilled quail, chopped up and bathed in a rich satsivi sauce, walnut and eggplant roll-ups, roast goose, an aromatic vegetable stew, chicken in a garlicky broth, and endless side dishes of cabbage, tomatoes, peppers, sour plum sauce, walnut sauce, and herb and pepper relish, as well as lavash and cheese-filled breads for dipping in the sauces. To drink, there was a white wine called Zinandali and bottles of Bojormi water. The meal ended some three hours later with a platter of fruits: watermelon, pears, apples, and persimmons.

Music, too, came and went throughout the meal, hovering over the feast. Georgians are known for their singing, traditionally unaccompanied and with extraordinary harmonies. Every so often Nino's father would hum a note quietly, then he and Nino would begin singing, her soprano threading its way around his sweet strong tenor, and soon joined by the bass voice of the man seated on my right, and then the baritone of the other men. The songs, like the toasts, were full of feeling and yearning and passion, about mother Georgia, and loyalty, and friendship, and partings. It all felt light-years from the gray streets and food queues, the passive gazes and faceless crowds of Moscow.

..▲▲▲▲▲▲▲▲•▲•▲▲•▲▲•▲▲•ι ▲

Satsivi is a walnut-based Georgian sauce with complex spicing, usually made in large quantities for festive occasions. We find it a novel way to serve leftover turkey, so successful that now we will often cook a turkey in order to have turkey meat the next day for satsivi. You can also boil a chicken for the stock and then use the meat in the recipe, or just make the sauce as a dip for bread or vegetables, raw or steamed.

The sauce is traditionally made even richer with an egg or two, but we prefer this relatively "light" version, easy to prepare and very satisfying to eat. Satsivi can be eaten warm or at room temperature and is best made at least an hour ahead so that the flavors can blend and settle.

s a u c e

1 cup walnut pieces

4 to 5 medium garlic cloves, crushed or coarsely chopped

½ cup packed fresh coriander leaves

1 dried red chile, broken in pieces, or 1 jalapeño (see page 410), seeded and finely chopped

¾ teaspoon salt

1 teaspoon olive oil

1½ cups finely chopped onions

1½ teaspoons unbleached all-purpose white flour

2½ cups turkey or chicken stock or water

1½ teaspoons Georgian Spice Blend (page 304; see Note)

¼ teaspoon turmeric

Pinch of ground cinnamon

1 tablespoon red wine vinegar

3 cups shredded cooked turkey or chicken

g a r n i s h

Pomegranate seeds (optional)

Fresh coriander leaves or mint leaves

You will need a large mortar and pestle or a food processor and a large heavy-bottomed saucepan with a lid.

To make the sauce: Combine the walnuts, garlic, coriander leaves, dried chile or jalapeño, and ½ teaspoon of the salt in a large mortar and pound until a smooth paste has formed. Or process in a food processor to a paste. Set aside.

In a heavy-bottomed saucepan heat the oil, and sauté the onions over medium heat, stirring constantly, until translucent and starting to brown, about 10 minutes. Reduce the heat to medium-low, stir in the flour, and cook, stirring for 1 minute. Gradually add the stock or water, stirring to blend. Bring to a boil, then reduce the heat and simmer gently, partially covered, for 5 minutes.

Add the walnut paste, and stir to blend well. Cook over low heat for 2 to 3 minutes. Add the spice blend and cinnamon and cook, stirring, for 2 to 3 more minutes. Remove from the heat, and stir in the vinegar and the remaining ½ teaspoon salt.

Place the turkey or chicken in a large shallow serving bowl. Pour the sauce over, and mix well. Let stand for 30 minutes before serving in order to allow the flavors to blend. (This can also be made a day ahead and refrigerated, covered. Bring to room temperature before serving.)

Serve garnished with optional pomegranate seeds and coriander or mint leaves.

Alternatives: If using as a dipping sauce for steamed vegetables, let cool to room temperature before serving. This is also delicious as a dressing for grilled eggplant. Cut 4 large or 6 medium eggplants crosswise into ¼-inch slices and grill until browned. Chop coarsely, and toss with the sauce. Let stand for an hour or more to let the flavors blend.

Note: If you do not have Georgian Spice Blend (page 304) on hand, you can substitute: 2 pinches fenugreek seed, dry-roasted and ground (or 2 pinches ground fenugreek); ¼ teaspoon coriander seed, ground, and ½ teaspoon dried spearmint or thyme or several fresh leaves, finely chopped; pinch of dried marigold leaves, several crushed saffron threads, or a pinch of turmeric.

··▲▲▲▲▲▲·▲·▲▲▲·▲▲▲·▲▲·▲

Serves 4.

Serve with stacks of warm Georgian Cheese-Filled Quick Bread (page 292) and Paperthin Lavash (page 283), and with a fresh green salad if you like. You can replicate the feast in Bojormi by serving Walnut and Eggplant Roll-ups (page 306), Green Bean Salad with Walnut Vinaigrette (page 303), and grilled lamb (try the Marinated Lamb Kebabs on page 176), with an Herb Plate (page 291), bowls of black olives, plates of goat cheese and mild string cheese, slices of cucumber and tomato, and pickled Balkan-style green peppers, along with bowls of Herb and Pepper Relish (page 301) and Sour Plum Sauce (page 309).

Herbed Red Snapper with Pomegranate and Walnut Sauce

We met on the train, the wrestling coach and I. When we reached Tbilisi, he said he'd be my host in Georgia. I didn't realize that Georgian tradition demands a great deal of a host, nor that he'd taken on a formal role and responsibility.

One evening he, his young son, and I went out to dinner. We had a room to ourselves and the food appeared in what seemed like an endless and wonderful stream. Most outstanding in the extraordinary array was a fish dish—sturgeon from the nearby Caspian Sea, dressed with pomegranate and walnut sauce. We drank a white Georgian wine with it, Manavi, and had a very pleasant evening, talking about anything and everything—miraculously, since he spoke not one word of English and my Russian was so broken that sustained conversation must have been as exhausting for him as it was for me. When I left Tbilisi, he drove me to the airport and made sure I had a good seat on the plane. He never allowed me to pay for anything, was happy to be thanked, but looked for nothing more. Georgian hospitality.

·· ▲▲▲▲▲▲▲▲·▲▲▲▲▲▲▲▲·▲ ▲

This recipe combines several Georgian specialties to produce a flavorful and decorative entrée. The red snapper (you can substitute another rich, firm-textured fish, such as sea bass) is coated with an adjika (chiles and herbs) paste, then baked and served with pomegranate and walnut sauce. The brilliant green of the herb paste is particularly pretty on the red snapper.

2 small red snapper (1¼ to 1½ pounds each), scaled and gutted

Olive oil

Scant 2 tablespoons salt

h e r b   p a s t e

¼ teaspoon coriander seed (see page 414), dry-roasted (see page 154) and ground

2 cloves garlic, peeled

1 banana pepper, chopped

1 fresh red chile pepper (see page 410), chopped, or 1 teaspoon crumbled dried red chile or chile flakes

½ cup mixed fresh herbs, chopped (use any 2 or 3: fresh coriander, thyme, mint, and lovage)

1 to 2 tablespoons fresh pomegranate juice or lemon juice

2 cups Pomegranate and Walnut Sauce (page 299)

You will need a large mortar and pestle or a food processor, foil or parchment, and a baking dish or roasting pan.

Preheat the oven to 400°F.

Rinse the fish and pat dry. Make three slashes on either side of each fish, cutting down to the bone. Brush the fish lightly with olive oil, then sprinkle on the salt. Place each fish on a piece of aluminum foil or parchment large enough to wrap the fish completely, and place them in a shallow baking pan.

Place the coriander seed, garlic, and both peppers in a large mortar and pound to a paste. Add the herbs and pound until well blended. Add the juice, and pound to produce a thick, moist paste. Alternatively, place all the ingredients in a food processor and process until a paste forms.

With a spatula, spread the paste on both sides and inside the cavity of each fish. Wrap the foil or paper around each fish to enclose, and place the pan in the center of the oven. Bake for 15 minutes, then fold back the foil or paper to expose the fish, and lower the oven temperature to 350°F. Bake for 5 to 10 minutes longer, or until the flesh visible at the slits is firm and a uniform white in color.

Transfer the fish to a decorative platter or shallow plate, and pour the cooking juices over. Serve with Pomegranate and Walnut Sauce (page 299).

Alternatives: The herb paste makes a good marinade for grilled chicken or quail as well as for fish.

··▲▲▲▲▲▲·▲·▲▲▲··▲▲▲··▲

Serves 4.

Begin the meal with Georgian Leek Pâté (page 305) and Paperthin Lavash (page 283) or Georgian Cheese-Filled Quick Bread (page 292), cut into wedges.

Prune-Stuffed Kufta Soup

Azeri kufta • Azerbaijan

Late on a chilly autumn afternoon I arrived by bus in Kuba, an old Azeri town in the Caucasus Mountains. As I got off the bus, everyone in the bus stand stared at me. For one thing, Kuba doesn't get many tourists, and on top of that, I'd arrived with no luggage, only a camera around my neck. Before starting out that morning from Baku, where I was staying, people had told me that I'd easily make it back that night. But they were wrong, and I was stranded.

As so often happens to us when traveling and feeling most vulnerable, strangers helped. Four men in a car offered, by gesturing, to drive me to a hotel. But the hotel was closed and wouldn't open until later. So we drove around, first up into the mountains outside town and then back into town, driving ever so slowly up and down the centuries-old streets. We drove by Kuba's three small mosques—with their humble, beautiful proportions—that looked absolutely exquisite at night as light came softly through their stained-glass windows. Kuba is ancient, but not at all grand. It feels like a town of perfect human scale, a town cared for and loved.

After a while we stopped, climbed out of the car, and walked into a restaurant. People turned and stared—a foreign face—but we walked

Kuba, Azerbaijan: Traditional house, cabbages

through the main room into a smaller room, and behind us the door was closed. A bottle of Russian vodka arrived, a bowl of *shor* (a very cheesey yogurt), *kabaso* (pork sausages), an herb plate (with fresh purple basil, coriander, parsley, and green onions), and small plates of a wonderful Azeri version of adjika (see page 301). As in Georgian tradition, one person at the table was in charge, filling empty glasses, tearing bread and distributing it around the table, calling for toasts. Shot glasses were filled with vodka, a toast was made, and we drank. Then we all took a wedge of pomegranate and chased the vodka with the sour-sweet pomegranate. Another glass of vodka, another toast, and then this time I was directed to another glass beside my plate: thick, fresh, unbelievably sweet pear juice. And so our meal went.

At some point our main course arrived, a hearty winter soup with prune-stuffed bulgur kuftas. It was hot and wonderful, and we began devouring it like people who hadn't eaten for days. The man in charge at last interrupted, calling another toast. Glasses were filled and lifted, and once they were all up in the air, he looked at me and said very slowly and carefully, in the first words of English I'd heard all day, "We love you."

Later that evening the hotel finally opened its doors, and I slept wonderfully on a cold night in Kuba.

...▲▲▲▲▲▲▲▲▲▲▲▲▲▲▲▲▲▲▲▲

Kufta is a bulgur-and-meat-paste mixture used either on its own or as a wrapping for other foods. Many different styles of kufta are found in Azerbaijan, as well as in Armenia and in the elaborate kibbehs of Syria.

This satisfying Azeri winter soup combines tender chunks of carrots and potatoes with large round balls of lamb kufta. Inside the kufta there is a delightful surprise: hot, juicy, plump, sweet prunes. Azeri cuisine is a close cousin to Persian cooking, and this recipe is a good example in its use of fruit as part of a savory dish. Kufta soup is served with bread and a side dish of fresh green herbs: tarragon, coriander, basil, mint.

m e a t b a l l s
½ pound lean ground lamb
1 cup fine bulgur
2 tablespoons minced onion
1 teaspoon salt
½ teaspoon cayenne
Approximately ½ cup water
15 to 16 pitted prunes

s t e w
1 tablespoon olive or vegetable oil
2 cloves garlic, minced
1 medium onion, diced

½ pound potatoes, peeled and cut into ½- to 1-inch cubes
½ pound carrots, peeled and cut into ½-inch slices
4 cups chicken or vegetable stock or water
1 teaspoon salt
½ teaspoon freshly ground black pepper
Generous quantity of fresh herbs, (mint, basil, tarragon, and coriander) (Herb Plate, page 291)

You will need a food processor (optional), a large bowl, and a large pot with a lid.

To make the meatballs: Combine the lamb, bulgur, onion, salt, and cayenne in a food processor. With the motor running, pour in the water a little bit at a time until a wet paste begins to form. Then process for 3 to 4 minutes to knead. Transfer the mixture to a large bowl. Alternatively, simply combine the lamb, bulgur, onion, salt, and cayenne in a large bowl and knead by hand for 10 minutes (the way it is traditionally done). The kneading will at first seem messy and difficult, but keep wetting your hands, and soon the mixture will become a kneadable mass.

continued

If you have the time, let the mixture rest covered in the refrigerator for 30 minutes. The pause is not essential but does allow the mixture to firm up and makes it easier to work with.

Tbilisi: Fresh cheese at the main market

To assemble the meatballs, scoop out a heaping tablespoon of the dough. Holding the piece of dough in your palm or in the spoon, make a depression in the middle of the dough with your thumb and insert a prune. Fold the dough over the prune and form a ball, hiding the prune inside. (The finished meatball will be about the size of a golf ball.) Continue shaping until all the meatballs have been formed, placing them on a large plate or a tray as you work.

To *prepare the soup:* Heat the oil in a large pot over medium-high heat. When hot, add the garlic and onion and cook until the onion is translucent. Carefully add the meatballs. Fry, stirring occasionally, for 3 to 4 minutes, until they start to brown. Add the potatoes and carrots, stir gently, and cook for 1 minute. Add the stock or water and bring to a boil over high heat. Reduce the heat and simmer, partially covered, for 30 minutes, or until the vegetables are tender. Stir in the salt and pepper.

Serve in bowls, with a plate of fresh herbs available for diners to garnish—and regarnish—their soup.

In the main market in Tbilisi, Georgia

**Serves 4 as a one-dish main course, accompanied by an Herb Plate (page 291)
and plenty of flatbreads.**

*Serve with Paperthin Lavash (page 283), Turcoman Sourdough Bread (page 63), or Pebbled
Persian Bread (page 55). You might open the meal with Georgian Leek Pâté
(page 305) or Herbs and Greens Egg Pie (page 58).*

1. Olive Ladder Bread
2. Sardinian Parchment Bread
3. Three-Color Focaccia
4. Pizza with Rosemary and Garlic
5. Norwegian Crispbread
6. Norwegian Wrapping Bread
7. Rye Hardtack Rings
8. Finnish Barley Bread
9. Scottish Oatcakes
10. Spelt Breakfast Bread

Europe

Although the shores of the northern Mediterranean are known for their bounty of olives, lemons, fruits, and vegetables, inland many rocky dry mountain valleys historically supported only herds of sheep and very marginal farms. Here barley and spelt were more suitable crops than *triticum aestivum* wheat. In several of these marginal agricultural areas, spurred by scarce fuel and grain resources, a flatbread tradition developed, most likely before the Roman era. The Romans were great bread eaters we are told, and some of the flatbreads of Italy and southern France are

A boulangerie in Alsace

probably descendants of Roman breads. Later, as the Arabs swept across North Africa, their influence was felt in the cuisine of Spain, Sicily, and southern Italy and undoubtedly also contributed to the development of Italian flatbreads such as pizza.

The northern shores of the Mediterranean share with North Africa and the Eastern Mediterranean an olive oil–based cuisine, which emphasizes simple combinations of fresh tastes, with ample use of fresh herbs and vegetables, garlic, and olives.

Northern Europe, on the other hand, with its harsh climate and short growing season, has limited food resources. In the cuisines of Finland, Sweden, and Norway, as well as in Scotland, distinctive and enduring flatbread traditions have long existed. In areas too cold for growing wheat, flatbreads are made from other grains. Oats, barley, and rye are used alone or in combination with wheat flour to make thin Norwegian crispbreads, Scottish oatcakes, and Finnish rye and barley flatbreads. Historically, in many parts of Northern Europe breads were used as a way of storing grain; they were baked only a few times a year and then stored in dried form.

A fisherman in Chartreuse

Many of the other foods in Northern Europe represent tasty and creative solutions to the food storage problems created by long cold winters. Root vegetables such as carrots, potatoes, and beets can be stored through the winter and are used in well-vinegared salads; fish, a major resource, is pickled or salted; and cheese is also an important part of the diet.

Jura: Cows near the village of Bendorf

Olive Ladder Bread

fougasse aux olives • France

One autumn we settled into a small house in a village in northern Provence, not far from Nyons, a town famous for its wonderful olives. We'd come to France interested in the renaissance of traditional bread making, in the revival of wood-fired village ovens and traditional whole-grain breads. And we'd come particularly to Provence because of its flatbreads: fougasse, socca, pissaladière.

Every day we drove from village to village, from market to market, tasting and filling the car with breads. The variety seemed limitless, each small bakery making its own unique version of the traditional regional breads. At the end of several months of wandering, we had many favorites, but the one we liked the most was a fougasse loaded with beautiful black Nyons olives.

Like the word *focaccia, fougasse* has its root in the Latin word for hearth: *focus.* It may have started as a simple flattened hearth bread, but it has now become a more fanciful-looking flat loaf. In this recipe, parallel slits are cut in the dough to make a ladder shape, one that invites pulling off pieces of bread. The blend of whole wheat and unbleached white, with a touch of buckwheat flour, gives this version its country flavor. The mix of all-purpose and pastry flours reproduces the softer flours found in Europe and gives it a very pleasing taste and texture.

This olive-laden fougasse is very filling, more like a main dish than plain bread. In Provence we found ourselves using it as the basis for a simple meal, accompanied by a bottle of red Côtes du Rhône.

1 teaspoon dry yeast

1½ cups lukewarm water

4 cups unbleached all-purpose flour, plus extra for kneading

2 tablespoons olive oil

2 teaspoons salt

1½ cups chopped and pitted black or purple olives (Nyons or Kalamata)

¼ cup buckwheat flour

2 cups soft whole wheat flour

You will need a large bread bowl, two 10- by 15-inch or larger baking sheets that will fit side by side in your oven, and a sharp knife or razor blade.

Place the warm water in a large bowl, sprinkle on the yeast, and then stir in 2½ cups of the all-purpose flour. Stir 100 times in the same direction, about 1 minute, to develop the gluten. Cover this sponge with plastic wrap and let rest for 30 minutes, or up to 2 hours.

continued

Stir the olive oil, salt, olives, and buckwheat flour into the sponge. Mix in the whole wheat flour and stir well. The dough will be sticky. Add the remaining

1½ cups all-purpose flour, stir as well as you can, and then turn the dough out onto a well-floured work surface. Using floured hands, knead gently until the dough feels smooth, then knead 5 minutes longer. (The dough will still feel soft, especially compared to doughs made entirely with hard flour.)

Clean the bread bowl, oil it lightly, place dough in the bowl, and roll around to coat with oil. Then cover with plastic wrap and let rise for 2

Provence: Breads at Bedoin market

hours, or until it has almost doubled in volume.

Oil two 10- by 15-inch (or larger) baking sheets.

Flatten the dough gently with your hands, then turn out onto a floured work surface. Cut the dough in half, return half to the bread bowl, and cover. Divide the remaining half in two. Knead each half into a ball and then flatten gently with the palm of your hand. Let stand for 5 minutes to rest.

Working with one piece of dough at a time, flatten it out with your palms into a rectangle or oval 10 to 12 inches long and 5 to 6 inches wide. It will be about ½ to ¾ inch thick. Transfer to a lightly oiled baking sheet and cover with plastic wrap or a damp towel while you shape the other dough; transfer it to the second baking sheet. Use a sharp knife or razor blade to make cuts through the breads: Starting 2 inches from the top and about 1 inch from one side, cut across and through the bread to within an inch of the other side. Make two more cuts parallel to the first, at about 2-inch intervals. The dough will separate at each cut so that the bread looks like a kind of fat-runged ladder; you can pull the dough apart even more if you wish and if your baking sheets are long enough, by tugging gently on each end of the breads to make the slits gape more. Let the loaves rise for 20 to 30 minutes, covered with plastic wrap.

Preheat the oven to 400°F and set a rack in the center of the oven, or slightly above.

Lightly brush the breads all over with olive oil, and bake for 20 minutes, or until golden.

Meanwhile, once the first loaves are in the oven, oil two more baking sheets, and shape and slash the remaining dough to form loaves. These breads should almost have finished rising by the time the first batch comes out of the oven. You can also store the remaining dough in the refrigerator, sealed in plastic wrap for up to 2 days. The color of the olives may leak into the dough a little during storage, so your breads may look a little mottled; the dough will also weaken a little, becoming softer. However, the breads will still be delicious. Uncover and bring to room temperature 1 hour before shaping and baking.

·.·▲▲▲▲▲·▲·▲▲·▲▲·▲▲·▲

Makes 4 rectangular loaves about 14 inches long and 6 to 8 inches wide.

Serve fougasse on its own or with Provençal Sautéed Wild Mushrooms (below) and Tender Greens Salad (page 327) as a simple, delicious meal. Olive Ladder Bread is great with many different soups or stews, as it is hearty, satisfying, and soaks up flavors very well. Try it with Okra and Chicken Stew (page 283), Luigi's Bean Soup (page 338), or Yemeni Stew (page 194). It makes a great contribution to a potluck.

Provençal Sautéed Wild Mushrooms
France

The Nyons weekly market was one of our favorites, not just for its marvelous olives, but also for its wild mushrooms. Each week we'd head straight for the wild

mushroom man's small stall, tucked away in a corner at the back. We never knew what we'd find, for the array of moist earth-toned mushrooms with their smell of damp leaves changed from week to week as the fall went on. "This one's finished for the year," he'd say, gesturing, "but these will go on for a while, I expect." Like any gathered wild food, the mushrooms had the aura of gifts mysteriously given, which could just as mysteriously vanish.

Nyons market

Home each Thursday evening from the market, we'd experiment with that week's haul of wild mushrooms. Our favorite cooking method was also the most direct, described in this recipe. The aroma that filled the house as the mushrooms cooked was heavenly.

continued

Now that shiitake mushrooms and chanterelles are available in North America for much of the fall and winter, you can use whichever you find or prefer for this dish.

1 pound chanterelles or shiitake mushrooms

2 tablespoons extra-virgin olive oil

3 cloves garlic, crushed

3 to 4 tablespoons fresh lemon juice

½ teaspoon salt, or to taste

Freshly ground black pepper to taste

You will need a cast-iron or other heavy skillet with a lid.

Brush or wipe any dirt from the mushrooms, then coarsely chop, discarding any tough, woody stems.

Heat the oil in a heavy skillet. Toss in the garlic and cook over medium-high heat until the garlic starts to turn golden. Add the mushrooms and cook, stirring constantly, until they begin to release their liquid and to soften. Lower the heat to medium and simmer, covered, for 2 to 3 minutes. Then raise the heat to high, add the lemon juice, and let cook for 30 seconds. Add the salt and pepper and taste for seasoning, then turn out into a warmed serving dish and serve immediately.

⸱⸱⸱▲▲▲▲▲⸱▲⸱▲▲⸱⸱⸱▲▲⸱⸱▲

Serves 2 as a centerpiece or 4 as an accompaniment to a larger meal.

We like to feature these mushrooms in an uncluttered lunch or supper accompanied by Tender Greens Salad (page 327), Olive Ladder Bread (page 323) or Three-Color Focaccia (page 331), and a bottle of red Côtes du Rhône.

Tender Greens Salad
salade de mâche • France

As the cool weather begins in early autumn in Provence, large wooden trays full of mâche appear in the markets. The leaves of this bright green salad, also known as lambs' lettuce, are harvested while still small and tender by pulling the whole plant out of the ground. Just recently we found mâche seeds available here in North America, and now have great hopes of growing it in our garden. You can of course substitute other tender salad greens, such as the inner leaves of Boston or bibb lettuce, or young leaf lettuce, but if you come across mâche, treat yourself to a generous quantity, then make a heap of lightly dressed salad to refresh your palate with its fine texture and delicate flavor.

4 cups loosely packed lambs' lettuce or
   other tender salad greens
¼ cup extra-virgin olive oil
2 tablespoons fresh lemon juice,
   or to taste

½ teaspoon salt, or to taste
¼ teaspoon freshly ground black pepper,
   or to taste

You will need a salad spinner or basket or a clean tea towel.

Wash the salad greens carefully, cutting off any roots and imperfections, and dry well in a salad spinner or by patting dry in a tea towel.

Assemble the salad just before you wish to serve it: In the bottom of your salad bowl, mix together the oil and lemon juice. Place the greens in the bowl and toss to coat with the dressing. Add the salt and pepper, toss again, and serve immediately.

Alternatives: You can vary this simple recipe if you have access to other fresh greens or herbs by stirring several very finely chopped young sorrel leaves or young nasturtium or dandelion leaves, or even basil or perilla leaves, into the vinaigrette before adding the salad greens.

⸺ ▲▲▲▲▲▲▲▲▲▲▲▲▲▲▲▲▲ ⸺

Serves 4 to 6.

Serve with Olive Ladder Bread (page 323), Pizza with Rosemary and Garlic (page 333),
or Three-Color Focaccia (page 331).

Sardinian Parchment Bread

carasau • Sardinia, Italy

*This shepherd's bread from Sardinia is a great introduction to unyeasted flat-*breads. Developed as an ideal portable food—light to carry and easy to store, a snack on its own and a meal when crumbled into soup—carasau is crisp and light, yet full of the taste of the grain. It takes about ten minutes to make (about as long as your oven needs to preheat) and only a few minutes baking time.

The essential ingredient in carasau is semolina, the coarsely ground heart of durum wheat; fine semolina flour should not be substituted. Semolina is granular, like coarse sugar, and the color of pale straw; it gives the breads a lovely crunchy bite, as well as a beautiful color.

1 cup coarse semolina (*not* semolina flour), plus extra for dusting

1 cup unbleached white flour, plus extra for dusting

Approximately ¾ cup warm water

¾ teaspoon salt

You will need unglazed quarry tiles (see page 20) to fit on a rack in your oven, a large bowl, a rolling pin, and a baker's peel or a large baking sheet.

Place quarry tiles on the bottom rack of your oven, leaving a 1-inch gap between the tiles and the oven walls, and preheat oven to 400°F.

In a large bowl, mix together the semolina, flour, and salt. Stir in the water gradually, until the dough is smooth and no longer sticky. Form the dough into a ball and transfer to a well-floured work surface. (We like to use a mixture of semolina and unbleached white flour to dust the work surface.) DO NOT KNEAD THE DOUGH.

Shepherd with flock

Cut the dough in half, then cut each piece in half and then again to make 8 equal pieces. Roll each piece in the flour and/or semolina, then flatten with the floured palm of your hand. Roll out one piece at a time, keeping the remaining pieces covered with a cloth:

Roll out one piece of dough as thin as possible on the lightly floured surface, rolling from the center out and rotating the bread slightly between each stroke of your rolling pin. If the bottom starts to stick, flour the surface a little more and turn the bread over; you can also try flouring your rolling pin. You should aim for a bread less than ¹⁄₁₆ inch thick, making a roughly circular bread 9 to 10 inches across. Don't worry that the circle is not perfect. Parchment breads are meant to be thin and handmade-looking, like old parchment.

After you finish rolling out the bread, transfer to a floured peel or the floured underside of a baking sheet, then slide gently onto the quarry tiles. Take your time when transferring the bread; if one side flips under, you can either lift it out and try again, using a large spatula, or let it bake on the first side and then try unfolding it. These breads are very forgiving and easy to work with, so after the first two or three you should feel very comfortable with them. Bake for 2 minutes, turn the bread over, and bake for 1 to 1½ minutes longer. The bread should have golden spots and be crisp. Place it on a rack (or a window ledge) to dry out further.

Proceed to roll out and bake remaining breads in the same fashion, starting to roll out the next bread as soon as you place one in the oven.

Eat carasau warm or keep them for several weeks, stored in a dry place, and snack on them as you would on crackers. To reheat, place in a 350°F to 375°F oven for several minutes. If you like, brush them lightly with olive oil, or olive oil and rosemary leaves, before you reheat them.

·· ▲ ▲ ▲ ▲ ▲ ·▪ ▲ ▲ ▲ ·▪ ▲ ▲ ·▪ ▲

Makes 8 thin, crisp round breads, about 9 to 10 inches in diameter.

Serve with Luigi's Bean Soup (page 338) and Tender Greens Salad (page 327). This is also a great bread to put out with an array of different salsas (see Chile Peppers and Flatbreads, page 390).

Salad of Tomatoes and Roasted Onions
insalata di pomodori e cipolle al forno • Southern Italy

Most wood-fired bread ovens take a long time to preheat, but they also tend to retain a significant amount of heat long after a batch of bread has finished baking. Wherever there is a tradition of baking bread in a wood-fired oven, there is also a host of other traditional foods, from slow-cooked casseroles to baked vegetables, that make use of the oven's waning heat. Roasted onions are one example, found almost everywhere across rural Europe. In southern Italy, they are first drizzled with a little oil. In this dish, inspired by a recipe in Carlo Middione's wonderful introduction to southern Italian cuisine—*The Food of Southern Italy*—the sweetness of the onions produces a caramelized ooze, which ends up glued to your baking sheet. We like to deglaze these drippings with a little vinegar and add them to the salad.

4 medium yellow onions, unpeeled

¼ cup extra-virgin olive oil, plus extra for baking

2 tablespoons red wine vinegar

2 sprigs fresh oregano, leaves only, finely chopped

½ teaspoon sea salt, or to taste

1 pound ripe tomatoes, coarsely chopped

Freshly ground black pepper

You will need a baking sheet with a rim and a small saucepan.

Preheat the oven to 350°F.

Rinse the onions, dry well, and place on a rimmed baking sheet lightly greased with extra-virgin olive oil. Brush the onions generously with oil. Bake in the center of the oven until soft but not completely collapsed (about 1 hour). Let cool slightly on the baking sheet.

When cool enough to handle, lift the onions off the baking sheet, and set the pan aside. Remove the outer skin and discard it. Coarsely chop the onions and set aside.

Pour the vinegar onto the baking sheet, and scrape up the caramelized onion juices. Pour the mixture into a shallow salad bowl. Add the oregano, the ¼ cup olive oil, and the salt, and stir well, mashing the oregano so it releases its flavor into the oil. Add the tomatoes and chopped onions and toss. Taste and add salt if necessary. Grind black pepper generously over the salad, and serve.

·••▲▲▲▲▲•▲•▲▲▮▮▲▲▲▲▲·▮▲

Serves 4 as a side dish or 2 as part of a bread and salad lunch.

Serve with Sardinian Parchment Bread (page 328), Three-Color Focaccia (page 331), or Pizza with Rosemary and Garlic (page 333) as a light meal centered around bread; for a classic bread, soup, and salad meal, include Luigi's Bean Soup (page 338).

Three-Color Focaccia
focaccia alla pugliese • Italy

Focaccia is a flatbread traditionally cooked on the hearth, often in a skillet covered with hot embers. Nowadays it is more often baked in an oven, though a skillet is still used, as in this recipe.

Focaccia comes in many forms; all tend to be thicker than most pizza and to carry their flavor in the dough rather than on the top surface. In the north of Italy focaccie are made with wheat-flour doughs and usually flavored with herbs. The potato-based dough used in this focaccia from Puglia, in the south, produces a dense-looking tender dough. This version of a focaccia recipe in Carol Field's classic *The Italian Baker* has the colors of the Italian flag: the red of sun-dried tomatoes and the green of sage and parsley, all floating in a pale dough—a pleasure to look at as well as a satisfying snack or accompaniment to soup.

1½ cups warm water

2 teaspoons dry yeast

4 to 5 cups hard unbleached white flour or unbleached all-purpose flour

1 teaspoon olive oil

½ yellow onion, finely chopped

2 cups chopped cooked peeled potatoes (about 4 medium potatoes)

½ cup potato-cooking water (or spring or tap water)

¾ cup packed flat-leafed parsley, coarsely chopped

¼ cup packed fresh sage leaves, finely chopped

2 tablespoons olive oil

2 teaspoons salt

½ cup sun-dried tomatoes, finely chopped (see Note)

Olive oil for brushing

½ teaspoon fine sea salt

You will need a large bread bowl, a medium skillet, a blender, a large bowl, and four heavy ovenproof skillets or metal pie plates 8 to 9 inches in diameter.

Place the warm water in a large bread bowl and add the yeast and 2 cups flour. Stir to blend, then stir 100 times, about 1 minute, in the same direction to develop the gluten. Let this sponge stand, covered, for 30 minutes to 2 hours.

Heat the oil in a medium skillet, and fry the onions over medium-high heat, stirring frequently, until translucent, about 5 minutes. Set aside.

Puree the potatoes in a blender with the potato cooking water or spring or tap water. Transfer to a large bowl and stir in the onion, parsley, sage, oil, and salt.

Add ½ cup flour to the sponge and stir well. Then add the potato mixture and stir thoroughly. Add the chopped tomatoes and stir well. Turn the dough out onto a well-floured surface and knead for 10 to 12 minutes, dusting both your hands and the kneading surface generously with the remaining 1 to 2 cups flour at intervals as you work, until the dough is no longer sticky, but soft and tender to the touch. Clean the bread bowl, oil lightly, and transfer the dough to the bowl. Cover with plastic wrap and let rise for 2 to 3 hours until at least doubled in volume.

Gently punch down the dough, and cut it in half. Set one half aside, covered with plastic wrap.

Cut the remaining dough in half. Form each piece into a ball. Generously oil two 8- or 9-inch cast-iron skillets or pie plates. Place a ball of dough in each skillet or pie plate. Press down on the center of each ball of dough and gently press it out toward the edges. Let rest for 5 minutes, then press each bread out again until it reaches or comes close to the edges of the pan. Cover with plastic wrap and let rise for 30 minutes.

Position a rack in the center of the oven, and preheat the oven to 400°F.

Just before the first batch of focaccia has finished rising, shape the remaining dough into 2 loaves. (Alternatively, refrigerate the remaining dough, well sealed in plastic wrap, for up to 2 days. Uncover and bring to room temperature before shaping and baking.)

When the first breads have risen, brush the tops gently but generously with olive oil. Press your fingertips firmly into the dough to create deep dimples all over. Lightly sprinkle each one witht ⅛ teaspoon sea salt. Bake in the center of the oven for 10 minutes, then lower the temperature to 375°F and bake for another 10 minutes, or until lightly golden. Turn the breads out onto a rack and let stand for at least 10 minutes to firm before slicing. Turn the oven temperature back up to 400°F, and bake the remaining breads. Serve warm or at room temperature, cut into wedges.

Note: If you use dry-packed sun-dried tomatoes, soak them in warm water for 30 minutes, drain, and pat dry before using.

··▴▴▴▴▴▴▴▴▴▴▴▴▴▴▴▴▴▴▴▴▴

Makes 4 round breads about 8 inches across and 2 inches thick.

Serve warm on its own or to accompany Luigi's Bean Soup (page 338). Focaccia freezes well; let cool completely, then seal the loaves in individual plastic bags and freeze. Reheat frozen breads before serving (see page 23 for defrosting and warming instructions).

Pizza with Rosemary and Garlic

pizza bianca • Italy

Talking to Luigi Orgera about food always makes us hungry. Raised in the small village of Spinio, south of Rome, he now owns a restaurant in Toronto called La Fenice. The restaurant is always crowded with customers there for Luigi's honest "country food": a wonderful array of antipasti; olive oil from his own trees in Spinio; lamb grilled with a little rosemary; carefully cooked risottos; and on and on.

One day over lunch he talked about pizza. His sister, Maria, was for years the village baker in Spinio. She has now made way for her son, Mauro, who regularly trucks his bread into Rome's specialty bread shops. "Traditionally," said Luigi, "in order to test whether the oven was at the right temperature, the baker would roll out a small piece of dough into a thin round, then toss it onto the hearth. If it puffed up without burning, the oven was right and the loaves could go in for baking. Later the Neapolitans added garlic and salt—so now we have pizza." Where did the word *pizza* come from? "Who knows? Maybe from the other side of the Mediterranean. It sounds like *pita,* doesn't it?"

In *The Classic Cuisine of the Italian Jews,* Edda Servi Machlin suggests that the first wave of Jewish immigrants to Italy, who probably came after the Roman conquest of the eastern Mediterranean brought pita with them. But it is doubtful that anything as refined as our modern-day pitas, which puff up during baking, could have been produced with the coarsely ground flour of that era. Perhaps thin round unleavened breads were called pita and then the breads evolved as milling techniques improved.

Pizza bianca is a classic morning or any-other-time snack in Rome. I once bought a piece from a small vendor in Rome right after arriving by plane from Turkey; it brought me quickly and delightfully into focus. Italy! It is often very thin, with good bite. At its most simple, it is dressed only with olive oil and salt—a very basic, very delicious bread. Our favorite is made of half white and half whole wheat flour, and adds a southern touch with chopped garlic and a sprinkling of rosemary.

continued

dough

1½ cups lukewarm water

½ teaspoon dry yeast

Approximately 4 cups unbleached all-purpose flour or unbleached hard white flour or a 50–50 blend of hard whole wheat flour and white flour

¼ teaspoon salt

2 tablespoons olive oil

topping

2 tablespoons olive oil

6 cloves garlic, finely chopped

3 sprigs rosemary, leaves only

1 teaspoon fine sea salt

You will need a large bread bowl, quarry tiles (see page 20) to fit on the bottom rack of your oven (optional), and a 12- by 18-inch baking sheet or two smaller sheets.

Place the warm water in a large bread bowl, stir in the yeast, and allow to dissolve. Stir in 1 cup flour, stirring constantly in the same direction. Stir in another cup of flour, and then stir 100 times in the same direction, about 1 minute, to help develop the gluten. Cover this sponge, and let stand for at least 30 minutes, or up to 3 hours.

Sprinkle the salt and oil over the sponge, and then add more flour, stirring it in ½ cup at a time. The dough will become heavier and harder to stir; when you can stir no longer, turn the dough out onto a well-floured surface. Knead, adding extra flour to your work surface as necessary to prevent the dough from sticking, for 10 minutes, or until smooth and easy to work. Clean the bread bowl, oil it lightly, and place the ball of dough into the bowl. Cover with plastic wrap and let rise until more than doubled in volume, about 3 hours. (The dough can be made ahead to this point. If you wish to postpone baking for a few hours, gently push down the dough, and leave, covered, in the bowl to rise again. Or store the dough in a plastic bag in the refrigerator for up to 5 days; remove from the plastic bag and bring to room temperature at least an hour before you want to work with it.)

Place quarry tiles, if using, on bottom rack of your oven. Preheat the oven to 500°F. Lightly oil a 12- by 18-inch baking sheet or two 9- by 12-inch sheets.

Turn the dough out onto a lightly floured work surface and flatten with the lightly floured palm of your hand. If working with two baking sheets, divide dough in half and work with one piece at a time. Pull and stretch the dough gently out into a rectangle slightly smaller than your baking sheet; take your time, and give the dough time to rest if it resists stretching. Then transfer the dough to the baking sheet and gently press and stretch it until it is of an even thinness across the bottom of the baking sheet and forms a slight rounded rim at the edges. (Don't worry if it tears; just patch the hole with a piece of dough and press firmly to join the edges.) Let rise, covered with plastic wrap, for 20 minutes.

Brush the top of the pizza with oil, then dimple the surface all over with your fingertips. Sprinkle the garlic and rosemary leaves as evenly as possible over the pizza, then sprinkle on the sea salt. Bake on the quarry tiles (see Note) or on the bottom rack of the oven until the crust is slightly golden around the edges, about 5 to 8 minutes. Remove from the oven, and lightly brush the edges with olive oil. Cut into large squares and serve hot or warm. (We often make pizza bianca several hours ahead, then wrap it in a clean kitchen towel to keep it moist until we are ready to reheat it for serving. To reheat, place in a dampened paper bag in a 300°F oven for about 10 minutes.)

Alternatives: You can, of course, use this dough to make other pizzas. For example, lay on tomato slices, lightly sautéed sliced onions, a generous sprinkling of chopped flat-leafed parsley, and strips of anchovy (rinsed if salted), then brush with a little oil, and sprinkle lightly with sea salt. Or spread with Basil and Garlic Sauce (page 336), then sprinkle on a little sea salt and bake.

Note: The pizza can also be baked directly on the quarry tiles instead of on a baking sheet. Use a peel (or the back of a baking sheet), liberally dusted with cornmeal, to transfer the pizza onto the hot tiles.

· · · ▴ ▴ ▴ ▴ ▴ · ▴ · ▴ ▴ ▴ · · ▴ ▴ ▴ ▴ · ▴ ▴

Makes 1 large (12- by 18-inch) pizza or 2 medium pizzas. Serves 6 to 8 as an appetizer or 3 to 4 as a light lunch accompanied by salad.

Cut into small squares to accompany antipasti, or serve as a light meal accompanied by Tender Greens Salad (page 327) or Salad of Tomatoes and Roasted Onions (page 329).

Basil and Garlic Sauce

pesto • Italy

Everyone has a favorite pesto sauce. This one is light on cheese and heavy on basil. Though pine nuts are usually used in pesto, walnuts can be substituted, as they often are in Livorno, for some or all of the pine nuts. If possible, make up pesto just before you wish to use it, to keep the basil's fresh flavor and bright green color.

Baking pesto on a quickly cooked thin-crust pizza gives the nuts a roasted taste and softens the edge of the garlic, without killing the fresh basil taste—a great treat. If you are making this as a fresh sauce for pasta, reduce the garlic to two or three large cloves.

6 cloves garlic, minced

1 teaspoon salt

2 tablespoons pine nuts or walnut pieces

2 cups packed fresh basil leaves (see Note)

3 to 4 tablespoons extra-virgin olive oil, or more if desired

3 tablespoons freshly grated Parmesan or Romano cheese, or more to taste

You will need a large mortar and pestle or a food processor.

Using a mortar and pestle, pound the garlic to a paste with the salt. Add the nuts and crush thoroughly. Chop basil leaves finely, then add to the mortar with 1 tablespoon of the olive oil and pound until you have a thick, coarse paste. Stir in another 2 tablespoons oil and then the cheese.

Alternatively, to produce a more even-textured but less traditional pesto, with the processor running, add garlic and salt, and process until a paste forms. Add the pine nuts and basil, and process briefly. Add 2 tablespoons of the olive oil and process briefly to form a paste; be careful not to process to a perfectly smooth paste. Turn out into a bowl and stir in 1 more tablespoon oil and the cheese.

Use to dress pizza dough just before baking, or as a pasta sauce—you may want to thin it by adding another tablespoon or so of oil—or store in the refrigerator in a well-sealed glass jar. To prevent the basil from darkening in the jar, cover the pesto with a layer of olive oil.

Alternatives: We also enjoy the completely (as far as we know) untraditional option of roasted unsalted pistachios as a substitute for the pine nuts. Their lively green adds to the rich color of the pesto paste and their slight sweet edge blends well with the basil. If basil is in short supply, you can extend it by substituting flat-leafed parsley for half of the basil, for a pesto with a fresher, less pungent taste.

Note: We like to put up basil in olive oil at the end of the summer for use in pesto during the winter months. We wash all the bunches of basil we can lay our hands on, dry them thoroughly, then pull off the leaves, discarding the stalks and any discolored leaves. We fill the food processor with the leaves, and pulse to chop them, drizzling in a little olive oil after the first pulse to coat the leaves and help to stop them darkening as they are crushed. We add enough oil to make a paste, processing in pulses and trying not to process the basil to a mush, then transfer the basil paste to small sterile jars, seal them, and refrigerate them. They can also be stored, unopened, for up to 6 months in a cool dark place. This method is simpler than putting up batches of pesto. It is also more flexible, since it yields a basil paste that can be combined with fresh ingredients to make pesto or with a vinaigrette to dress a salad.

....

Makes ½ cup dense paste.

Spread on pizza before baking or on hot pasta before tossing and serving, thinning with extra olive oil if you wish. If using with the pizza dough from Pizza with Rosemary and Garlic (page 333), spread on the pesto, thinning with a little olive oil if it seems too thick, then sprinkle with an additionalt ¼ teaspoon sea salt.

Luigi's Bean Soup
fagioli • Italy

Beans, legumes, peas—whatever term you use, they're wonderful foods. Their proteins complement those in grains, so they pair well with breads. We tend to think of the combination of legumes and grains as typically South or Central Asian, but Europe too has wonderful country bean dishes that are always eaten with bread. Try this simple meatless soup with Three-Color Focaccia or Sardinian Parchment Bread for a satisfying one-dish supper.

2 cups dried navy beans, washed and picked over

2 medium tomatoes, coarsely chopped

2 scallions, coarsely chopped

2 tablespoons olive oil

1 stalk celery, coarsely chopped

3 to 4 large cloves garlic, coarsely chopped

½ teaspoon freshly ground black pepper

¼ cup loosely packed fresh basil leaves

1½ teaspoons salt

Freshly grated Parmesan or aged goat cheese for serving

Freshly ground black pepper for serving

You will need a large pot with a lid.

Place the beans in a large pot, add water to cover by 3 to 4 inches, and bring to a boil, skimming off any foam. Drain the beans, and add cold water to cover by 3 to 4 inches. Place over medium-high heat, and add the tomatoes, scallions, oil, celery, garlic, black pepper, and basil. Cover and bring to a boil. Lower the heat and simmer, covered, for 2 to 3 hours, until the beans are tender. Check the beans every so often, and add more water if necessary.

Add the salt, bring back to a rolling boil, and cook for 3 to 5 minutes to thicken. Transfer to a serving bowl. Serve hot, with a bowl of freshly grated Parmesan or aged goat cheese for those who wish to sprinkle it on their beans. Grind pepper generously over each serving.

Makes 4 to 5 cups soup. Serves 2 as a main course or 4 to 5 as part of a larger meal.

Serve as a satisfying meal-in-one, with plenty of Three-Color Focaccia (page 331), Sardinian Parchment Bread (page 328), or Pizza with Rosemary and Garlic, (page 333).

Spelt Breakfast Bread

pain d'épeautre • Swiss Alps

Spelt (triticum speltum) is a wheat that was widely cultivated in Europe until the beginning of this century. With the rise of industrial farming, spelt was largely abandoned in favor of modern wheat strains, which gave higher yields under intensive cultivation. There has been a spelt revival in Europe and North America over the last decade; spelt can now be found easily in North American natural food stores. The spelt flours we have tested have excellent bread-making characteristics and can usually be substituted for whole wheat flour.

These are very simple breads, delicious on their own or with honey. This recipe is adapted from one passed on to us by Aline Lemordant of Grenoble. The breads are easy to prepare and ideal for breakfast. They don't keep well, so we make only as many as can be eaten when fresh.

1 cup warm water	1 tablespoon olive oil
1 tablespoon honey	3 to 3½ cups spelt flour (see page 403)
1 teaspoon salt	

You will need a large baking sheet and a bread bowl.

Preheat the oven to 450°F. Lightly oil a large baking sheet.

Combine the water, honey, salt, and oil in a medium-sized bread bowl. Stir in the flour 1 cup at a time until a dough begins to form. Turn the dough out onto a lightly floured bread board and knead until well mixed, 3 to 5 minutes. Let rest for 10 minutes.

Divide the dough into 8 equal pieces. Flatten each piece between floured palms into flat discs approximately 3 inches in diameter. Arrange the breads on the baking sheet.

Bake on the middle rack of the oven for 17 to 20 minutes, until firm to the touch. Cool briefly on a rack. Serve warm.

··▲▲▲▲▲▲▲··▲▲··▲▲▲▲··▲

Makes 8 small round flatbreads, about 3 inches across.
Serves 2 to 4 for breakfast.

Serve for breakfast with honey, jam, or marmalade, or serve plain as an afternoon snack.

Norwegian Crispbread

flatbrød • Norway

These cracker-like breads are paperthin, full of flavor, and good on their own or with any number of accompaniments. They take less time to make than a trip to the store to buy a commercial version: This recipe takes less than half an hour from start to finish.

Virtually any combination of flours can be used. In this four-flour combination, the wheat flour makes for easy kneading and the other three give an intriguing depth of flavor. If you can't find oat flour (available in many health food stores), increase the amounts of each of the others to one and a third cups.

Traditionally flatbrød were large round thin discs, up to eighteen inches across, baked over a fire on a metal plate called a *takke*. One way to reproduce the traditional takke method of baking is to use a baking sheet laid over two burners, but we prefer oven baking because of its reliably even heat.

1 cup oat flour	1½ teaspoons salt
1 cup light rye flour	1½ cups warm water
1 cup hard unbleached wheat flour	Oat flour or barley flour for kneading and rolling out
1 cup barley flour	

You will need a large bowl, a food processor (optional), a rolling pin, and baking sheets (see Note).

Mix all the flours and salt together in a large bowl. Stir in the warm water, and form the dough into a ball. Turn out onto a work surface generously dusted with flour. Knead with well-floured hands, working the dough gently until it gains elasticity and loses its stickiness. Continue kneading for 5 minutes longer. This will develop the gluten in the wheat and rye flours and make rolling out a pleasure.

Alternatively, to use a food processor, divide the ingredients in half and make two batches instead of one large batch. Put the flours and salt into the processor, then pour in the water as the machine is running, and process until a dough forms. Continue to process for 1 minute, then turn out onto a well-floured work surface. Repeat with the remaining ingredients, combine the two doughs, and knead briefly. (For more details about kneading with a food processor, see High-Tech Crackers, page 392.)

Let the dough rest for 10 minutes, covered with a towel. Preheat the oven to 375°F.

Divide the dough into four. Flour your work surface and each piece of dough generously, and flatten each piece with the palm of your hand. Cover three of the pieces with a towel. Working with the fourth, flatten it further with your palm into a rectangle about 6 to 8 inches across. Then start rolling it out, working from the center outward, into a rectangle the size of your baking sheet and less than ⅛ inch thick. Trim off the edges to make a neat rectangle and transfer it to an ungreased baking sheet. (Keep the trimmed edges, without combining them, to make other crispbreads; see Note, below.)

Using a knife or pizza cutter, cut the dough lengthwise into 1½-inch-wide strips. Then cut the strips crosswise in thirds. If your oven is large enough to accommodate two baking sheets at once, roll out and cut another piece of dough. Place the baking sheet(s) in the center of the oven, and bake for 5 to 10 minutes, depending on how thin the flatbread is. You will see the crispbreads separate from each other as they curve away from the hot surface; start checking them after 5 minutes—once you see them starting to brown, they're done. Transfer to a rack to cool.

Roll out and bake the remaining dough. Store the completely cooled flatbreads in a well-sealed plastic bag or a cookie tin.

Note: When we make these crispbreads, we make four baking sheets' worth, using 10- by 15-inch sheets. The instructions given here assume that you have two baking sheets that size. If you have only 12- by 18-inch baking sheets, divide the dough into three, not four. You will then be able to roll each piece out to almost fill a sheet. The important thing is to have a baking sheet large enough to hold the rolled-out dough; since it is then cut into crackers, it doesn't matter if your sheet is larger than the sheet of dough.

We like to play around with the trimmed edges, rolling them out even thinner, then cutting them into odd-shaped crackers, a nice contrast to the regular rectangles. We bake them after the others are done.

Makes approximately 50 thin rectangular crackers, 1 to 1½ inches wide and 5 to 6 inches long.

These are great on their own or with Marinated Herring (page 352) or Anna's Cured Salmon (page 342) as a snack, an appetizer, or part of a smorgasbord (see page 348).

Anna's Cured Salmon

gravad laks, gravlax • Sweden and Norway

In summer, the North Sea coast of Norway is an exhilarating place to visit with its tall mountains, deeply cut fjords, and idyllic-looking farmhouses tucked into hillsides patterned with carefully tended fields. As you travel even farther north, the terrain gets rockier, and outside every house in the small fishing settlements there is a wooden rack for hanging and drying salt cod. Life here revolves around the sea and depends upon fishing. Fish are traditionally salted, smoked, or brine-cured and versions of all of these methods are still used at both the local and commercial levels.

Scandinavians also developed a method of fermenting fish by burying it in the ground, the most easily available cold storage. Centuries before the modern freezer, fishermen learned to preserve their catch by burying it along the shore pressed between two layers of birch bark. The modern version of "buried fish" (*gravad* means buried) is not allowed to ferment, but merely to cure with spices and herbs in a cool place. Trout or mackerel are delicious cured by this method, but by far its best-known application is with salmon, or *lax*—hence the famous *gravlax.*

Gravlax has become popular outside Scandinavia and is available at many delicatessens and specialty stores. The best is still homemade, using a simple method of rubbing the fish with sugar and spices, strewing it with herbs, pressing it under a weight for twenty-four to forty-eight hours, and slicing it just before serving. The salt draws moisture from the fish, leaving it firmer, while the sugar, pepper, and dill lightly flavor it. In Sweden, gravlax is an essential dish on the Christmas table, traditionally served with a sweet-tasting mustard and dill dressing, made right at the table or prepared just before serving.

Our neighbor Anna is from Sweden, born in Göteberg on the west coast and raised in Stockholm. This is a version of her recipe, though she bemoans the fact that farmed salmon or Pacific salmon usually is the only fish available here in North America; Atlantic salmon, traditionally preferred for its firm flesh and subtle flavor, has been so overfished that it is difficult to find and extremely expensive when you do come across it. Fresh salmon from fish farms is both affordable and very flavorful when cured.

2 to 2½ pounds salmon, preferably the midsection of the fish, or 2 pounds salmon fillet, in two matching pieces, skin on

1 tablespoon sugar

1 tablespoon kosher or other coarse salt

1½ teaspoons coarsely crushed white pepper (black pepper will leave black traces on the fish)

2 bunches fresh dill

garnish and accompaniments

½ bunch fresh dill, coarsely chopped

Lemon wedges (optional)

You will need a cleaver or sharp knife if your fish is unfilleted, a large shallow plate, a flat plate, and a weight (such as a 2-quart jar filled with water).

Wipe the fish clean and dry; do not scale or rinse with water. If using unboned salmon, cut into two fillets and remove the backbone. Remove the pin bones from the fish.

Combine the sugar, salt, and pepper, and rub it into the flesh of each piece. Place one piece skin side down on a large shallow plate, and spread 1 bunch of dill on top. Place the other piece skin side up over the first piece. Cover with a flat plate and put a weight on top of the plate. Place in the lower part of the refrigerator for 24 to 36 hours, turning the salmon twice in that time. The fish releases water as it is pressed, so drain off liquid before turning it over. The second time you turn the fish, replace the dill with the second bunch.

To serve, discard the dill, and scrape the sugar and spices off the salmon. Slice the fish with a very sharp knife at an angle; if you wish, cut out and discard the triangular grayish patch from the center of each slice. Place the slices on a serving platter surrounded by fresh dill. Serve with plenty of lemon wedges, if desired.

Alternatives: If you make gravad trout or mackerel, let the fish cure for 2 to 3 days. Instead of dill, try using coarsely chopped scallions between the layers of fish. Coriander, with its distinctive flavor, will also perfume a gravad fish very pleasingly.

Serves 8 as an appetizer or as part of a smorgasbord (see page 348).

Serve with lemon wedges, accompanied by Norwegian Crispbread (page 340) and Midnight Sun Potato Salad (page 346).

Norwegian Wrapping Bread

lefse • Norway

Our friend Judy is from Minnesota, from a family of Norwegian extraction.
Whenever she talks of lefse, she gets a dreamy, faraway look in her eye. One day
she called to say that she'd received a shipment of lefse in the mail from her Aunt
Effie. She arrived at the door ten minutes later and we feasted on it, in the traditional way—spread with fresh sweet butter and lightly sprinkled with sugar, then
rolled up. We washed our excesses down with strong coffee.

Lefse are indeed a great treat, one Judy particularly associates with
Christmas and other festive occasions. Every region, every family, seems to have a
preferred style: Some are fine and supple, rich with butter and cream, and soft with
cooked mashed potato; others are made only with potato, flour, and water. Judy
also describes another traditional way of eating lefse, wrapped around slices of
smoked meat or cheese and meat combinations, like a rolled-up sandwich.

Lefse are easier to roll out if the dough is made a day ahead and refrigerated overnight, as described below. They need an even heat, so an electric frying
pan (or a lefse maker) is ideal, but a heavy well-seasoned cast-iron skillet will do.
The rolling pin commonly used for lefse has fine grooves in it to help prevent the
dough from sticking to the pin as you roll. We manage without a grooved pin, using
instead a very small lightweight wooden pin and keeping it well floured.

Though it is tempting to knead the dough, try to resist, for kneading produces a tougher lefse than tradition finds acceptable, though still soft and of course
somewhat easier to roll out.

2 pounds old or mealy potatoes, peeled and coarsely chopped (about 4 cups)	1½ teaspoons salt
⅓ cup soft unsalted butter	Approximately 2 cups unbleached all-purpose flour, plus extra for rolling
½ cup heavy cream (35% butterfat)	

You will need a large pot, a large bowl, a rolling pin, preferably with
grooves, a potato masher, and an electric frying pan or lefse maker or a large cast-
iron skillet.

T*he day before you wish to serve lefse, prepare the dough:* Place the potatoes in a
large pot and add water to just cover. Bring to a boil and cook until soft. Drain, and
mash thoroughly; there must be no small lumps to interfere with rolling out the
breads. (We're told that many lefse makers now use instant mashed or flaked potatoes because of the need to have the potatoes absolutely smooth and lump-free.)

Transfer the potatoes to a bowl. Stir in butter, cream, and salt, and blend well. Sift and stir in 2 cups flour. Work the dough into a ball; DO NOT KNEAD. If the dough feels very sticky, add a little more flour; potatoes vary in moisture content, so the amount of flour you need to make a workable dough will vary. Cover and refrigerate overnight, well sealed in plastic wrap.

Turn the dough out onto a well-floured surface. Divide in two, and set one half aside, covered with plastic wrap. (You can also wrap the dough in plastic wrap and store it in the refrigerator for up to 5 days.)

Divide the piece of dough into 16 equal pieces. (This will yield lefse slightly smaller than those made by Judy's Aunt Effie, and therefore easier to handle and to cook evenly in a skillet.) Keeping your hands and work surface lightly floured, flatten one piece of dough with the palm of your hand, turning it over once or twice as you do so. Using a light touch and a rolling pin, (ideally, a grooved pin), roll the dough out, rolling from the center outward and rotating it an eighth to a quarter-turn between each stroke, to a very thin round, 8 to 10 inches across. Turn the dough over occasionally and keep your work surface and rolling pin very lightly floured to prevent sticking. Slide the bread to one side of your work surface and start rolling out the next one.

At first you may wish to roll out eight breads and cook them before you start rolling out the others. As you develop a rhythm, you will be able to roll out breads while you cook. Remember as you roll them out that even slightly-thicker-than-perfection lefse will still look and taste wonderful.

Heat an electric frying pan to 350°F or heat a lefse maker or large cast-iron skillet over medium-high heat. When the pan is hot, transfer a rolled-out bread to the pan and cook for 45 seconds to 1 minute, or until lightly speckled with gold, but not brown. Turn over and cook the other side. (The butter in the dough will keep it from sticking.) Lift the bread out gently and transfer to a plate. Continue cooking the rolled-out breads, then roll out and cook the remaining

Potatoes

dough. If you plan on storing the lefse in the refrigerator, place a sheet of waxed paper between each, since they tend to stick to each other when cooled. In our house they are devoured almost as they are made, so we don't bother with the waxed paper. You can store them for several days on a plate, well wrapped in plastic wrap, at room temperature, or for up to 2 weeks in the refrigerator; reheat in a dry medium-hot skillet just before eating.

···▲▲▲▲▲··▲▲··▲▲▲··▲

Makes 32 thin, supple round breads, 8 to 10 inches in diameter.

Serve with granulated sugar or honey or homemade berry jam for breakfast, a late afternoon snack, or for dessert. Sprinkle each bread lightly with sugar, or brush lightly with honey or jam, and roll it up neatly before eating. A friend raised on English pancakes suggested we try a squeeze of lemon on the sugared bread before rolling it up—delicious, if untraditional. Lefse also make a great addition to a smorgasbord (see page 348) as a sweet course, accompanied by fresh berries and strong coffee.

Midnight Sun Potato Salad

Norway

One summer I traveled in a tiny Fiat van up the coast of Norway from Bergen to the Nordkapp and back down through Finland. The trip was long and interesting; the international music festival in Bergen seemed light-years away from isolated farms by the side of steep-walled fjords farther up the coast and from reindeer grazing in Lapland.

On a tight budget, I found the only affordable foods in the far north of Norway were bread, potatoes, and yogurt, all three were excellent. The potatoes were particularly good, even though they were the last of the previous year's crop. Perhaps they tasted so good because they were almost all I ate, but maybe it was because they were locally grown and had the true flavor of the landscape I was traveling through.

In this simple potato salad, the potatoes stay potatoes; they don't disappear into a jumble of mushy tastes and textures, so it's important to start with good ones.

3 pounds new potatoes

½ medium white onion, finely chopped (approximately ½ cup)

⅔ cup cider vinegar, or to taste

6 tablespoons finely chopped fresh dill

2 teaspoons salt

½ teaspoon freshly ground black pepper, or more to taste

You will need a large pot and a small bowl.

Place the potatoes in a large pot and cover with cold water. Bring to a boil, and boil gently, partially covered, until cooked through but not mushy. Drain, return the potatoes to the still-hot pot, and let stand until ready to proceed; we find this helps firm them up.

When the potatoes are cool (we often cook them ahead and refrigerate them for several hours or overnight before making the salad), slide the skins off if you like, and cut the potatoes into 1-inch cubes. Place in a large serving bowl, and add the onion.

In a small bowl, mix together the vinegar, dill, salt, and pepper. Pour the dressing over the salad and toss gently to coat. Serve at once, or let sit for several hours, covered, in a cool place, to give the dressing time to penetrate the potatoes.

Alternatives: You can also make this salad a rustic meal in one, accompanied only by flatbread, such as Finnish Barley Bread (page 354), by adding 6 to 8 anchovy fillets, soaked to wash away excess salt, and chopped. If using the anchovies, omit the salt in the dressing. Taste the salad once it is assembled, then add salt to taste.

Makes about 6 cups salad. Serves 4 to 6 as part of a simple meal or 8 to 10 as one of many dishes on a smorgasbord.

Serve with Norwegian Crispbread (page 340) and Marinated Herring (page 352) for lunch, or place on a smorgasbord (see page 348).

SCANDINAVIAN SMORGASBORD

In 1975, travel to the Soviet Union was complicated to arrange and expensive. But in Helsinki it was possible to book a short boat trip to Tallinn in Estonia to have at least a glimpse behind the Iron Curtain. A friend and I boarded the boat in Helsinki's busy harbor, not far from the summertime vegetable market, with its late-July stacks of tomatoes and cucumbers. Our fellow passengers were almost all Finns enjoying a forty-eight-hour jaunt across the Baltic. We'd been told that the Estonians referred to them as "whiskey Finns," because the liquor sold on board was duty-free, a far cry from the highly taxed spirits sold in Finland.

From our point of view, after two months of camping in Norway and Finland, the outstanding luxury on board was the food: a traditional Finnish-style spread of dishes, called in Finnish *seisova poyta* ("stand-up table") or, more colloquially, *voileipa poyta* ("sandwich table"). There were six or eight kinds of bread, most of them flatbreads—crisp and soft, made of rye, wheat, or barley—accompanied by a large array of fish dishes and northern salads. Herring in all its forms, as well as colorful bowls of roe and plates of gravlax (sliced cured salmon) and smoked trout, caught the eye. Nearby were bowls of cucumber slices tossed in sour cream and dill, or dressed simply with vinegar and capers. Tufts of dill were scattered through one kind of potato salad, while another was pink with beet juice. There were pickles of various shapes and sizes, as well as an array of cheeses, fresh and aged, all produced in Finland. It seemed ambitious to try to taste everything, but no one else appeared the least bit restrained. We never even reached the main courses—roast this and that—or the desserts.

All the Scandinavian countries have a version of this "stand-up table." The Swedish word for it is the most familiar: *smorgasbord,* literally "bread and butter table." The Norwegians and Danes call their version *koldt bord.*

The smorgasbord is a flexible, bread-based way to feed a crowd and a festive start to a sit-down celebration such as Christmas or Thanksgiving. (A special version of smorgasbord, called a *joulebord,* is served at Christmas in Sweden.) Like the mezze table (see page 203), the smorgasbord can be either an appetizer preceding a main course or a full meal in itself, laid out buffet-fashion for guests to help themselves. Many of the northern European dishes in this chapter can be assembled into a smorgasbord.

Always place a selection of breads on the table. Include at least two of the following: Norwegian Crispbread (page 340), Finnish Barley Bread (page 354), Rye Hardtack Rings (page 350), Norwegian Wrapping Bread (page 344), and Scottish Oatcakes (page 357). A traditional buffet also has several Scandinavian cheeses, fresh and aged. Lumpfish roe or smoked herring roe, served in a bowl with a side plate of lemon wedges, a bowl of sour cream, and some chopped onion, is great for heaping onto crispbread, as well as pleasing to the eye. A simple salad of sliced cucumbers in cider vinegar adds crispness and a Beet and Dill Salad (page 356) gives color. Marinated Herring (page 352) and Midnight Sun Potato Salad (page 346) are two essentials. You could also offer Anna's Cured Salmon (page 342) with lemon wedges. To add a slightly crosscultural twist, serve a Georgian Leek Pâté (page 305) and a Salad of Tomatoes and Roasted Onions (page 329), which will also help provide for vegetarians in the crowd.

Schnapps, aquavit, beer, or fruit juice: Almost anything goes well with this heavily flavored array of food. At a festive meal you could go on to serve roast turkey or goose, though the smorgasbord on its own feels very festive. When your guests have finished the savory part of the meal, set out more lefse and fresh berries to round it off.

Rye Hardtack Rings
ruisleipa • Finland

Rye, secale cereale, *is a grain similar in composition to wheat. It is a hardy*
grass that can tolerate cold winter temperatures and poor soils, traits that have made
its cultivation of rye possible in areas where no other cereals can flourish. Rye can
be cultivated farther north than any other winter cereal, which is why it is still the
dominant grain grown in northern Europe and parts of Russia. As far as domesticated cereal grains go, however, rye is a relative newcomer. While barley and wheat
were being cultivated as early as 4000 B.C., rye lived the life of a weed until around
400 B.C.; even today it is considered a weed in Central Asia.

For bread making, what distinguishes rye is not its similarity to wheat, but
the ways in which it is different. Rye has roughly the same proportion of protein,
carbohydrate, fiber, and fat as wheat, and like wheat—and unlike many of the other
cereal grains—it also has gluten. Gluten is essential for making raised breads and
loaf breads (see Flatbread Basics, pages 7–27). But the gluten in rye is made up only
of gliadin, whereas the gluten in wheat is made up of both gliadin and glutenin, giving wheat superiority in bread making. Rye also differs from wheat in that it has a
large number of carbon sugars, called pentosans. These pentosans have a high
water-binding capacity, so that a dough made from rye flour retains more water
than a wheat dough, the reason rye doughs are so often sticky. This higher water-
binding capacity also means that crisp dry rye breads—like those made in
Scandinavia—tend to swell in the stomach as they absorb more moisture, making
us feel full over a longer period of time. Rye has sometimes been called a "poverty
grain," in part because it tends to grow in marginal areas and in part because of its
ability to make one feel fuller longer, an important characteristic if you can't afford
enough to eat. In many parts of central and northern Europe, rye breads have traditionally been eaten by the poor and wheat breads by the rich.

···▲▲▲▲▲·▲·▲▲▲▲▲▲▲·▲··▲

Ohrarieska are lightly yeasted Finnish rye flatbreads with a wonderful rye
flavor. They can be eaten either fresh and soft, or crisp and crackly. A hole is cut out
of the center of each because they are traditionally made in large batches only once
or twice a year and then hung on poles or cords high up near the ceiling to dry. A
similar technique is used for storing breads in parts of Norway and Sweden, as well
as in central Anatolia in Turkey.

Bread, and flatbread in particular, is still a very important part of life in
Finland. When a young couple moves into a new apartment, friends give rye rings

and salt to bring them good luck: If these essentials are taken care of, life will go well.

2 teaspoons dry yeast

2 cups warm water

4 to 4½ cups rye flour, plus extra for kneading and rolling

1½ teaspoons salt

You will need a medium-sized bread bowl, two 12- by 18-inch baking sheets, and a rolling pin.

In a medium-sized bread bowl, dissolve the yeast in the warm water. Add 2 cups rye flour and stir 50 times in the same direction. Sprinkle on the salt and stir well. Stir in 2 more cups flour, and turn out onto a lightly floured surface. Knead 3 to 4 minutes, dusting with flour as necessary. Clean out and lightly oil the bread bowl. Return the dough to the bread bowl and cover. Let rise for 1½ hours; you can let it sit for longer, but the dough will become stickier and more difficult to work with.

Preheat the oven to 425°F. Oil and lightly flour two large baking sheets, at least 12 inches by 18 inches.

Gently punch down the dough. Divide into four pieces. Flatten each piece between floured palms, and let rest for 2 to 3 minutes.

Gently roll out each piece of dough into a round approximately 8 inches in diameter, or as large as your baking sheets will accommodate. The dough can be quite sticky, so add flour as necessary to prevent sticking. Using a sharp knife, cut a circular hole approximately 2 inches in diameter in the center of each bread. Transfer the breads to the baking sheets and cover with damp towels or with plastic wrap. Let rise for 15 to 20 minutes. The pieces of dough from the cut-out holes can be gathered together and made into another bread, or—as we prefer—simply rolled out into several thin flatbreads and baked on a hot griddle on top of the stove for immediate consumption.

Using a fork, prick the tops of the breads at 1- to 2-inch intervals. Bake for 15 minutes. Remove and cool on a rack. These breads are delicious sliced into wedges and eaten when just baked, but they are traditionally strung on a cord and hung up in the kitchen in order to dry out completely. In their dried form they can be broken up into soups or eaten as flavorful crackers.

·‥▲▲▲▲▲▲▲‥·‥▲▲‥▲▲▲‥·‥▲

Makes four 8-inch round flatbreads about ½ to 1 inch thick.

Excellent as part of a smorgasbord (see page 348) or served with Marinated Herring (page 352) and Midnight Sun Potato Salad (page 346).

Marinated Herring

Brining is an ancient method of preserving fish, still widely used for herring.
Fresh-caught fish stored in barrels of brine become firm, almost stiff, and keep

almost indefinitely. As a result, salt herring is generally available year-round.

Marinated herring has always been a great treat for us—somewhat rationed because of the relatively high cost of even a small jar. But recently we learned an easy way of making it in our own kitchen, at a fraction the cost of the commercial versions and with better flavor. The balance of vinegar and sweet and the proportion of onion to herring are the most important elements. We love the spicing in this marinade, adapted from the version

Scotland: Fishing village on North Sea

in Elizabeth Luard's *The Old World Kitchen*. A simpler version made without carrot, allspice, or mustard seed is also delicious.

Marinated herring keeps well and is an excellent accompaniment to Norwegian Crispbreads or Rye Hardtack Rings.

2 salt herring (about 1 pound headless; see Note)

Approximately 3 cups milk

1 cup white vinegar (5% to 6% acidity)

⅓ cup sugar

1 teaspoon black peppercorns

1 teaspoon whole allspice berries

2 to 3 bay leaves

1 teaspoon mustard seed

1 to 2 carrots, thinly sliced

1 medium red onion, cut in half lengthwise and thinly sliced crosswise

You will need a shallow dish, a small saucepan, and a sterilized 1-pint wide-mouthed mason or other well-sealed glass jar.

Gut the herring, scale, cut off the tails, and rinse well with water. Place in a shallow dish and add enough milk to cover. Place in the refrigerator or a cool corner and let soak for 12 to 24 hours to draw out salt; the fish will soften during soaking, making filleting much easier.

Drain the herring, rinse well, and dry. Remove and discard the skin, and fillet the fish. Check the flesh by feeling it with your fingers to make sure all bones have been removed. Cut the herring into ¼-inch strips less than 1 inch long.

Combine the vinegar, sugar, peppercorns, allspice, bay leaves, and mustard seed in a saucepan. Bring to a boil, stirring to dissolve the sugar, and boil for 2 to 3 minutes. Let cool for 10 minutes.

In a sterilized 1-pint wide-mouthed glass jar, layer the carrot, onion, and herring, repeating the layers until the jar is half-full. Spoon half the vinegar marinade, including the spices, into the jar. Layer the remaining carrot, onion, and herring in the jar, pressing down to compress if necessary, and then pour over the remaining marinade. Seal the jar, and let stand for 4 to 5 days before serving. The herring keeps indefinitely when sealed; once opened, it will keep for 10 days to 2 weeks in the refrigerator.

Note: If you can buy filleted salt herring, do so, since it will eliminate the need to skin and fillet the fish yourself. You will need about 14 ounces filleted herring. The fillets must still be soaked, but soaking time can be reduced to 8 hours.

Makes 2 cups marinated herring.

Serve with Norwegian Crispbread (page 340), Finnish Barley Bread (page 354), or Rye Hardtack Rings (page 350) as a snack or appetizer, or as part of a smorgasbord (see page 348).

Finnish Barley Bread

ohrarieska • Finland

As a cereal crop barley is very versatile, much like oats. It grows in Tibet at very high altitudes and in extremely cold weather, and it also grows in the hot, dry climates of India and the Middle East. It can adapt itself to a very short growing season, making it superior to other grains in places susceptible to summer drought.

Field of barley in summer

Most of the barley now grown in the world goes to feed animals or is processed into malt, but this is a relatively recent phenomenon. The domestication of barley took place at roughly the same time as wheat, and for thousands of years barley was a staff of life in Europe, the Eastern Mediterranean, and in parts of Central Asia and China. The barley flatbreads of the Arab world, like Bedouin Barley Bread (page 212), represent some of the longest uninterrupted bread traditions in the world. With the introduction of leavening in bread (a feat usually attributed to the Egyptians), barley, which has no gluten, gradually fell from favor as a bread grain and was generally replaced by wheat.

I first tasted this Finnish barley bread one summer night in the far north of Finland (spring barleys can be grown even farther north than winter ryes). A Lapp family, settled on a lakeside farm north of the Arctic Circle, had a traditional wooden sauna house that travelers could enjoy. In rural Finland, the sauna is traditionally a place of warmth, comfort, and conviviality, a place where people relax. After soaking up the heat in the cedar-lined sauna room, I finally got the courage to dash out for a dip in the cold, cold tree-rimmed lake.

A traditional after-sauna snack of strong black coffee with ohrarieska, butter, and jam gave new energy, so I kept watch as the sun dipped down toward the horizon around midnight, then started its long, slow climb back up into the crisp, clear northern sky.

At home we've experimented with several different versions of ohrarieska, and this is our favorite by far. The pearl barley soaks in buttermilk overnight, becoming tender and absorbing moisture and flavor. Even after it's ground in the blender, the barley gives a satisfying chewiness and body to the bread, as well as an aromatic and slightly nutty flavor, without being tough. Apart from the overnight soaking, the bread takes very little time; it requires no kneading, just thorough mixing.

2 cups pearl barley	2 cups barley flour
2 cups buttermilk	1 teaspoon baking soda
1 cup water	1 teaspoon salt

You will need a medium-sized bread bowl, an 8-inch cast-iron skillet, and a blender.

Combine the pearl barley and buttermilk in a medium-sized bread bowl, cover, and let soak overnight.

Preheat the oven to 350°F. Lightly oil and flour an 8-inch cast-iron skillet.

Add the water to the buttermilk and barley mixture, then transfer to the blender and blend until the barley is well pulverized (it won't become a smooth puree). Return this batter to the bread bowl, add the barley flour, soda, and salt, and mix well. Turn the batter out into the skillet. Bake in the center of the oven for 50 minutes. Let cool on a rack before serving.

Makes 1 flat loaf, 8 inches across and about 1½ inches thick.

Cut into slices or wedges and serve with coffee or tea and berry jam or honey as a snack. Slice and place on the smorgasbord table (see page 348) or serve as part of a bread and soup meal, with, for example, Luigi's Bean Soup (page 338) or Red Beans with Sour Plum Sauce (page 308).

Beet and Dill Salad

This salad, earthy with beets and tart with vinegar, aromatic with ground car- away seed and dill, is a wonderful addition to a smorgasbord table and a great companion for Marinated Herring. You can also do as we do, and eat vast quantities of it on its own with fresh bread.

2 pounds small to medium beets	1 teaspoon salt
7 to 8 tablespoons cider vinegar	½ cup sour cream (optional)
1 teaspoon ground caraway	Freshly ground black pepper (optional)
½ cup coarsely chopped fresh dill	

You will need a large saucepan with a lid and a bowl.

Rinse the beets, then place in a large saucepan and add cold water just to cover. Bring to a boil, and boil gently, partly covered, until a fork penetrates easily to the center of the beets; depending on the size of your beets, it may take up to 2 hours. Drain and let cool completely. (If you are in a hurry, rinse with cold water to help speed cooling.)

Slice off the beet stems and tails and peel. Cut the beets into ½-inch cubes and place in a serving bowl.

In a bowl, mix together the vinegar, caraway, dill, and salt. If you wish, add the optional sour cream; we prefer the salad without it, but it's traditional in many households. Mix it in with the vinegar dressing. (It will make your salad pink rather than deep red). Pour the dressing over the beets. Grind pepper over if you like. Mix well, and let stand, covered, for at least 1 hour to blend the flavors; if you include sour cream in the dressing, refrigerate the salad.

Serve at room temperature.

··▲▲▲▲▲·▲·▲▲▲▲▲▲▲▲▲·▲

Makes 4 cups salad. Serves 6 to 8.

Serve with Midnight Sun Potato Salad (page 346) and one or more breads, such as Rye Hardtack Rings (page 350), Finnish Barley Bread (page 354), or Norwegian Crispbread (page 340). Makes a colorful addition to a smorgasbord (see page 348).

Scottish Oatcakes

bannock, farls • Scotland

There were always oatcakes in our house while I was growing up. We took them for granted, thin and not at all sweet, great on their own or with cheese. My mother, an instinctive cook, rolled them out with ease, then baked them in the oven; the only tricky part was judging the correct cooking time—there's just a brief moment when they're perfectly done, lightly golden, before they start to burn.

Traditionally in Scotland, oatcakes were cooked on a griddle, or girdle, an iron plate suspended over the fire; oven-baked versions are relatively modern. We prefer the stove-top method to oven-baking; it's much easier to tell when the oatcakes are done. This recipe is a straightforward and very quick stove-top version of the oatcakes my mother made. We have called for the oatcake to be cut into quarters, or *farls,* before baking. The rolled-out farls are smaller and therefore easier to transfer to the skillet than a full-sized round oatcake.

1 cup fine or medium oatmeal (see Note), plus extra for rolling

¼ teaspoon salt

½ teaspoon bacon drippings or lightly salted butter

⅓ to ½ cup boiling water

You will need two griddles or cast-iron skillets, a medium-sized bowl, a rolling pin, and a wide spatula.

Preheat the oven to 350°F.

Place two ungreased griddles or cast-iron skillets on the stove to preheat over medium heat.

Combine the oatmeal and salt in a bowl. Stir the drippings or butter into ⅓ cup boiling water and blend well. Gradually pour the liquid into the dry ingredients, stirring as you pour, just until all of the oatmeal is moistened. Add more boiling water as necessary.

Dust a work surface with oatmeal and turn out the dough. Form the oatmeal mixture into two balls. Flatten each with oatmeal-dusted hands and then, working quickly and lightly, roll out each one into a 6- to 8-inch round. (You want to get the rolling done before the dough cools and stiffens.) Trim and patch the edges as necessary to make them even. Cut each round into four wedges (farls) and transfer the quarters to the preheated griddles or skillets. Cook over medium heat until the edges curl and the undersides are light brown, 3 to 5 minutes. Then transfer the skillets to the preheated oven for about 1 minute to dry out the top surface. Alternatively, turn the farls over and cook for 30 seconds.

Serve immediately, or store, once completely cooled, in a well-sealed tin. Reheat before serving.

A boulangerie in Grenoble

Note: Oatmeal, as opposed to rolled oats, is coarsely ground oats. It comes in fine, medium, and coarse. Medium is the easiest to find. We have tried making oatcakes with rolled oats, just to see if it is possible. The results are edible, but not tender like the oatmeal oatcakes; they have a toughness and coarseness that comes from the size of the pieces of rolled oats, even in the "fine" grade.

⋅⋅▲▲▲▲▲▲▲⋅▲⋅▲▲▲⋅▲▲▲▲▲⋅⋅▲ ▲

Makes 8 thin wedge-shaped oatcakes.

Serve with Anna's Cured Salmon (page 342) or Marinated Herring (page 352). These are also delicious with marmalade.

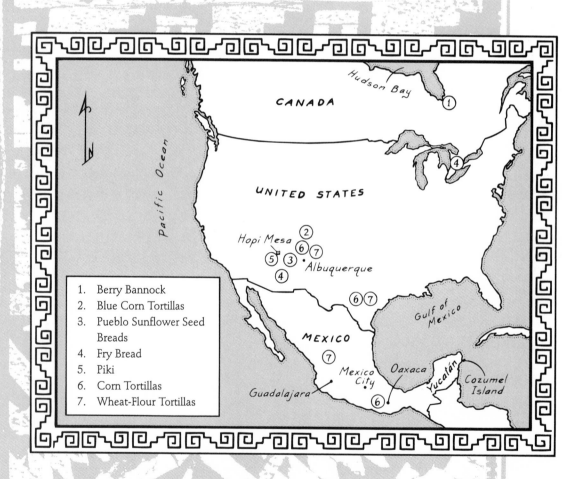

CANADA

Hudson Bay

①

④

UNITED STATES

Pacific Ocean

Hopi Mesa

②

⑥ ⑦

⑤ ③

④

•Albuquerque

⑥ ⑦

Gulf of Mexico

MEXICO

⑦

Mexico City

Oaxaca

Yucatán

Cozumel Island

Guadalajara

⑥

1. Berry Bannock
2. Blue Corn Tortillas
3. Pueblo Sunflower Seed Breads
4. Fry Bread
5. Piki
6. Corn Tortillas
7. Wheat-Flour Tortillas

North America

In the fertile valleys of Mexico and Central America, and in the mesas and valleys of the American Southwest, corn was domesticated and used as the staple grain long before the Spanish Conquest. Corn grows well if the soil is fertile and can survive with relatively little moisture. Wheat originated in Central Asia and was not found in the Americas until it was introduced after the Conquest.

Taos Pueblo: Adobe houses and horno (oven)

The dominant pre-Conquest bread was the corn tortilla, made from lime-soaked ground corn and baked on a clay comal. The tortilla tradition still rules in Mexico and the Southwest United States and has made converts across North America. The introduction of wheat added flexibility and new versions to the tortilla repertoire, but the breads are still used in the traditional way to scoop up sauces and to wrap around morsels of meat. Like pita in the Eastern Mediterranean, tortillas are also dried or toasted and used as flavoring and texture in soups, casseroles, and other dishes.

With wheat flour introduced from Europe, native peoples and traders in the northern regions of Canada developed bannock, an ideal traveler's bread, cooked quickly over a fire and flavored with animal fat or berries or with meat from the hunt. In more settled areas farther south, where supplies of oil were more available, deep-fried wheat-flour quick breads, known as fry bread, became a staple.

In the last four hundred years, immigrants from all over the world have settled in North America, bringing their food traditions with them and adapting them to ingredients available in the New World. Many of the flatbreads described in other chapters—the most notable being pizza—are now widely made in North America.

Oaxaca market: Making tlayudas

Others in this category include lefse, lavash, naan, chapatti, focaccia, oatcakes, and injera. Crackers, an adaptation of several flatbread traditions, have become a whole new genre.

Chiles in all their wonderful variety, as well as tomatoes, corn, and beans—all given to the rest of the world by the Americas—are still the main elements in Native American and Mexican cuisines. Beans are slow-cooked and flavored with herbs and garlic and sometimes a little meat to make rich-tasting dishes that are natural partners to wheat or corn tortillas.

Berry Bannock

Canada

"Of course you'll have a recipe for bannock," said a friend who grew up in the north of Canada. But in researching bannock we found, even more than with other breads, that everyone has a firm idea about how to make it and that these ideas seldom match up. The original bannock was a Scottish bread baked on a griddle and made from oatmeal, barley, or wheat (see Scottish Oatcakes, page 357). It probably came to North America with the Hudson's Bay Company, as the company was the first to introduce wheat flour to the northern parts of Canada. As flour sold by the company's trading posts gradually became a part of the local diet, so too did bannock, but in a form not necessarily resembling its plain Scottish ancestor. When berries were available, they went into the bannock batter. When there was meat or fish, it was chopped up and included.

Bannock is now made all across the north of Canada, in households and in hunting and fishing camps, by native peoples and newcomers alike. It's a quick and fuel-efficient way to make bread, and almost foolproof as well, even when made over a campfire.

Our recipe for oven-baked blueberry bannock is simple and fast, and comes out of the oven with deep bursts of color (from the berries) on pale bread. Unlike most bannock, it has no fat. If blueberries are unavailable, substitute cranberries, fresh or frozen, and balance their tartness by adding sugar.

3 cups unbleached all-purpose flour or
   hard unbleached white flour

1 teaspoon salt

1 tablespoon baking powder

1 cup fresh blueberries (or 1 cup fresh
   or frozen cranberries plus
   ½ cup sugar)

1½ cups water

You will need a cast-iron or other heavy ovenproof skillet 9 to 10 inches in diameter and a medium-sized mixing bowl.

Preheat the oven to 425°F. Lightly grease a 9- or 10-inch heavy ovenproof skillet.

In a bowl, mix the flour, salt, and baking powder until thoroughly blended. Add the berries (or berries and sugar) and stir to mix in. Make a well in the middle of the dry ingredients, pour in the water, and stir quickly to mix. The dough should be fairly stiff, but evenly moistened.

continued

Transfer the batter to the skillet. With wet fingers, lightly pat out the batter to fill the skillet. Place in the center of the oven and bake for 20 to 25 minutes, or until the bannock is firm to the touch in the center. Carefully remove the bannock from the skillet and transfer to a rack to cool. Serve warm or at room temperature.

Alternatives: To bake bannock over a campfire or on a stove top, use a heavy skillet and cook over a medium-hot fire or medium heat, covered, for 10 minutes, or until browned on the bottom. Then slide out onto the lid, flip over, and bake until lightly browned on the other side. Remove from the skillet and cool.

‥▲▲▲▲▲▲‥▲▲▲‥▲▲▲▲‥▲

Makes one 9- to 10-inch round loaf, about 1½ inches high.

Cut into wedges and eat warm on its own, or try dunking it in yogurt for breakfast or a snack. This bannock is a great companion to a Thanksgiving dinner, particularly when made with cranberries, or delicious as part of an autumn bread and soup meal. If serving the cranberry version for breakfast or a snack, you may want to provide honey or maple syrup as a sweetener to spread on the bread to balance the tartness of the cranberries.

Blue Corn Tortillas

Southwest United States

Blue corn is one of many different varieties of corn grown by the Hopi and Pueblo Indians in the southwestern United States. Ranging in color from gray to blue to almost black, it is used in breads, dumplings, sauces, and in drinks. Blue corn is of particular significance to the Hopi, who use it extensively in conjunction with ceremonial events and believe it is "a compass, for wherever it can grow, we can go. Blue corn survives where others die."

Blue corn flour has a slightly nutty taste and texture, unlike other varieties of corn. Hopi blue corn tortillas are traditionally made without salt, for salt is thought to mask the full but subtle taste of the corn. These tortillas are soft, and not at all tough. Because they contain a little wheat flour, they are also relatively easy to handle; you can pat them out by hand, then roll them to an even thickness if need be. They are cooked quickly in a hot ungreased skillet, then wrapped in a towel to stay soft and warm until ready to be eaten.

1½ cups blue cornmeal
1½ cups boiling water
¾ to 1 cup unbleached all-purpose flour

You will need a medium-sized bowl, a griddle or heavy skillet at least 8 inches in diameter, and a rolling pin.

Place the cornmeal in a bowl, pour the boiling water over, and stir to mix well. Let sit for 15 minutes. Stir ½ cup flour into the cornmeal, and turn this mixture out onto a work surface spread with ¼ cup more flour. Knead for 2 to 3 minutes, incorporating the flour into the dough, and, if necessary, adding a little more. The dough will be soft but not at all strong. Return the dough to the bowl, cover, and let rest for 30 minutes.

Divide the dough into 8 pieces. Between well-floured palms, form each piece into a flat disc and set aside.

Heat an 8-inch or larger griddle or heavy skillet over medium-high heat until hot.

On a well-floured surface (as the dough is quite sticky), roll out a tortilla until it is approximately 7 to 8 inches in diameter. (We find it easiest to pat out the dough first with our fingers or between our palms, and then roll out the tortilla at the very last just to make it uniform in thickness.) Cook the tortilla for approximately 1 minute on each side, or until flecked with brown on both sides and cooked through. Remove and wrap in a kitchen towel. Continue shaping and cooking the tortillas, stacking the cooked tortillas one on top of another.

.. ▲▲▲▲▲▲▲▲.▲▲▲▲▲▲▲▲.▲

Makes 8 tortillas approximately 8 inches in diameter.

These are great on their own as a snack, or served with a salsa such as Cascabel Chile Salsa (page 394), Cutting-Board Salsa (page 178), or Tomatillo Salsa (page 397). They are also a natural accompaniment to Pumpkin and Sweet Corn Soup (page 366) and Hopi Bean Stew (page 376).

Pumpkin and Sweet Corn Soup

Pumpkins (or squash), corn, and beans—the "three sisters" in Iroquois myth-ology—were the mainstays of many of the agricultural societies in the Americas before the European conquest. Native cultures in the Americas knew that corn and beans should be planted together in order to maintain the soil's fertility. Corn extracts large amounts of nitrogen from the soil, while beans, planted near the corn, help restore nitrogen to the soil.

Fat orange pumpkins sitting all alone in a field surrounded by the yellowing debris of their vines is still a quintessential autumn image in many parts of North America, but in general the hearty and nutritious pumpkin sadly has been relegated to providing pie fillings and jack-o'-lanterns. In traditional native cooking, the pumpkin was and still is revered as an abundant and versatile vegetable. The flesh is used in soups and stews, as well as in breads (pumpkin not only lends its soft orange hue to breads, but conditions a dough in a way similar to the way potatoes do). Roasted pumpkin seeds are a source of protein, traditionally used to flavor and to thicken stews and sauces, just as they are still used in many Mexican moles.

This soup combines two of the three sisters—corn and pumpkin. The soup is quick and straightforward to prepare and yields a substantial, beautifully golden-orange puree, warming on a cool day and yet delicious served cold on a still-warm early autumn evening.

---

2 tablespoons corn oil

1 medium yellow or white onion, diced

1½ pounds peeled and seeded pumpkin (see page 417), cut into 1-inch cubes (approximately 4 cups)

1 large ear sweet corn, husked and kernels cut off

4 cups beef broth

3 sprigs fresh mint, coarsely chopped

3 sprigs fresh oregano, coarsely chopped

1 teaspoon salt, or more to taste

g a r n i s h

¼ cup New Mexico piñon nuts or pine nuts

1 dried red New Mexico chile

You will need a large cast-iron or other heavy-bottomed saucepan, a food processor or blender, and a small cast-iron or other heavy skillet.

In a large heavy saucepan, heat the oil over medium-high heat. Toss in the onion and cook, stirring occasionally, until translucent, about 5 minutes. Add the pumpkin cubes, lower the heat to medium, and cook, stirring occasionally, for 5 minutes. Add the corn kernels, and cook for 4 to 5 minutes, stirring frequently. Add the beef broth and bring to a boil, then reduce the heat and simmer, partially covered, for 45 minutes, or until the pumpkin is tender.

Add the mint, oregano, and salt, stir well, and simmer for another 5 minutes. Remove from the heat. Using a food processor, puree the soup, in two or more batches, as necessary. Taste for salt, and stir in more if you wish. (The soup can be made ahead and stored, covered, in the refrigerator for up to 3 days, or frozen for up to 1 month. Reheat just before serving.) Return the pureed soup to the pot, and set aside.

Prepare the garnish: Heat a small skillet over medium-high heat. Toss in the pine nuts and dry-roast, stirring constantly, until golden brown, about 4 minutes. Turn the nuts out onto a cutting board and chop coarsely. Transfer to a small serving bowl.

Place the skillet back over medium-high heat and dry-roast the chile for 3 to 4 minutes, turning the chile and moving it around to keep it from burning. It will soften and puff up a little as it heats up. Transfer to a cutting board and let cool for a minute. Cut off the stem and discard with the seeds. Chop the chile as fine as possible and place in a small serving bowl.

Reheat the soup over low heat. Serve in individual soup plates, and garnish each serving with a generous tablespoon of chopped nuts and a good pinch of chile flakes. Place the remaining garnishes on the table so guests can add more as they wish.

▲▲▲▲▲▲▲·▲▲▲·▲▲▲▲▲▲·▲·▲▲

*Makes 6 to 7 cups. Serves 6 as part of a larger meal or
4 as part of a soup, salad, and bread meal.*

*We enjoy this soup as a warming lunch or supper dish accompanied only by Pueblo
Sunflower Seed Breads (page 368) or Wheat-Flour Tortillas (page 395) and perhaps a green
salad. It is also dazzling as the opening course of a more substantial meal, followed by
Pueblo Chile-Bathed Pork (page 369) with Blue Corn Tortillas (page 364) and Red and
Yellow Pepper Salad (page 387). Finish the meal with fresh fruit and sage tea.*

Pueblo Sunflower Seed Breads

Southwest United States

An unmistakable feature of Pueblo villages in New Mexico is the presence of large adobe ovens, called hornos, that sit out in front of every house. Of ancient origin, these beehive-shaped ovens are approximately four feet tall and four feet in diameter at the base. Bread is baked on the floor of the ovens, as it is in Italian wood-fired bread ovens.

Acoma Pueblo: Horno (oven) outside house

The bread most commonly associated with the Pueblo Indians is a round white-floured cottage loaf that is made in the horno, and often put out for sale. It is a pleasant fresh loaf with a good texture, but not nearly so interesting as other Pueblo breads such as these sunflower seed breads. They are tender when they first come out of the oven, but if left out on a rack to cool they become crisp. They taste more like crackers—or hard cookies—than breads, making them ideal for breakfast or for snacking. They are often made with piñon nuts, but we sometimes have problems ordering piñon nuts through mail order sources; sunflower seeds are always available and inexpensive, and their flavor transforms during baking into a great nutty taste.

These breads can be made either by hand or in the food processor, which grinds the sunflower seeds and makes for a different texture in the breads.

½ cup unsalted raw sunflower seeds
   (or piñon nuts)

1½ cups hard whole wheat flour

2 teaspoons baking powder

½ teaspoon salt

1 tablespoon brown sugar

1 tablespoon unsalted butter or
   vegetable oil

¾ cup water

You will need a large bowl or a food processor, a rolling pin, and one large or two small baking sheets.

Preheat the oven to 400°F. Lightly grease one large or two small baking sheets. If making the breads by hand, mix together all the dry ingredients in a large bowl. Cut in the butter. Add the water, and stir to form a dough. If using a processor, put the sunflower seeds, flour, baking powder, salt, sugar, and butter in the processor and process until a fine meal is formed. With the motor running, slowly add the water, and continue to process until a ball of dough forms, 15 to 20 seconds.

Turn the dough out onto a lightly floured surface and knead briefly until smooth. Cover and let rest for 10 minutes.

Cut the dough into 8 pieces. Roll out each piece to a round approximately 5 inches in diameter and ⅛ inch thick. Place on the baking sheet(s) and bake for 8 to 9 minutes. The breads will be a little bit soft, a little crisp. Wrap in a cloth or plastic bag to keep soft, or transfer to racks to cool and crisp.

·· ▲▲▲▲▲·▲·▲▲·▲▲▲▲·▲

Makes 8 thin cracker-like breads, about 5 inches in diameter.

Serve as a snack for kids, or with coffee or tea. These are a great accompaniment to Pumpkin and Sweet Corn Soup (page 366).

Pueblo Chile-Bathed Pork
Pueblo carne adobado • Southwest United States

Carne adobado ("marinated meat") is found in various guises all across the American Southwest and in Mexico. The Pueblo Indians of central New Mexico marinate and cook the meat in a sauce made of dried red New Mexico chiles; as a result, the dish has a rich red sauce, ideal for mopping up with tortillas. Dried red New Mexico chiles are not particularly hot, but they are full of flavor and give the sauce depth as well as a beautiful color.

1½ pounds lean boneless pork

red chile sauce

1½ to 2 ounces dried red New Mexico chiles (or 10 dried guajillos) (see page 410), stems removed and coarsely chopped

¾ cup water

½ teaspoon salt

1 clove garlic, minced

3 sprigs fresh oregano, leaves only, or 1 tablespoon dried oregano

2 tablespoons corn oil

You will need a shallow nonreactive bowl, a blender or food processor, and a deep cast-iron skillet or heavy-bottomed saucepan.

Cut the pork into long strips 1 to 2 inches wide and ¼ inch thick. Place in a shallow nonreactive dish.

Prepare the chile sauce: Combine the chiles, including the seeds, and water in a blender or processor and blend to a smooth paste. Add the salt, garlic, and oregano and blend well.

continued

Pour the sauce over the pork. Turn to coat. Let stand for 12 to 24 hours in the refrigerator or a cool place, covered, to marinate.

Lift the pork out of the marinade, and cut into approximately ½-inch lengths. Reserve the marinade.

Heat a deep skillet or heavy-bottomed saucepan over medium-high heat. Add the oil. When hot, add the meat and sauté until browned, stirring frequently. Pour in the marinade and simmer over medium-low heat for 1 hour. Serve with fresh tortillas.

·· ▲▲▲▲▲·▲·◄▲▲◄▲▲▲▲◄·▲

Serves 4.

Apart from plenty of warm Wheat-Flour Tortillas (page 395) or Blue Corn Tortillas (page 364), this pork is well complemented by a fresh sauce such as Tomatillo Salsa (page 397) or a salad such as Tender Greens Salad (page 327) or Red and Yellow Pepper Salad (page 387).

Fry Bread

This is the quickest and most common stove-top bread in many native com-munities across North America. A soft soda-risen white-flour dough is shaped into flatbreads and fried—traditionally in lard, for which we substitute peanut oil—then eaten hot on its own or as part of a meal. We've tasted some that look more like dumplings, about three inches across, and others, like the ones in this recipe, that are five to six inches wide. All are fried, usually in several inches of oil. They are turned over partway through cooking to expose both sides to the heat of the pan; the larger breads have a hole punched through them that allows the oil to bubble up and helps ensure that both sides get well cooked. They come out of the pan softly puffed, with a golden, slightly crispy outer layer and a chewy interior.

Fry breads have become popular fast food items at fairs and powwows throughout North America. They are served hot and sometimes dressed with cooked ground beef, tomatoes, salsa, and a little cheese, to make what is known as an "Indian taco." They're delicious on their own or with stews and sauces.

2 cups unbleached all-purpose flour or hard unbleached white flour

1 teaspoon baking powder

½ teaspoon salt

1 cup warm water

Peanut oil or lard for deep-frying

You will need a wok or deep heavy pot for deep-frying, a medium-sized bowl, and tongs.

Fill your wok or pan with 2 inches of peanut oil or lard and heat over medium to medium-high heat.

Meanwhile, combine the dry ingredients in a bowl. Make a well in the center and stir in the water. Mix to form a dough, and knead briefly. The dough should be soft but not sticky. Add a little more flour or water if necessary.

Cut the dough into 4 equal pieces. Flatten one piece to a thin disc about 5 inches in diameter and less than ¼ inch thick. Cut a 1-inch triangular wedge out of the center of the bread, and test the oil temperature by dropping the wedge into the oil. The oil should sizzle quietly and the dough wedge should begin to change color. If it burns or sizzles fiercely, the temperature is too high; adjust it accordingly. Slide the bread into the oil (the oil will sizzle and bubble up through the hole in the middle), and cook until golden on the bottom, about 2 to 3 minutes. Then turn over, taking care not to splash yourself with oil, and cook until golden, approximately 1½ to 2½ more minutes. As the bread cooks, shape the next one and cut a triangular hole in the center.

Place the cooked bread on a plate lined with paper towels to drain while you prepare and cook the remaining breads. Serve warm.

⸱⸱▲▲▲▲▲▲▲⸱⸴▲▲⸳⸳▲▲⸳⸳⸳▲⸳⸳ ▲

Makes 4 fried flatbread rounds approximately 5 inches across.

Serve these on their own or with jam, honey, or maple syrup for breakfast or a snack, or serve with Pueblo Chile-Bathed Pork (page 369) or Juniper Lamb Stew (below) as part of a meal.

✳

Juniper Lamb Stew

Southwest United States

Juniper berries are an important spice in the culinary traditions of many native peoples across North America, just as they are in Scandinavian, German, and rural Italian cooking. Their bittersweet aroma and taste stand up well in marinades and are particularly good paired with game. Because the diuretic properties of juniper are beneficial in treatment of colds and chest infections, the berries are also commonly used in medicinal teas.

continued

In this modern interpretation of a traditional Navajo recipe, small chunks of lamb are browned, then simmered in an aromatic and mildly spicy broth. Juniper berries give the broth a slightly tart edge, while fresh yellow corn and chunks of sweet green pepper give it color and sweetness. Similar corn and meat stews are found farther north among the Mohawk, Iroquois, Seneca, and Chippewa tribes. In these more agricultural societies, beef and pork are used instead of lamb.

½ teaspoon juniper berries, ground

2 teaspoons finely ground dried red chile (see page 410) or 1 tablespoon dried chile pepper flakes

1 teaspoon salt

1 teaspoon freshly ground black pepper

1 tablespoon all-purpose flour

1 pound lean lamb, trimmed of all fat and sinew and cut into ½-inch cubes

1 tablespoon vegetable oil

Kernels from 4 ears sweet corn or 2 medium carrots, thinly sliced

4 scallions, finely chopped

2 medium green bell peppers, cut into ½-inch chunks

3 cups stock or water

You will need a medium-sized bowl and a large heavy saucepan with a lid.

In a medium bowl, combine the juniper berries, powdered chile, salt, pepper, and flour, and mix well. Add the lamb, and rub with your hands to ensure the meat is well coated.

In a large heavy saucepan, heat the oil over medium-high heat. When hot, add the meat (reserving any excess seasoning mixture) and cook, stirring constantly for 3 to 4 minutes, until evenly browned. Add the corn, scallions, and bell pepper, stir, and cook for 1 minute. Add the stock or water together with any flour and seasoning mixture remaining in the bowl. Bring to a boil, stirring to prevent lumps. Reduce the heat to a gentle simmer, partially cover, and cook for 1 to 1½ hours, until the lamb is very tender. Taste, and adjust the seasoning before serving.

·· ▲ ▲ ▲ ▲ ▲ ▲ · ▲ · ▲ ▲ · · · ▲ ▲ · · ▲ ▲

Serves 3 to 4.

Have plenty of warm, fresh Blue Corn Tortillas (page 364) or Wheat-Flour Tortillas (page 395) to serve with the stew, or offer Fry Bread (page 370). Serve also with Red and Yellow Pepper Salad (page 387).

PIKI

Hopi Mesa, Arizona

I'd read about piki and been told stories about the bread, but I wanted to see it, to hold it, to taste it. So from Toronto I flew to Denver, then drove five hundred miles south into New Mexico and over to Arizona. Mid-July, hot, dry, and bright: It is lovely driving in an air-conditioned car with a good stereo, stopping in small-town Mexican restaurants along the way.

Early the next morning I drive to Hopi Mesa, arriving in the village of Shongopovi just around midday, and begin looking for a man I've been sent to see, named Steven. I'm directed to a large, outstretched mobile home. I turn off the car engine, and the air-conditioning. Hot dry air comes in like a strong wind through the open window. The village is quiet, and the view from atop the mesa breathtaking.

"Piki?" Steven laughs in response to my questions. "Piki, that's for women." But he doesn't mean it. I can go with his daughter Isabel, he says. I'll find her in the garden. Just then she walks in. "Sure," she says, "our neighbor is making piki. We can go now."

We cross a dirt road and walk through a field. I feel a little bit silly in my Toronto clothes and sunglasses. As we approach a small cinder-block one-room building set off by itself, I suddenly catch the fragrance of burning juniper. Burning juniper in dry air, a smell that is a way of life, just like the smell of bread baking. With my eyes closed, I could be in Tibet, or in Afghanistan.

We enter the room—the "piki house," where only piki is made—by pulling back a curtain that hangs in the doorway. Inside a woman is sitting by a fireplace making piki. She may be sixty years old, she may be seventy, maybe eighty. She has the face of someone who has lived most of her life outside. She passes a fresh

Piki breads

gray-blue piki bread my way. The bread tastes warm but crisp; it almost melts in my mouth. ("Piki tastes great with watermelon," Isabel whispers.) We sit down on two wooden crates around the fire; it's hot inside the cinder-block room, extremely hot. And wonderful. I no longer feel out of place.

Piki is remarkable. I can't give a recipe for it, but I can describe the process: First you make a batter from blue cornmeal, water, and ash. The batter looks like a thin pancake batter, and I'm told it is sometimes even thinner. The ash usually comes from the chamisa bush. It gives the piki its beautiful gray-blue color; without the ash, it wouldn't stay so blue. The ash also helps make available certain amino acids, but it's the color that's important.

Once you have the batter made, the next thing that must be done is to heat the piki stone. Piki stones come in different sizes, but most are long rectangles of granite around twenty-five inches long by eighteen inches wide and approximately two inches thick. A stone is passed down from a mother to her daughter. The stone's top surface is made perfectly smooth by rubbing it over and over again with oil from a sheep's brain, or oil made from watermelon seeds. It is rubbed between every bread, batch after batch of piki, year after year, generation after generation.

The piki stone rests on top of two parallel rock walls, approximately fourteen inches tall, leaving room for the fire to burn underneath. Once the stone is hot, the piki maker picks up some batter with her fingertips and rubs it across the stone, covering the stone entirely and carefully. Obviously, one of the first things to acquire in learning the art of making piki are calluses on your fingers. It is a little like rubbing your fingers across the surface of a very hot cast-iron skillet. Difficulty number one.

The piki now bakes on the stone for what seems like an unusually long time given how thin it is, about three minutes. Difficulty number two comes in pulling the bread off the hot stone at exactly the right time, and without tearing it—a task I'm told is far more of a problem than developing calluses on your fingers. After it is carefully taken from the stone, the paperthin bread is laid out on a flat woven tray while a second bread is started. After about two minutes, the first bread is put on top of the second bread as it's cooking. In a few seconds, and with a few gentle pushes, the stiff sheet becomes somewhat pliable; it is folded in half, then rolled into a cylinder about two inches wide and nine or ten inches long. And then it's done.

Difficulty number three has all to do with endurance. Piki making isn't quick, and great quantities of the bread must be made at one time. Large black plastic garbage bags and cardboard boxes are filled with piki: piki for ceremonies, piki for gifts, piki simply for eating.

"Do you like watching piki making?" Isabel asks as we sit around the fire, perspiring profusely.

"Yes, very much. And you?"

"Yes, very much. I just like sitting here."

Isabel is recently married. Ideally, she should have learned to make piki before now, but she is still learning. She also comes to the piki house to practice speaking Hopi; she was raised speaking English while her grandparents' generation speaks primarily Hopi.

At last we have to leave; Isabel has work to do. It's no longer bright outside. The sun has disappeared behind a thundering afternoon storm cloud, and there is even a chill in the air. Rain is on its way.

Hopi Bean Stew

chil-il ou gya va • Hopi Mesa, Arizona

The traditional Hopi diet relies primarily upon corn and beans; meat and other foods are used in smaller quantities as a supplement to the carbohydrates. At a simple piki-based meal, each person around the table might have a soup bowl filled with water or a thin soup, and a piki bread or two to be broken up into the liquid. In the middle of the table there will be one or two savory dishes, such as this meat and bean stew, from which everyone can take spoonfuls from time to time to add to their bowl. As in so many other grain-based diets around the world, meat is used to flavor the grain, not eaten as a meal in itself.

This particular stew is a good example of how a relatively small amount of meat can be used for flavor in what is essentially a high-carbohydrate dish. The beef and pinto beans are simmered with onion, garlic, and dried chile to make a thick and satisfying stew. The recipe calls for the beef to be finely chopped with a cleaver; you can substitute lean ground meat, but the texture will be different and the dish less successful.

½ pound boneless sirloin or other lean beef, trimmed of all fat

1½ tablespoons corn oil

1 medium onion, finely chopped

1 clove garlic, minced

1 teaspoon finely ground dried red chile (see page 410), or 1½ teaspoons dried chile pepper flakes

2 cups pinto beans, soaked overnight in 4 cups cold water and drained

½ teaspoon salt

You will need a cleaver and cutting board, a deep heavy skillet, and a large pot with a lid.

Chop the beef with a cleaver to the texture of coarse ground meat.

Heat a deep heavy skillet over medium-high heat, and add the oil. When hot, add the onion and garlic and cook, stirring, until the onion is translucent. Add the beef and brown it, stirring constantly. Stir in the chile, remove from the heat, and set aside.

Place the pinto beans in a large pot and add water to cover by 1 inch. Bring to a boil. Add the meat, reduce the heat, and simmer, partially covered, until the beans are tender, about 1½ hours. Check occasionally to ensure that there is enough water to keep the beans from sticking or burning. Stir in the salt, and remove from the heat. Adjust seasonings.

Serve with tortillas.

Makes 5 cups stew. Serves 3 to 4 hungry people as a meal-in-one.

Serve accompanied by Blue Corn Tortillas (page 364), or Corn Tortillas (below).

Corn Tortillas

Mexico and Southwest United States

In the markets of Oaxaca, around noontime and again in the late afternoon and early evening, women stand or squat by deep round baskets lined and draped with cotton. If you express interest, a vendor will flip back a corner of the fabric to

show you her tortillas—fresh, fine, and supple, pale yellow or blue-gray—while calling out to other passersby, "blandas, blanditas," the local name for the large, refined tortillas of Oaxaca. If you ask for a thousand pesos' worth (less than thirty-five cents), you'll find yourself handed a warm aromatic bundle of four or five large folded tortillas. And unless you already have a bag for them, chances are another woman standing nearby will persuade you to buy a plastic bag from

Julia patting out a corn tortilla

her, to keep your tortillas soft and warm until you can sit down to enjoy them. You can step up to the nearest *fonda,* or fast-food counter, and order a chicken in broth or enchiladas or some kind of meat, then sit next to others, each with his or her tortilla stash, eating and mopping up the flavors with your marvelous tortillas. For travelers and bread lovers, this is as good as it gets.

One day I took a local bus out to Zaachila, a small town half an hour from Oaxaca. It wasn't market day, so the main square was quiet. Down the lanes I walked past half-open doors leading into peaceful courtyards, which were often home to a cow or several goats or a pig. I'd been invited to visit by Julia, a woman of about fifty whom I'd met several days earlier at the big Saturday market in Oaxaca. She met me at her doorway, then led me across the courtyard past the pig to the cooking area. She showed me a pile of corn kernels, large dried-out lumps as big across as my thumbnail. They're often stored on the cob, then cut off as needed. Julia had also already soaked some corn so that I could see how it looked and felt. Lime, called *cal,* is dissolved in water, and the corn kernels are soaked for several hours until their outer husk comes loose and they feel softened and a bit slimy to the touch. Then it's time to drain and grind them.

Traditionally grinding was women's work, done kneeling before a shallow curved stone surface, the *metate,* against which the kernels were ground with a stone roller. The work was laborious and back-breaking. Nowadays, wherever there is electricity, there is usually an electric mill to grind the corn. I watched at a small mill down the lane from Julia's, run by a grandmother next to her house, as the mill ground a large pail's worth of soaked corn into moist dough (*masa*) in minutes. Then the masa is taken home to be patted and pressed and patted again into tortillas.

All the women I have watched make tortillas have the same look of effort-less ease as they work, the result of thousands of tortillas made over the course of a lifetime. First a lump of dough is pulled from the masa and flattened between the palms. Then the tortilla press—usually a wooden press—is opened and the flattened patty laid on a piece of plastic (traditionally it was a banana leaf), then covered with another piece of plastic. The tortilla is pressed, then sometimes flipped over and pressed again, before the two plastic sheets are carefully peeled off. To achieve the large fine Oaxaqueña tortilla, the uncooked bread is then patted out even thinner between the palms until it is twelve inches across or more. Once the *comal,* a spe-cial large shallow clay plate, has been placed over the fire and heated up, it is rubbed with a lime-soaked rag, making it look whitewashed. Then the first tortilla is placed on it to cook while the cook goes on to press and pat out the next one. As they're lifted off the comal, the tortillas are placed in a basket and carefully wrapped in a cotton cloth.

And so it goes, in thousands of households, every day: fresh corn tortillas, made by hand. For those who can't make their own, the vendadoras in the market supply home-style tortillas. Cheaper, and not nearly as pleasurable to touch or to taste, are the machine-made tortillas that come trundling off conveyor belts in mar-kets and bakeries all across Mexico. Still, even they have that freshly-made-from-corn flavor.

So how can tortillas made from masa harina, or "masa flour"—the flour made when lime-soaked corn is ground to masa, dried out so it will keep, and pul-verized to a flour-like powder—possibly taste like old-style tortillas? Well, they can come close, and they're certainly much more flavorful and tender than the store-bought frozen variety. If you do have access to freshly ground masa, use it. The rest of us will make do with masa harina (available from grocery stores and shops stocking Mexican and Southwest specialties), and our tortillas, too, will be wonderful.

··▲▲▲▲▲▲▲·▲▲▲▲▲▲▲▲▲·▲

The consistency of the dough is everything. If it is too dry, the tortillas will be dry and stiff; if it is too wet, you will have a fragile, sticky mess on your hands. But tortillas are easy to make. If you press a tortilla and it doesn't feel right—either too wet or too dry—knead a little more flour or warm water into the dough. Once you have the hang of it, the rest is clear sailing.

2 cups masa harina

Approximately 1¼ cups hot water

You will need a medium-sized bowl, a tortilla press, several Ziploc plastic bags (see Note), and two large cast-iron griddles or skillets.

In a medium-sized bowl, mix the masa harina into the water. Turn out onto a work surface and knead briefly until a dough is formed; add more water or more flour as necessary. The dough should be very soft to the touch. Return the dough to the bowl, cover with plastic wrap, and let rest for at least 30 minutes.

Divide the dough into 16 equal pieces. Flatten each piece between your palms into a small round disc. Set all the discs to one side (do not stack) and cover with plastic wrap.

Start with one disc to practice with your tortilla press. Open the press and place a plastic bag on the bottom of your press. Place the disc on the bag, setting it just off center, toward the hinge connecting the two plates. Place another plastic bag over the dough, matching the position of the first bag. Bring the top plate down over the bottom plate, and bring the handle down over both plates. Push the handle down forcefully and then pull it up. Peel off the top bag, starting from the hinge side first. Then check to see that your tortilla is not too dry and crackly at the edges. If it is, combine all the pieces of dough and add a little water, and knead gently once again to make a softer dough. Divide the dough and proceed to cooking.

Heat one large cast-iron griddle over fairly low heat, and another over medium-high heat. When the griddles are hot, peel the bottom plastic bag from the first tortilla by picking up the bag, placing the tortilla on your fingers bag side up, and carefully peeling off the bag. (If you wish to try to make the tortilla thinner, à la *Oaxaqueña,* try flipping it gently back and forth between your palms until it is somewhat larger.)

continued

Place the tortilla onto the griddle set over low heat. Let it rest there for 10 to 15 seconds, then transfer it to the hotter griddle, flipping it over as you make the transfer. (Traditionally, a comal placed over an open fire has hotter and cooler areas on its cooking surface, so the tortillas can be easily moved around; using two griddles is a substitute technique.) Cook until it starts to speckle with brown on the bottom, about 30 to 40 seconds. Flip it one more time (still on the hot griddle), and cook for another 30 to 40 seconds. (If the tortilla is going to balloon, it will happen now.) When it has browned a little bit, remove and wrap in a clean towel.

Continue pressing and cooking the remainder of the tortillas. Because tortillas dry out very quickly when exposed to the air, it is important to keep them wrapped in a cloth; as you add a tortilla to the growing stack, some steam will escape and thus keep the tortillas from getting soggy.

Alternatives: Try making *tlayudas,* a Oaxacan street food that is a kind of open-faced tortilla sandwich, and a distant cousin to the Tex-Mex tostado. Dry-toast a cooked tortilla on a hot griddle until it crisps up, then spread some black beans (page 386) or Black Bean Dip (page 385) over it. Drizzle on some Tomatillo Salsa with Árbol Chiles (page 381) and crumble on some Mexican white cheese or grated Monterey Jack and shredded lettuce. Place the hot tlayuda on a plate, and eat it by breaking bits off the edges until gradually the whole crisp flavor-laden bread has disappeared.

Note: You can use any heavy pieces of plastic for pressing the tortillas; Ziploc bags are durable and have the advantage that they tend to lie flat and wrinkle-free.

᛫᛫▲▲▲▲▲▲᛫▲᛫▲▲▲▲▲▲▲▲᛫᛫▲

Makes 16 tortillas about 6 inches across.

Eat corn tortillas on their own or dipped into any of the salsas in this book as a snack. Or serve tortillas to accompany main dishes such as Pueblo Chile-Bathed Pork (page 369), Pumpkin and Sweet Corn Soup (page 366), Hopi Stew (page 376), and Lime-Marinated Fresh Fish Salad (page 399). You can use tortillas to wrap up other foods, sandwich-style; good fillings include the chile-bathed pork, and Black Bean Dip (page 385).

Tomatillo Salsa with Árbol Chiles

Mexico

When tomatillos are in season, they can be easily cooked by peeling off the paper-like husk, and then simply boiling them in water until softened. We also freeze cooked tomatillos in pint containers for use in the cold months. This salsa has great flavor and a little heat. It can be made with precooked, frozen, and defrosted tomatillos with no loss of flavor, as well as with canned or fresh cooked tomatillos. It brings a welcome reminder of summer in the middle of winter.

1 tablespoon vegetable oil

3 to 4 large cloves garlic, minced

1 medium white onion, finely chopped

3 to 4 árbol chiles (see page 410), finely chopped (about 1 tablespoon)

1 pound freshly cooked tomatillos (see page 419) or canned tomatillos, drained

1 cup chicken broth

1 teaspoon sugar

½ teaspoon salt, or to taste

½ cup fresh coriander leaves, chopped

You will need a large skillet or heavy saucepan and a blender or food processor (optional).

Heat the oil in a large heavy skillet or saucepan over medium-high heat. Add the garlic and onion and cook, stirring occasionally, until the onion is translucent. Add the chiles and cook for 1 minute, then add the tomatillos, broth, sugar, and salt. Bring to a boil, lower the heat, and simmer gently, uncovered, for 30 minutes. Remove from heat and let cool. Taste for salt and adjust if necessary.

You can either mash the tomatillos with a fork to produce a coarse-textured salsa, or transfer the sauce to a food processor or blender and process briefly to a smooth texture. Transfer to a serving dish. Just before serving, stir in the coriander.

‣‣▲▲▲▲▲▲‣‣‣▲▲‣‣‣▲▲‣‣‣▲

Makes approximately 2 cups salsa.

Serve with fresh Corn Tortillas (page 377), Wheat-Flour Tortillas (page 395), or High-Tech Crackers (page 392). We also enjoy this salsa as a dip for Central Asian breads such as Afghan Snowshoe Naan (page 40) and as a condiment for grilled meats such as Spicy Cumin Kebabs (page 33).

Tortilla Soup

sopa de tortilla • Mexico

Tortillas have so many different personalities. They can be warm, soft, and pliable with a wonderful smell of fresh corn. They can be dry and bland, crisp and salty, stale and almost impossible to bite into. Yet no matter what their form, there are many ways in which they can be made to come alive. In Mexican cooking, as well as in the native cuisines of the Southwest, old, stale tortillas are as important as warm, fresh ones. Nothing is wasted, especially not corn. Chilaquiles (page 383) is a versatile—and always popular—simmered casserole based on stale tortillas. Tortilla chips, often referred to as *totopos* in Mexico, are another solution to the problem of what to do with dried-out tortillas.

Sopa de tortilla, a much-loved soup served all over Mexico, uses stale tortillas as if they were croutons. Once the tortillas have dried out, they are cut into thin strips and lightly fried. The strips are added to the soup just before it is served. The hot soup softens the tortilla strips, while the tortillas add body and flavor to the soup.

2 pasilla chiles (see page 410)

2 cloves garlic, chopped

1 small onion, chopped

1 pound (2 large or 4 medium) tomatoes

¼ cup vegetable oil

6 stale corn tortillas, cut into ¼-inch-wide strips

6 cups chicken broth

1 tablespoon chopped fresh epazote leaves (see page 414) or chopped fresh thyme

½ teaspoon salt, or more to taste

garnish and accompaniments

2 to 3 limes or lemons, cut into wedges

⅓ cup grated mild Cheddar cheese or Monterey Jack

You will need a small bowl, a blender, a large heavy nonreactive saucepan, and a small skillet.

Soak the pasilla chiles in hot water for 10 minutes; drain. Slice open the chiles and take out the seeds, reserving them. Coarsely chop the chiles and transfer to a blender. Add the garlic, onion, and tomatoes, and blend until roughly pureed.

In a heavy saucepan, heat the oil over medium-high heat. Toss in the tortilla strips and fry, stirring frequently, until they begin to crisp. Remove the strips to paper towels to drain.

Drain off all but 1 tablespoon of the oil remaining in your saucepan. Heat the oil over medium-high heat. Add the chile and tomato mixture, being careful not to get splattered, and cook, stirring frequently, for 8 to 10 minutes, until the sauce has reduced slightly.

Meanwhile, in a small skillet, dry-roast the reserved chile seeds over medium heat until they just begin to brown. Remove and put on a small serving plate.

Add the broth to the tomato-chile sauce and bring to a boil. Add the tortilla strips, epazote or thyme, and ½ teaspoon salt. Cook for 3 to 4 minutes longer, then taste and adjust seasoning. Serve in individual bowls. Add the lime or lemon wedges to the plate of toasted chile seeds, and set on the table along with the cheese, so each person eating can garnish with cheese, chile seeds, and a squeeze or two of lemon or lime juice (which really brings out the flavor of the soup).

..▲▲▲▲▲▲▲▲..▲▲..▲▲..▲▲..▲

Makes 6 to 7 cups soup. Serves 4 to 6.

Serve with fresh Corn Tortillas (page 377) and Red and Yellow Pepper Salad (page 387).

Black Bean and Tortilla Casserole
chilaquiles • Mexico

A few years ago the television coverage of the final day of the Tour de France included a short feature on what the different riders liked (or forced themselves) to eat each day. The twenty-plus days of the race are so excruciating that the number of calories riders must consume daily—just to make up for what they are burning—is staggering.

At the end of the race, American rider Andy Hampsten had done especially well, finishing in the top ten. When he was interviewed afterward, he vowed that he would do better the next year by taking more control over his food: He would have more of the food he likes, more Mexican food in particular.

New Mexico

When I heard this, I understood exactly. After a year in Thailand, or Taiwan, eating some of my favorite foods in the world every day, still I end up craving enchiladas, chimichangas, chilaquiles—a Tex-Mex meal on a cold winter night in a steamy small-town restaurant with chips and a very hot fresh salsa on the table. Not comfort food, but craving food.

·· ▲ ▲ ▲ ▲ ▲ ▲ ▲ ⸱ ⸱ ▲ ▲ ▲ ⸱ ⸱ ⸱ ▲ ▲ ⸱ ⸱ ▲

There seem to be almost as many versions of chilaquiles as there are regions in Mexico with leftover tortillas, and more. This one is a quickly assembled dish of black beans and stale tortillas simmered in a smoky chile sauce. Prepared and served in a well-seasoned cast-iron skillet, it is one of our favorite potluck dishes; the black of the skillet and the beans contrasts beautifully with the deep red chunks of tomato.

6 New Mexico chiles (see page 410), stems and seeds removed

2 chipotle chiles (see page 410), stems removed

1½ cups hot water

¼ cup sunflower or other vegetable oil

9 dried corn tortillas, broken into bite-sized bits (about 4 cups chips)

3 cloves garlic, minced

1 medium mild onion, finely chopped

1 pound (2 large or 4 medium) tomatoes, chopped into bite-sized chunks

2 sprigs fresh epazote (see page 414) or 2 large sprigs fresh oregano or 1½ teaspoons dried oregano

2 cups cooked black beans (see page 386)

1 teaspoon salt

½ cup (packed) fresh coriander leaves, finely chopped

a c c o m p a n i m e n t s

1 cup grated Monterey Jack or crumbled Mexican white cheese or mild feta

1 cup plain yogurt (optional)

You will need a medium-sized bowl, a large cast-iron skillet 10 to 12 inches in diameter or a heavy saucepan, and a blender.

Place the chiles in a bowl and add the hot water. Let soak for 15 minutes.

Heat the oil in a large skillet or heavy saucepan over medium-high heat. When hot, add the tortilla bits and fry, stirring constantly, until golden but not crisp, about 6 minutes. Drain, on paper towels. Set the pan aside.

Transfer the chiles and soaking water to a blender and blend to a puree. Set aside.

The recipe can be prepared ahead to this point. Store the cooled tortilla chips in a plastic bag and the chile puree, covered, in the refrigerator for up to 5 days.

Reheat the skillet or saucepan over medium-high heat. (There should remain a light coating of oil from frying the tortillas; if not, add just enough oil to lightly coat the pan.) When the oil is hot, add the garlic and onion, and cook, stirring constantly, for 5 minutes. Add the pureed chiles, tomatoes, and epazote or oregano and stir well, then simmer gently for 10 minutes, stirring occasionally.

Stir in the black beans, tortilla bits, and salt and simmer for about 8 minutes. Stir in the chopped coriander, and simmer for 1 to 2 minutes longer. Serve hot, with the grated or crumbled cheese to be sprinkled on top, along with plain yogurt if you wish.

..▲▲▲▲▲▲.▲▲▲▲▲▲▲▲▲..▲

Serves 4.

We like to serve chilaquiles for breakfast. You can spice it up further by setting out dishes of salsa; we recommend Tomatillo Salsa with Árbol Chiles (page 381) or Cutting-Board Salsa (page 178). Chilaquiles also makes a satisfying light lunch or supper, accompanied by a fresh green salad.

Black Bean Dip
frijolemole

Black beans, sometimes called turtle beans, are one of nature's great gifts to creative cooks. Combining them with deep red or bright green salsa and homemade yellow corn tortillas makes one of the jazziest flatbread meals we can think of. It's nutritious, easy to prepare, and absolutely delicious. The beans can be cooked simply with a bay leaf and dried oregano and garnished with chopped red onion, or they can be transformed—as they are in this dip—into a well-seasoned puree of contrasting tastes.

Often, when we're making frijolemole, we'll cook a large batch of beans (we usually start with four cups dried beans) and freeze what we won't need right away, as two- or three-cup servings are always useful to have in the freezer for short-notice meals. The beans can be frozen (with their cooking liquid) until you want to use them, or will keep for several days in a covered container in the refrigerator.

continued

beans (see Note)

1 cup dried black beans, rinsed and picked over

3 cups water

½ small yellow onion, coarsely chopped

1 large clove garlic, peeled

1 sprig fresh epazote (see page 414), or generous pinch of fresh or dried thyme

seasonings

½ pound (1 large or 2 medium) tomatoes, cut into ½-inch dice

2 scallions, chopped (white and tender green parts)

2 large cloves garlic, minced

2 jalapeños, stemmed, seeded, and finely chopped

½ teaspoon salt, or more to taste

¼ cup fresh lime juice, or more to taste

½ cup tightly packed fresh coriander leaves, coarsely chopped

You will need a large pot with a lid and a food processor or blender.

Place the beans in a large pot, and add the water, onion, and garlic. Bring to a boil, then reduce the heat to medium-low. Cover and simmer until the beans are tender, 1½ to 2 hours, stirring occasionally to ensure that the beans don't burn or stick. Add ½ cup more water if necessary.

Transfer the beans and cooking liquid to a food processor or blender and puree until smooth.

Place the pureed beans in a serving bowl, and stir in the tomatoes, scallions, garlic, jalapeños, and salt. Mix well. Add the lime juice and mix well. Stir in the coriander. Taste and adjust for seasoning.

Serve at room temperature, with tortillas or crackers for dipping.

Alternatives: Cooked black beans can also be served warm, simply dressed with olive oil and a little salt and garnished with chopped white onion and fresh coriander leaves. Accompany with Corn Tortillas (page 377).

Note: You can also substitute 2½ cups cooked beans, pureed in a food processor or blender, for the dried beans mixture.

·· ▲ ▲ ▲ ▲ ▲ ▲ ·▲ ▲ ▲ ▲ ▲ ▲ ▲ ·▲ ▲

Makes 2½ to 3 cups dipping sauce.

Serve as a dip with Corn Tortillas (page 377) or Blue Corn Tortillas (page 364), or with High-Tech Crackers (page 392). This is also delicious with Pueblo Sunflower Seed Breads (page 368). Or serve frijolemole on the side to accompany Chicken and Tortilla Casserole (page 388).

Red and Yellow Pepper Salad

Oaxaca, Mexico

Golden yellow and rich red rounded chiles were laid out invitingly on a tarp by the side of the road. "They're called canarios," said the Zapotec woman selling them, "because of the yellow color, of course." Their firm round shape made the red ones look like small shiny apples. "Taste," she said, as she handed me a pepper. They were thick-walled and very crisp, with a sweet, almost aromatic, taste, followed by a small jolt of heat. Delightful. And, alas, unobtainable outside southern Mexico, as far as we know.

As a result, this recipe, though inspired by a Oaxacan dish made of sliced canarios, onions, lime juice, coriander leaves, and salt, is only an approximation, but still very good. It should be prepared and tossed together at the last moment, for its fresh crispness is part of its appeal. A combination of red and yellow bell peppers, dressed with lime juice blended with a jalapeño, reproduces both the sweetness and the slight heat of the canarios, as well as the color.

1 medium yellow bell pepper

1 medium red bell pepper

1 small to medium white onion

½ cup packed fresh coriander leaves, coarsely chopped

¼ cup fresh lime juice

¼ teaspoon salt, or more to taste

1 jalapeño, minced

Freshly ground black papper

You will need a small bowl.

Cut the bell peppers into quarters, discarding the seeds, stem, and membranes. Slice into narrow strips about ¼ inch wide, and place in a shallow serving bowl.

Cut the onion in half lengthwise, then finely slice. Add to the serving bowl, along with the coriander.

Place the lime juice in a small bowl, add the salt and jalapeño, and blend well. Pour over the salad, and toss well to coat. Grind black pepper over the salad, taste for seasonings, and serve immediately, to accompany a meal of tortillas and stew or tortillas and soup.

Serves 4.

Serve with Corn Tortillas (page 377) and Hopi Bean Stew (page 376), Pueblo Chile-Bathed Pork (page 369), or Chicken and Tortilla Casserole (page 388).

Chicken and Tortilla Casserole

enchiladas Alejandro • Mexico

Luisa and Alejandro came to California from Guadalajara. They were a young couple with a little money, a lot of energy, and a dream. They took over the lease of a small place in a medium-sized town and opened a restaurant serving "fine continental cuisine." Lucky for me, I applied for a job just when they had decided that they would need an extra set of hands.

The three of us worked hard, but the restaurant never took off. We served the old continental standbys: steamed fish du jour in a wine sauce, grilled steaks topped with mushrooms. Late every night, after waiting patiently for the last lonely customer to finish eating and pay, we all sat down to supper. It was always Mexican, and always fantastic, like these enchiladas. It was prepared and served with ease, and it was always appetizing, even after a long night of cooking.

"Why not put Mexican dishes on the menu?" I'd ask Alejandro. "No," he'd answer, shaking his head with some uncertainty. Their dream was to serve "continental cuisine," not Mexican food. Yet inevitably, as we'd finish our meal and be washing dishes, I'd hear nostalgic stories about life in Guadalajara, about dressing up and going to dances, about all the great food.

The restaurant eventually closed; Alejandro and Luisa went off to become students at a culinary institute. We lost touch, so whether they opened another restaurant later I don't know. But I still make Alejandro's enchiladas.

1½ pounds chicken breasts

1 yellow onion, diced

Pinch of dried thyme

1 bay leaf

8 cups water

4 ancho chiles (see page 410), washed and stemmed

1 pound potatoes, peeled and cut into ½- inch chunks

2 cloves garlic

1 teaspoon salt

½ pound Monterey Jack cheese, grated

12 Corn Tortillas (page 377)

You will need a large pot, a medium-sized bowl, a blender, a shallow bowl, a shallow rectangular baking dish, and a heavy griddle or skillet.

Place the chicken, onion, thyme, and bay leaf in a large pot and add the water. Bring to a boil, then reduce the heat and simmer, partially covered, for 1½ hours. Remove the chicken, reserving the stock, and let cool. When cool, shred the chicken, discarding the bones and skin, and set aside.

In a medium bowl, soak the chiles in 1½ cups of the reserved hot chicken stock for 30 minutes.

Meanwhile, in the large pot, boil the potatoes in the remaining stock until tender, about 15 minutes; drain. (Set aside the stock for another use.)

In a blender, combine the chiles and their soaking liquid, the garlic, and salt. Blend until smooth. Pour this sauce into a shallow bowl.

Preheat the oven to 350°F.

To assemble, have ready a large rectangular baking dish, approximately 10 by 14 inches. Heat a heavy griddle or skillet over medium-high heat. Start with one tortilla: First heat the tortilla on the griddle or skillet, turning it with your fingers and flipping it until the tortilla is soft. Now slide it through the sauce until the tortilla is lightly but completely covered with sauce. Lay it in the baking dish and place about 2 tablespoons shredded chicken in the center. Place about 1 tablespoon of the potatoes and 1 tablespoon of the cheese on top. Roll up like a jelly roll and fit neatly, seam side down, against the end of the dish. Repeat with the remaining tortillas, placing them side by side in the dish. Pour any remaining sauce over the enchiladas, and sprinkle with any remaining cheese. Bake for 15 to 20 minutes, until heated through and bubbling.

Serve hot, with an assortment of salsas as condiments.

··▲▲▲▲▲▲·▲·▲▲··▲▲▲▲··▲

Serves 4.

For a substantial meal, you might start with Pumpkin and Sweet Corn Soup (page 366),
which can be served hot or cool. We like to serve enchiladas with a variety of condiments,
which double as salads: try Tomatillo Salsa with Árbol Chiles (page 381) and
Cutting-Board Salsa (page 178).

CHILE PEPPERS AND FLATBREADS

Many of the world's oldest flatbread traditions had been going strong for over a thousand years before even a hint of chile pepper crossed their paths, but since the Spanish carried the magical little fruit home from the Americas some five hundred years ago—and then left it to the Portuguese to introduce them to the rest of the world—flatbreads and chiles have been inseparable. It's no accident that chiles and salsas appear in seven out of eight chapters in this book, as well as in a number of breads: for example, Hot Chile Bread (page 201), Coriander, Ginger, and Chile Crêpes (page 157), and Savory Country Corn Bread (page 136). Chiles are now the world's most widely eaten spice, as well as the most common single accompaniment to a grain-based meal.

Flatbreads sustain the body while chiles stimulate the appetite—a natural partnership of the best kind. There is a Chinese expression about all the tasty dishes (*tsai*) that appear on the table meant to be eaten with rice: The role of tsai is to "send" the rice, to make the rice come alive. Similarly we find that chiles, and chile sauces, can help "send" a bread. People who don't like chiles sometimes complain that the sensation of "hot" overpowers the subtle tastes of other foods. Most chile eaters—ourselves included—find just the opposite.

Taos Pueblo: Ristra of dried chiles

While you're allowing a dough to rest for fifteen minutes before rolling out flatbreads, use the time to make a fresh salsa. Once the breads are baked, you not only have fresh bread but a tasty combination. We always like to have one or two salsas in the refrigerator to pull out to accompany a light meal or afternoon snack, especially ones that keep well—Spicy Peanut Sauce is a good example. One salsa we always have in the kitchen as a condiment is a simple Thai chile sauce called *nam pla prik,* or "fish sauce with chile." To make nam pla prik, simply pour one to two cups of bottled fish sauce (nam pla) into a glass jar and add a cup of very finely chopped chiles, seeds and all. The chile traditionally used in this sauce is the tiny, and fiercely hot, bird chile, which has become increasingly available here in Thai and Vietnamese groceries. But serranos or jalapeños also work well. One of the beauties of this sauce is that it is a very good keeper, simply add more fish sauce and chiles as the supply gets low—a little bit like replenishing a sourdough starter. Keep the jar covered in the refrigerator, and anytime you want a hit of hot, pull it out.

When it comes to salsas and flatbreads, the absolute best combinations depend upon a salsa as fresh as the bread. Coconut Chutney, Tomatillo Salsa, and Cutting-Board Salsa all taste wonderful with almost any flatbread; their freshness and flavor are irresistible. Another salsa in this category is Herb and Pepper Relish, a Georgian specialty that combines chiles with loads of fresh herbs. Try it with Fenugreek Corn Bread (page 223) or Afghan Snowshoe Naan (page 40).

Listed below are all the sauces with chiles included in the book. We think they're all wonderful.

Herb and Pepper Relish (page 301)

Pomegranate Sauce (page 299)

Cutting-Board Salsa (page 178)

Spicy Yemeni Salsa (page 191)

North African Chile Paste (page 245)

Ethiopian Chile and Spice Paste (page 275)

Spicy Peanut Sauce (page 82)

Peanut Dipping Sauce (page 105)

Vietnamese Dipping Sauce (page 109)

Armenian Tomato and Eggplant Salsa (page 287)

Spicy Tomato Chutney (page 139)

Nepali Green Chile Chutney (page 141)

Hot Peanut Chutney (page 161)

Coconut Chutney (page 156)

Sesame-Tamarind Chutney Powder (page 167)

Tomatillo Salsa with Árbol Chiles (page 381)

Cascabel Chile Salsa (page 394)

Tomatillo Salsa (page 397)

High·Tech Crackers
processor crackers

The only problem with being an embarrassingly slow reader in a graduate program in English literature was that the required reading took up an incredibly large proportion of my existence. At my speed of twenty-five to thirty pages an hour, it's a good thing that *Tom Jones* is as humorous as it is long. But I survived, thanks to my comfortable rocking chair and, of course, my crackers.

I kept them in large brown paper shopping bags within arm's length of the rocker. Rock, read, and eat crackers. Every five or six days I'd replenish my supply, starting at three or four in the afternoon and working madly until five or six. With baking sheets, a pizza cutter, a rolling pin for rolling, a spritzer for spritzing, and a very hot oven, this rocking chair reader became an assembly-line cracker maker. And then the moment I loved most: two bags, sometimes three bags, full of crackers. Cayenne crackers, sesame, tamari, Romano, sunflower—some thick, some paperthin, some almost crisp burnt, some still soft to the bite. Whole wheat crackers, never white. In my one-room apartment I'd move from the oven to my rocker, carrying a bag of crackers, ready to read.

This may all sound like a borderline unbalanced diet, but the crackers were great. The reading wasn't all that bad. And, well, as for the rocking chairs . . .

·· ▲▲▲▲▲ ◂ ◂ ▴ ▴ ▴ ▴ ◂ ◂ ◂ ·· ▲

This recipe is an updated version of my original, using a food processor to mix and knead the dough. Processors seem tailor-made for unyeasted wheat doughs. Once the ingredients are mixed and a ball of dough has formed, be sure to process for only one minute. If you go on longer, you risk overkneading the dough.

3 cups hard whole wheat flour, or more as necessary	Cayenne
	Coarse salt
1 teaspoon salt	Sesame seeds
1½ cups warm water	Grated unsweetened coconut
o p t i o n a l t o p p i n g s	Cumin seed
Grated Parmesan	

You will need a food processor, several 10- by 14-inch baking sheets or 14-inch pizza pans, a pizza cutter or a sharp knife, and a clean spray bottle or plant mister.

Place the flour and salt in a food processor and process for 10 seconds to mix thoroughly. With the motor running, add the water in a steady stream, then process for 10 seconds longer. The dough should have formed into one large ball; if not, feel the dough: If it feels very sticky, add 3 to 4 tablespoons more flour and process briefly until a ball forms. If the dough feels dry and floury, start the processor again, add 2 to 3 tablespoons more water, and process until a ball of dough forms.

Once you have a ball of dough, process for 1 minute more, no longer. Turn the dough out onto a lightly floured surface and knead for 30 seconds or so. Cover with plastic wrap and let rest for 30 minutes.

Preheat the oven to 500°F, and place two racks near the center of the oven.

Divide the dough into 8 pieces. Work with one piece at a time, leaving the other pieces covered. On a lightly floured surface, with lightly floured hands, flatten a piece of dough with your palms. Then roll it out to a very thin rectangle or round, as even a thinness as possible to ensure even cooking. Gently lift the dough from your rolling surface and place it on a large baking sheet or pizza pan. Sprinkle on one of the optional toppings or leave plain (see Note). Using a knife or a pizza cutter, cut through the dough to make rectangular crackers. (Don't worry if they are not all exactly the same size. Variations in size and flavor will make your crackers interesting.) Spray the dough lightly with water and place on the upper oven rack.

Begin rolling out the next piece of dough, keeping an eye on the crackers already baking. (Crackers brown from underneath.) Check on them 2½ to 3 minutes after they go in. As soon as the thinnest patches of the dough have started to brown, take them out. If necessary, continue baking, checking every 30 seconds, but it is better to take the crackers out a little early than too late.

You will soon get a feel for timing and degree of doneness. Variables that affect timing are the heat of your oven and how thin you managed to roll out your dough. When they come out of the oven, some of the crackers will be crisp, while others will need a little time in the air to crisp up. Transfer to a large bowl, breaking up any incompletely separated crackers. Roll out the remaining dough, season, and bake. When completely cool, crackers can be stored in a well-sealed plastic bag or cookie tins for up to a month.

Note: You can also sprinkle sesame seeds or cumin seed or grated coconut on your baking sheet before laying down the dough. You may have other flavors you wish to experiment with. We like to serve these crackers all mixed up in a large bowl, to keep an element of surprise: Which flavor will my next cracker be?

Makes about 13 dozen very thin crackers of varying size, averaging approximately 1½ inches by 2½ inches.

These are good with almost any sauce, dip, or spread.

Cascabel Chile Salsa

Mexico

We heard a call-in radio program not long ago on why people buy and collect cookbooks. The title of the hour-long program was "The Cookbook Addiction," but from the very first caller onward, the suggestion that collecting cookbooks was anything but honorable was quickly dispelled. For lovers of cookbooks, it was an hour's worth of great entertainment. One caller described herself as an armchair eater, a person who reads cookbooks that describe the foods of faraway places, then shows up in foreign-food groceries walking up and down the aisles, mumbling exotic words and carrying a cookbook half-open in one hand.

As armchair eaters, we put chiles high on our list of "foods we like most to explore." Dried chiles, fresh chiles, preserved chiles—and in the last few years there's been a great deal more written on the subject, making identification of chiles much easier (see pages 410–411).

Cascabel chiles are dried chiles that are deep maroon and smooth-textured. The dried pods rattle if you shake them; their Spanish name means "little rattle." Cascabel salsa has a good rich chile flavor, but is only slightly hot.

7 to 8 dried cascabel chiles	2 to 3 cloves garlic, peeled
½ pound (2 medium) tomatoes, quartered	½ cup water
1 tablespoon vegetable oil	½ teaspoon salt

You will need a heavy skillet and a blender or food processor.

Preheat the broiler.

Lightly roast the chiles in a cast-iron skillet over medium heat until soft, turning so they do not burn. Remove and discard the stems. Transfer the chiles to a blender or food processor.

Place the tomatoes in a broiler pan and broil until well softened, about 5 minutes. Transfer to the blender or processor, add the remaining ingredients, and blend well. Serve as a dipping sauce for tortillas.

‥▲▲▲▲▲▲‥▲▲‥▲▲‥▲▲▲‥▲

Makes approximately 1½ cups sauce.

The rustic rich flavor of this salsa is particularly good with Blue Corn Tortillas (page 364) and with Wheat-Flour Tortilla Quesadillas (see page 395).

Wheat-Flour Tortillas

Wheat-flour tortillas are now so widely available in supermarkets that they've been absorbed into mainstream North American culture. This is great, because tortillas, are generally unadulterated with chemical additives, unlike much commercially available bread. Kids just home from school all across the United States now grab a tortilla, sprinkle on some cheese, and warm it in the microwave to make a "quesadilla"—in many homes the alternative to the peanut butter and jam sandwich of yesteryear. The only downside to this pop-Mexican cooking is that it obscures or obliterates the real thing: fresh home-cooked tortillas, and quesadillas made with care and eaten with a wonderful array of salsas.

Wheat-flour tortillas are simple to make at home and better tasting than the commercially available versions. Though these tortillas are traditionally made with lard, we use corn oil instead and they turn out just fine.

2 cups hard unbleached white flour	3 tablespoons corn oil
½ teaspoon salt	½ to ¾ cup warm water

You will need a medium-sized bowl, a cast-iron or other heavy griddle or skillet at least 8 inches in diameter, and a rolling pin.

Combine the flour and salt in a bowl. Sprinkle on the corn oil, and blend it in thoroughly. Gradually add ½ cup warm water, stirring with a fork to moisten the dough evenly. If it is too dry to gather into a dough that will hold together, add a little more water. Gather the dough into a ball, turn out onto a work surface, and knead briefly. The dough should be neither particularly wet nor especially dry, but easily kneaded.

Divide the dough into 8 equal pieces. Flatten each between lightly floured palms to a disc approximately 3 inches in diameter. Cover with plastic wrap, and let rest for 30 minutes.

Heat an 8-inch or larger cast-iron griddle over medium-high heat until very hot (make sure your griddle is hot enough before beginning to cook the tortillas).

On a lightly floured surface, using a rolling pin, roll out a tortilla until it is 7 to 8 inches in diameter. Place the tortilla on the griddle; if the griddle is sufficiently hot, the first side should cook and become speckled with brown in approximately

45 seconds. Turn the tortilla and cook for 45 seconds longer. Remove and wrap in a kitchen towel.

As each tortilla is cooking, you should have just enough time to roll out the next tortilla. Stack the finished tortillas one on top of the other, and keep them wrapped in the towel. Serve warm.

Tortilla dough can be stored in the refrigerator, well sealed in plastic bags for up to a week. Before rolling out the tortillas, let the dough come to room temperature.

You can also store leftover tortillas in the freezer, well sealed in plastic. To reheat a cold tortilla, place on a hot dry cast-iron or other heavy skillet or griddle for 30 seconds, flipping it over halfway through. Once reheated, tortillas toughen quickly, so reheat them only as you need them.

Alternatives: Once you've made your own wheat-flour tortillas, you can go on to turn them easily into quesadillas. Spread each with a little Mexican-style queso or any crumbly white cheese, add a sprig of epazote or a sprinkle of oregano, and fold over to make a half-moon shape. Place on a hot cast-iron griddle, and heat the first side until starting to brown on the bottom. Then turn over and heat a minute or so longer. Serve a stack of 2 or 3 per person on a plate with bowls of several of the salsas mentioned above.

Makes 8 thin tortillas about 8 inches in diameter.

Serve with Black Bean Dip (page 385) or Tomatillo Salsa (page 397), Tomatillo Salsa with Árbol Chiles (page 381), and/or Cascabel Chile Salsa (page 394), or to accompany any Mexican or Southwestern dishes. We—and our children especially—enjoy them warmed and spread with peanut butter, then rolled up and eaten for breakfast or a snack.

Tomatillo Salsa

salsa verde cruda • Mexico

***Tomatillos are often referred to as* tomates verdes, *or green tomatoes.* The** tomatillo is related not to the tomato, but to the ground cherry or cape gooseberry. It's a tough, hardy, self-seeding annual that grows wild by the side of the road in many parts of North America. For centuries, it has been an important source of food for many native peoples.

One summer we grew tomatillos in our garden to see how they would do. Heaven, we thought, to have an abundance of tomatillos! The summer weather was cool and rainy, the tomatoes were terrible, okra was impossible, the garden sagged and cried out for sun. But through it all the tomatillos flourished. They grew tall and branched out rapidly, at first appearing graceful and happy with bright yellow flowers popping out everywhere. Soon they reached four feet in height, then five feet, and before long we started to feel invaded.

Eventually the flowers became bright green papery spheres like Chinese lanterns, each sheltering a tiny green tomatillo inside. As the tomatillos ripened, they filled out their paper-like covering, and then finally they were ready for harvest. And harvest we did. We had salsa after salsa, and what we didn't eat we cooked and froze. All winter we had tomatillo salsas, and we still love them. But the next year, we decided to buy our tomatillos, rather than inviting them into our garden.

..▲▲▲▲▲▲.▲.▲▲..▲..▲▲.▲.▲

This salsa is noteworthy for its unique flavor and its simplicity; it is a wonderful accompaniment to tortillas, and many other flatbreads. Although it is an uncooked ("cruda") salsa, the tomatillos should be cooked before being combined with the other ingredients; it softens them and mellows their acidity.

½ pound fresh tomatillos or 1 cup canned tomatillos (see page 419), drained

1 clove garlic, finely chopped

¼ teaspoon salt, or more to taste

1 jalapeño, stemmed, seeded, and coarsely chopped

¼ cup packed fresh coriander leaves, coarsely chopped, plus several sprigs for garnish (optional)

2 scallions, finely chopped (white and tender green parts)

Pinch of sugar

You will need a medium-sized nonreactive saucepan, a shallow bowl, and a large mortar and pestle or a blender or food processor. *continued*

Peel off the outer paper-like husk of the tomatillos. Place the tomatillos in 2 inches of water in a saucepan and bring to a boil. Reduce the heat and simmer for 10 minutes, or until tender. You do not want them to burst open, just to soften. Drain and let stand in a shallow bowl to cool . When cool enough to handle, remove the stem ends and coarsely chop. Set aside (see Note).

Place the garlic in a large mortar and pestle and pound several times. Add the salt and pound to a paste. Add the jalapeño, and pound to break up further. Add the coriander and scallions and pound to blend. Add the tomatillos, and pound and blend to break up further. (Be careful not to splash yourself; the tomatillos are rather watery when they first break up.)

Alternatively, if using a blender or food processor: Add the ingredients in the same order, pulsing after each addition, but be careful not to overprocess. The salsa should not be a puree, but still be somewhat rough in texture.

Turn out into a bowl and stir in the sugar. Garnish with a few sprigs of fresh coriander if you wish, and serve immediately, with fresh tortillas or tortilla chips or as a sauce to accompany a meal. This salsa should always be served very fresh; it loses flavor and balance after several hours.

Note: Cooked tomatillos can be frozen for later use. Place in sealed plastic containers and freeze until ready to use. To use frozen tomatillos, defrost, then remove the tough stem ends and coarsely chop.

Makes approximately 1 cup sauce.

We like to have a bowl of this salsa on the table whenever we serve Mexican food. It brings out the flavor of Chicken and Tortilla Casserole (page 388), Black Bean Dip (page 385), egg dishes, and meats like Juniper Lamb Stew (page 371). It is also great just scooped up with Blue Corn Tortillas (page 364) or regular Corn Tortillas (page 377).

Lime-Marinated Fresh Fish Salad
ceviche • Mexico

Long ago, friends fed me ceviche on the first hot day of summer. They'd learned the recipe during a stay in Mexico. It was a revelation with its chile heat, sour lime, crunchy onion, and tender pieces of fish. Almost ten years later, while staying at a coastal town in the Yucatán where the local market featured fresh conch, I decided to try making conch ceviche. The fish vendors were generous with advice on ingredients and proportions, and the dish that resulted was splendid, with plenty of Yucatán-style chile heat—a great accompaniment to beer on a hot day.

This version uses firm saltwater fish—kingfish or mackerel, as did the original recipe I was given, since conch is hard to come by and fairly tough when you do find it. Be sure the fish is very fresh; freezing seems to weaken the flesh, resulting in a somewhat soggy texture after marinating. Serve with fresh corn or blue corn tortillas, which can be used for scooping up the ceviche as well as for mopping up the sauce.

1 pound skinless fresh kingfish or
    mackerel fillets

¾ cup fresh lime juice (use Key limes
    if possible)

½ teaspoon sea salt, or more to taste

½ small white onion, finely chopped

1 jalapeño, stemmed, seeded, and
    minced

½ cup loosely packed chopped coriander
    leaves

1 medium to large tomato, finely
    chopped

¼ teaspoon freshly ground black pepper,
    or to taste

You will need a shallow nonreactive bowl or container.

Shred the fish, and check the flesh with your fingers for any ends of bone. Place in a shallow nonreactive container and add the lime juice, salt, onion, and jalapeño. Stir well to coat. Place, well covered, in the refrigerator to marinate for at least 4 hours, or up to 2 days.

Less than 1 hour before serving, add the remaining ingredients, and stir well. Just before serving, taste and adjust the seasonings. Serve in a serving bowl or in a shallow dish lined with lettuce leaves.

·· ▲ ▲ ▲ ▲ ▲ ▲ ▲ ·▲ ·▲ ▲ ▲ ·▲ ▲ ▲ ▲ ·· ▲

Serves 6 to 8 as an appetizer or snack.

Serve with cold Mexican beer and Wheat-Flour Tortillas (page 395), Corn Tortillas
(page 377), or Blue Corn Tortillas (page 364).

More About Wheat

WHEAT BERRIES

One of my great pleasures as a child was feeding the hens on my grandparents' farm. I would go with my grandmother to the granary, a compact log building, and there get the grain for the hens. As the granary door swung open, a familiar smell of grain—slightly sweet and slightly tickle-the-nostrils dusty—would greet us. What we'd scoop up to take to the hens was wheat: small, hard, reddish kernels, too hard for chewing. We could run our hands through it and let it slide between our fingers like cool, smooth, evenly shaped small pebbles. Then we'd walk across the yard and into the large grassy hen run, where the hens would come running toward us at the sight of the tin of grain. We'd sprinkle and toss the wheat in small trails, clucking and calling the hens and watching the busy action as they scrambled for each precious morsel. It was completely exhilarating. Too soon the tin would be empty, eke out the grain as we might, and we'd head into the henhouse to look for eggs, while the hens continued to peck at the last of the wheat.

As an adult, when I first heard the term *wheat berry,* I didn't connect it with those little pebble-like grains of wheat. But if *berry* means fruit, I realized, then wheat berries are well named: As the fruit of the wheat plant, each berry contains an embryo and the nutrients necessary for it to germinate into an entirely new plant.

Wheat Berry Structure: On the outside, wheat berries are very hard, barely yielding when we try to bite into one. These tough outer layers are called the pericarp and the seed coat. Beneath the outer coatings is a layer of cells called the aleurone. When wheat is milled, the outer layers (pericarp and seed coat) together with the aleurone layer are removed; together they are called the bran. The pericarp and seed coat are primarily cellulose and contain only a small proportion of the vitamins, proteins, and minerals in the grain. The aleurone layer, however, contains niacin and other B vitamins as well as valuable proteins and minerals.

Beneath the outer layers, at one end of the grain is the germ, or embryo, the reason for all this protection and structure. When a grain of wheat is given moisture, the germ will start to sprout into a new plant, feeding its initial growth with the proteins and starches stored in the endosperm, the grain's bulk storage area. Between the germ and the endosperm is the scutellum, another source of nutrients for the embryo as it develops.

The germ or embryo contains proteins and sugar-like carbohydrates as well as important amounts of B vitamins. The germ is also approximately 30 percent oil by weight. The oil is rich in vitamin E, and a high proportion of it is unsaturated. This means that wheat germ, once milled from the grain, turns rancid very quickly unless stored in airtight containers and refrigerated. The scutellum, next to the embryo, has a similar composition and also contains much of the phosphorous and thiamine of the grain.

The endosperm, or storage area, accounts for more than four fifths of the total weight of the grain. It is made up of starches and proteins, the fuel for the growth of the embryo. Because it is by far the largest part of the grain, the endosperm, even in lower-protein wheats, contains the highest proportion of the grain's protein. It is the makeup of the endosperm that largely determines the baking characteristics of the flour milled from a particular variety of wheat.

Varieties of Wheat: Hard wheat, soft wheat, winter wheat, durum, semolina, all-purpose flour . . . the terms float by. Pinning them down and understanding their significance takes time, at least it has for us.

In the last one hundred years, plant geneticists have developed strains of wheat that can cope with short growing seasons and water shortages, as well as strains resistant to diseases like rust. There are, however, still places and situations where wheat does not thrive. In warm, moist climates, wheat is subject to destruction by disease, and because it is a cool-season crop, it does not do well in extreme dry heat. Wheat can grow in dry climates, but it requires a location that receives at least thirty inches of rain per year.

The dominant wheat species now grown in the world is *Triticum aestivum* subspecies *vulgare.* It is by far the most significant species commercially and, as a result, it is the species most tinkered with by the plant geneticists. Varieties of *vulgare* include hard and soft red wheats and white wheats, discussed in detail here. These are milled to produce bread flours, all-purpose flours, and cake flours.

Other wheat species and subspecies that are still commercially available include:

Club wheat (*Triticum aestivum* subspecies *compactum*)   This is a soft wheat grown in North America to produce pastry flour. A related wheat, called Indian club wheat (*Triticum sphaerococcum),* is grown, though decreasingly, in India.

Durum wheat (*Triticum durum*)   Durum is the "hardest" wheat of all, with a protein-laden endosperm. It is a tetraploid wheat, having only twenty-eight chromosomes, compared to *Triticum aestivum*'s forty-two. When the endosperm of durum wheat is milled, the product is called semolina. Because it consists largely of protein molecules, semolina is tough and gritty, with a texture rather like that of slightly coarse granulated sugar. In Italy, it is often used to dust baking sheets to prevent loaves from sticking, and it is also used for making pasta. Couscous is also made from semolina. To make couscous, angular pieces of semolina are moistened and then rolled in fine flour to produce rounded yellow granules.

If semolina is ground more finely, semolina flour, also called durum flour, is produced. Semolina flour is used for making some regional Italian breads (particularly in Sicily), but it has too much gluten for most breads. Too much gluten produces a stiff dough that is difficult to knead and results in quite a tough bread.

Spelt (*Triticum aestivum* subspecies *spelta*)   Spelt is a subspecies of *Triticum aestivum* wheat that grows well in agriculturally marginal areas. It has a slightly different protein content than *vulgare*. There is some dispute as to whether it is an older form of wheat than *vulgare*, but the archaeological evidence seems to be that *vulgare* preceded it. However, spelt has not been genetically manipulated the way *vulgare* has, so in that sense it could be described as an older grain. Before the large-scale commercialization of *Triticum vulgare,* spelt was much more widely grown in Europe. Spelt's major disadvantage in the era before modern milling was that it is not free-threshing; that is, traditionally it had to be parched (heated) in order to separate the husk from the grain. Because heating the grain destroys its gluten-forming properties, parched grain cannot be used to make risen loaves, so spelt was more commonly used for porridge and unleavened breads.

With modern husking techniques, spelt can now be threshed without parching, but it has not supplanted the commercial exploitation of the *vulgare* subspecies. It is, however, experiencing a revival in the mountainous and less-fertile farming areas of Europe as well as in parts of North America. Spelt flour is now sold in most health food stores, as a wheat-berry or as a whole-grain flour. The spelt flours we have tried in pita and matzoh behave like whole wheat flour and produce breads with a pleasant whole wheat-like taste.

Kamut (*Triticum polonicum*) Often described as an old Egyptian variety of wheat, kamut is now sold in health food stores in North America. Whatever its origins, kamut is a tetraploid wheat, having, like durum, only twenty-eight chromosomes. Like spelt, it is often touted as a grain that has good bread-baking characteristics, but one that people who are normally allergic to wheat can eat without difficulty. It has been suggested that because kamut has been less genetically manipulated than *Triticum aestivum,* it triggers fewer allergies in wheat-sensitive people. However, in the case of people with celiac disease—where there is an allergy to the gluten-forming protein gliadin—kamut is almost certainly of no help, as gliadin is found in every grain with good bread-baking characteristics.

We have made both pita and matzoh using kamut flour. The flour looks and feels rather like semolina flour—pale yellow in color, fine, and apparently high in gluten. Because of the strong gluten, it is a little stiff to knead and roll out. It makes a smooth dough with a pleasing pale yellow color. The breads taste very good once they've cooled; for some reason, immediately out of the oven, they have a slightly bitter taste.

WHEAT CHARACTERISTICS

Hard wheat versus soft wheat: "Why soft and hard?" we always wondered. The answer lies in the makeup of the endosperm. Starch molecules tend to be soft and relatively large, while protein molecules are smaller and harder. "Hard" wheats have an endosperm with a higher proportion of hard protein molecules. "Soft" wheats have an endosperm with a larger proportion of soft starch molecules and fewer protein molecules.

The endosperm of hard wheat thus produces a flour containing proportionately more protein particles than flour made from soft wheat. As a result, flour made from hard wheat feels more granular and "harder" to the touch. When proteins in wheat flour are mixed with water and kneaded, they form strands of gluten, the structure necessary for leavened breads to rise. Often the percentage of protein in a particular flour is spoken of loosely as percentage gluten, because gluten-forming proteins are the largest proportion of proteins present in wheat flour, and they are also the most significant for bread-making.

When soft wheat is ground, the flour produced is generally finer and softer to the touch. There are fewer protein granules in the flour, so although they will form gluten when mixed with water, it will be relatively weak and inelastic. Soft flour is ideal for soft-textured cakes, but not strong enough to support leavened bread. On the other hand, if hard flour is used for cakes, it produces a tough bread-like crumb because there is too much gluten in the flour.

Winter wheat and spring wheat: Winter wheat is planted in the fall and grows slowly through the winter, then matures in the spring and early summer for harvest in the summer. It is grown where summers are very hot—too hot to be ideal for wheat—and winters are sufficiently mild. In North America, winter wheat is grown in the Pacific Northwest, in parts of the Midwest, and in southern Ontario. Most of the wheat grown in England, France, and Italy is winter wheat.

Spring wheat is planted in the early spring and grows through the summer for harvest in late summer or early fall. Most wheat grown in the climatically harsher parts of the North American wheat belt is spring wheat. In India, spring wheats are the only kind grown, but they are planted in the fall after the monsoon, then harvested in April and May in the hot season.

Winter and spring wheats can both be "hard" or "soft" varieties, although generally winter wheats are slightly softer and lower in protein than spring wheats.

Red wheat and white wheat: Some varieties of *Triticum aestivum* subspecies *vulgare* are red in color and others are white. The red varieties are generally associated with a bundle of other characteristics, the most important being hardness; some people also believe they produce a better-flavored bread. White wheats, which are primarily grown in the Pacific Northwest, are usually softer, with a protein content of 8 to 10 percent.

WHEAT FLOURS

Wheat flour is made by milling or grinding wheat berries. The flour produced depends upon the variety of wheat being used, the particular method of grinding, the proportion of the original berry that ends up in the flour, and whether or not any additives are added to the flour.

Bread flour versus cake flour: As we mentioned earlier, in North America and Europe, bread flour is flour that makes a good risen loaf. In North America bread flour, also commonly called hard wheat flour or strong flour, is generally made from hard winter or hard spring wheat and has a high protein content, between 12 and 15 percent. Most wheat grown in England, France, and Italy, apart from durum grown primarily for pasta, is "softer"; it generally has a lower protein content than wheat grown in the dry plains of North America.

Cakes and pastries require less gluten than breads. Cake and pastry flours are milled from varieties of *Triticum aestivum* that are generally referred to as soft red and soft white wheats. The softest flours of all are milled from a different species (*Triticum compactum*) called club wheat. Soft wheat flour has only 5 to 9 percent protein and is sold as cake flour; pastry flour, from club wheats, has as little as 4 percent protein.

The all-purpose flour sold in grocery stores is a blended flour that can, as its name suggests, be used for baking both bread and cakes. It generally has a protein content of about 11 percent.

Extraction rates: Transforming the wheat berry into flour requires grinding or milling. Originally wheat and other grains were ground using a mortar and pestle (related to the Roman term for bakers and millers, *pistores)* or a hand-turned grindstone (hand-turned grindstones are *still* used in rural areas in Morocco and Tunisia). Water- and animal-powered mills made the job more specialized: People took their grain to the mill for grinding rather than milling their own grain at home. The miller took grain in payment for his work, rather than having to grow his own.

Today most commercially ground flour is ground as it passes through steel rollers. If wheat berries are ground up into fine particles and nothing is subtracted—in other words the resulting flour contains ground-up germ and bran as well as endosperm—the flour is described as having an extraction rate of 100 percent (high-extraction flour). At the other end of the scale, flour containing none of the bran or germ has an extraction rate of about 70 percent (low-extraction flour).

The differences between a 100 percent and a 70 percent extraction flour, if both are ground from the same batch of wheat berries, are in color, nutritional composition, ease of storage, and baking characteristics. High-extraction flour has flecks of pale brown bran and germ, giving it an overall light tan color, while the low-extraction flour is a uniform off-white. Low-extraction flour lacks fiber and has substantially lower levels of niacin, thiamine, vitamin E, and various other vitamins and minerals. On the other hand, there is phytic acid in the bran of high-extraction flour, which can interfere with the body's absorption of calcium, iron, and zinc unless the phytic acid is given time during fermentation (at least one hour) to break down. This is the main reason for allowing whole wheat doughs (such as chapatti doughs) time to rest before baking.

Because of the oils in the germ, high extraction flour can turn rancid quickly unless stored well sealed in a very cool place. As a result, in countries where food storage and food distribution are a problem, such as China, the government has emphasized production of low-extraction flour in order to reduce spoilage.

When used for baking bread, high-extraction flour takes longer to absorb water and requires more kneading. It also requires more time to rise and may not rise as high, since the particles of bran and the oils in the germ interfere with the formation of gluten. The bread will be chewier and will have a wheatier taste.

Most commercially available whole wheat flours have an extraction rate of 90 to 100 percent. White flours in Europe have an extraction rate of about 80 percent, while in North America it tends to be closer to 70 percent. Atta flour, used for making chapattis, is very finely ground hard whole wheat flour of 90 to 100 percent extraction. Graham flour, developed by the nineteenth-century American nutritionist Sylvester Graham, is 100 percent extraction flour that has had the bran and germ separated out, finely ground, then mixed back into the flour. White all-purpose flour has an extraction rate of 70 percent.

Bleaching and aging: The low-extraction white flour described above isn't really white, but slightly off-white. Most white flours in North America are also bleached to produce a very white flour. Bread baked from unbleached flour can have an off-white tinge, which is said—by commercial bakeries—to displease the consumer. Bleaching used to be done with alum; now chlorine dioxide is generally used. Semolina flours, ground from durum wheat, may have a low extraction rate, but they are never bleached; they keep their characteristic pale yellow color.

Freshly ground flour is said not to bake loaves as well or as consistently as flour aged approximately two months, because aged flour has oxidized sulfur compounds, which allow for the formation of stronger gluten strands and hence better-risen loaves. Rather than waiting for time to pass, most commercial bakeries age their flour artificially with chlorine dioxide, iodate, or potassium bromate. Though the baking characteristics of freshly milled flour may displease commercial bakers, with their modern equipment, rushed production techniques, and need for uniformity, we find freshly ground flour to be superior in taste to any commercially available flour and a delight to bake with. A baker's wife in a small village in Alsace told us that the bakery's flour (which was untreated) always behaved skittishly in spring during the period that the wheat in the fields was in bloom. When we asked how the bakery coped, she laughed, shrugged her shoulders, and said, "The bread is just different and people buy it and eat it just the same. It's nature's way, the wheat calling out to the flour."

Glossary

Asafoetida: Used in Indian recipes and available from South Asian groceries, this spice comes from the rhizomes of a species of giant fennel. On its own, the taste and smell of asafoetida is altogether unpleasant, but when it is fried in oil, the bad smell gives way to an appetizing oniony aroma and taste.

Atta flour: Available from South Asian grocery stores and from some health food stores, atta flour is a very finely ground wheat flour, cream or pale yellow in color. To approximate atta flour, use whole wheat flour and sift out the coarsest particles of bran. Atta is ideal for chapattis and unyeasted flatbreads in general.

Candlenuts: We have substituted macadamias for the candlenuts traditionally used in Malay and Nonya cooking to thicken sauces and curry pastes; both are rich nuts, and in fact they are virtually indistinguishable. Use whichever of the two you can find more easily. They are sold shelled in Southeast Asian groceries.

Cardamom: You will find cardamom pods in South Asian groceries and in the spice sections of well-stocked grocery stores. Some are pale green in color, others almost white, and others black. Brown cardamom, also known as false cardamom, is quite different from white or green cardamom. It is used in some Ethiopian dishes and spice mixtures and is available from well-stocked spice shops or from groceries serving the Ethiopian community. Seeds from green or white cardamom pods are often called for in Indian dishes, ground to a powder. If you have a choice, buy the green rather than the white; they have a more aromatic flavor.

Chickpeas: Also known by their Spanish name, garbanzos, chickpeas are large round legumes sold dried or canned, and eaten in soups, salads, and dips. Dried chickpeas require long soaking and boiling. Rather than buying them canned, we prefer to soak and cook large batches of chickpeas and then freeze them in pint containers for use whenever needed (see method described in Note, page 200). A smaller variety of chickpea, called *channa,* is a favorite legume in India; it is most often available hulled and split.

Chickpea flour: Known in India as *besan*—the name you should use if asking for it in Asian groceries—chickpea flour can also be found in well-stocked health food stores. It is used in Ethiopia and in South Asia to make vegetarian specialties and in breads.

Chiles:

Fresh

Anaheim: also called *New Mexico chiles:* medium-hot; red or green; 6 to 7 inches long, tapering to a blunt point.

bird: also called *santaka:* less than 1 inch long; green, orange, or red; very hot; available in Thai groceries.

banana: similar in appearance to Hungarian yellow wax; 5 to 8 inches long, tapering to a wide point; pale green to yellow; mild to mildly hot; available in Chinese and Thai groceries, and frequently in supermarkets.

cayenne: 6 to 8 inches long, 1 inch wide, tapering to a point; red when mature but sometimes available dark green; hot.

fresh green, fresh red: term for cayennes used in South Asian and Southeast Asian recipes; term for Anaheims/New Mexico chiles in North America.

jalapeño: 2 to 3 inches long, ¾ to 1 inch wide, with a wide rounded tip; smooth shiny green surface, sometimes blotched with purple; moderately hot; available in large supermarkets (see chipotle).

poblano: lumpy-looking, almost square-shouldered, with a pointed tip; dark green or, when fully mature, dark red; mildly hot (*see* ancho).

serrano: 1½ to 3 inches long, slender and pointed; dark green to red and other colors; hot; frequently available in supermarkets.

Dried

ancho: dried poblano; flat, 4 to 5 inches long, about 3 inches wide; dark red, almost black; mildly hot.

de árbol: 2 to 3 inches long, narrow and tapered; red to deep reddish-brown; hot; available in Mexican groceries.

dried red: dried cayenne; variable size; hot; available in Southeast Asian groceries.

cascabel: round, smooth; 1 to 1½ inches in diameter; purplish-black; medium-hot; nutty flavor; available in Mexican groceries.

chipotle: smoke-dried jalapeño; about 2 inches long; dark brown or almost black; pronounced smoky flavor; often available canned, in Mexican groceries.

quajillo: 5 to 6 inches long and 1 inch wide; medium hot; dark red; smooth; available in Mexican groceries.

pasilla: 5 to 6 inches long, 1 inch wide, and wrinkled; almost black; medium-hot with an almost sweet taste; available in Mexican groceries.

Chile oil: Also known as *hot oil,* chile oil is made by infusing hot red chile flakes in vegetable oil or peanut oil. It is used as a flavoring and condiment in Chinese cuisine. Available at Chinese and other Asian groceries.

Coconut: Living far from the tropics, we have found that the most satisfactory way of buying coconut is shredded and frozen. Packages of frozen shredded coconut are now commonly available in the freezer sections of Asian groceries; make sure that it is unsweetened. Once it thaws, it is moist and can be easily dry-roasted in a skillet to bring out its flavor. If you are forced to use dessicated shredded coconut, be sure to buy it unsweetened. Soak it in a little warm water until it softens, chop it with a sharp knife or in a food processor to make it finer-textured, then roast it as directed in the recipe. The reason we don't recommend using the fresh coconuts available in supermarkets is that too frequently they are overripe and bad. Furthermore, you need a special tool for shredding; grating a coconut is not the same as shredding it.

Coconut milk: Where fresh coconuts are available, coconut milk and coconut cream are traditionally made in the kitchen by hand. The coconut is split open and then the flesh is laboriously scraped out. The scrapings are then soaked and pressed, releasing the "milk." The thicker liquid, or first pressing, is coconut cream, while later pressings yield a thinner product. Again, far from the tropics, we recommend using canned unsweetened coconut milk.

Coriander leaf (cilantro): *Cilantro* is the Spanish name for the leaf of the coriander plant. It is probably the most widely used herb in Southeast Asia, South Asia, and Mexico, and is also frequently used in Russian-Georgian food. We love its intense aromatic flavor. You can grow it in your garden, where it does best in the less intense warmth of May and September, or you can find it at many grocery stores and at Southeast Asian stores. Try to find bunches of coriander with the roots still on. Stored in the refrigerator with the roots in water and a plastic bag loosely over the top, it will keep for about a week. When recipes call for fresh coriander, discard the thick stalks and chop the fine stalks and leaves. The roots are widely used as a flavoring in Thai dishes.

Coriander seed: Coriander seed, from the coriander plant, is a widely used spice commonly available in well-stocked supermarkets. You can also grow coriander, in the garden or indoors, and let it go to seed. The flavor of coriander seed is enhanced if it is dry-roasted for several minutes in a skillet before being ground in a spice grinder or mortar and pestle. You can buy ground coriander seed, but it is apt to be somewhat stale and generally lacks the flavor and aroma of the freshly ground seed.

Corn flour, cornmeal: Corn flour is finely ground corn, ground to the consistency of fine flour. It is available in health food stores and other specialty shops. Cornmeal is coarsely ground corn and most commonly used dusted on baking sheets to prevent breads from sticking. It is available in well-stocked supermarkets.

Curry leaves: Used mainly in curries to flavor the oil in which other ingredients are fried, these are of South Indian origin. When the leaves hit the hot oil, they give off a warm, welcoming aroma, a smell that stimulates the appetite; the taste of the leaves in the finished dish is not nearly so dramatic as the first aroma. Fresh curry leaves are dark green and glossy; in North America they are more commonly available dried. Look for them in Indian markets.

Dal: In India and most of South Asia, *dal* is a generic term used to refer to any legume, whether it be a dried bean, a lentil, or a split pea, although, by precise definition, only split peas are truly *dal*. The dals that are most commonly used, described here, are all "hulled" or skinned, and some are "split"—two processes that make the legumes easier and faster to cook. When you shop for dal, in a South Asian grocery or a well-stocked health food store, it is generally the hulled or split varieties that you want.

channa dal: Made from hulled and split small chickpeas, channa dal is creamy to pale yellow in color, with a delicious taste.

masur dal: Also referred to as *red lentils,* masur dal is a small hulled split pea with a beautiful orange color. It cooks very quickly, making it a favorite in our kitchen.

mung dal: One of the most widely eaten dals, mung dal, or *mung bean,* is split and generally hulled, yellow in color, with no traces of its green exterior. Whole mung beans are also commonly prepared in India, particularly in the north, and are often for sale alongside the hulled variety. Mung dal has a very good taste and goes well with other flavors, making it a good household staple.

toovar dal: A split pea, ochre in color, with a taste quite unlike most other dals. It sometimes appears in shops with an oily surface; if using, the oily coating should be washed off before you start cooking the dal.

urad dal: Also referred to as *black gram dal,* though when hulled it is off-white in color. This dal is used more in the south of India than anywhere else, where it is an important ingredient in dosas.

Dried black mushrooms: The more expensive black mushrooms, also called "flower" mushrooms, distinguished by a lighter-colored pattern of cracks on the caps, are prized for their superior texture and appearance. The other main type, which is unbroken in its color, is less expensive, but also has very good flavor; if the mushroom is to be sliced or chopped, these are generally the ones used. Because black mushrooms offer so much flavor for an ingredient that keeps so well, they are an ideal food to have on hand in your kitchen. They are available in Chinese and Vietnamese groceries.

Dried pork: Dried pork is generally sold shredded, in Asian groceries, in plastic containers. We keep ours in the refrigerator, for use as a garnish for Savory Hot Soy Milk (page 81) or congee (rice soup).

Dried shrimp: Dried shrimp are used as a flavoring agent, giving a salty and slightly pungent depth to curry pastes and other blends in a number of Chinese and Southeast Asian dishes. Available in small cellophane packages in Chinese and

Asian groceries, they often have a strong smell when you open the package. Once opened, they should be kept well wrapped in plastic in the refrigerator.

Eggplant, Chinese and Japanese: Chinese eggplants are slender and mauve or pale purple in color, while Japanese eggplants, also slender and often very long (up to twelve inches), are dark purple. Unlike the plump dark eggplants we are accustomed to in the West, Chinese and Japanese eggplants require no salting and draining before being stir-fried.

Epazote: Though it is only occasionally available in Mexican groceries, we have successfully grown this Mexican herb in our garden, then watched it reseed itself and spring up all over the garden. The plant grows up to two and a half feet tall, with jagged-edged fine leaves all along its stems and branches. The seeds are tiny and appear in small clusters. There are several different varieties of epazote, but all those we've encountered here or in Mexico have the same distinctive shoe-polish-tinged-with-turpentine smell when first crushed. However, used in cooked dishes such as black beans or Black Bean and Tortilla Casserole (page 383), epazote leaves add a definite and delightful herby aroma. The closest substitute is a mixture of thyme and oregano.

Fagara: See Xichuan peppercorns.

Fava beans: Similar in appearance to lima beans, favas are available fresh, canned, or dried. Once dried, they require soaking and long cooking like other dried beans. Canned favas, available at Middle Eastern grocery stores and specialty shops, require only a very short cooking time; rinse and drain them before using; many are salted, so taste for salt before seasoning your dish.

Fenugreek: The seeds of the fenugreek plant are used as a spice in Georgian and Indian food, and around the Horn of Africa, but it is actually a legume. The seeds are small and light yellowish-brown in color, with little aroma until dry-roasted and ground. We have been told that in Ethiopia pregnant women, and infants who are being weaned, are often fed a protein-rich gruel made of boiled fenugreek. Fenugreek leaves, usually in their dried form (called *methi*), are used in a number of North Indian dishes.

Fish sauce: Known as *nam pla* in Thai and *nuoc mam* in Vietnamese, fish sauce can be found in Southeast Asian groceries as well as in many well-stocked grocery stores. Look for lighter-colored versions, which tend to be subtler-tasting. Fish sauce is made from fermented fish, but has more of a salty, briny taste than an overtly fishy flavor. It is used to enhance the flavor of many dishes in Thai and Vietnamese cuisine, is often used instead of salt, and is the basic ingredient in most Vietnamese dipping sauces.

Ful medames: *Ful* is the Arabic word for beans, and ful medames are a kind of flat dried legume widely used in Egypt, also known as *Egyptian brown beans.* They can often be found, canned or dried, in Eastern Mediterranean or Arab groceries. Fava beans or broad white beans are an excellent substitute.

Garlic chives: Also called *Chinese chives,* these long, slender, flat-bladed chives are available wherever fresh Chinese produce is sold. Look for chives with very slender leaves, as they are the most delicate in flavor. We store them wrapped in plastic in the refrigerator, but they won't keep for longer than a week.

Ginger: Ginger is a rhizome, widely used fresh as a flavoring ingredient in Indian and East Asian cooking. It adds heat as well as flavor. It is also known for its medicinal properties; sliced and boiled in water, it makes a tea that, flavored with honey, is both a favorite and effective cold remedy (because of its diuretic properties) and a delicious warming drink in the winter. Look for ginger that is firm and pale tan in color; wrinkled ginger has dried out and will have less flavor. We store ginger in the refrigerator.

Goat's milk, goat's milk yogurt: Both can be found at most well-stocked health food stores. In addition, farmers' markets often offer goat's milk products: cheese, milk, and yogurt. The milk is richer than cow's milk and stronger-tasting. When it is called for in bread recipes, you can substitute regular whole milk, with no change in texture but a slight loss of flavor. Similarly, the yogurt has a tangier taste and thus makes a more flavorful cheese (see Yogurt Cheese balls, page 206) than does yogurt made from cow's milk.

Hot pepper paste: There are a great many different hot pepper pastes (*la jiou*) available in small bottles wherever Chinese groceries are sold. Look at the ingredients, and at least for the purpose of making Mapo Dofu (page 90), avoid hot pepper pastes that include garlic or soybeans. Also called chile paste, hot pepper paste has a strong hot salty taste, more suitable for use in a stir-fry than eaten on its own as a hot sauce.

Lemon grass: An aromatic, fibrous stalk used widely in Southeast Asian cooking. Available fresh in Asian groceries, lemon grass adds a citrus tang and aroma to many dishes. Only the bottom white portion is used. Shredded dried lemon grass is also available in Asian markets; it must be soaked for thirty minutes before using.

Substitute approximately a tablespoon of dried lemon grass for each stalk of fresh called for in a recipe.

Lily buds: Lily buds, also called *golden needles,* are sold dried, in small cellophane bags, at Chinese groceries. They must be soaked and shredded before using. Store any leftover lily buds well sealed in a plastic bag; they can smell strong when dried, but are mild after cooking. They add texture, color, and a little flavor to traditional Xichuan and Beijing dishes.

Lime, slaked: Known as *cal* in Mexico, this white powder is calcium hydroxide; we know it as the lime used in making mortar for brick and stone walls. In Mexican cooking, it is used, dissolved in water, to soften corn kernels and, more important, to make them more digestible before they are ground into masa for making corn tortillas or tamales (*see also* Masa harina).

Mahleb: Mahleb is the kernal—looking like a miniature almond—inside the pit of a species of black cherry that grows in the Eastern Mediterranean. You may need to seek out a Lebanese or Arabic grocery to find it, but many well-stocked spice shops also carry mahleb, either ground or whole. We prefer to buy mahleb whole and then grind it as we need it, because the taste is stronger and because, like any other product containing natural oils, once ground, it can easily turn rancid. It gives a delightful aroma to baked goods.

Masa harina: This is "flour from masa"; in other words, dough from lime-treated ground-up corn that has been dried out and pulverized. Unlike fresh masa, which sours very quickly, it can be stored for long periods if kept dry and well sealed. It is available in supermarkets and in Mexican and Southwestern groceries. It is the main ingredient in corn tortillas for those with no access to fresh masa. Like other dried forms of fresh ingredients (fresh versus dried herbs come to mind), it is an acceptable and necessary substitute that produces a similar but not identical end product.

Mung bean threads: Also known as *cellophane noodles,* these are dried, translucent, noodle-like strands, made from the starch of processed mung beans. They are very hard, stiff, and surprisingly tough until soaked or cooked, when they become transparent, delicate, soft threads. They are available, usually in eight-ounce packages, in Asian groceries. Use scissors to cut off the amount you want from the larger bundle of bean threads. They are usually soaked before using to make them easier to cut into short lengths.

Mustard seed: Yellow mustard seeds are milder than the black. In Indian cooking, black mustard seeds are often used to flavor cooking oil; tossed into hot oil before other ingredients are added, they pop and spit as they heat, giving the oil a pleasing and distinctive taste. Yellow mustard seeds can be substituted if you are unable to find black. These tiny seeds are also used in pickling mixtures, not only in India, but in Northern Europe as well.

Nigella: This spice, sometimes referred to as black onion seed, is in fact the seed of a culinary annual, with a tangy, slightly oniony taste. The seeds are small and black, with one rounded end and one pointed. Nigella is widely used in Central Asia and in North India as a flavoring sprinkled on breads before baking, and it is also used more generally in India for pickling.

Orange blossom water: Sold in bottles in Arab and South Asian groceries and often available as well in health food stores and pharmacies, this scented water is used to scent desserts and for handwashing. Use sparingly in order not to overwhelm.

Palm sugar: Palm sugar is made from sap that is taken from one of several different kinds of palm trees; the sap is boiled down to produce the sugar. Its taste resembles that of maple sugar, very mellow and agreeable. Palm sugar is sold in many different forms and can often be found in Mexican, Southeast Asian, or Indian groceries. Indian *jaggery* is a palm sugar, but the name can also refer to a crude cane sugar that looks like palm sugar.

Pine nuts: Known in Italy as *pignoli,* these small pale yellow nuts of the umbrella pine are about ½ inch long and narrow with one rounded end and one pointed end. Pine nuts are used in small quantities to thicken sauces and, dry-roasted, as a garnish. They are rich with oil and relatively expensive. Store in the refrigerator to keep from becoming rancid.

Pumpkin: Although jack-o'-lantern pumpkins can be used in cooking, the best pumpkin for savory dishes is found in shops selling Caribbean and African foods, or tropical fruits and vegetables. It usually has a green to yellow skin and is sold by the pound cut in wedges. Look for deep orange-colored flesh; it is more flavorful than the paler, yellow flesh.

Roasted sesame oil: The only sesame oil used in these recipes is roasted sesame oil, which is pale brown and has a nutty toasted taste and aroma. It is usually used in small amounts as a flavoring agent, rather than for stir-frying or other cooking. Roasted, or dark, sesame oil should not be confused with unroasted sesame oil. It is available in Chinese, Japanese, and Southeast Asian groceries; our preferred brand is Kadoya.

Rose water: Like orange blossom water, this aromatic water is used to scent desserts (and hand-washing water). It is available from Arab and Asian groceries and often from health food stores.

Semolina and semolina flour: Made from the ground endosperm of wheat—usually durum wheat—semolina is coarse, granular, and generally pale yellow in color. Semolina flour is finely ground semolina, powdery and very fine. For a more detailed discussion of wheat semolina and durum wheat, see page 402.

Sesame Oil: See Roasted sesame oil.

Sorghum: Sorghum is a grain related to millet that grows well in dry marginal lands, and different varieties are grown in many parts of the world, including China, Yemen, Turkmenistan, and India. Sorghum flour is available in some health food stores and in South Asian grocery stores. Ask for it by its Hindi name, *jowar.*

Soy milk: Now widely available in health food stores and some supermarkets, soy milk has become popular as a milk substitute for those with lactose intolerance. It is sold sweet and flavored as well as plain, with a neutral, slightly nutty taste.

Spelt and spelt flour: Spelt is a species of wheat with certain special characteristics, discussed in more detail on page 403. Spelt flour is available at most well-stocked health food stores. The grain is now being grown in North America as well as in Europe, where its revival began ten to fifteen years ago. Often people who are allergic to regular wheat find they can eat moderate amounts of spelt without ill effect.

Sumac: Sold ground in Middle Eastern groceries, this reddish spice (it looks like chili powder) is made from dried sumac berries, ground up. It gives a pleasant acid taste to spice blends and other dishes. Lemon juice can sometimes be substituted.

Tahini: Tahini is a yellowish-brown paste made of crushed sesame seeds, widely used in Lebanese, Israeli, Egyptian, and Syrian cooking. It is usually blended with lemon juice or used to flavor legume dishes. Tahini is sold in Middle Eastern groceries, specialty shops, and in health food stores, usually in glass jars. It should be kept in the refrigerator to prevent the oil from turning rancid.

Tamarind paste or pulp: Tamarind paste or pulp, from the pods of the tamarind tree, is used in Indian, Thai, Nyonya, Persian, and Malaysian cooking to add a sour element to a blend of spices. The paste is sold in jars in Asian groceries and other specialty stores. The pulp is sold in Asian groceries in cellophane-wrapped moist, black squares. Both the paste and pulp must be dissolved in warm water before use. As the pulp has bits of seed and fibers in it, it must then be strained before adding it to other ingredients.

Teff and teff flour: Teff is a grain related to millet, with very small grains. Until very recently, teff was grown only in Ethiopia; now some farmers in North America are growing teff. Teff flour (see Teff Injera, page 269) is fine-textured and almost violet-brown in color. Teff and teff flour can be found in Ethiopian groceries and sometimes in health food stores.

Tomatillos: Also known as *tomates verdes,* or green tomatoes, tomatillos are related to the cape gooseberry and are not tomatoes at all. They grow with a papery outer covering and are sold fresh in Mexican and specialty produce stores with the brownish cover still on; remove it before cooking. Tomatillos are hard—like unripe plums—and are generally cooked before using. They are also sold canned in specialty shops.

Tree ears: These mushrooms are available dried in Chinese and Southeast Asian groceries, packed in small cellophane bags. Choose tree ears that look like small dull black bits in their plastic bag; they are better than the light-on-one-side kind. Tree ears, also called *tree fungus* by the Chinese, must be soaked before using. They add texture to a number of classic northern Chinese and Xichuanese dishes; there is no substitute.

Xichuan peppercorns: Also called *fagara* or *brown pepper,* these small reddish-brown dried berries are aromatic rather than hot and give a distinctive woody flavor to Xichuan and other dishes. They are available in most Chinese groceries or in well-stocked spice stores.

Bibliography

Amma, P. Lakshmikutty. *Mama's Treasure Chest*. Trivandrum, India: Kerala Home Science Association, 1972.

Anderson, E. N. *The Food of China*. New Haven: Yale University Press, 1988.

Aykroyd, W. R., and Joyce Doughty. *Wheat in Human Nutrition*. Rome: FAO, 1970.

Babbar, Purobi. *Rotis and Naans of India*. Bombay: Vakils, Feffer and Simons, 1988.

Baboian, Rose. *The Art of Armenian Cooking*. Garden City, N.Y.: Doubleday, 1971.

Bailey, Adrian. *The Blessings of Bread*. London: Paddington Press, 1975.

Barer-Stein, T. *You Eat What You Are*. Toronto: McClelland and Stewart, 1979.

Barreiro, José, ed. "Indian Corn of the Americas," *Northeast Indian Quarterly*, Vol. 4 (spring/summer 1989).

Batmanglij, Najmieh. *Food of Life*. Washington, D.C.: Mage, 1986.

Bayless, Rick and Deann. *Authentic Mexican*. New York: Morrow, 1987.

Beard, James. *Beard on Bread*. New York: Knopf, 1978.

Benkirane, Fettouma. *Secrets of Moroccan Cookery*. Paris: Jean-Pierre Taillandier, 1985.

Bennani-Smires, Latifa. *La Cuisine Marocaine*. Casablanca: Société d'Edition et de Diffusion, 1988.

Bremzen, Anya von, and John Welchman. *Please to the Table*. New York: Workman, 1990.

Caceres, Benigno. *Si le 'Pain M'Etait Conte . . . .* Paris: Editions la Découverte, 1987.

Carson, Dale. *Native New England Cooking*. Madison, Conn.: Peregrine Press, 1980.

Chang, K. C., ed. *Food in Chinese Culture*. New Haven: Yale University. Press, 1978.

Chirinian, Linda. *Secrets of Cooking Armenian, Lebanese, Persian*. New Canaan, Conn.: Lionhart, 1987.

Cribb, Roger. *Nomads in Archaeology*. London: Cambridge University Press, 1991.

David, Elizabeth. *English Bread and Yeast Cookery*. Middlesex, England: Penguin, 1977.

Dewitt, Dave, and Nancy Gerlach. *The Whole Chile Pepper Book*. Boston: Little, Brown, 1990.

Dissanayake, Chandra. *Ceylon Cookery*. Colombo, Sri Lanka: Metro, 1968.

Dodwell, Christina. *A Traveller on Horseback in Eastern Turkey and Iran*. London: Sceptre, 1988.

Donovan, Holly, Peter Donovan, and Harvey Mole. *A Guide to the Chinese Cuisine and Restaurants of Taiwan*. Taipei: 1977.

Fernandez, Adela. *La Tradicional Cocina Mexicana*. Mexico: Panorama Edit, 1985.

Field, Carol. *The Italian Baker*. New York: Harper & Row, 1985.

Fitzgibbon, Theodora. *A Taste of Scotland*. London: Pan Books, 1971.

Fukuoka, Masanobu. *The One-Straw Revolution*. Emmaus, Penn.: Rodale Press, 1978.

Ganor, Avi, and Ron Maiberg. *Taste of Israel*. Toronto: McClelland & Stewart, 1990.

Goldstein, Darra. "Georgia on My Mind," *Eating Well,* October 1990.

Govinda, Lama Anagorika. *The Way of the White Clouds*. New Delhi: B. I. Publications, 1974.

Gray, Patience. *Honey from a Weed*. New York: Harper & Row, 1985.

Hamady, Mary Laird. *Lebanese Mountain Cookery*. Boston: Godine, 1987.

Hogrogian, Rachel. *The Armenian Cookbook*. New York: Atheneum, 1971.

Hughes, Phyllis, ed. *Pueblo Indian Cookbook*. Santa Fe: Museum of New Mexico, 1972, 1979.

Iny, Daisy. *The Best of Baghdad Cooking with Treats from Teheran*. New York: Saturday Review Press, 1976.

Iturriaga de la Fuente, José N. *De Tacos, Tamales, y Tortas*. Mexico: Editorial Diana, 1987.

Jacob, H. E. *Six Thousand Years of Bread*, trans. R. and C. Winston. Garden City, N.Y.: Doubleday, Doran, 1944.

Jenkins, Myra Ellen, and Albert H. Schroeder. *A Brief History of New Mexico*. Albuquerque: University of New Mexico, 1974.

Kahn, E. J., Jr. *The Staffs of Life*. Boston: Little, Brown, 1985.

Kavasch, Barrie. *Native Harvests*. New York: Vintage, 1979.

Kavena, Juanita Tiger. *Hopi Cookery*. Tucson, Ariz.: University of Arizona Press, 1980.

Kegan, Marcia. *Southwest Indian Cookbook*. Santa Fe: Clear Light, 1987.

Kennedy, Diana. *The Cuisines of Mexico*. New York: Harper & Row, 1972.

Kim, Yeap Joo Kim. *The Penang Palate*. Penang, Malaysia: Phoenix, 1990.

Lal, Premila. *Vegetable Dishes*. Bombay: IBH, 1970.

Lappé, Frances Moore, and Joseph Collins. *Food First*. New York: Ballantine, 1977.

Louis, André. *Nomades d'Hier et d'Aujourd'hui dans le Sud Tunisien*. Aix-en-Provence, France: Edisud, 1979.

Lovesick Lake Native Women's Association, ed. *The Rural and Native Heritage Cookbook*. Toronto: Totem Books, 1987.

Luard, Elizabeth. *The Old World Kitchen: The Rich Tradition of European Peasant Cooking*. New York: Bantam, 1989.

McGee, Harold. *On Food and Cooking*. New York: Collier, 1984.

———. *The Curious Cook*. San Francisco: North Point Press, 1990.

Machlin, Edda Servi. *The Classic Cuisine of the Italian Jews*. New York: Giro, 1981.

Maiberg, Ron. *Taste of Israel*. London: Multimedia Books, 1990.

Maillart, Ella. *Forbidden Journey*. London: Century Publishing, 1937, 1983.

———. *Turkestan Solo*. London: Century Publishing, 1934, 1985.

Majupuria, Indra. *Joys of Nepalese Cooking*. Gwalior, Nepal: S. Devi, 1988.

Man, Rosamond. *The Complete Meze Table*. London: Ebury Press, 1986.

Margvelashvili, Julianne. *The Classic Cuisine of Soviet Georgia*. New York: Prentice Hall, 1991.

Mathew, K. M. *Kerala Cookery*. Kottayam, India: Manorama Publishing.

May, Jacques M. *The Ecology of Malnutrition in the Far and Near East*. New York: Hafner, 1961.

————. *The Ecology of Malnutrition in North Africa*. New York: Hafner, 1967.

————. *The Ecology of Malnutrition in Mexico and Central America*. New York: Hafner., 1972.

Mazda, Maideh. *In a Persian Kitchen*. Rutland, Vt.: Charles Tuttle, 1960.

Mesfin, Daniel. *Exotic Ethiopian Cooking*. Falls Church, Va.: Ethiopian Cookbook Enterprise, 1987.

Middione, Carlo. *The Food of Southern Italy*. New York: Morrow, 1987.

Ngo, Bach, and Gloria Zimmerman. *The Classic Cuisine of Vietnam*. New York: Plume, 1979, 1986.

Ojakangas, Beatrice. *The Finnish Cook Book*. New York: Crown, 1964.

————. *The Great Scandinavian Baking Book*. Boston: Little, Brown, 1988.

The Oxford Book of Food Plants. London: Oxford University Press, 1969.

Philips, Roger, and Martyn Rix. *The Random House Book of Vegetables*. New York: Random House, 1993.

Pomeranz, Y., and J. A. Shellenberger. *Bread Science and Technology*. Westport, Conn.: Avi Publishing, 1971.

Pruthi, J. S. *Spices and Condiments*. New Delhi: National Book Trust, 1976.

Robertson, Laurel. *The Laurel's Kitchen Bread Book*. New York: Random House, 1984.

Roden, Claudia. *A Book of Middle Eastern Food*. London: Thomas Nelson, 1968.

Routhier, Nicole. *The Foods of Vietnam*. New York: Stewart, Tabori and Chang, 1989.

Sahni, Julie. *Classic Indian Vegetarian and Grain Cooking*. New York: Morrow, 1985.

Salikhov, S. G. *Blyuda, Uzbekskoi Kukhny (Uzbek Cuisine)*. Tashkent, Uzbek: 1991.

Santa Maria, Jack. *Indian Vegetarian Cookery*. Bombay: B. I. Publications, 1973.

Schrecker, Ellen. *Mrs. Chiang's Szechwan Cookbook*. New York: Harper & Row, 1976.

Shahrani, M. Nazif Mohib. *The Kirghiz and Wakhi of Afghanistan*. Seattle: University of Washington Press, 1979.

Shulman, Martha Rose. *Mediterranean Light*. New York: Bantam, 1989.

Simmons, Shirin. *Entertaining the Persian Way*. Luton, England: Lennard Publishing, 1988.

Skrine, C. P. *Chinese Central Asia*. New York: Barnes & Noble, 1926.

Spicer, Arnold, ed. *Bread: Social, Nutritional, and Agricultural Aspects of Wheaten Bread*. London: Applied Science Publishers, 1975.

Stark, Freya. *The Southern Gates of Arabia*. London: Century Publishing, 1936, 1982.

Suzuki, Shunryu. *Zen Mind, Beginner's Mind*. New York: Weatherhill, 1970.

Tan, Cecilia. *Penang Nyonya Cooking*. Singapore: Times Books International, 1983.

Tannahill, Reay. *Food in History*. New York: Stein and Day, 1973.

Tanttu, Anna-Maija and Juha. *Food from Finland*. Helsinki: Otava, 1989.

Tropp, Barbara. *The Modern Art of Chinese Cooking*. New York: Morrow, 1982.

van der Post, Laurens. *African Cooking*. New York: Time-Life Books, 1970.

Visser, Margaret. *Much Depends on Dinner*. Toronto: McClelland and Stewart, 1987.

Wolfert, Paula. *Couscous and Other Good Food from Morocco*. New York: Harper Perennial, 1973.

———. "A Feast of Flavors," *Food & Wine*, October 1990.

Index

Page numbers in **bold type** refer to recipes.